Sociology
An international bibliography of serial publications 1880–1980

Sociology

An international bibliography of serial publications 1880–1980

JAN WEPSIEC

Mansell Publishing Limited

ISBN 0 7201 1652 X

Mansell Publishing Limited, 6 All Saints Street,
London N1 9RL

First published 1983

Distributed in the United States and Canada by
The H.W. Wilson Company, 950 University
Avenue, Bronx, New York 10452.

British Library Cataloguing in Publication Data

Wepsiec, Jan
Sociology : an international bibliography of serial publications 1880–1980.
1. Sociology — periodicals — Bibliography
I. Title
016.301'05 Z7164.S67

ISBN 0-7291-1652-X

Printed and bound in Great Britain
at The Pitman Press, Bath

Contents

Introduction

The aim of this bibliography is to serve a wide range of students of sociology — research workers, teachers, historians — and various groups concerned with the applications of sociology or with serving government agencies throughout the world, as they develop social policies. Scope of such breadth requires the inclusion of not only publications devoted entirely to sociology but also those which deal primarily with other subject fields within the social sciences and include information that pertains to the sociological aspects of those fields. Publications that ceased to be published at an early stage in the development of sociology are included specifically to serve the needs of historians of sociology.

Criteria applied to the inclusion of publications on the periphery of sociological investigation are not defined in detail. The compiler acknowledges, as a cautionary alert, Parsons' statement: 'Not only there is no "official" sociological point of view, but there is no authoritative catalog, to say nothing of logically symmetrical classification, of sectors and subdivisions of the discipline'.[1] Published outlines of the field of sociology were consulted, such as comprehensive handbooks, the areas of sociology as listed by the International Sociological Association and the particular areas studied by its committees, Lasswell's structured list of concepts in the study of society,[2] and lists of publications abstracted in *Sociological Abstracts* over the past 30 years, or indexed in *International Bibliography of Sociology*. Another source helpful in the selection of peripheral serials was a study — the largest ever undertaken — of users' needs and related aspects in the social sciences. It was conducted by the Library of the University of Bath, under the direction of M. B. Line, and reported in three multi-volume works.[3] When the present bibliography was approaching completion, useful criteria for the inclusion of peripheral literature were also found to be applied in three extensive bibliographies.[4,5,6] These three works, and the names of the institutions that sponsored the literature cited in them, demonstrate a spread of sociological literature reaching far beyond journals devoted solely to sociological studies.

Based, then, on both compromise and consensus, signposts were eventually erected to mark boundaries and general rules for the selection of publications to be included in the bibliography as follows:

1. publications devoted entirely to sociology;
2. the more comprehensive publications in social psychology that deal with social interaction and socialization — especially those which, according to Layder,[7] can be called sociologically oriented — and, selectively, publications in social anthropology whose interest in recent years has extended beyond simple societies;
3. serial publications in the general social and behavioral sciences that contain a significant amount of sociological literature;
4. social science publications that appeared during the early stages of the development of sociology in Western Europe and North America, and those of recent origin, published in some countries of South and Central America, Africa and Asia, which do not have separate publications for sociology (India, Australia, New Zealand and Japan do, of course, have separate sociological publications);
5. publications in the social sciences and philosophy, especially those on dialectical materialism and social history, published in the Soviet Union and the countries of the People's Democracies, until the end of the Stalinist period, when separate sociological publications were not published;

6. interdisciplinary and, more frequently, multidisciplinary publications containing studies on the social aspects of some social institutions, e.g., urban planning and socioeconomic development;
7. selectively, publications on population (especially its composition, spatial distribution, occupation and migration), social history, social problems (especially deviant behavior, delinquency and crime) and social work;
8. very selectively, publications on eugenics, social psychiatry and social biology — the latter not always considered by sociologists to be a subfield of sociology;
9. selectively, publications that occasionally contain studies but are primarily collections of raw data, e.g., statistics of population composition and migration. Population censuses are excluded but a continuously updated bibliography of censuses[8] is included;
10. comprehensively, secondary information serials such as abstracts, indexes, bibliographies, review journals and survey journals — they provide access to the primary sociological literature and enable the user to extend the range of his search for studies that are scattered.

Serial publications in sociology are published in various literary forms: regularly and irregularly published journals; learned and educational institutions' numbered reports of both completed and ongoing research, and monograph series. In addition to these categories, two other types of work usually considered by librarians to be monographs, are included in this bibliography, namely, transactions (papers delivered at various conferences), some of which are published regularly over a long period, and a few directories which are or are planned to be published in updated editions and whose contents provide access to research pertaining to society.

Form of Description

Bibliographic description consists of the following elements: title, or name of issuing agency and title; designation of first issue ('v.' and 'n.' designating both the English abbreviations and their foreign equivalents); date of first issue, designated in English (year only, for monograph series, or publications that appear less frequently than once a year, or irregularly; year and month for semi-annuals, quarterlies, bimonthlies and monthlies; year, month and day for biweeklies and weeklies). When the first issue was not available for examination and bibliographic sources did not give the precise date, a probable date is given, followed by a question mark. The date of last issue of a ceased irregularly published serial is difficult to determine (even occasionally when the issue number is known) and question marks are used to indicate lack of positive evidence; change in the place of publication is given and when the change occurs frequently, as in the case of congresses and conferences, the phrase 'Place of publication varies' is used; the name of the publisher is given either in full or in its commonly known designation, e.g. Macmillan; publications edited and published by learned institutions, if entered under their titles, receive the phrase 'issued by...' which indicates 'edited and published by...'; if entered in the form of a corporate entry, it is to be understood (unless otherwise indicated) that the institution, under whose name the publication is entered, is also the publisher; frequency of publication is given on the basis of the editorial statement, unless it is known that the actual publishing does not correspond with that statement — in which case 'irregular' is added parenthetically. When publication is planned to be irregular, the word 'irregular' is used without parentheses. In the few cases where a corporate entry is entered under a geographical name which has undergone change, cross-reference from the later to the earlier name is given, e.g., Poznan *see* Posen.

Changes of title that occurred before the new Anglo-American cataloguing rules were implemented, begin with the phrase 'Title varies', followed by volume or issue number and date applicable to the previously used title; cross-reference from the earlier to the later title is given in alphabetical sequence. For a publication catalogued according to the new rules, the phrase 'Title varies' is not used and the publication changing its title is regarded as ceased; it receives the phrase 'Continued by...' and the publication with the new title receives in its description the phrase 'Continues ...', followed by the title of its predecessor. The merger of two publications, or the fact that a publication absorbs or is absorbed by another publication, is appropriately indicated, as also is the fact that a publication is a subseries of another publication.

The publication of supplements is indicated, and if the supplement is a serial publication, its title is given and also listed in the main alphabetical sequence.

A subtitle that sheds light on the scope or perspective of the publication is included in quotation marks. The language of the text is stated, if other than Latin, English, French or German, or if the text is in more than one language. Summaries and their languages are given. Descriptions of publications abstracted or indexed in secondary information journals include the latters' titles in abbreviated form; a list of the full titles and abbreviations precedes the bibliography section. Some of the publications, that commenced 1979–1980, have not yet been documented in secondary information sources such as the *International Bibliography of Sociology* and *Sociological Abstracts*.

Because works in the form of monograph series and numbered research reports are catalogued by some libraries as individual works, the user is advised to consult also the monograph catalogue whenever the catalogue is divided into separate sections for periodicals and monographs.

Despite the existence and application of the Anglo-American cataloguing rules in North America and the United Kingdom, inconsistencies sometimes occur in library practice in these countries; the library rules in European countries and in other parts of the world also complicated decisions as to the form of entry to be adopted. Three works that list a large number of serials, namely: *Union List of Serials in the United States and Canada* (3rd ed.); *New Serial Titles* 1953–), and *British Union-Catalogue of Periodicals* (1955–80) were used as models for the type of entry, as they are the largest and most frequently used bibliographical lists of serial publications published anywhere in the world.

Arrangement

Entries are arranged alphabetically, letter-by-letter; titles consisting of, or beginning with, an acronym are listed at the beginning of the given letter section; a hyphenated word precedes a non-hyphenated word with the same initial morpheme. The initial article in a title is disregarded for purposes of the alphabetical arrangement.

Transliteration

The romanization of titles in Chinese, Japanese, Korean, or a Slavic language in the Cyrillic alphabet, presented a problem that could not be solved to the satisfaction of everyone. A choice had to be made from among the systems for transliteration accepted in various countries. One of the most favoured systems was that of Unesco, but unfortunately the majority of the publications listed in this bibliography had not yet been included in the published lists of Unesco. On the other hand, the bibliographic publications of the Library of Congress — the most widely distributed throughout the world — and the Library of Congress catalogue did together include the vast majority of the publications listed. The practice of the Library of Congress for the romanization of titles was therefore accepted as the model most likely to assure a degree of consistency in the transliterations included in this bibliography.

Supplements

Two short supplements have been added at the end of the bibliography, each with their own alphabetical sequence, but continuing the running numerical sequence. These are items which came to light after the initial compilation, and are included so as to ensure as complete a coverage as possible at the time of going to press.

Index

A subject index is supplied in order to facilitate search for subfields, perspectives, or aspects. The number of headings under which a publication appears may vary, from one to several. Secondary information publications are listed in the Index by form, as 'abstract', 'bibliography', 'index', 'directory', 'review', or 'survey', and also by subject matter, with the above terms used as form subdivisins.

*

* *

Contemplating this work, the compiler regrets that more complete information was not available for the descriptions of certain titles; the desired completeness could have been achieved only if entire sets of publications had been available for examination or, in some cases, if more complete information could have been secured from bibliographies. Declining growth of the collections in many libraries since the late 1970s hampered the gathering of data. When a library's holdings of publications were incomplete, or when bibliographies compiled some years ago did not include all the needed information, it was occasionally possible to piece together data obtained from two or even more libraries. As a last resort, attempts were made to obtain data from the publisher — if still existent, or the editor — if his whereabouts were known. At the same time, search brought some satisfaction and even, occasionally, amusement — as when the compiler was addressed as Ms., due to the first name, Jan; or Rev., because the relevant publication contained some material about religion. But perhaps the most refreshing response was the one accompanied by the address and cordial recommendation of a public house.

Acknowledgments

The completion of this bibliography has been made possible through the facilities offered by numerous libraries and the information supplied by many editors and librarians; to all of them, my thanks and appreciation. Special mention should be made of The Library of Congress, which allowed me direct access to the shelves and to the records of its collections, reducing significantly the amount of time needed for collecting information; the staff of the Reading Room of the Lending Division of the British Library; the University of London Library, and the Diet of Japan Library, which supplied information concerning publications that were entirely in Japanese.

I would like to express my gratitude to the following individuals: Ms. Cynthia Adams, University of North Carolina Library; Mr. W. Anderson, University of Strathclyde Library; Mr. D. Beagle, Virginia Polytechnic Institute and State University; Mrs. P. M. Blackwell, Pergamon Press, Oxford; Mr. John Campbell, University of Georgia Library; Ms. Mary Canada, Duke University Library; Ms. Aileen Claridge, National Library of New Zealand; Mrs. Jane Clark,

University of Toronto Library; Mrs. M. Coleman, University of Salisbury, Zimbabwe; Mrs. Edith K. Connelly, State University of New York, at Albany, Library; Prof. A. P. M. Coxon, University College, Cardiff; Mr. Hilary Cummings, Southern Illinois University at Carbondale; Mrs. Edna L. Dolber, Brandeis University Library; Mr. David K. Evans, Overseas Research Center, Wake Forest University; Ms. Gwynneth Evans, National Library of Canada; Dr. Lidia Ferenczy, Orzagos Szechenyi Konyvtar, Budapest; Miss Elizabeth C. Foushee, Ohio State University Library; Miss Janet R. Gardner, University of Birmingham Library; Ms. Charlotte R. Howard, University of Mississippi; Mr. Lawrence C. Johnson, Michigan State University Library; Mrs. Libby Kahane, Jewish National & University Library, Jerusalem; Mr. David Langenberg, Stanford University Library; Mrs. Eileen Libby, University of Chicago Library; Mr. Dennis Lien, University of Minnesota Library; Mr. David McChesney, University of Connecticut Library; Mrs. Kathryn McGrodden, University of California, at Berkeley, Library; Mr. Y. Morita, National Diet Library, Tokyo; Ms. Erika Rother, Institut für Leihverkehr und Zentralkataloge, Berlin; Ms. Marcia Segal, Editor of *Newsletter*, Sociologists for Women in Society; Ms. Miriam Seltzer, Boston (Mass.) Public Library; Ms. Betty Smith, Information Retrieval System for the Sociology of Leisure and Sport, University of Waterloo, Canada; Mr. Richard G. Smith, University of Illinois, at Urbana, Library; Ms. Caroline Tengstrom Spicer and Mrs. Jean Warholic, Program in Urban and Regional Studies, Cornell University; Ms. Doris Ann Sweet, Boston University Library; Ms. Cassie Taylor, Utah State University, at Logan, Library; Mr. Stephen J. Tordellam, Applied Population Laboratory, University of Wisconsin — Extension; Ms. Diana Twelves, University of Texas, at El Paso, Library; Mr. Stephen White, Joint Editor, *Co-existence*, Glasgow; Ms. Katharine M. Wood, University of Delaware Library, Mr. Rudolph Clay, Jr., Washington University Libraries; Ms. Anna-Karin Kollind, Library Service of the Sociological Institute, Goteborgs Universitet; Ms. Eeva Peltonen, Sociological Institute in Helsinki; Mr. Thomas V. Schmidt, Catholic University of America Library; Mr. Torbjorn Soderholm, Abo Akademis Bibliotek; Mr. Frederick L. Arnold, Princeton University Library; Ms. Marguerite A. Christensen, University of Wisconsin Library; Ms. Ellen Hjortsaeter, University of Oslo Library; Mrs. Marian B. Hughes, The National Library of Wales; Mr. Mark O'Donnell, The Johns Hopkins University Library; I. Schwartz, United Nations Library; Ms. Jacqueline A. Smith, University of Minnesota Library; Miss Annamaria Tasca, Instituto Nazionale per la Storia del Movimento di Liberazione in Italia; Mr. Wm. Jerry Thornton, The University of Michigan Library; Mr. Willy Venderpijpen, *Bibliographie de Belgique*; and Ms. Lynn Wiley, American Museum of Natural History Library.

Finally, special thanks to my wife for typing the manuscript and for sharing the work throughout its final stages.

J.W.
December, 1981

References

1. Talcott Parsons, 'Introduction', in Talcott Parsons, ed., *American Sociology. Perspectives, Problems, Methods* (New York, Basic Books, 1968), p. x.
2. Harold D. Lasswell, 'Human Society', in *The New Encyclopaedia Britannica*, 15th ed. (Chicago, Chicago University Press, 1974), v. 'Propaedia', pp. 280–310.
3. Bath, England. University. Library. *Design of Information Systems in the Social Sciences. Research Reports. Series A.*, no. 1–5, (Bath, 1975–1980); *Design of Information Systems in the Social Sciences. Research Reports. Series B.*, no. 1–7 (Bath, 1973–1978); *Design of Information Systems in the Social Sciences. Working Paper*, no. 1–11 (Bath, 1971–1973).
4. Tor W. Holm and Erkki J. Immonen. *Bibliography of Finnish Sociology, 1945–1959, Transactions*, v.13 (Helsinki, Westermarck Society, 1966. 179 p.)
5. Hilkka Sisko Lamminen. *Bibliography of Finnish Sociology, 1960–1969, Transactions*, v.19 (Helsinki, Westermarck Society, 1973. 370 p.)
6. Illinois. University. Center for International Comparative Studies (CICS), and Informationszentrum Sozialwissenschaften, Bonn. *Bibliographie zür deutschen Soziologie. Bibliography of German Sociology 1945–1977.* (Göttingen, Otto Schwartz & Co., 1980. 800 p.)
7. Derek Layder. *Structure, Interaction and Social Theory*. (London, Routledge & Kegan Paul, 1981).
8. Texas. University. Bureau of International Business Research. Population Research Center. *International Census Bibliography*, no. 1–6, 1965–1967; and Supplement, 1968–   . (Austin, Texas. Irreg.)

Abbreviations for Titles of Abstracting and Indexing Journals

ABC Pol. Sc.
ABC Political Science (1969–)

Abstr. Soc. Work.
Abstracts for Social Workers (1965–1977. Continued by *Social Work Research & Abstracts*)

Abstr. Anth.
Abstracts in Anthropology (1970–)

Afr. Abstr.
African Abstracts (1950–)

Anth. Ind.
Anthropological Index (1963–)

APAIS
Australian Public Affairs Information Service (1945–)

Brit. Hum Ind.
British Humanities Index (1915–)

Bull. sig. soc. eth.
Bulletin signaletique. Pt. 521. Sociologie — Ethnologie (1961–)

Can. Per. Ind.
Canadian Periodical Index (1975–)

Cath. Per. Ind.
The Catholic Periodical and Literature Index (1930–)

Crime Del. Abstr.
Crime and Delinquency Abstracts (1963–1972)

Crime Del. Lit.
Crime and Delinquency Literature (1970–)

Curr. Cont.
Current Contents, Social and Behavioral Sciences (1969–)

Eth. Stud. Bibl.
Ethnic Studies Bibliography (1975–)

Int. Bibl. Soc.
International Bibliography of Sociology (1951–)

Int. Bibl. Soc. Cult. Anth.
International Bibliography of Social and Cultural Anthropology (1955–)

Int. Ind.
International Index (Titled later, *Humanities and Social Sciences Index*)

Int. Pol. Sc. Abstr.
International Political Science Abstracts (1951–)

LLBA
Language and Language Behavior Abstracts (1967–)

PAIS
Public Affairs Information Service. Bulletin (1915–)

PHRA
Poverty and Human Resources Abstracts (1966–)

Peace Res. Abstr. J.
Peace Research Abstracts Journal (1964—)

Pop. Ind.
Population Index (1935–)

Psych. Abstr.
Psychological Abstracts (1927–)

Sage Fam. Stud. Abstr.
Sage Family Studies Abstracts (1979–)

Sage Race Rel. Abstr.
Sage Race Relations Abstracts (1975–)

Sage Urb. Stud. Abstr.
Sage Urban Studies Abstracts (1973–)

SSCI
Social Sciences Citation Index (1973–)

SSHI
Social Sciences and Humanities Index (1913–1974)

Soc. Abstr.
Sociological Abstracts (1952–)

Soc. Ed. Abstr.
Sociology of Education Abstracts (1965–)

Soc. Sc. Ind.
Social Sciences Index (1974–)

Soc. Work Res. Abstr.
Social Work Research Abstracts (1977–). *Continues Abstracts for Social Workers*)

Urb. Aff. Abstr.
Urban Affairs Abstracts (1971–)

Wom. Stud. Abstr.
Women Studies Abstracts (1972–)

The Bibliography

ABS AMERICAN BEHAVIORAL SCIENTIST
See AMERICAN BEHAVIORAL SCIENTIST

ABS QUARTERLY CHECK LIST OF ETHNOLOGY & SOCIOLOGY
See QUARTERLY CHECK LIST OF ETHNOLOGY & SOCIOLOGY

ABT. SOZIOLOGIE
See DAS WISSENSCHAFTLICHE TASCHENBUCH; ABT. SOZIOLOGIE

A.E. & R.S.
See Pennsylvania. State University. Department of Agricultural Economics and Rural Sociology. A.E. & R.S.

AKD QUARTERLY; THE ALPHA KAPPA DELTA QUARTERLY
See SOCIOLOGICAL INQUIRY

ASA DIRECTORY
See American Sociological Association. DIRECTORY

ASR. AMERICAN SOCIOLOGICAL REVIEW
See AMERICAN SOCIOLOGICAL REVIEW

ABHANDLUNGEN. GESELLSCHAFTSWISSENSCHAFTEN
See Akademie der Wissenschaften der DDR. ABHANDLUNGEN. GESELLSCHAFTSWISSENSCHAFTEN

ABHANDLUNGEN ZUR MITTELSTANDFORSCHUNG
See SCHRIFTEN ZUR MITTELSTANDFORSCHUNG

1 ABHANDLUNGEN ZUR PHILOSOPHIE, PSYCHOLOGIE, SOZIOLOGIE DER RELIGION UND ÖKUMENIK. no.1–52/53, 1922–1941; n.s. no.1– , 1948– . München, later Würzburg.

Title varies: no.1–27, *Abhandlungen zur Philosophie, Psychologie und Soziologie der Religion.*

ABHANDLUNGEN ZUR PHILOSOPHIE, PSYCHOLOGIE UND SOZIOLOGIE DER RELIGION
See ABHANDLUNGEN ZUR PHILOSOPHIE, PSYCHOLOGIE, SOZIOLOGIE DER RELIGION UND ÖKUMENIK

ABSTRACT-BIBLIOGRAPHY SERIES
See Population Center Foundation. Population Information Division. ABSTRACT-BIBLIOGRAPHY SERIES

2 ABSTRACTS FOR SOCIAL WORKERS. v.1–13, no.1, Spring 1965–summer 1977. Albany, N.Y., National Association of Social Workers.

Continued by: *Social Work Research & Abstracts.*

3 ABSTRACTS OF BULGARIAN SCIENTIFIC LITERATURE. PHILOSOPHY, SCIENCE OF SCIENCE, PSYCHOLOGY AND PEDAGOGICS. 17– , 1974– . Sofia. Semi-annual. Issued by the Bulgarian Academy of Sciences. Scientific Information Centre for Natural, Mathematical and Social Sciences.

Continues: *Abstracts of Bulgarian Scientific Literature. Philisophy, Psychology and Pedagogics.*

ABSTRACTS OF PAPERS PRESENTED AT THE ANNUAL MEETING OF THE:
- American Society of Criminology
- American Sociological Association
- Association for the Humanist Sociology
- Association for the Sociology of Religion
- Canadian Sociology and Anthropology Association
- Eastern Sociological Society
- Georgia Sociological & Anthropological Association
- Illinois Sociological Association
- International Society for Research on Aggression
- International Symposium on Victimology
- Mid-South Sociological Association
- Midwest Sociological Society
- North Central Sociological Association
- Pennsylvania Sociological Association
- Rural Sociological Society
- Society for the Study of Social Problems
- Southern Sociological Society
- Southwestern Sociological Association

See SOCIOLOGICAL ABSTRACTS. SUPPLEMENT

ABSTRACTS OF PAPERS PRESENTED AT THE CONGRESS OF THE INTERNATIONAL INSTITUTE OF SOCIOLOGY
See SOCIOLOGICAL ABSTRACTS. SUPPLEMENT

ABSTRACTS OF PAPERS PRESENTED AT THE WORLD CONGRESS OF RURAL SOCIOLOGY
See SOCIOLOGICAL ABSTRACTS. SUPPLEMENT

ABSTRACTS OF PAPERS PRESENTED AT THE . . . WORLD CONGRESS OF SOCIOLOGY

See SOCIOLOGICAL ABSTRACTS. SUPPLEMENT

4 ABSTRACTS ON CRIMINOLOGY AND PENOLOGY. v.1–19, Jan/Feb. 1961–Nov/Dec. 1979. Amsterdam, Excerpta Criminologica Foundation. Bimonthly.
Title varies: v.1–8, 1961–68, *Excerpta criminologica*. Continued by: *Criminology & Penology Abstracts*. In English. Includes author and subject indexes.

5 Academia de Ciencias Politicas y Sociales. BOLETIN. v.1– , 1937– . Caracas. Irreg.
Issued in cooperation with the Universidad Central de Venezuela.

6 Academia Republicii Populare Romîne. Filiala Cluj. STUDI ȘI CERCETĂRI ȘTIINȚIFICE: SERIA 3: ŞTIINȚE SOCIALE. v.5, no.3/4–v.6, no.3/4, July/Dec. 1954–July/Dec. 1955. Cluj.
Continues (with Seria 1 and 2) its *Studii şi Cercetări Științifice*. Superseded by: *Studii şi Cercetări de Lingvistica,* and *Nyelv-es Irodalamon Tudományi Közlemények*.

ACTA AFRICANA
See GENÈVE AFRIQUE. GENEVA AFRICA

7 ACTA CRIMINOLOGICA. ÉTUDES SUR LA CONDUITE ANTISOCIALE. STUDIES OF ANTISOCIAL BEHAVIOUR. v.1–7, 1968–1974. Montréal, Presses de l'Université de Montréal. Annual.
Issued by the Université de Montréal. Departement de Criminologie. Continued by: *Criminologie*. In French and English; summaries in English, French, German, Spanish and Russian.
Indexed: Soc. Abstr.

ACTA SCIENTIARUM SOCIALIUM
See HSIA-MEN TA HSÜEH HSÜEH PAO; SHE HUI K'O HSÜEH PAN

8 ACTA SOCIOLOGICA. SCANDINAVIAN REVIEW OF SOCIOLOGY. SCANDINAVISCHE ZEITSCHRIFT FÜR SOZIOLOGIE. REVUE SCANDINAVE DE SOCIOLOGIE. v.1– , 1955– . Copenhagen. Quarterly.
Issued by the Danish Sociological Society, Norwegian Sociological Society, Lund Sociological Society, and Westermarck Society. In English; occasionally in one of the Scandinavian languages.
Indexed: Bull. sig. soc. eth.; Int. Pol. Sc. Abstr.; PAIS; SSCI; Soc. Sc. Ind.

9 ACTA SOCIOLOGICA. SERIE B: CIUDAD. 1– , 1969– . Mexico City. Irreg.
Issued by the Centro de Estudios del Desarrollo. Universidad Autonoma Nacional.

10 ACTA SOCIOLOGICA. SERIE PROMOCIÓN SOCIAL. no.1– , 1969– . Mexico City. Annual.
Issued by the Centro de Estudios de Desarrollo. Universidad Autonoma Nacional.

ACTES SOCIAUX
See Action Populaire, Rheims. ACTES SOCIAUX

11 Action Populaire, Rheims. ACTES SOCIAUX. 1–80, 1906–1913. Rheims.

12 Action Populaire, Rheims. ANNÉE SOCIALE INTERNATIONALE. 1910–1914. Rheims.

13 Action Populaire, Rheims. REVUE. 1–6, 1908–Jan. 1914. Rheims.
Continued by its *Dossiers,* a series of monographs.

ACTUALITÉS SOCIALES
See Brussels. Université Libre. Institut de Sociologie. ACTUALITÉS SOCIALES

14 ADMINISTRATION & SOCIETY. v.6– , May 1974– . Beverly Hills, Calif., Sage Publications. Quarterly.
Continues: *Journal of Comparative Administration*. Published in cooperation with the Comparative Administration Group, American Society for Public Administration.
Indexed: Int. Bibl. Soc.; SSCI; Soc. Abstr.

15 ADOLESCENCE, SPORT AND LEISURE. 1975– . Waterloo, Ont. Three issues a year.
Issued by SIRLS, the Faculty of Human Kinetics and Leisure Studies, University of Waterloo.

16 ADULTHOOD, SPORT AND LEISURE. 1975– , Waterloo, Ont. Three issues a year.
Issued by SIRLS, the Faculty of Human Kinetics and Leisure Studies, University of Waterloo.

17 ADVANCES IN APPLIED SOCIAL PSYCHOLOGY. v.1– , 1980– . Hillsdale, N.J., Lawrence Erlbaum Associates. Annual.

18 ADVANCES IN BEHAVIOUR RESEARCH AND THERAPY. 1– , 1978– . London, Pergamon Press. Quarterly.
Indexed: Soc. Ed. Abstr.

19 ADVANCES IN EXPERIMENTAL SOCIAL PSYCHOLOGY. v.1– , 1964– . New York, Academic Press. Annual (Irreg.)

20 ADVANCES IN FAMILY INTERVENTION; ASSESSMENT AND THEORY. 1– , 1980– . Greenwich, Conn., JAI Press. Annual.

ADVANCES IN THE SOCIOLOGY OF LANGUAGE
See CONTRIBUTIONS TO THE SOCIOLOGY OF LANGUAGE

21 AFGHANISTAN JOURNAL. 1974– . Graz, Akademische Druck und Verlagsanstalt. Quarterly.

22 AFRICA. no.1– , Apr. 1928– . London, Oxford University Press; Manchester University Press, v.52– , 1982– . Quarterly.
Issued by the International African Institute (called, Jan. 1928–Dec. 1945, International Institute of African Languages and Cultures). Publication suspended Oct. 1940–Oct. 1942. In English, French, and German.
Indexed: Afr. Abstr.; Soc. Abstr.

23 AFRICA. v.1– , Aug. 1946– . Roma, Edizioni africane. Quarterly.
Issued by the Istituto Italiano per l'Africa. Title varies: Aug. 1946, *Notiziario della Associazione Frale; Impresse Italiane in Africa.* In Italian; summaries in English and French.

24 AFRICAN ABSTRACTS. v.1– , Jan. 1950– . London. Quarterly.
Issued by the International African Institute. Title varies: 1950–66, *African Abstracts. Bulletin analytique africaniste.* Published also in a French edition titled *Analyses africanistes,* Mar/Apr. 1967– . Ethnic, linguistic, and author indexes supplied.

25 AFRICAN PERSPECTIVES. 1976– . Leiden. Two issues a year.
Issued by the Afrika-Studiecentrum. Continues: *Kroniek van Afrika.* In English. Some issues thematic.

AFRICAN POPULATION NEWSLETTER
See United Nations. Economic Commission for Africa. AFRICAN POPULATION NEWSLETTER

26 AFRICAN SOCIAL RESEARCH. no.1– , June 1966– . Manchester, Manchester University Press. Semi-annual.
Issued by the Institute for Social Research, University of Zambia. Supersedes: *Rhodes-Livingstone Journal. Human Problems in British Central Africa.*
Indexed: Afr. Abstr.; Soc. Abstr.

27 AFRICAN SOCIAL RESEARCH DOCUMENTS. v.1– , 1970– . Leiden. Irreg.
Issued jointly by the Afrika Studiecentrum at Leiden and African Studies Centre, Cambridge University. In English.
Monograph series.
Indexed: Afr. Abstr.; Anth. Ind.; Int. Bibl. Soc.; Bull. sig. soc. eth.; Peace Res. Abstr. J.

28 AFRICAN STUDIES REVIEW. v.13– , Apr. 1970– . East Lansing, Mich. Three issues a year.
Issued by the African Studies Center, State University of Michigan, for the African Studies Association. Continues: *African Studies Bulletin,* 1958–69.
Indexed: Soc. Sc. Ind.

29 AFRICAN URBAN NOTES. v.1–7, 1966–1972. Los Angeles, Calif. Irreg.
Issued by the Department of Political Science, University of California at Los Angeles. Superseded by: *African Urban Notes. Series B.*

30 AFRICAN URBAN NOTES. SERIES B. winter 1974/1975–1977. East Lansing, Mich. Three issues a year.
Issued by the African Studies Center, State University of Michigan. Supersedes: *African Urban Notes.* Continued by: *African Urban Studies.*

31 AFRICAN URBAN STUDIES. no.1– , 1972– . Evanston, Ill. Irreg.
Monograph series.

32 AFRICAN URBAN STUDIES (AFRICAN STUDIES). n.s. no. 1– , spring 1978– . East Lansing, Mich. Three issues a year.
Issued by the African Studies Center, State University of Michigan. Continues: *African Urban Notes. Series B.*

AFRICAN WOMEN
See WOMEN TODAY

33 AFRICANA RESEARCH BULLETIN. v.1– , 1970– . Freetown. Quarterly (irreg.).
Issued by the Institute of African Studies. Fourah Bay College, University of Sierra Leone.

34 AFRO-AMERICAN RESEARCH BIBLIOGRAPHY. no. 1– , 1970– . St. Louis. Irreg.
Issued by the Pius XII Memorial Library, St. Louis University. Title varies: *Black America; A Research Bibliography.*

35 AFRO-AMERICAN STUDIES. v.1–3, 1970–1975. London, Gordon and Breach Science Publishers. Quarterly.
Issued by the City University of New York. Superseded by: *Ethnic Groups.*
Indexed: Psych. Abstr.

36 AGGIORNAMENTI SOCIALI. 1– , 1950– . Milan.
Issued by the Centro di Studi Sociali. Cumulative index, 1950–69.
Indexed: Bull. sig. soc. eth.; Int. Bibl. Soc.; Int. Pol. Sc. Abstr.

37 AGGLOMÉRATION BRUXELLOISE; APPROCHE GÉOGRAPHIQUE ET SOCIOLOGIQUE. 1– , 1971– . Brussels. Irreg.
Issued by the Institut de Sociologie, Université Libre de Bruxelles.

38 Agrarsoziale Gesellschaft. MATERIAL-SAMMLUNG. no.1– , 1953– . Göttingen. Irreg.

39 Ahmadu Bello University, Zaria, Nigeria. Sociology Department. OCCASIONAL PAPERS. no.1– , 1972– . Irreg.
Title varies: no.1, 1972, *Occasional Publications*.
Series of papers.

40 Akademie der Wissenschaften der DDR. ABHANDLUNGEN. GESELLSCHAFTSWISSENSCHAFTEN. 1– , 1975– . Berlin, Akademie Verlag GmbH. Irreg.

41 Akademiia nauk Armianskoi S.S.R. IZVESTIIA. SERIIA OBSHCHESTVENNYKH NAUK. 1945–1965. Erivan. Monthly.
Superseded by its *Vestnik obshchestvennykh nauk*. Text and summaries in Armenian and Russian.

42 Akademiia nauk Armianskoi S.S.R. VESTNIK OBSHCHESTVENNYKH NAUK. 1966– . Erivan.
Supersedes its *Izvestiia. Seriia obshchestvennykh nauk*. Text and summaries in Armenian and Russian.

43 Akademiia nauk Estonskoi S.S.R. IZVESTIIA. SERIIA OBSHCHESTVENNYKH NAUK. 1958– . Tallin. Quarterly.
Supersedes: *Izvestiia Akademii nauk Estonskoi S.S.R.*, 1952–55. Text in Russian and Estonian; summaries in English, Estonian, German and Russian.
Indexed: Int. Bibl. Soc.

44 Akademiia nauk Kazakhskoi S.S.R. IZVESTIIA. SERIIA OBSHCHESTVENNYKH NAUK. 1954– . Alma Ata. Bimonthly.
Title varies: 1954–57, *Izvestiia. Seriia istorii, ekonomiki, prava*; 1958–62, *Izvestiia. Seriia istorii, arkheologii i etnografii,* and *Seriia ekonomiki, filosofii i prava*. In Russian; summaries in Kazakh.
Indexed: Int. Bibl. Soc.

45 Akademiia Kirghizskoi S.S.R. IZVESTIIA. SERIIA OBSHCHESTVENNYKH NAUK. 1959– . Frunze. Three issues a year, 1960–61; two issues a year 1964– . Suspended in 1962.
Text in Kirghiz and Russian.

Akademiia nauk Litovskoi S.S.R.
See Lietuvos TSR Mokslu Akademija, Vilnius.

46 Akademiia nauk Moldavskoi S.S.R. IZVESTIIA. SERIIA OBSHCHESTVENNYKH NAUK. 1968– . Kishenev, Izdatel'stvo Shtiintsa. Three issues a year.
Test in Ukrainian and Russian.
Indexed: Bull. sig. soc. eth.; Int. Bibl. Soc.

47 Akademiia nauk S.S.S.R. IZVESTIIA. OTDELENIE OBSHCHESTVENNYKH NAUK. 1928–1935; n.s., 1936–38. Moskva. Ten issues a year, 1928–1935; monthly (irreg.), 1936–1938.
Supersedes, in part, its *Izvestiia. VI Seriia.* Title varies: 1928–30, its *Izvestiia. VII Seriia. Otdelenie humanitarnykh nauk*; 1931–35, *Izvestiia. VII Seriia. Otdelenie obshchestvennykh nauk*. In Russian.

48 Akademiia nauk S.S.S.R. Sibirskoe Otdelenie. IZVESTIIA. SERIIA OBSHCHESTVENNYKH NAUK. 1963– . Novosibirsk, 'Nauka'. Three issues a year.
Supersedes, in part, its *Izvestiia.* In Russian.
Indexed: Int. Bibl. Soc.

49 Akademiia nauk Tadzhiskoi S.S.R. Otdelenie obshchestvennykh nauk. IZVESTIIA. no.1–24, 1952–1957; n.s. v.1– , 1958– . Dushanbe. Four issues a year.
Text and summaries in Tadjik and Russian.
Indexed: Int. Bibl. Soc.

50 Akademiia nauk Turkmenskoi S.S.R. IZVESTIIA. SERIIA OBSHCHESTVENNYKH NAUK. 1952– . Ashabad.
Title varies: 1952–59, *Izvestiia Akademii nauk Turkmenskoi S.S.R.* Supersedes: *Izvestiia Turkmenskogo filiala Akademii nauk S.S.S.R.*, 1944–51. Text and summaries in Turkman and Russian.
Indexed: Int. Bibl. Soc.

51 Akademiia Navuk Belaruskai S.S.R., Minsk. VESTSI. SERYIA HRAMADSKIKH NAVUK. 1956– . Minsk, Izd. 'Nauka i tekhnika'.
Superseded: *Izvestiia Akademii navuk Belaruskai S.S.R. Seryia hramadskikh navuk*, 1948–55. In White Russian; summaries in Russian.

52 Akademiia za obshchestveni nauki i sotsialno upravlenie. NAUCHNI TRUDOVE. Sofia.

In Bulgarian; summaries in Russian; occasionally in English or French.

53 Akademija nauka i umjetnosti. Odjeljenie drustvenikh nauka. SPOMENIK. n.s. 1– , 1950– . Beograd. Irreg.
In Serbocroatian; summaries in English, French, German or Russian.

54 Akademija nauka i umjetnosti Bosne i Hercegovine. Odjeljenie drustvenikh nauka. [RADOVI]. Sarajevo.
Subseries of the Academy's *Radovi*. Summaries in English, French and German.

55 AKADEMIKA: JOURNAL OF HUMANITIES AND SOCIAL SCIENCES. 1, 1972. Kuala Lumpur, Publications Committee, National University of Malaysia. One issue published.
Subtitle also in Malay. Text and summaries in English or Malay. Superseded by *Humanisma*.

56 Alabama. Agricultural Research Station, Auburn. Department of Agricultural Economics and Rural Sociology. RURAL SOCIOLOGY SERIES. no.1– , Apr. 1974– . Auburn. Irreg.

57 ALLENSBACHER JAHRBUCH DER DEMOSKOPIE. v.1– , 1947/55– . Vienna, Verlag Fritz Molden. Irreg.
Issued by the Institut für Demoskopie. Title varies: v.1–5, 1947/53–73, *Jahrbuch der öffentlichen Meinung*.

THE ALPHA KAPPA DELTA QUARTERLY
See SOCIOLOGICAL INQUIRY

ALPHA KAPPA DELTIAN
See SOCIOLOGICAL INQUIRY

58 ALTERNATIVE FUTURES. v.1– , spring 1978– . Troy, N.Y. Quarterly.
Issued by the Human Dimensions Center, Renssalaer Polytechnic Institute, the University of Michigan Rackham Graduate School, and the Humanities Department, College of Engineering.
Indexed: Soc. Abstr.

59 ALTERNATIVE LIFE-STYLES. 1– , Feb. 1978– . Beverly Hills, Calif., Sage Publications. Quarterly.
Issued by the Department of Sociology and Anthropology, University of New Hampshire. Subtitle reads 'Changing patterns in marriage, family & intimacy'.

60 ALTERNATIVE ROUTES. 1977– . Ottawa, Ont. Annual.
Issued by the Department of Sociology and Anthropology, Carleton University.

61 AMERASIA JOURNAL. v.1– , Mar. 1971– . Los Angeles, Calif. Semi-annual.
Issued by the Asian American Studies Center, University of California.

62 AMERICA LATINA. v.1– , 1958– . Rio de Janeiro. Quarterly.
Issued by the Centro Latino-Americano de Pesquisas em Ciências Sociais. Title varies: v.1–4, 1958–61, *Boletim* of the Centro Latino-Americano de Pesquisas em Ciências Sociais. In Portuguese.
Indexed: Anth. Ind.; Int. Bibl. Soc.

AMERICA LATINA. ESTUDIOS SOCIOLÓGICOS
See ESTUDIOS SOCIOLÓGICOS LATINO-AMERICANOS

63 American Academy of Political and Social Science. ANNALS. v.1– , July 1890– . Philadelphia, Pa. Quarterly, 1890/91; bimonthly, 1891/92– , forming two volumes annually since 1895.
Indexed: ABC Pol. Sc.; Bull. sig. soc. eth.; Int. Bibl. Soc.; Int. Pol. Sc. Abstr.; Soc. Sc. Ind.; Soc. Abstr.

64 AMERICAN ANTHROPOLOGIST. 1888–1898; n.s. v.1– , 1899– . Washington, D.C. Monthly.
Issued originally by the American Anthropological Society of New York, Anthropological Society of Washington, D.C., and American Ethnological Society of New York; currently by the American Anthropological Association. Supersedes: Anthropological Society of Washington. *Transactions*. Cumulative indexes: 1888–1928, in v.32, no.3, part 2; includes index to *Current Anthropological Literature*, and *Memoirs* of the American Anthropological Association, 1929–38, in v.42.
Indexed: Afr. Abstr.; Bull. sig. soc. eth.; Int. Pol. Sc. Abstr.; PHRA; Soc. Sc. Hum. Ind.; Soc. Sc. Ind.; Soc. Abstr.

65 THE AMERICAN BEHAVIORAL SCIENTIST. v.1– , Sept. 1957– . Beverly Hills, Calif., Sage Publications. Bimonthly.
Issued by the Institute of Political Science, Princeton University, Dec. 1959–June 1960. Title varies: v.1–3, 1957–59, *PROD*; v.3, no. 2,4,6,8,10, *PROD Translations*. At head of title; 1957–June 1960, *Political Research; Organization and Design*. Other title: *ABS American Behavioral Scientist*. Separately paged supplements accompany some issues.

Indexed: Bull. sig. soc. eth.; Crime Del. Abstr.; Int. Bibl. Soc.; Int. Pol. Sc. Abstr.; Soc. Sc. Ind.; Sage Urb. Abstr.; Soc. Abstr.; Wom. Stud. Abstr.

THE AMERICAN CATHOLIC SOCIOLOGICAL REVIEW
See SOCIOLOGICAL ANALYSIS

66 American Country Life Conference. PROCEEDINGS OF THE CONFERENCE. 1st– , 1918– . Berlin, Wis. Annual.
Title varies: 1916–28, *Proceedings of the American Country Life Conference* (earlier called National Country Life Conference) No conference held in 1941–43, 1945.

67 AMERICAN JOURNAL OF COMMUNITY PSYCHOLOGY. 1– , Jan/Mar. 1973– . Washington, D.C., V. H. Winston & Sons. Quarterly.
Issued by the Association of Community Psychology in cooperation with the American Psychological Association.
Indexed: Curr. Cont.

68 AMERICAN JOURNAL OF ECONOMICS AND SOCIOLOGY. v.1– , Oct. 1941– . New York. Quarterly.
Sponsored by the Robert Schalkenback Foundation; co-sponsored by the Francis Neilson Fund.
Indexed: Abstr. Soc. Work; Bull. sig. soc. eth.; Int. Bibl. Soc.; Peace Res. Abstr. J.; SSCI; Soc. Abstr.

69 AMERICAN JOURNAL OF ORTHOPSYCHIATRY. v.1– , Oct. 1930– . Menasha, Wis., George Banta Publishing Co.
Issued by the American Orthopsychiatry Association. Indexes: v.1–10, 1930–40, 1 v.; v.11–20, 1941–50, 1 v.
Indexed: Abstr. Soc. Work; Int. Bibl. Soc.; Psych. Abstr.; Soc. Abstr.; Wom. Stud. Abstr.

THE AMERICAN JOURNAL OF RELIGIOUS PSYCHOLOGY AND EDUCATION
See JOURNAL OF RELIGIOUS PSYCHOLOGY, INCLUDING ITS ANTHROPOLOGICAL AND SOCIOLOGICAL ASPECTS

70 THE AMERICAN JOURNAL OF SOCIOLOGY. v.1– , July 1895– . Chicago, The University of Chicago Press. Bimonthly.
Indexed: Curr. Cont.; Int. Bibl. Soc.; SSCI; Soc. Sc. Ind.; Soc. Abstr.

AMERICAN LEARNED JOURNALS
See A LIST OF AMERICAN LEARNED JOURNALS DEVOTED TO HUMANISTIC AND SOCIAL STUDIES

71 AMERICAN MEN AND WOMEN OF SCIENCE. URBAN COMMUNITY SCIENCES. 1974– . New York, R. R. Bowker. Irreg.

72 American Planning Association. JOURNAL. v.1– , May/June 1935– . Boston, Mass., G. H. Ellis. Bimonthly, 1935–Feb. 1939; quarterly.
Title varies: 1935/43, *The Planner's Journal*. Publication suspended 1943–summer 1944. Issuing agency called American Institute of Planners through v.44, 1978.
Indexed: Bull. sig. soc. eth.; PAIS; PHRA; Soc. Work Res. Abstr.

73 THE AMERICAN SCHOLAR. v.1– , Jan. 1932– . New York, United Chapters of Phi Beta Kappa. Quarterly.
Indexed: Int. Bibl. Soc.; Soc. Abstr.

74 American Sociological Association. ANNUAL PROCEEDINGS. 1972– . Washington, D.C.

75 American Sociological Association. DIRECTORY. Dec. 1950– . New York. Triennial.
Other title: *ASA Directory*.

76 American Sociological Association. FOOTNOTES. 2– , 1974– . Washington, D.C. Nine issues a year.
Indexed: Soc. Abstr.

77 American Sociological Association. PUBLICATIONS. v.1–29, 1907–1935. Washington, D.C.

78 AMERICAN SOCIOLOGICAL FORUM. 1– , 1963– . Durham, N.C., Duke University Press.
Monograph series.

79 AMERICAN SOCIOLOGICAL REVIEW. v.1– , Feb. 1936– . Menasha, Wis., subsequently Washington, D.C. Bimonthly.
Issued by the American Sociological Association. Cover title: *ASR. American Sociological Review*. Book review section discontinued when *Contemporary Sociology* established, Jan. 1972. Indexes: v.1–15, 1936–50; v.1–20, 1936–55.
Indexed: Int. Bibl. Soc.; Int. Pol. Sc. Abstr.; Sage Urb. Abstr.; Soc. Abstr.; Soc. Work Res. Abstr.; Wom. Stud. Abstr.

80 AMERICAN SOCIOLOGIST. v.1– , Nov. 1965– . Albany, N.Y., subsequently, Washington, D.C. Quarterly.
Indexed: Bull. sig. soc. eth.; Int. Bibl. Soc.; Int. Pol. Sc. Abstr.; SSCI; Soc. Abstr.; Wom. Stud. Abstr.

ANALELE UNIVERSITATII BUCUREŞTI. SOCIOLOGIE
See Bucharest. Universitatea. ANALELE. SOCIOLOGIE

81 ANALES DE CIENCIAS SOCIALES. no.1– , Dec. 1971– . Panama City, Editoriale Universitaria. Semi-annual.
Issued by the Centro de Investigaciónes Sociales y Económicas, Universidad de Panama.

82 ANALES DE SOCIOLOGIA. v.1– , June 1966– . Barcelona. Two issues a year.
Issued by the Departamento de Sociologia del Centro de Estudios Económicos y Sociales de la Delegación del Consejo Superior de Investigaciónes Cientificas en Barcelona. In Spanish.
Indexed: Soc. Abstr.

ANALES. ECONOMIA Y SOCIOLOGIA AGRARIAS
See Spain. Instituto Nacional de Investigaciónes Agrarias. ANALES. ECONOMIA Y SOCIOLOGIA AGRARIAS

ANALES INTERNACIONALES DE CRIMINOLOGIA
See ANNALES INTERNATIONALES DE CRIMINOLOGIE

83 ANALISE SOCIAL. v.1– , Jan. 1962– . Lisboa, Editorial Imperio. Annual.
Issued by the Instituto Superior de Ciências Economicas e Financieras, Cabinete de Investigações Sociais. Supersedes: *Revista do Cabinete de Estudos Corporativos*. In Portuguese; table of contents and summaries also in English and French.
Indexed: Bull. sig. soc. eth.; Int. Pol. Sc. Abstr.; Peace Res. Abstr. J.; Soc. Abstr.

84 ABALIZY I PRÒBY TECHNIK BADAWCZYCH W SOCJOLOGII. v.1– , 1966– . Wrocław, Zakład Narodowy im. Ossolińskich. Irreg.
Issued by the Instytut Filozofii i Socjologii, Polska Akademia Nauk.
Monograph series.

ANALYSE DE POLITIQUES
See CANADIAN PUBLIC POLICY

85 ANALYSE & PREVISION; ÉTUDES, FUTURIBLES, BIBLIOGRAPHIE. v.1–8, no.4/6, 1966–Oct/Dec. 1974. Paris. Bimonthly.
Issued by the Société d'Études et de Documentation Économiques, Industrielles et Sociales. Superseded by: *Futuribles*.
Indexed: Int. Bibl. Soc.; Soc. Abstr.

ANALYSES AFRICANISTES
See AFRICAN ABSTRACTS

ANALYSIS OF POPULATION RESEARCH REPORT
See United States. Interagency Committee on Population Research. INVENTORY AND ANALYSIS OF FEDERAL POPULATION RESEARCH.

ANNALES
See Brussels. Université Libre. Institut de Sociologie. Centre d'Études des Religions. ANNALES

ANNALES
See Institut des Sciences Sociales, Brussels. ANNALES

ANNALES
See Musée Sociale, Paris. ANNALES

ANNALES
See Toulouse. Université des Sciences Sociales. ANNALES

86 ANNALES D'ÉCONOMIE ET DE SOCIOLOGIE RURALES. v.1– , 1972- . Paris, Service des Publications, I.N.R.A. Two or three issues a year.
Issued by the Departement d'Économie et de Sociologie Rurales, Institut National des Recherches Agronomiques. Supersedes: *Recherches d'Économie et de Sociologie Rurales,* 1967–71. Table of contents and summaries in English.

87 ANNALES D'HISTOIRE ÉCONOMIQUE ET SOCIALE. v.1–10(no.1–54), Jan. 15, 1929–Nov. 1938. Paris.
Superseded by: *Annales d'Histoire Sociale.* Index to v.1–10 in v.10.

88 ANNALES D'HISTOIRE SOCIALE. v.1–3, no.3/4, Jan. 1939–July/Dec. 1941. Paris.
Supersedes: *Annales d'Histoire Économique et Sociale.* Superseded by a publication of the same title.

89 ANNALES D'HISTOIRE SOCIALE. 1–8, 1942–1945. Paris.
Title varies: 1942–44, *Mélanges d'Histoire Sociale.* Supersedes a publication of the same title. Superseded by: *Annales; Économies, Sociétés, Civilisations.*

90 ANNALES DE DÉMOGRAPHIE HISTORIQUE. 1964– . Paris, Éditions Sirey. Annual.
Issued by the Société de Démographie Historique. Title varies: 1964, *Études et Chroniques de Démographie Historique.*

ANNALES DE L'ASSOCIATION INTERNATIONALE POUR LE PROGRÈS DES SCIENCES SOCIALES

See Association Internationale pour le Progrès des Sciences Sociales. ANNALES.

91 ANNALES DE L'EST. v.1– , 1949– . Nancy, Berger-Lavrault. Quarterly.
Issued by the Université de Nancy.

ANNALES DE L'INSTITUT DE SOCIOLOGIE
See International Institute of Sociology. ANNALES

92 ANNALES DE SOCIOLOGIE. v.1–6, 1900–1910. Paris, Bruxelles.
Issued by the Société Belge de Sociologie. Title varies: v.1, *Annales de Sociologie et Mouvement Sociologique Internationale.*

ANNALES DE SOCIOLOGIE ET MOUVEMENT SOCIOLOGIQUE INTERNATIONALE
See ANNALES DE SOCIOLOGIE

93 ANNALES; ÉCONOMIES, SOCIÉTÉS, CIVILISATIONS. 1– , Jan/Mar. 1946– . Paris, A. Colin. Bimonthly.
Supersedes: *Annales d'Histoire Sociale.*
Indexed: Afr. Abstr.; Bull. sig. soc. eth.; Peace Res. Abstr. J.; SSCI.

94 ANNALES INTERNATIONALES DE CRIMINOLOGIE. INTERNATIONAL ANNALS OF CRIMINOLOGY. ANALES INTERNACIONALES DE CRIMINOLGIA. v.1– , 1962– . Paris. Semi-annual.
Issued by the Société Internationale de Criminologie. Continues: *Bulletin* of the Société Internationale de Criminologie. In English and French; summaries in English and French.
Indexed: Int. Bibl. Soc.

95 ANNALES MAROCAINES DE SOCIOLOGIE. 1968– . Rabat.
Issued by the Institut de Sociologie de Rabat. Title also in English and Arabic; text in Arabic, English or French; summaries in two of these languages, other than language of text. Title in English: *Moroccan Annals of Sociology.*
Indexed: Soc. Abstr.

96 ANNALES SOCIOLOGIQUES. SÉRIE A: SOCIOLOGIE GÉNÉRALE. 1–4, 1934–1941. Paris.
Published during suspension of *l'Année Sociologique,* by which it was later absorbed.

97 ANNALES SOCIOLOGIQUES. SÉRIE B: SOCIOLOGIE RELIGIEUSE. v.1/3–4, 1939–1940. Paris.
Published during suspension of *l'Année Sociologique*, by which it was later absorbed.

98 ANNALES SOCIOLOGIQUES. SÉRIE C: SOCIOLOGIE JURIDIQUE ET MORALE. v.1–3, 1934–1940. Paris.
Published during suspension of *l'Année Sociologique,* by which it was later absorbed.

99 ANNALES SOCIOLOGIQUES. SÉRIE D: SOCIOLOGIE ÉCONOMIQUE. v.1–3/4, 1934–1940. Paris.
Published during suspension of *l'Année Sociologique,* by which it was later absorbed.

100 ANNALES SOCIOLOGIQUES. SÉRIE E: MORPHOLOGIE SOCIALE, LANGAGE, TECHNOLOGIE, ESTHETIQUE. v.1–3/4, 1935–1942. Paris.
Published during suspension of *l'Année Sociologique,* by which it was later absorbed.

ANNALES UNIVERSITATIS MARIAE CURIE-SKŁODOWSKA. SECTIO I. PHILOSOPHIA — SOCIOLOGIA
See Lublin. Uniwersytet. ANNALES. SECTIO I. PHILOSOPHIA — SOCIOLOGIA

ANNALES UNIVERSITATIS SCIENTIARUM BUDAPESTIENSIS DE ROLANDO EÖTVÖS NOMINATAE. SECTIO PHILOSOPHICA ET SOCIOLOGICA
See Budapest. Tudomány-Egyetem. ANNALES. SECTIO PHILOSOPHICA ET SOCIOLOGICA

ANNALI
See Fondazione Luigi Einaudi. ANNALI

101 ANNALI DI SOCIOLOGIA. v.1– , 1964– . Milano. Annual.
Issued by the Centro di Studi Sociologici. In Italian.
Indexed: Bull. sig. soc. eth.; Int. Bibl. Soc,; Soc. Abstr.

ANNALS
See Hungary. Központi Statisztikai Hivatal. Demográfiai Elnökségi Bizottság. ANNALS

ANNALS
See Tokyo Daigaku. Shakai Kagaku Kenkyūjo. ANNALS

102 THE ANNALS OF PHENOMENOLOGICAL SOCIOLOGY. 1– , 1976– . Dayton, Ohio. Annual.
Issued by the Wright State University.

ANNALS OF RURAL SOCIOLOGY — STUDIES AND MATERIALS
See ROCZNIKI SOCJOLOGII WSI. STUDIA I MATERIALY

ANNALS OF THE AMERICAN ACADEMY OF POLITICAL AND SOCIAL SCIENCE

See American Academy of Political and Social Science. ANNALS

ANNALS OF THE INSTITUTE OF SOCIAL SCIENCE
See Tokyo Daigaku. Shakai Kagaku Kenkyūjo. ANNALS

ANNALS OF THE SOCIETY FOR THE HISTORY OF SOCIAL THOUGHT
See SHAKAI SHISO SHI KENKYU

103 L'ANNÉE SOCIALE. 1960– . Bruxelles. Annual.
Issued by the Institut de Sociologie, Université Libre.

ANNÉE SOCIALE INTERNATIONALE
See Action Populaire, Rheims. ANNÉE SOCIALE INTERNATIONALE

104 L'ANNÉE SOCIOLOGIQUE. 1–12, 1896/97–1909/12; n.s. v.1–2, 1923/24–1924/25; serie 3, v.1– , 1940/48– . Paris, Presses Universitaires de France. Annual.
Absorbed: *Annales Sociologiques,* série A, B, C, D, E.
Indexed: Bull. sig. soc. eth.; Int. Bibl. Soc.; Int. Pol. Sc. Abstr.; Soc. Abstr.

105 ANNUAIRE DE L'U.R.S.S.: DROIT, ÉCONOMIE, SOCIOLOGIE, POLITIQUE, CULTURE. 1965–1969. Paris. Quarterly.
Issued by the Centre de Recherches sur l'U.R.S.S. et des Pays de l'Est, Université des Sciences Juridiques Politiques et Sociales. Supersedes a two-volume publication titled: *l'U.R.S.S. Droit, Économie, Sociologie, Politique, Culture.* Continued by: *Annuaire de l'U.R.S.S. et des Pays Socialistes Européens.*
Indexed: Int. Pol. Sc. Abstr.

106 ANNUAIRE DE L'U.R.S.S. ET DES PAYS SOCIALISTES EUROPÉENS. 1972/73– . Strasbourg, Librarie Iskra.
Issued by the Centre de Recherches sur l'U.R.S.S. et des Pays de l'Est, Université de Strasbourg. Continues: *Annuaire de l'U.R.S.S. Droit, Économie, Sociologie, Politique, Culture.* In English and French.

107 ANNUAIRE DE STATISTIQUE INTERNATIONALE DES GRANDES VILLES. INTERNATIONAL STATISTICAL YEARBOOK OF LARGE TOWNS. 1961–1972. The Hague. Biennial.
Issued by the International Statistical Institute in cooperation with the International Union of Local Authorities.

ANNUAIRE DE STATISTIQUES SOCIALES
See SOZIALSTATISTIK; JAHRBUCH

ANNUAIRE DÉMOGRAPHIQUE
See Portugal. Instituto Nacional de Estatistica. STATISTIQUES DÉMOGRAPHIQUES

108 ANNUAIRE DES DÉPARTEMENTS DE SOCIOLOGIE, D'ANTHROPOLOGIE, D'ARCHÉOLOGIE DES UNIVERSITÉS ET DES MUSÉUMS DU CANADA. GUIDE TO DEPARTMENTS OF SOCIOLOGY, ANTHROPOLOGY, ARCHEOLOGY IN UNIVERSITIES AND MUSEUMS IN CANADA. 1978–1979– . Ottawa, National Museum of Man.
Compiled by the Canadian Sociology and Anthropology Association. Subseries of *Mercury Series* and *Directorate Paper.* Continues: *Guide to Departments of Sociology and Anthropology in Canadian Universities.*

ANNUAIRE DES DÉPARTEMENTS DE SOCIOLOGIE ET D'ANTHROPOLOGIE DU CANADA
See GUIDE TO DEPARTMENTS OF SOCIOLOGY AND ANTHROPOLOGY IN CANADIAN UNIVERSITIES

109 ANNUAIRE DES SOCIOLOGUES ET ANTHROPOLOGUES AU CANADA ET LEUR RECHERCHE COURANTE. A DIRECTORY OF SOCIOLOGISTS AND ANTHROPOLGISTS IN CANADA AND THEIR CURRENT RESEARCH. 1968–1972/1973. Montréal. Annual.
Issued by the Société Canadienne de Sociologie et d'Anthropologie. Continued by: *Guide to Departments of Sociology and Anthropology in Canadian Universities.* In French and English.

ANNUAL ADMINISTRATION REPORT ON SCHEDULED AREAS IN GUJURAT STATE
See Gujurat, India (State). ANNUAL ADMINISTRATION REPORT ON SCHEDULED AREAS IN GUJURAT STATE

ANNUAL BULLETIN OF SOCIOLOGY
See SHAKAIGAKU NENSHI

ANNUAL MEETING PROCEEDINGS
See National Council on Family Relations. ANNUAL MEETING PROCEEDINGS

ANNUAL PROCEEDINGS
See American Sociological Association. ANNUAL PROCEEDINGS

ANNUAL REPORT
See Canadian Consultative Council on Multiculturalism. ANNUAL REPORT

ANNUAL REPORT
See Center for Intergroup Studies. ANNUAL REPORT

ANNUAL REPORT
See Eugenics Society, London. ANNUAL REPORT

ANNUAL REPORT
See Institute of Race Relations. ANNUAL REPORT

ANNUAL REPORT
See Intergovernmental Committee for European Migration. ANNUAL REPORT

ANNUAL REPORT
See Kenya. Department of Community Development. ANNUAL REPORT

ANNUAL REPORT
See Michigan. University. Population Studies Center. ANNUAL REPORT

ANNUAL REPORT
See Northern Ireland. Community Relations Commission. ANNUAL REPORT

ANNUAL REPORT
See Social Science Research Council. ANNUAL REPORT

ANNUAL REPORT
See South African Institute of Race Relations. ANNUAL REPORT

ANNUAL REPORT OF MEIJI GAKUIN UNIVERSITY REVIEW. SPECIAL EDITION FOR SOCIOLOGY
See MEIJI GAKUIN RONSO KENKYU NENPO — SHAKAIGAKU SHAKAI JIGYO

ANNUAL REPORT OF SOCIOLOGY
See OHTANI DAIGAKU SHAKAIGAKU NENPO

ANNUAL REPORT OF THE EXECUTIVE DIRECTOR
See Harvard University. Program on Technology and Society. ANNUAL REPORT OF THE EXECUTIVE DIRECTOR

110 ANNUAL REVIEW OF PSYCHOLOGY. v.1– , 1950– . Stanford, Calif. Annual.
Issued by the Stanford University.
Indexed: Soc. Abstr.

111 ANNUAL REVIEW OF SOCIOLOGY. 1– , 1975– . Palo Alto, Calif., Annual Reviews, Inc.

ANTHROPOLOGY AND SOCIOLOGY PAPERS
See Montana. State University, Missoula. Department of Anthropology and Sociology. ANTHROPOLOGY AND SOCIOLOGY PAPERS

112 ANUARIO COLOMBIANO DE HISTORIA SOCIAL Y DE LA CULTURA. 1–5, 1963–1971. Bogotá, D.E. Annual.
Issued by the Departamento de Historia, Faculdad de Ciencias Humanas, Universidad Nacional de Colombia. In Spanish.

113 ANUARIO DE SOCIOLOGIA DE LOS PUEBLOS IBERICOS. 1955–1967. Madrid, Instituto de Estudios Sindicales, Sociales y Cooperativos. Annual.
Issued by the Asociación de Sociologos de Lengua Espanola y Portuguesa (ASLEP) and the Instituto de Cultura Hispanica. In Spanish.

ANUARIO — DEMOGRAFIA; ANUARIO DE DEMOGRAFIA
See Chile. Instituto Nacional de Estadisticas. DEMOGRAFIA

ANUARIO DEMOGRAFICO
See Bolivia. Dirección Nacional de Estadistica y Censos. ANUARIO DEMOGRAFICO

ANUARIO DEMOGRAFICO
See Colombia. Departamento Administrativo Nacional de Estadistica. ANUARIO DEMOGRAFICO

ANUARIO DEMOGRAFICO
See Portugal. Instituto Nacional de Estatistica. STATISTIQUES DEMOGRAFIQUES

114 APORTES. July 1966–Oct. 1972. Paris. Quarterly.
Issued by the Instituto Latinoamericano de Relaciónes Internacionales. In Spanish.
Indexed: Bull. sig. soc. eth.; Int. Bibl. Soc.; Int. Pol. Sc. Abstr.; Soc. Abstr.

APPLIED ANTHROPOLOGY
See HUMAN ORGANIZATION

115 APPLIED SOCIAL PSYCHOLOGY ANNUAL. v.1– , Feb. 1980– . Beverly Hills, Calif., Sage Publications.
Sponsored by the Society for the Psychological Study of Human Issues.

ARAB JOURNAL FOR SOCIOLOGICAL DEFENCE
See AL MAJALLAH AI-ARABIYAH LIL-DIFA' AL-IJTIMA

116 Araraquara, Brazil. Faculdade de Filosofia, Ciências e Letras. Cadeira de Sociologia e Fundamentos Sociologicos da Educação. BOLETIM. 1965– . Araraquara. Irreg.
In Portuguese.

ARBEITSBERICHTE AUS DEM INSTITUT FÜR SOZIOLOGIE DER UNIVERSITÄT
See Bern. Universität. Institut für Soziologie. ARBEITSHEFTE

ARBEITSHEFTE
See Berlin (West). Technische Universität. Institut für Soziologie. SOZIOLOGISCHE ARBEITSHEFTE

117 ARBEITSHEFTE FÜR GEMEINSCHAFTSKUNDE. no.1–11, 1963–1969. Frankfurt-am-Main-Hoechst, Wochenschau Verlag. Irreg.
Includes subseries: *Gesellschaft, Staat und Wirtschaft*. no.1–6, 1965–1969.

118 ARBEITSPAPIERE ZUR POLITISCHEN SOZIOLOGIE. no.1–9, 1972–1973. München. Irreg.
Title on back cover, *Ein Forum Junger Sozialwissenschaftler*.

119 ARCHIVES AFRICAINES DE SOCIOLOGIE. v.1– , 1971– . Paris, Éditions Classiques d'Expression Francaise. Irreg.
Issued by the Centre de Recherche et d'Information Socio-Politiques.
Monograph series.

120 ARCHIVES DE SOCIOLOGIE DES RELIGIONS. v.1–17(no.1–34), Jan/June 1956–1972. Paris, Centre Nationale de la Recherche Scientifique. Two issues a year.
Issued by the Groupe de Sociologie des Religions, Centre d'Études Sociologiques, Centre Nationale de la Recherche Scientifique. Continued by: *Archives des Sciences Sociales et Religions*.
Indexed: Bull. sig. soc. eth.; Int. Bibl. Soc.; Int. Pol. Sc. Abstr.; Soc. Abstr.

121 ARCHIVES DES SCIENCES SOCIALES DE LA COOPÉRATION ET DU DÉVELOPPEMENT. v.43– , Jan/Mar. 1978– . Paris.
Issued by the Bureau d'Études Coopératives et Communautaires. Continues: *Archives Internationales de Sociologie de la Coopération*. At head of title: *Communautés*

122 ARCHIVES DES SCIENCES SOCIALES DES RELIGIONS. v.18(no.35)– , Jan/June 1973– . Paris, Centre National de Recherche Scientifique. Semi-annual.
Issued by the Institut des Sciences des Religions. Continues: *Archives de Sociologie des Religions*.
Indexed: Soc. Abstr.

123 ARCHIVES EUROPÉENNES DE SOCIOLOGIE. v.1– , 1960– . Paris. G. P. Maisonneuve et Larose. Semi-annual.
Issued by the 6e Section des Sciences Économiques et Sociales, École Pratique des Hautes Études. Other titles: *European Journal of Sociology* and *Europaisches Archiv für Soziologie*.
Indexed: Bull. sig. soc. eth.; Int. Bibl. Soc.; Int. Pol. Sc. Abstr.; Sage Urb. Abstr.; SSCI; Soc. Sc. Ind.; Soc. Abstr.

124 ARCHIVES INTERNATIONALES DE SOCIOLOGIE DE LA COOPERATION. ARCHIVIO INTERNAZIONALE DI SOCIOLOGIA DELLA COOPERAZIONE. INTERNATIONAL ARCHIVES OF SOCIOLOGY OF COOPERATION. no.1–41/42, Jan/June 1957–1977. Paris. Semi-annual.
Issued by the Bureau d'Études Coopératives et Communataires, International Council for Research in Sociology of Cooperation. Supersedes: *Communauté et Vie Coopérative*. Continued by: *Archives des Sciences Sociales de la Coopération et du Développement*. Issued as a supplement to *Communauté*. In French; some articles in English.
Indexed: Int. Bibl. Soc.; Soc. Abstr.

125 ARCHIVES MAROCAINES. v.1–34, 1904–1936. Paris.
V.1–24 published by the Mission Scientifique de Maroc; v.26–34 by the Section Sociologique de la Direction des Affaires Indigènes. V.25 not published.

126 ARCHIVES OF SEXUAL BEHAVIOR. v.1– , 1971– . New York, Plennum Publishing Co. Bimonthly.
Subtitle reads: 'An interdisciplinary research journal'.
Indexed: Curr. Cont.; Soc. Abstr.

ARCHIVES SOCIOLOGIQUES
See Brussels. Université Libre. Institut de Sociologie. BULLETIN

127 ARCHIVO DI STUDI URBANI E REGIONALI. v.1– , May 1969– . Milan, Novita Marsiglio Editore, subsequently Franco Angeli, Editore. Originally monthly, now quarterly.
Each issue is thematic.

ARCHIVO INTERNAZIONALE DI SOCIOLOGIA DELLA COOPERAZIONE
See ARCHIVES INTERNATIONALES DE SOCIOLOGIE DE LA COOPÉRATION

128 Argentina Republic. Dirección General de Estadistica. INFORME. SER. D: DEMOGRAFIA. no.1–12, 1926–1944. Buenos Aires.

129 ARKANSAS JOURNAL OF SOCIOLOGY. 1– , May 1972– . Fayetteville, Ark.

'A journal published by the graduate students, Department of Sociology, University of Arkansas'.

130 ARMED FORCES AND SOCIETY. 1– , fall 1974– . Chicago, subsequently Beverly Hills, Calif., Sage Publications. Quarterly.
Issued by the Inter-University Seminar on Armed Forces and Society.
Indexed: Soc. Abstr.

131 ASIA QUARTERLY. v.1– , 1971– . Bruxelles, Éditions de l'Institut de Sociologie. Four issues a year.
Issued by the Centre d'Études du Sud-Est Asiatique et de l'Extrême-Orient, Institut de Sociologie, Université Libre. Supersedes: *Revue du Sud-Est Asiatique et de l'Extrême-Orient, Journal of Southeast Asia and the Far East.*
Indexed: Curr. Cont.; Int. Bibl. Soc.; PAIS; Soc. Abstr.

132 ASIAN FOLKLORE AND SOCIAL LIFE MONOGRAPHS. v.1– , 1971– . Taipei, Oriental Culture Service. Irreg.
Monograph series; some reprints.

133 ASIAN POPULATION STUDIES SERIES. no.1– , 1966– . New York. Irreg.
Issued by the United Nations (U.N. Document E/CN.11).
Monograph series.

134 ASIAN SOCIAL SCIENCES BIBLIOGRAPHY WITH ANNOTATIONS AND ABSTRACTS. v.1– , 1952– . Delhi, Vicas Publishing House. Annual.
Issued by the Research Centre on the Social Implications of Industrialization in Southern Asia, Unesco. Title varies: 1952–56, *Social Science Bibliography, India;* 1957, *Social Science Bibliography, India, Pakistan;* 1958, *South Asia Social Science Bibliography;* 1959–65, *Southern Asia Social Science Bibliography* (with Annotations and Abstracts). Absorbed: *South Asia Social Science Abstracts* in 1959.

135 ASIAN SURVEY. v.1– , Mar. 1961– . Berkeley, Calif., University of California Press. Monthly.
Issued by the University of California at Berkeley. Subtitle reads: 'A monthly review of contemporary Asian affairs'.
Indexed: Int. Bibl. Soc.; Int. Pol. Sc. Abstr.; SSCI; Soc. Sc. Ind.

136 ASIAN THOUGHT AND SOCIETY. v.1– , Apr. 1976– . Oneonta, N.Y. Three issues a year.
Issued by the Department of Political Science, State University of New York, in cooperation with the Center of East Europe, Russia and Asia, Boston College.

137 Asociación Española de Economia y Sociologia Agrarias. REUNIÓN DE ESTUDIOS. [1]– , 1967– . Madrid, Institute de Estudios Agro-Sociales.

138 Asociación Venezolana de Sociologia. SOCIOLOGIA. no.1–2, Apr. 1961–Dec. 1962. Caracas.

139 Association for Sociologists in Southern Africa. PAPERS FROM THE CONGRESS. 1972?– . Durban. No more information available.

140 Association Internationale pour le Progrès des Sciences Sociales. ANNALES. 1–4 session, 1863–1866. Bruxelles.

141 Association of Social Anthropologists. MONOGRAPH. no.1– , 1965– . New York, Praeger. Irreg.
Monograph series.

ASYLUM; JOURNAL OF MENTAL SCIENCE
See BRITISH JOURNAL OF PSYCHIATRY

142 ATISBOS. Summer 1975– . Stanford, Calif., subsequently Phoenix, Ariz. Three issues a year.
Issued by the Stanford University; since 1981 by the American Studies and Research Center, University of Arizona.

143 ATTITUDE TOWARD LEISURE. 1975– . Waterloo, Ont. Three issues a year.
Issued by the SIRLS, Faculty of Human Kinetics and Leisure Studies, University of Waterloo.

144 ATTITUDE TOWARD SPORT AND PHYSICAL ACTIVITY. 1975– . Waterloo, Ont. Three issues a year.
Issued by the SIRLS, Faculty of Human Kinetics and Leisure Studies, University of Waterloo.

145 Auckland, N.Z. University. SOCIOLOGY SERIES. no.1– , 1954– . Auckland. Irreg.
Subseries of its *Bulletin.*

146 Auckland, N.Z. University. Department of Sociology. PAPERS IN COMPARATIVE SOCIOLOGY. no.1–4, 1974. Auckland. Irreg.
Continued by: *Working Papers in Comparative Sociology.*

147 AUGUSTE COMTE MEMORIAL TRUST LECTURE. no.1–10, 1954–1974. London, Athlone Press.
Sponsored by the London School of Economics and Political Science, University of London.

148 Australia. Bureau of Census and Statistics. DEMOGRAPHY. BULLETIN. no.1– , 1900/06– . Canberra, Government Publishing Service. Quarterly.

Title varies: no.1–39, *Population and Vital Statistics;* no.40–55, Australian Demography. No.1–44 published in Melbourne.

149 Australia. Bureau of Census and Statistics. INTERNAL MIGRATION. 1969/1973– . Melbourne.

First report covers May 1969–Apr. 1973. Report year-end, Apr. 30.

150 Australia. Bureau of Census and Statistics. POPULATION: PRINCIPAL CITIES AND TOWNS. 1966/1972– . Canberra.

151 Australia. Department of Immigration and Ethnic Affairs. AUSTRALIAN IMMIGRATION. Jan. 1952– . Canberra. Quarterly.

Early issues published under the Department's earlier name, Department of Immigration.

152 Australia. Department of Immigration and Ethnic Affairs. AUSTRALIAN IMMIGRATION; CONSOLIDATED STATISTICS. no.1– , 1966– . Canberra, Government Publications Service.

Early issues published under the Department's earlier name, Department of Immigration.

153 THE AUSTRALIAN AND NEW ZEALAND JOURNAL OF SOCIOLOGY. v.1– , Apr. 1965– . Melbourne, Pitman and Sons. Three issues a year.

Issued by the Sociological Association of Australia and New Zealand. Mimeographed. Indexes: v.1–2, with v.2.

Indexed: Curr. Cont.; Int. Bibl. Soc.; Int. Pol. Sc. Abstr.; SSCI; Soc. Abstr.

154 AUSTRALIAN DEMOGRAPHIC REVIEW. no.1– , Jan. 1951– . Canberra. Irreg.

Issued by the Bureau of Census and Statistics.

AUSTRALIAN DEMOGRAPHY
See Australia. Bureau of Census and Statistics. DEMOGRAPHY

155 AUSTRALIAN GALLUP POLLS. 1941– Melbourne, Vic. Irreg.

Issued by the Ray Morgan Research Centre Pty., Ltd.

AUSTRALIAN IMMIGRATION
See Australia. Department of Immigration and Ethnic Affairs. AUSTRALIAN IMMIGRATION.

156 AUSTRALIAN IMMIGRATION: A BIBLIOGRAPHY AND DIGEST. [1]– , 1966– . Canberra.

Issued by the Department of Demography, Australian National University.

AUSTRALIAN IMMIGRATION; CONSOLIDATED STATISTICS
See Australia. Department of Immigration and Ethnic Affairs. AUSTRALIAN IMMIGRATION: CONSOLIDATED STATISTICS

157 AUSTRALIAN IMMIGRATION: MONOGRAPH SERIES. no.1– , 1974– . Canberra. Irreg.

Issued by the Department of Demography, Institute of Advanced Studies, The Australian National University.

158 THE AUSTRALIAN JOURNAL OF SOCIAL ISSUES. v.1– , spring 1961– . Sydney. Semiannual.

Issued by the University of Sydney, and New South Wales Branch of the Australian Association of Social Workers.

Indexed: APAIS; Soc. Abstr.

159 AUSTRALIAN PUBLIC AFFAIRS INFORMATION SERVICE. v.1– , 1945– . Canberra. Eleven issues a year, cumulated annually.

Issued by the National Library of Australia.

160 AUSTRALIAN SOCIAL SCIENCE ABSTRACTS. 1–18, Mar. 1946–Nov. 1964. Melbourne.

Issued by the Committee on Research in the Social Sciences, Australian National Research Council, Nov. 1946–Oct. 1951; by the Social Science Research Council of Australia, May 1952–Nov. 1964.

161 Austria. Statistisches Zentralamt. NATÜRLICHE BEVÖLKERUNGSBEWEGUNG. 1966–1974. Wien.

Continued by: *Demographisches Jahrbuch Österreichs.*

162 AUTONOMOUS GROUPS. v.1–15, Feb. 1945–Winter 1960. New York. Quarterly.

Issued by the Committee on Autonomous Groups. Title varies: Feb. 1945–summer 1955, *Autonomous Groups Bulletin.*

AUTONOMOUS GROUPS BULLETIN
See AUTONOMOUS GROUPS

163 AUTREMENT. no.1– , spring 1975– . Paris, Autrement. Four issues a year.

164 AVANCES DE INVESTIGACIÓN. 1975– . San José. Irreg.

Issued by the Instituto de Investigaciónes Sociales, Faculdad de Ciencias Sociales, Universidad de Costa Rica.

165 'AVARYANUT VE-HEVRAH. DELINQUENCY AND SOCIETY. 1966–1970. Jerusalem. Irreg.
Issued by the Israel Institute of Criminology, Faculty of Law, Hebrew University.
Indexed: Soc. Abstr.

AZTLAN
See AZTLAN — INTERNATIONAL JOURNAL OF CHICANO STUDIES RESEARCH

166 AZTLAN — INTERNATIONAL JOURNAL OF CHICANO STUDIES RESEARCH. 1– , spring 1970– . Los Angeles, Calif. Three issues a year.
Issued by the Mexican American Cultural Center, subsequently by Chicano Studies Center, University of California at Los Angeles.
Indexed: Soc. Sc. Ind.; Soc. Abstr.

167 Bangor, Wales. University College of North Wales. Department of Social Theory and Institutions. OCCASIONAL PAPERS. no.1– , 1975– . Bangor. Irreg.
Monograph series; some volumes are thematic collections of papers.

168 Barnaul. Pedagogicheskii institut. TRUDY KAFEDR OBSHCHESTVENNYKH NAUK. no.1– , 1966– . Barnaul, U.S.S.R.
In Russian.

BASIC DOCUMENTATION
See World Fertility Survey. BASIC DOCUMENTATION.

169 Bath, England. University. Centre for the Study of Organizational Change and Development. WORKING PAPERS. 1– , 1975– . Bath. Irreg.
Series of papers.

BEFÖLKNINGS FÖRÄNDRINGAR
See Sweden. Statistiska Sentralbyraa. BEFÖLKNINGS FÖRÄNDRINGAR

170 BEHAVIOR AND ENVIRONMENT; THE USE OF SPACE BY ANIMALS AND MAN. 1971– . New York, Plenum Publishing Co. Quarterly.

171 BEHAVIOR CHANGE. v.4– , 1974– . Chicago, Aldine Publishing Co. Quarterly.
Continues: *Psychotherapy and Behavior Change.*

172 BEHAVIOR MODIFICATION. v.1– , Jan. 1977– . Beverly Hills, Calif. Sage Publications. Quarterly.

BEHAVIOR SCIENCE NOTES
See BEHAVIOR SCIENCE RESEARCH

173 BEHAVIOR SCIENCE RESEARCH. v.1– , 1966– . New Haven, Conn., Human Relations Area Files, Inc. Quarterly.
Title varies: v.1–8, 1966–73, *Behavior Science Notes*. Supersedes: *HRAF News*. Index: v.1–11 in v.11.
Indexed: Abstr. Anth.; Int. Bibl. Soc.; Int. Pol. Sc. Abstr.; Psych. Abstr.; SSCI.

174 BEHAVIORAL SCIENCE. v.1– , Jan. 1956– . Ann Arbor, Mich.; subsequently Louisville, Ky., Systems Science Publications. Bimonthly.
Issued by the Mental Health Research Institute, University of Michigan; later by the Society for General Systems Research in cooperation with the Institute of Management Sciences.
Indexed: Abstr. Anth.; Abstr. Soc. Work; Int. Bibl. Soc.; Peace Res. Abstr. J.; Psych. Abstr.; Soc. Abstr.; Wom. Stud. Abstr.

175 BEHAVIORAL SCIENCE IN PROGRESS. 1– , 1971– . Washington, D.C.
Issued by the American Psychological Association.

176 BEHAVIOR RESEARCH AND THERAPY. v.1– , May 1963– . Oxford, New York, Pergamon Press. Bimonthly.
Subtitle reads: 'An international multidisciplinary journal'.
Indexed: Soc. Work Res. Abstr.; Soc. Abstr.

177 BEHAVIORAL ANALYSIS AND MODIFICATION. v.2– , 1977– . München, Baltimore, Urban and Schwarzenberg. Quarterly.
Continues: *European Journal of Behavioral Analysis and Modification*. Text in English; summaries in French and German.

178 BEHAVIORAL SCIENCES AND COMMUNITY DEVELOPMENT. v.1–11, Mar. 1967–Sept. 1977. Hyderabad, India. Semiannual.
Issued by the National Institute of Community Development. Superseded by: *Behavioral Sciences and Rural Development.*
Indexed: Int. Bibl. Soc.; Int. Pol. Sc. Abstr.; Soc. Abstr.

179 BEITRÄGE ZU EINER HISTORISCHEN STRUKTURANALYSE BAYERMS IM INDUSTRIALZEITALTER. v.1– , 1968– . Berlin, Duncker & Humblot.
Monograph series.

BEITRÄGE ZUR BEZIEHUNGSLEHRE. ERGÄNZUNGSHEFTE ZU DEN ZWEITEN TEILE DER KÖLNER VIERTELJAHRESHEFTE FÜR SOZIOLOGIE
See KÖLNER VIERTELJAHRESHEFTE FÜR SOZIOLOGIE. ERGÄNZUNGSHEFTE. BEITRÄGE ZUR BEZIEHUNGSLEHRE

180 BEITRÄGE ZUR KONFLIKTFORSCHUNG v.1– , 1971– . Köln, Markus-Verlagsgesellschaft GmbH. Quarterly.
Indexed: Soc. Abstr.

181 BEITRÄGE ZUR PSYCHOLOGIE UND SOZIOLOGIE DES KRANKEN MENSCHEN. 1– , 1974– . München. Irreg. Vol. 2 published in 1973.
Monograph series.

182 BEITRÄGE ZUR SOZIALKUNDE: REIHE B: STRUKTUR UND WANDEL DER GESELLSCHAFT. 1– , 1965– . Opladen, C. W. Leske. Irreg.
Other title: *Beiträge zur Wirtschaft- und Sozialkunde. Reihe B: Struktur und Wandel der Gesellschaft*. Subseries of *Veröffentlichungen der Akademie für Wissenschaft und Politik*, Hamburg. Each volume is accompanied by separately paged *Soziologische Lehrbeispiele*.

183 BEITRÄGE ZUR SOZIALWISSENSCHAFTLICHEN FORSCHUNG. 1– , 1968– . Opladen, Westdeutscher Verlag. Irreg.
Title varies: 1–8, 1968–72, *Beiträge zur Soziologischen Forschung*.
Monograph series.

184 BEITRÄGE ZUR SOZIOLOGIE AFRIKAS. 1– , 1976– . Freiburg, Br., Klaus Schwarz Verlag. Irreg.
Monograph series.

185 BEITRÄGE ZUR SOZIOLOGIE DES BILDUNGSWESEN. v.1– , 1960– . Heidelberg, Quelle & Meyer. Irreg.
Monograph series.

186 BEITRÄGE ZUR SOZIOLOGIE UND SOZIALKUNDE LATEINAMERICAS. v.1–10, 1967–1971. Berlin, Gehlin. Irreg.
Includes some works in translation.
Monograph series.

187 BEITRÄGE ZUR SOZIOLOGIE UND SOZIALPHILOSOPHIE. v.1–13, 1946–1967. Bern, Regio-Verlag. Irreg.
Monograph series.

BEITRÄGE ZUR SOZIOLOGISCHEN FORSCHUNG
See BEITRÄGE ZUR SOZIALWISSENSCHAFTLICHEN FORSCHUNG

BEITRÄGE ZUR WIRTSCHAFTS- UND SOZIALKUNDE. REIHE B: STRUKTUR UND WANDEL DER GESELLSCHAFT
See BEITRÄGE ZUR SOZIALKUNDE. REIHE B: STRUKTUR UND WANDEL DER GESELLSCHAFT

188 BEITRÄGE ZUR WISSENSSOZIOLOGIE, BEITRÄGE ZUR RELIGIONSSOZIOLOGIE. CONTRIBUTIONS TO THE SOCIOLOGY OF KNOWLEDGE, CONTRIBUTIONS TO THE SOCIOLOGY OF RELIGION. 1975– . Opladen, Westdeutscher Verlag. Irreg.
Subseries of *Internationales Jahrbuch für Wissens- und Religionssoziologie*. In English, French, and German; summaries in English or German.

189 Belfast. Queen's University. Department of Social Anthropology. QUEEN'S UNIVERSITY PAPERS IN SOCIAL ANTHROPOLOGY. no.1– , 1976– . Belfast. Irreg.
Monograph series.

190 Belgium. Institut National de Statistique. RELEVE OFFICIEL DU CHIFFRE DE LA POPULATION DU ROYAUME. Bruxelles. Annual.
Issued by the Administration des Affaires Electorales et de la Statistique Générale, through 1926. Text in French and Flemish.

191 Belgium. Institut National de Statistique. STATISTIQUES DÉMOGRAPHIQUES. no.1– , 1969– . Bruxelles. Irreg.

192 Belgium. Ministère de la Santé Publique et de la Famille. Centre d'Étude de la Population et de la Famille. CAHIERS. PUBLIKATIES. no.1– , 1964– . Bruxelles. Three issues a year.
Monograph series.

193 Belgium. Ministère de la Santé Publique et de la Famille. Centre d'Étude de la Population et de la Famille. STUDIES EN DOCUMENTATEN. 1– , 1972– . Antwerpen, Nederlandsche Boekhandel. Irreg.
Monograph series, in French and Flemish.

BERICHTE
See Wien. Hochschule für Welthandel. Institut für Allgemeine Soziologie. BERICHTE

BERICHTEN UIT HET VERNE OOSTEN
See COURRIER DE L'EXTRÊME ORIENT. BERICHTEN UIT HET VERNE OOSTEN

194 BERKELEY JOURNAL OF SOCIOLOGY: A CRITICAL REVIEW. v.1– , 1955– . Berkeley, Calif. Annual (Irreg.)
Title varies: v.1–4, 1955–58, *Berkeley Publications in Society and Institutions*.
Indexed: Bull. sig. soc. eth.; Int. Bibl. Soc.; Int. Pol. Sc. Abstr.; Soc. Abstr.

BERKELEY PUBLICATIONS IN SOCIETY AND INSTITUTIONS
See BERKELEY JOURNAL OF SOCIOLOGY; A CRITICAL REVIEW

195 Berlin (West). Statistisches Landesamt. BEVÖLKERUNGSENTWICKLUNG IN BERLIN [West]. Feb. 1968– . Berlin.

196 Berlin (West). Statistisches Landesamt. NATÜRLICHE BEVÖLKERUNGSBEWEGUNG IN BERLIN [West]. 1956– . Berlin.

197 Berlin (West). Statistische Landesamt. DIE WANDERUNG IN BERLIN [West]. 1956– . Berlin. Quarterly, with annual summary.
Title varies: 1956–59, *Die Wanderungsbewegung in Berlin* [West].

198 Berlin (West). Freie Universität. Osteuropa Institut. PHILOSOPHISCHE UND SOZIOLOGISCHE VERÖFFENTLICHUNGEN. 1– , 1959– . Berlin. Irreg.
Monograph series.

199 Berlin (West). Freie Universität. Wirtschafts- und Sozialwissenschaftliche Fakultät. SOZIOLOGISCHE ABHANDLUNGEN. no. 1–13, 1961–1971. Berlin, Duncker & Humblot. Irreg.
Monograph series; includes some doctoral dissertations.

200 Berlin (West). Technische Universität. Institut für Soziologie. SOZIOLOGISCHE ARBEITSHEFTE. no.1– , 1969– . Berlin. Irreg.
Title varies: no.1–7, 1969–71, *Arbeitshefte*. Includes subseries: Berlin (West). Technische Universität. Arbeitsgruppe für Bevölkerungsforschung. *Heft*.

201 Bern. Universität. Institut für Soziologie. ARBEITSBERICHTE AUS DEM INSTITUT FÜR SOZIOLOGIE DER UNIVERSITÄT. Bern. Irreg.

BERNER BEITRÄGE ZUR SOZIOLOGIE
See BERNESE STUDIES IN SOCIOLOGY

202 BERNESE STUDIES IN SOCIOLOGY. 1– , 1959– . Bern, Stuttgart. Irreg.
Issued by the Institute für Soziologie, und Sozio-Ökonomische Entwicklungsfragen, Universität, Bern. Title varies: 1–15, 1959–75, *Berner Beiträge zur Soziologie*.

BEVÖLKERUNG UND ERWERBSSTÄTIGKEIT
See Germany (Federal Republic). Statistisches Bundesamt. BEVÖLKERUNG UND ERWERBSSTÄTIGKEIT. REIHE 1.1; 1.2.2; 1.3

BEVÖLKERUNG NACH ALTER UND FAMILIENSTAND
See Germany (Federal Republic). Statistisches Bundesamt. BEVÖLKERUNG UND ERWERBSSTÄTIGKEIT. REIHE 1.3: BEVÖLKERUNG NACH ALTER UND FAMILIENSTAND

BEVÖLKERUNG UND FAMILIENSTAND
See Germany (Federal Republic). Statistisches Bundesamt. BEVÖLKERUNG UND FAMILIENSTAND

BEVÖLKERUNG UND KULTUR. REIHE 2; 3; 5
See Germany (Federal Republic). Statistisches Bundesamt. BEVÖLKERUNG UND KULTUR. REIHE 2; 3; 5

BEVÖLKERUNGSBEWEGUNG IN DER SCHWEIZ
See Switzerland. Statistisches Amt. BEVÖLKERUNGSBEWEGUNG IN DER SCHWEITZ

BEVÖLKERUNGSENTWICKLUNG IN BERLIN [West]
See Berlin (West) Statistisches Landesamt. BEVÖLKERUNGSENTWICKLUNG IN BERLIN [West]

BEVOLKING DER GEMEENTEN VAN NEDERLAND
See Netherlands. Centraal Bureau voor Statistiek. BEVOLKING DER GEMEENTEN VAN NEDERLAND

203 BEVOLKING EN GEZIN. no.1– , June 1972– . Kapellen, N.V. de Nederlansche Boekhandel and N.V. de Sikkel. Semi-annual.
Issued by the Centrum voor Bevolking-en Gezinstudien (CBGS). Supersedes: *Bevolking en Gezin. Population et Famille*. 1963–1971. In Dutch; summaries in English.
Indexed: Int. Bibl. Soc.

BEVOLKING EN OPPERVLAKTE DER GEMEENTEN VAN NEDERLAND
See Netherlands. Centraal Bureau voor de Statistiek. BEVOLKING DER GEMEENTEN VAN NEDERLAND

BIBLIOGRAFIA
See Centro Latinoamericano de Pesquisas de Ciências Sociais. BIBLIOGRAFIA

204 BIBLIOGRAFIA BRASILEIRA DE CIÊNCIAS SOCIAIS. v.1– , 1954– . Rio de Janeiro. Annual (Irreg.)

Issued by the Instituto Brasileiro de Bibliografia e Documentação, Conselho Nacional de Pesquisas. Supersedes: *Bibliografia economico-social.* In Portuguese.

205 BIBLIOGRAFIA ITALIANA DELLE SCIENZE SOCIALI. [1]– , 1957 [published 1958]– . Milano, Società Editrice 'Vita e Pensiero'.

Issued by the Istituto di Scienze Economiche dell'Università Cattolica del Sacro Cuore. Vols. for 1957–58 are extracts from *Rivista Internazionale di Scienze Sociali,* v.6, Nov–Dec. 1958, and v.6, Nov.–Dec. 1959. In Italian.

206 BIBLIOGRAFIA POLSKIEGO PIŚMIENNICTWA DEMOGRAFICZNEGO. 1945/1960– Warszawa.

Issued by the Pracownia Demograficzna, Polska Akademia Nauk. Vol. 1945/1960 published in *Biuletyn,* no.5(7) of the Komitet Przestrzennego Zagospodarowania Kraju, Polska Akademia Nauk. In Polish.

207 BIBLIOGRAFIE VAN IN NEDERLAND VERSCHENEN DEMOGRAFISCHE STUDIES. BIBLIOGRAPHY OF POPULATION STUDIES PUBLISHED IN THE NETHERLANDS. 1970– . Vooburg, Vereniging voor Demografie. Annual.

In Dutch and English.

208 BIBLIOGRAFIJA JUGOSLAVIJE. SERIJA A. DRUSTVENE NAUKE: ČLANCI I KNJIŽEVNI PRILOŽI U ČASOPISIMA I NOVINAMA. Jan/Mar. 1952– Beograd, Bibliografski institut.

Supersedes, in part, and continues the volume numbering of *Bibliografija Jugoslavije. Članci i književni priloži u casopisima i novinama.* Title varies slightly, 1950–51. In Serbo-Croatian.

BIBLIOGRAPHIC SERIES
See Michigan. State University, East Lansing. Institute for Community Development and Services. BIBLIOGRAPHY

BIBLIOGRAPHIC SERIES
See Toronto. University. Centre for Urban and Community Studies. BIBLIOGRAPHIC SERIES

BIBLIOGRAPHIC SERIES: ANNOTATED BIBLIOGRAPHY ON LEISURE
See European Centre for Leisure and Education. BIBLIOGRAPHIC SERIES. ANNOTATED BIBLIOGRAPHY ON LEISURE

209 BIBLIOGRAPHIE DER SOZIALWISSENSCHAFTEN. 1905–1943; n.s. 1950–1967. Dresden; Berlin, Vandenhoeck & Ruprecht.

Title varies: 1921–24, *Sozialwissenschaftliches Literaturblatt;* 1937–43, *Bibliographie der Staats- und Wirtschaftswissenschaften.* Vol. 1–3, 1905–07, published as supplement to *Kritische Blätter für die gesammten Sozialwissenschaften;* v.4–8, 1908–12, as supplement to *Blätter für die gesammten Sozialwissenschaften.* Publication suspended 1944–49; resumed with v.42, 1950, covering 1948–50. Two volumes, covering 1943/45 and 1946/47, to be published. Vol.42 called also n.s. v.1.

BIBLIOGRAPHIE DER SOZIALWISSENSCHAFTEN
See BIBLIOGRAPHIE DES SCIENCES ÉCONOMIQUES, POLITIQUES ET SOCIALES

BIBLIOGRAPHIE DER STAATS- UND WIRTSCHAFTSWISSENSCHAFTEN
See BIBLIOGRAPHIE DER SOZIALWISSENSCHAFTEN

210 BIBLIOGRAPHIE DES SCIENCES ÉCONOMIQUES, POLITIQUES ET SOCIALES. BIBLIOGRAPHIE DER SOZIALWISSENSCHAFTEN. BIBLIOGRAPHY OF SOCIAL SCIENCE. v.1–12, 1909–1910. Paris, Marcel Revieure. Monthly, with annual author index.

Merged with: *Bibliographie der Sozialwissenschaften.*

BIBLIOGRAPHIE INTERNATIONALE D'ANTHROPOLOGIE SOCIALE ET CULTURELLE
See INTERNATIONAL BIBLIOGRAPHY OF SOCIAL AND CULTURAL ANTHROPOLOGY

BIBLIOGRAPHIE INTERNATIONALE DE SCIENCE ÉCONOMIQUE
See INTERNATIONAL BIBLIOGRAPHY OF ECONOMICS

BIBLIOGRAPHIE INTERNATIONALE DE SOCIOLOGIE
See INTERNATIONAL BIBLIOGRAPHY OF SOCIOLOGY

211 BIBLIOGRAPHIE SOZIOLOGIE (DDR). 1965– . Berlin [East]. Irreg. (6–10 issues).

Issued by the Zentralstelle für die soziologische Information und Dokumentation im Institut für Gesellwissenschaften, Akademie für Gesellwissenschaften beim Zentral Komitee der SED. Bibliography, loose leaf, arranged by decimal classification. Each issue supplied with author and title indexes. No cumulations.

212 BIBLIOGRAPHIES IN SOCIAL RESEARCH. 1– , 1974– . Bundoora, Vic. Irreg.
Issued by the Department of Sociology, La Trobe University.

BIBLIOGRAPHY
See Institute of Applied Social and Economic Research. BIBLIOGRAPHY

BIBLIOGRAPHY
See Michigan. State University, East Lansing. Institute for Community Development and Services. BIBLIOGRAPHY

BIBLIOGRAPHY
See Princeton University. Research Center for Urban and Environmental Planning. BIBLIOGRAPHY

213 BIBLIOGRAPHY OF DOCTORAL DISSERTATIONS. SOCIAL SCIENCES & HUMANITIES, 1975/1976– . New Delhi, Association of Indian Universities. Annual.

214 BIBLIOGRAPHY OF FAMILY PLANNING AND POPULATION. v.1–2, no.3, July 1972–1973. Cambridge, England.
Issued by the Simon Population Trust. Geographical and author indexes included.

BIBLIOGRAPHY OF SOCIAL SCIENCE
See BIBLIOGRAPHIE DES SCIENCES ÉCONOMIQUES, POLITIQUES ET SOCIALES. BIBLIOGRAPHIE DER SOZIALWISSENSCHAFTEN. BIBLIOGRAPHY OF SOCIAL SCIENCE

215 BIBLIOGRAPHY OF URBAN STUDIES IN AUSTRALIA. 1– , 1966/1968– . Canberra. Annual.
Issued by the Australian Institute of Urban Studies. Subseries of *A.I.U.S. Publication.* Preceded by the Preliminary Edition.

BIBLIOGRAPHY ON SCHEDULED CASTES, SCHEDULED TRIBES AND SELECTED MARGINAL COMMUNITIES OF INDIA
See India (Republic). Census. BIBLIOGRAPHY ON SCHEDULED CASTES, SCHEDULED TRIBES AND SELECTED MARGINAL COMMUNITIES OF INDIA

216 BIBLIOTECA MODERNA DI SOCIOLOGIA. 1– , 1968– . Torino, Unione Tipografico-Editrice Torinese. Irreg.
Monograph series.

217 BIBLIOTHÈQUE D'ÉCONOMIE POLITIQUE ET DE SOCIOLOGIE. no.1–7, 1909–1923. Paris. Irreg. No.7 published in 1914; no.3 in 1923.
Monograph series.

218 BIBLIOTHÈQUE D'HISTOIRE ET DE SOCIOLOGIE. 1–7, 1903?. Paris. Irreg.
Monograph series.

219 BIBLIOTHÈQUE INTERNATIONALE DE SOCIOLOGIE DE LA COOPÉRATION. v.1– , 1955– . Paris, Éditions de Minuit. Irreg.
Monograph series.

220 BIBLIOTHÈQUE INTERNATIONALE DES SCIENCES SOCIOLOGIQUES. v.1–11, 1890–1901. Paris.
Monograph series.

BIBLIOTHÈQUE SOCIOLOGIQUE
See Instituts Solvay. Institut de Sociologie. BIBLIOTHÈQUE SOCIOLOGIQUE

221 BIBLIOTHÈQUE SOCIOLOGIQUE INTERNATIONALE. 1– , 1896– . Paris. Ceased publication.

222 Bilbao, Spain. Universidad de Deusto. Instituto de Ciencias Sociales. SOCIOLOGIA. 1– , 1972– . Bilbao. Irreg.
Monograph series.

BIOLOGY
See BIOLOGY AND HUMAN AFFAIRS

223 BIOLOGY AND HUMAN AFFAIRS. 1– , 1935– . London. Three issues a year.
Issued by the British Social Biology Council. Title varies: 1–12, no.3, 1935–spring 1947, *Biology;* beginning with v.45, 1980, *Social Biology and Human Affairs.*
Indexed: Brit. Ed. Ind.

224 Birmingham. University. Centre for Russian and East European Studies. DISCUSSION PAPERS. SERIES RC/C: SOCIOLOGY AND POLITICAL SCIENCE. no.1– , 1964– . Birmingham. Irreg.
Series of papers.

225 Birmingham. University. Centre for Urban and Regional Studies. OCCASIONAL PAPER. 1– , 1968– . Birmingham. Irreg.
Series of papers.

226 Birmingham. University. Centre for Urban and Regional Studies. URBAN AND REGIONAL STUDIES. no.1– , 1970– . London, Allen & Unwin. Irreg.
Monograph series.

227 Birmingham. University. Faculty of Commerce and Social Science. DISCUSSION PAPERS. SERIES C: SOCIOLOGY AND POLITICS. no.1– , Aug. 1960– . Birmingham. Irreg.
Series of papers.

228 Birmingham. University. Faculty of Commerce and Social Science. DISCUSSION PAPERS. SERIES F: BIRMINGHAM SOCIETY AND POLITICS. 1960–1973. Birmingham. Irreg.
Series of papers.

BLACK AMERICA; A RESEARCH BIBLIOGRAPHY
See AFRO-AMERICAN RESEARCH BIBLIOGRAPHY

229 THE BLACK SCHOLAR. v.1– , Nov. 1969– . San Francisco, Calif., Black World Foundation. Monthly, except July and August.
Indexed: PHRA; Soc. Sc. Ind.; Soc. Abstr.; Wom. Stud. Abstr.

230 BLACK SOCIOLOGIST. v.7– , 1977– . New Brunswick, N.J., Transaction Periodicals Consortium. Quarterly.
Issued by the Association of Black Sociologists, Department of Sociology, Princeton University. Continues: *CBS Newsletter*.
Indexed: Soc. Abstr.

BLUEPRINT OF AN IDEA
See Hawaii. University, Honolulu. Center for Cultural and Technical Interchange between East and West. REPORT

231 Bogazici Üniversitesi. BOGAZICI ÜNIVERSITESI DERGISI; YONETICILIK, EKONOMI, VE SOSYAL BILIMLER. BOGAZICI ÜNIVERSITY JOURNAL: MANAGEMENT, ECONOMICS AND SOCIAL SCIENCES. v.1– , 1973– . Istanbul. Annual.
Title varies: v.1, 1973, *Bogazici Üniversitesi Dergisi; Sosyal Bilimler; Bogazici University Journal; Social Sciences.* In English and Turkish; summaries in Turkish or English.

BOGAZICI ÜNIVERSITESI DERGISI; SOSYAL BILIMLER
See Bogazici Üniversitesi. BOGAZICI ÜNIVERSITESI DERGISI; YONETICILIK, EKONOMI, VE SOSYAL BILIMLER. BOGAZICI ÜNIVERSITY JOURNAL: MANAGEMENT, ECONOMICS AND SOCIAL SCIENCES

BOGAZICI ÜNIVERSITESI DERGISI; YONETICILIK, EKONOMI, VE SOSYAL BILIMLER
See Bogazici Üniversitesi. BOGAZICI ÜNIVERSITESI DERGISI; YONETICILIK, ECONOMI, VE SOSYAL BILIMLER. BOGAZICI UNIVERSITY JOURNAL; MANAGEMENT, ECONOMICS AND SOCIAL SCIENCES

BOGAZICI UNIVERSITY JOURNAL; SOCIAL SCIENCES
See Bogazici Üniversitesi. BOGAZICI ÜNIVERSITESI DERGISI; YONETICILIK, EKONOMI, VE SOSYAL BILIMLER. BOGAZICI UNIVERSITY JOURNAL: MANAGEMENT, ECONOMICS AND SOCIAL SCIENCES

BOLETIM
See AMERICA LATINA

BOLETIM
See Araraquara, Brazil. Faculdade de Filosofia, Ciências e Letras. Cadeira de Sociologia. BOLETIM

BOLETIM
See Brazil. Instituto Joaquim Nabuco de Pesquisas Sociais. BOLETIM

BOLETIM DA CADEIRA DE SOCIOLOGIA E FUNDAMENTOS SOCIOLOGICOS DA EDUCAÇÃO
See Araraquara, Brazil. Faculdade de Filosofia, Ciências e Letras. Cadeira de Sociologia e Fundamentos Sociologicos da Educação. BOLETIM

BOLETIM INFORMATIVO DA FUNDAÇÃO ESCOLA DE SOCIOLOGIA E POLITICA DE SÃO PAULO
See São Paulo. Universidade. Fundação Escola de Sociologia e Politica. BOLETIM INFORMATIVO

BOLETIN
See Academia de Ciencias Politicas y Sociales. BOLETIN

BOLETIN
See Chile. Universidad, Santiago. Instituto de Sociologia. BOLETIN

BOLETIN
See Cordóba, Argentina. Universidad Nacional. Faculdad de Derecho y Ciencias Sociales. BOLETIN

BOLETIN
See Museo Social Argentino, Buenos Aires. BOLETIN

BOLETIN
See Panama (City). Universidad. Instituto de Investigaciónes Sociales y Economicas. BOLETIN

BOLETIN DE ANALISIS DEMOGRAFICO
See Peru. Dirección Nacional de Estadistica y Censos. BOLETIN DE ANALISIS DEMOGRAFICO

232 BOLETIN DE CIENCIAS POLITICAS Y SOCIALES. no.1–16, 1951–1967. Mendoza. Annual.
Issued by the Faculdad de Ciencias Politicos y Sociales, Universidad Nacional de Cuyo. Title varies: 1951–61, *Boletin de Estudios Politicos*. In Spanish.

BOLETIN DE ELAS
See Escuela Latinoamericana de Sociologia. BOLETIN DE ELAS

BOLETIN DE ESTADISTICA
See Nicaragua. Dirección General de Estadisticas y Censos. BOLETIN DE ESTADISTICA. ESTADISTICAS DEMOGRAFICAS

BOLETIN DE ESTUDIOS LATINO-AMERICANOS
See BOLETIN DE ESTUDIOS LATINO-AMERICANOS Y DEL CARIBE

233 BOLETIN DE ESTUDIOS LATINO-AMERICANOS Y DEL CARIBE. v.1– , 1967– . Leiden. Semi-annual.
Issued by the Studie- en Documentatie-centrum Latin America, in Amsterdam, and Instituto Real de Linguistica y Antropologia, Departamento de Estudios del Caribe in Leiden. Title varies: 1967–71, *Boletin Informativo de Estudios Latinoamericanos;* 1972–73, *Boletin de Estudios Latinoamericanos*. In Spanish and English.

BOLETIN DE ESTUDIOS POLITICOS
See BOLETIN DE CIENCIAS POLITICAS Y SOCIALES

BOLETIN DE POBLACIÓN
See POPULATION BULLETIN

BOLETIN DEL INSTITUTO DE SOCIOLOGIA
See Buenos Aires. Universidad Nacional. Instituto de Sociologia. BOLETIN

BOLETIN DEMOGRAFICO
See United Nations. Regional Centre for Demographic Training and Research in Latin America. BOLETIN DEMOGRAFICO

BOLETIN INFORMATIVO
See Programa Avanza do Latinoamericano de Sociologia Rural. BOLETIN INFORMATIVO

BOLETIN INFORMATIVO
See United Nations. Centro Latinoamericano de Demografia. BOLETIN INFORMATIVO

BOLETIN INFORMATIVO DE ESTUDIOS LATINOAMERICANOS
See BOLETIN DE ESTUDIOS LATINO-AMERICANOS Y DEL CARIBE

234 BOLETIN SOCIOGRAFICO. v.1– , 1933– . Santiago. Irreg.
Issued by the Fundación Juan Enrique Lagarrique.

235 BOLETIN URUGUAYO DE SOCIOLOGIA. v.1– , June 1961– . Montevideo. Three issues a year.
Issued by the Sociedad Uruguaya de Sociologia. In Spanish; summaries in English, French, Portuguese and Spanish.
Indexed: Int. Bibl. Soc.; Int. Pol. Sc. Abstr.; Soc. Abstr.

236 BOLGARSKII SOTSIOLOGICHESKII ZHURNAL. v.1– , 1978– . Izd-vo Bolgarskoi akademii nauk. Annual.
Issued by the Institut Sotsiologii Bolgarskoi akademii nauk and Sotsiologicheskaia assotsiatsiia. In Bulgarian.

237 Bolivia. Dirección Nacional de Estadistica y Censos. ANUARIO DEMOGRAFICO. 1936– , La Paz. Annual.
Title varies: 1936–44, *Demografia.*

BOLLETINO DI PSICOLOGIA APPLICATA
See BOLLETINO DI PSICOLOGIA E SOCIOLOGIA APPLICATE

238 BOLLETINO DI PSICOLOGIA E SOCIOLOGIA APPLICATE. 1/3– , Feb/June 1954– . Firenze.
Title varies: no.1–3, 1954–Feb/Apr. 1955, *Bolletino de Psicologia Applicata*.

BOLLETINO DI SOCIOLOGIA DELL'ISTITUTO LUIGI STURZO
See Istituto Luigi Sturzo. BOLLETINO DI SOCIOLOGIA

BOLLETINO. SERIE SOCIOLOGICA
See Milan. Università Commerciale L. Bocconi. Centro per la Ricercha Operativa. BOLLETINO. SERIE SOCIOLOGICA.

239 BONNER BEITRÄGE ZUR SOZIOLOGIE. no.1– , 1964– . Stuttgart, F. Enke. Irreg.
Issued by the Institut für Soziologie, Universität Bonn.
Monograph series.

240 BOOK REVIEW INDEX TO SOCIAL SCIENCE PERIODICALS. 1– , 1978– . Ann Arbor, Pierian Press. Irreg.

241 Boston College, Boston, Mass. Bureau of Public Affairs. COMMUNITY ANALYSIS AND ACTION SERIES. MONOGRAPH. no.1– , Sep. 1964– . Boston. Irreg.
Monograph series.

242 Boston University. Center for Applied Social Science. RESEARCH REPORTS AND TECHNICAL NOTES. no.1–218, 1955–1971. Boston.
Earlier name of Center, Human Relations Center.

243 Boston University. School of Public Relations and Communications. Communications Research Center. REPORT. no.1–71, Sep. 1970–Aug. 1975. Boston.

244 Brazil. Centro Brasileiro de Estudos Demograficos. ESTUDOS Y ANALISES. no.1– , 1968– . Rio de Janeiro. Irreg.

245 Brazil. Instituto Joaquim Nabuco de Pesquisas Sociais. BOLETIM. 1952–1972. Recife. Annual (Irreg.)
Continued by: *Ciência & Tropico*.

BREVIARIOS DE CULTURA. SERIE SOCIOLOGIA
See Instituto Otavaleno de Antropologia. BREVIARIOS DE CULTURA. SERIE SOCIOLOGIA.

246 Brigham Young University. Department of Sociology. SOCIAL SCIENCE RESEARCH BULLETIN. no.1– , 1962– . Provo, Utah.
Title varies: no. 2–3, *Social Science Bulletin*.

247 Brighton, England. University of Sussex. Research Unit for the Study of Multi-Racial Societies. OCCASIONAL PAPERS. no.1– , 1966– . Brighton. Irreg.
Series of papers.

248 THE BRITISH JOURNAL OF CRIMINOLOGY. v.14– , 1974– . London, Stevens. Quarterly.
Issued by the Institute for the Study and Treatment of Delinquency. Continues: *British Journal of Criminology, Delinquency and Deviant Social Behaviour*, which title appears also on the added title page.
Indexed: Soc. Abstr.

249 BRITISH JOURNAL OF CRIMINOLOGY, DELINQUENCY AND DEVIANT SOCIAL BEHAVIOUR. v.1–13, 1961–1973. London, Stevens. Quarterly.
Issued by the Institute for the Study and Treatment of Delinquency. Supersedes: *British Journal of Delinquency*. Continued by: *The British Journal of Criminology*.
Indexed: Soc. Sc. Ind.; Soc. Abstr.

250 BRITISH JOURNAL OF DELINQUENCY. v.1–10, July 1950–Apr. 1960. London. Quarterly.
Superseded by: *British Journal of Criminology, Delinquency and Deviant Social Behaviour*.
Indexed: Soc. Abstr.

251 BRITISH JOURNAL OF LAW AND SOCIETY. 1– , summer 1974– . London, Professional Books Ltd. Quarterly.
Indexed: Int. Pol. Sc. Abstr.; Soc. Work Res. Abstr.; Soc. Abstr.

252 BRITISH JOURNAL OF MATHEMATICAL AND STATISTICAL PSYCHOLOGY. v.1– , Oct. 1947– . London, subsequently Bristol. Three issues a year.
Issued by the British Psychological Society. Title varies: Oct. 1947–Nov. 1952, *The British Journal of Psychology. Statistical Section*; May 1953–Nov. 1964, *British Journal of Statistical Psychology*.
Indexed: Bull. sig. soc. eth.; Psych. Abstr.; SSCI; Soc. Abstr.

253 BRITISH JOURNAL OF PSYCHIATRY. 1853– . London, Lewis & Co. Ltd. Quarterly.
Issued by the Royal Medical-Psychological Association. Title varies: 1853–55, *Asylum, Journal of Mental Science*; 1856–1962, *Journal of Mental Health*.
Indexed: SSCI; Soc. Abstr.; Wom. Stud. Abstr.

THE BRITISH JOURNAL OF PSYCHOLOGY. STATISTICAL SECTION.
See BRITISH JOURNAL OF MATHEMATICAL AND STATISTICAL PSYCHOLOGY

254 THE BRITISH JOURNAL OF SOCIAL AND CLINICAL PSYCHOLOGY. v.1–19, Feb. 1962–1980. London, Cambridge University Press. Three issues a year.
Issued by the British Psychological Society. Institute of Experimental Psychology. Continued, in part, by *The British Journal of Social Psychiatry*.
Indexed: Bull sig. soc. eth.; Int. Bibl. Soc.; Soc. Sc. Ind.; Soc. Abstr.; Wom. Stud. Abstr.

255 BRITISH JOURNAL OF SOCIAL PSYCHIATRY. v.1–3, winter 1966/67–1969. London, Avenue Publishing Co. Quarterly.
Issued by the British Association of Social Psychiatry. Continued by: *British Journal of Social Psychiatry and Community Health*.
Indexed: Int. Bibl. Soc.; SSCI.

256 BRITISH JOURNAL OF SOCIAL PSYCHIATRY AND COMMUNITY HEALTH. v.4– , 1970– . London, Avenue Publishing Co. Quarterly.

Issued by the British Association of Social Psychiatry. Continues: *British Journal of Social Psychiatry*.

257 THE BRITISH JOURNAL OF SOCIAL PSYCHOLOGY. v.20, pt.1– , Feb. 1981– . Leicester.
Issued by the British Psychological Society. Continues, in part, *The British Journal of Social and Clinical Psychology*.

258 THE BRITISH JOURNAL OF SOCIOLOGY. v.1– , Mar. 1950– . London, Routledge & Kegan Paul. Quarterly.
Issued by the London School of Economics and Political Science (until Mar. 1957, called the London School of Economics). Includes annual index. Indexes: v.1–10, 1950–59, in v.10, no.5.
Indexed: Afr. Abstr.; Brit. Hum. Ind.; Bull. sig. soc. eth.; Int. Bibl. Soc.; PAIS; Psych. Abstr.; Soc. Sc. Hum. Ind.; Soc. Sc. Ind.; Soc. Work Res. Abstr.; Soc. Abstr.

259 BRITISH JOURNAL OF SOCIOLOGY OF EDUCATION. v.1– , 1980– . Oxford, Carfax Publishing Co. Three issues a year.
Indexed: Soc. Abstr.

BRITISH JOURNAL OF STATISTICAL PSYCHOLOGY
See BRITISH JOURNAL OF MATHEMATICAL AND STATISTICAL PSYCHOLOGY

260 British Library. Lending Division. INDEX OF CONFERENCE PROCEEDINGS. 1966– . Boston Spa, England. Annual. Quinquennial and decennial cumulations.

261 BRITISH POLITICAL SOCIOLOGY YEARBOOK. v.1– , 1974– . New York, Halsted Press. Annual.
Indexed: Int. Pol. Sc. Abstr.

262 BRITISH PUBLIC OPINION QUARTERLY. 1– , 1979– . London. Quarterly.

263 British Sociological Association. INDUSTRIAL STUDIES. 1–2, 1973. London, Allen & Unwin. Irreg.
Monograph series.

Brno
See Brünn

264 Brünn. Univerzita. Filozoficka fakulta. SBORNIK PRACI. RADA SOCIALNE VEDY. no.1– , 1957– . Praha, Knižni Velkoobched. Annual.
Title varies slightly. Table of contents in German and Russian. In Czech.

265 Brussels, Belgium. Université Libre. Institut de Sociologie. ACTUALITÉS SOCIALES. 1904–1913; n.s. no.1– , 1945– . Bruxelles. Irreg.
During the suspension, the Institut published *Travaux*.
Monograph series.

266 Brussels, Belgium. Université Libre. Institut de Sociologie. COLLECTION DE SOCIOLOGIE GÉNÉRALE ET DE PHILOSOPHIE SOCIALE. 1–5, 1954–1963. Bruxelles, Éditions du Parthenon, S.P.R.I. Irreg.
Continued by an unnumbered monograph series.

267 Brussels, Belgium. Université Libre. Institut de Sociologie. ÉTUDES AFRICAINES. v.1– , 1953– . Bruxelles. Irreg.
Title varies: 1–7, 1953–59, *Études Coloniales*. Number 7 repeated.

268 Brussels, Belgium. Université Libre. Institut de Sociologie. ÉTUDES D'AGGLOMÉRATIONS. 1– , 1955– . Bruxelles. Irreg.
Monograph series.

269 Brussels, Belgium. Université Libre. Institut de Sociologie. RAPPORT ANNUEL ET PROGRAMME DES TRAVAUX. 1956/57– . Bruxelles. Annual.
Title varies: *Rapport d'Activité. Programme des Travaux*.

270 Brussels, Belgium. Université Libre. Institut de Sociologie. REVUE. 1– , July 1920– . Bruxelles, Éditions de l'Université Libre de Bruxelles. Bimonthly, 1920–May 1926; quarterly. Forms two volumes annually.
Supersedes the Institut's *Bulletin*. Publication suspended Apr. 1940–47.
Indexed: Bull. sig. soc. eth.; Int. Bibl. Soc.; Int. Pol. Sc. Abstr.; Soc. Abstr.

271 Brussels, Belgium. Université Libre. Institut de Sociologie. Centre d'Études des Religions. ANNALES. 1– , 1962– . Bruxelles. Irreg.
Monograph series.

272 Brussels, Belgium. Université Libre. Institut de Sociologie. Centre d'Histoire Économique et Sociale. CONTRIBUTIONS À L'HISTOIRE ÉCONOMIQUE ET SOCIALE. 1962– . Bruxelles. Irreg.
Monograph series.

273 Brussels, Belgium. Université Libre. Institut de Sociologie. Centre de Sociologie du Travail. CAHIERS. 1– , 1951– . Bruxelles. Irreg.
Monograph series.

274 Brussels, Belgium. Université Libre. Institut de Sociologie. Centre de Sociologie du Travail. TRAVAUX. 1–4, 1953–1958. Bruxelles. Irreg.
Monograph series.

Brussels, Belgium. Université Libre. Institut de Sociologie
See also Instituts Solvay. Institut de Sociologie

275 Bucharest. Universitatea. ANALELE. SOCIOLOGIE. no.1–22, 1951–1973. Bucureşti. Annual.
In various languages. Summaries in French and Russian.

276 Bucharest. Universitatea. BULETIN DE INFORMĂRE ŞTIINŢIFICĂ: FILOZOFIE, LOGICA, SOCIOLOFIE, PSIHOLOGIE. 1964– . Bucureşti. Monthly.
Issued jointly with the Centrul de Documentare Ştiinţifica, Academia Republicii Socialiste România. Author and subject indexes.

277 Budapest. Tudomány-Egyetem. ANNALES. SECTIO PHILOSOPHICA ET SOCIOLOGICA. v.1– , 1968?– . Budapest.
In English, French, German, Italian and Russian.

278 Buenos Aires. Universidad. Instituto de Sociologia. BOLETIN DEL INSTITUTO DE SOCIOLOGIE. no.1– , May 1942– . Buenos Aires. Irreg.
Title varies: 1942–59, *Cuadernos del Boletin*; 1960, *Cuadernos de Sociologia*. 1942–47 numbered 1–5; 1952–54 designated ano 10–12(no.6–9); 1957–59 designated tomo 10. In Spanish.

279 Buenos Aires. Universidad. Instituto de Sociologia. TRABAJOS E INVESTIGACIÓNES. PUBLICACIÓN INTERNA. no.1– , 1962– . Buenos Aires. Irreg.
In Spanish.
Series of papers.

BUHUT AL-QAHIRAH FI AL'ULUM AL-IJTIMA'IYAH
See CAIRO PAPERS IN SOCIAL SCIENCE

280 Bulgaria. Durzhavno upravlenie za informatsiia. NESELENIE. 1968– . Sofia. Annual.
Supersedes: Bulgaria. Tsentralno statistichesko upravlenie. *Demografska statistika*.

281 Bulgaria. Tsentralno statistichesko upravlenie. DEMOGRAFSKA STATISTIKA. 1960–1967. Sofia.
Superseded by: Bulgaria. Durzhavno upravlenie za informatsiia. *Neselenie*.

282 BULGARIAN JOURNAL OF SOCIOLOGY. 1– , 1978– . Sofia, Bulgarian Academy of Science Press. Annual.
Issued by the Institute of Sociology, Bulgarian Academy of Sciences and the Bulgarian Sociological Association. In English.

BULLETIN
See Canadian Ethnic Studies Association. BULLETIN

BULLETIN
See Carnegie Institution of Washington. Eugenics Records Office, Cold Spring Harbor, N.Y. BULLETIN

BULLETIN
See Cultural Research Institute. BULLETIN

BULLETIN
See Eugenics Society, London. BULLETIN

BULLETIN
See Glasgow. University of Strathclyde. Regional Studies Group. BULLETIN

BULLETIN
See Institut Fondamental d'Afrique Noire. BULLETIN. SÉRIE B: SCIENCES HUMAINES

BULLETIN
See Instituts Solvay. Institut de Sociologie. BULLETIN

BULLETIN
See International Institute for Social History, Amsterdam. BULLETIN

THE BULLETIN
See Oregon Social Hygiene Society. THE BULLETIN

BULLETIN
See PROBLÈMES SOCIAUX CONGOLAIS

BULLETIN
See The Public Affairs Information Service. BULLETIN

BULLETIN
See Social Science Research Council. BULLETIN

BULLETIN
See Société Canadienne de Sociologie et d'Anthropologie. BULLETIN

BULLETIN
See Société Francaise de Sociologie. BULLETIN

BULLETIN
See Société Internationale de Science Sociale. BULLETIN

BULLETIN
See Society for the History of Medicine. BULLETIN

BULLETIN
See Socio-Economic Research Institute. BULLETIN

BULLETIN
See Zambia. University. Institute for Social Research. BULLETIN

BULLETIN
See Zürich. Universität. Soziologisches Institut. BULLETIN

BULLETIN ANALYTIQUE AFRICANISTE
See AFRICAN ABSTRACTS

BULLETIN BIBLIOGRAPHIQUE
See NOTES CRITIQUES SCIENCES SOCIALES: BULLETIN BIBLIOGRAPHIQUE

BULLETIN D'INFORMATION
See SONDAGES

BULLETIN D'INFORMATION SUR LES RECHERCHES DANS LES SCIENCES HUMAINES CONCERNANT L'AFRIQUE
See International Centre for African Economic and Social Documentation. BULLETIN OF INFORMATION ON CURRENT RESEARCH ON HUMAN SCIENCES CONCERNING AFRICA

BULLETIN D'INFORMATION SUR LES THÈSES ET LES ÉTUDES EN COURSE OU EN PROJET
See International Centre for African Economic and Social Documentation. BULLETIN OF INFORMATION ON CURRENT RESEARCH ON HUMAN SCIENCES CONCERNING AFRICA

BULLETIN DE INFORMÁRE ŞTIINŢIFICĂ: FILOZOFIE, LOGICA, SOCIOLOGIE, PSIHOLOGIE
See Bucharest. Universitatea. BULLETIN DE INFORMÁRE ŞTIINŢIFICĂ: FILOZOFIE, LOGICA, SOCIOLOGIE, PSIHOLOGIE

BULLETIN DE RECHERCHES URBAINES
See URBAN RESEARCH BULLETIN

BULLETIN DES ÉTUDES AFRICAINES AU CANADA
See BULLETIN OF AFRICAN STUDIES IN CANADA

BULLETIN DES RELATIONS INDUSTRIELLES
See RELATIONS INDUSTRIELLES

BULLETIN DU CENTRE D'ÉTUDE DES PAYS DE L'EST ET DU CENTRE NATIONAL POUR L'ÉTUDE DES ÉTATS DE L'EST
See REVUE DES PAYS DE L'EST

BULLETIN ÉCONOMIQUE DU MAROC
See BULLETIN ÉCONOMIQUE ET SOCIAL DU MAROC

283 BULLETIN ÉCONOMIQUE ET SOCIAL DU MAROC. v.1– , 1933–1939; 1945–1963; 1966– . Rabat. Quarterly.
Issued by the Société d'Études Économiques, Sociales et Statistiques. Title varies: 1933–39, *Bulletin Économique du Maroc*.
Indexed: Int. Bibl. Soc.

284 BULLETIN ÉCONOMIQUE ET SOCIAL DU MAROC. SÉRIE SOCIOLOGIE. (1)– , 1971?– . Rabat. Irreg.
Issued by the Société des Études Économiques, Sociales et Statistiques.

BULLETIN MENSUEL
See Instituts Solvay. Institut de Sociologie. BULLETIN

BULLETIN MENSUEL
See Musée Social, Paris. BULLETIN MENSUEL

BULLETIN. NEWSLETTER
See International Sociological Association. ISA BULLETIN

285 BULLETIN OF AFRICAN STUDIES IN CANADA. BULLETIN DES ÉTUDES AFRICAINES AU CANADA. v.1–3, no. 2, 1963–1966. Edmonton, Alberta. Semi-annual.
Issued by the Comité des Études Africaines au Canada. Superseded by: *Canadian Journal of African Studies*.
Indexed: Int. Bibl. Soc.

BULLETIN OF INFORMATION ON CURRENT RESEARCH ON HUMAN SCIENCES CONCERNING AFRICA
See International Centre for African Economic and Social Documentation. BULLETIN OF INFORMATION ON CURRENT RESEARCH ON HUMAN SCIENCES CONCERNING AFRICA.

BULLETIN OF INFORMATION ON THESES AND STUDIES IN PROGRESS OR PROPOSED

See International Centre for African Economic and Social Documentation. BULLETIN OF INFORMATION ON CURRENT RESEARCH ON HUMAN SCIENCES CONCERNING AFRICA

286 BULLETIN OF QUANTITATIVE AND COMPUTER METHODS IN SOUTH ASIAN STUDIES. no.1– , June 1973– . London.

Issued by the School of Oriental and African Studies, University of London, and the South Asian Institute, University of Heidelberg.

BULLETIN OF THE ACADEMY OF MEDICINE
See JOURNAL OF SOCIOLOGIC MEDICINE

287 BULLETIN OF THE ATOMIC SCIENTISTS. v.1– , 1945– . Chicago. Biweekly (irregular); currently monthly.

Title varies: 1945–Mar. 1946, *Bulletin of the Atomic Scientists of Chicago*. Absorbed: *Atomic Engineer and Scientist*. Subtitle reads: 'A magazine of science & public affairs'.

Indexed: Int. Bibl. Soc.; SSCI; Soc. Abstr.

BULLETIN OF THE ATOMIC SCIENTISTS OF CHICAGO
See BULLETIN OF THE ATOMIC SCIENTISTS

BULLETIN OF THE CULTURAL RESEARCH INSTITUTE
See Cultural Research Institute. BULLETIN

BULLETIN OF THE KOREAN RESEARCH CENTER
See Hang'guk You'Guwon, Seoul, Korea. BULLETIN. JOURNAL OF SOCIAL SCIENCES AND HUMANITIES

288 BULLETIN ON HUMAN ECOLOGY. v.1– , May 1969–1971?. Elsan, Ill. Quarterly.

Issued by the Human Ecological Society.

289 BULLETIN SCIENTIFIQUE. SECTION B. SCIENCES HUMAINES. v.1– , 1965– . Zagreb. Monthly.

Issued by the Council des Académies des Sciences et des Arts de la RSF de Yugoslavie.

BULLETIN. SÉRIE B. SCIENCES HUMAINES
See Institut Fondamental d'Afrique Noire. BULLETIN. SÉRIE B: SCIENCES HUMAINES

BULLETIN SIGNALÉTIQUE. 521. SOCIOLOGIE. ETHNOLOGIE
See France. Centre National de la Recherche Scientifique. BULLETIN SIGNALÉTIQUE. 521. SOCIOLOGIE — ETHNOLOGIE

BULLETIN SIGNALÉTIQUE. 521. SOCIOLOGIE, ETHNOLOGIE, PRÉHISTOIRE ET ARCHÉOLOGIE
See France. Centre National de la Recherche Scientifique. BULLETIN SIGNALETIQUE. 521. SOCIOLOGIE, ETHNOLOGIE, PRÉHISTOIRE ET ARCHÉOLOGIE

BULLETINS
See Centre International d'Études de Problèmes Humains. BULLETINS

290 BUNKA TO SHAKAI. no.1–5, 1957–July 1965. Kyoto. Irreg.

Issued by the Ryūkoku Daigaku Shakai-Gakkai (Ryokoku University Sociological Society). Title in English: *Culture and Society*. Continued by: *Shakai to fukushi*.

BUSOLA SOCIALE
See SOCIAL COMPASS

CBS NEWSLETTER
See BLACK SOCIOLOGIST

CES RESEARCH PAPER
See Centre for Environmental Studies. OCCASIONAL PAPERS

CES REVIEW
See Centre for Environmental Studies. CES REVIEW

CEUR
See Centro de Estudios Urbanos y Regionales. CEUR [CUADERNOS]

CICRED BULLETIN
See Committee for International Coordination of National Research in Demography. CICRED BULLETIN

291 CADERNOS DE ESTUDOS RURAIS E URBANOS. v.1– , 1969– . São Paulo. Annual.

Issued by the Centro de Estudos Rurais e Urbanos.

Indexed: Bull. sig. soc. eth.

CAHIERS
See Belgium. Ministère de la Santé Publique et de la Famille. Centre d'Étude de la Population et de la Famille. CAHIERS.

CAHIERS
See Brussels. Université Libre. Institut de Sociologie. Centre de Sociologie du Travail. CAHIERS

LES CAHIERS
See Centre Haitien d'Investigation en Sciences Sociales. CAHIERS

CAHIERS
See Fédération des Groupes d'Études et des Recherches Institutionelles. CAHIERS

CAHIERS
See France. Centre National de la Recherche Scientifique. Institut d'Aménagement et d'Urbanisme de Région Parisienne. CAHIERS

CAHIERS
See Musée Social, Paris. CAHIERS

CAHIERS
See Paris. École Pratique des Hautes Études. 6e Section des Sciences Économiques et Sociales. Laboratoire de Sociologie de la Connaissance. CAHIERS

CAHIERS CANADIENNE DE SOCIOLOGIE
See THE CANADIAN JOURNAL OF SOCIOLOGY

292 CAHIERS D'ÉTUDE DE SOCIOLOGIE CULTURELLE. no.1– , 1971– . Bruxelles Éditions de l'Université de Bruxelles. Irreg.
Issued by the Institut de Sociologie, Université Libre.

293 CAHIERS D'ETUDES AFRICAINES. v.1– , Jan. 1960– . Paris, The Hague, Mouton. Quarterly.
Issued by the 6e Section des Sciences Économiques et Sociales, Division des Affaires Culturelles, École Pratique des Hautes Études. In French and English.
Indexed: Afr. Abstr.; Bull. sig. soc. eth.; Int. Bibl. Soc.; Int. Pol. Sc. Abstr.; Soc. Abstr.

CAHIERS DE L'I.A.U.R.P.
See France. Centre National de la Recherche Scientifique. Institut d'Aménagement et Urbanisme de Région Parisienne. CAHIERS

294 CAHIERS DE PSYCHOLOGIE SOCIALE. no.1– , Oct. 1978– . Liège.
Issued by the Service de Psychologie Sociale, Université de Liège.

295 CAHIERS DE SOCIOLOGIE. no.1– , Sep/Nov. 1965– . Rabat. Irreg.
Issued by the Institut de Sociologie, Université Mohammed V. In French; summaries in Arabic.

296 CAHIERS DE SOCIOLOGIE ÉCONOMIQUE. June 1959–1972. Le Havre, Société des Amis du Centre Universitaire Havrais. Two issues a year.
Issued by the Centre de Recherches et Études de Psychologie des Peuples et de Sociologie Économique, Institut Havrais de Sociologie Économique et de Psychologie des Peuples.
Indexed: Int. Bibl. Soc.; Soc. Abstr.

297 CAHIERS DE SOCIOLOGIE ET DE DÉMOGRAPHIE MÉDICALES. 1– , June 1961– . Paris, Éditions du Centre de Sociologie et de Démographie Médicales.
Indexed: Bull. sig. soc. eth.; Int. Bibl. Soc.; Soc. Abstr.

298 LES CAHIERS DE TUNISIE; REVUE DES SCIENCES HUMAINES. v.1– , 1953– . Tunis. Quarterly.
Issued by the Faculté des Lettres et Sciences Humaines, Université de Tunisie. In Arabic, English, French, German, Italian and Spanish.
Indexed: Int. Bibl. Soc.

299 CAHIERS DES ÉTUDES RURALES. no.1– , 1963– . Paris. Irreg.
Issued by the 6e Section des Sciences Économiques Sociales, Laboratoire d'Anthropologie Sociale, École Pratique des Hautes Études.

CAHIERS DU C.E.R.E.S. SÉRIE DÉMOGRAPHIQUE
See Tunis. Al-Jami'ahal-Tunisiyah. CAHIERS. SERIE DÉMOGRAPHIQUE

CAHIERS DU LABORATOIRE DE SOCIOLOGIE DE LA CONNAISSANCE
See Paris. École Pratique des Hautes Études. 6e Section des Sciences Économiques et Sociales. Laboratoire de Sociologie de la Connaissance. CAHIERS

300 CAHIERS DURKHEIMIENS. no.1– , 1976– . Bruxelles.
Issued by the Institut de Sociologie, Université Libre de Bruxelles.

301 CAHIERS ÉCONOMIQUES ET SOCIAUX. v.1– , Oct. 1962– . Kinshasa, Zaire. Four issues a year.
Issued by the Institut de Recherches Économiques et Sociales, Université Lovanium. Vols. for 1962–63 bear title also in English, *Economic and Social Papers*. Supersedes: Leopoldville, Congo. Université Lovanium. Institut de Recherches Économiques et Sociales. *Notes et Documents*.
Indexed: Afr. Abstr.; Bull. sig. soc. eth.; Curr. Cont.; Int. Bibl. Soc.; Int. Pol. Sc. Abstr.; Soc. Abstr.

302 CAHIERS INTERNATIONAUX D'HISTOIRE ÉCONOMIQUE ET SOCIALE. QUADERNI INTERNAZIONALI DI

STORIA ECONOMICA E SOCIALE. INTERNATIONAL JOURNAL OF ECONOMIC AND SOCIAL HISTORY. 1– , 1972– . Geneva.
Issued by the Istituto Italiano per la Storia dei Movimenti Sociali e delle Strutturi Sociali, beginning with v.9. Supersedes: *Annali di Storia Economica e Sociale.*

303 CAHIERS INTERNATIONAUX DE SOCIOLOGIE. v.1– , 1946– . Paris, Presses Universitaires de France. Two issues a year (irreg.). Some double issues.
Issued by the 6e Section des Sciences Économiques et Sociales, École Pratique des Hautes Études.
Indexed: Afr. Abstr.; Int. Bibl. Soc.; Int. Pol. Sc. Abstr.; Urb. Aff. Abstr.; Soc. Abstr.; Wom. Stud. Abstr.

304 CAHIERS QUÉBECOIS DE DÉMOGRAPHIE. v.4– , Mar. 1975– . Montréal. Quarterly.
Issued by the Association de Démographie du Québec. Continues: Association de Démographie du Quebéc. *Bulletin.*
Indexed: Pop. Ind.

305 LES CAHIERS RURAUX. 1– , 1953– . Bruxelles. Quarterly.
Issued by the Centre d'Études Rurales.
Indexed: Int. Bibl. Soc. Cult. Anth.

CAHIERS. SOCIOLOGIE DE L'ÉDUCATION
See Paris. École Pratique des Hautes Études. Centre de Sociologie Européenne. CAHIERS. SOCIOLOGIE DE L'ÉDUCATION

306 CAHIERS VILFREDO PARETO; REVUE EUROPÉENNE D'HISTOIRE DES SCIENCES SOCIALES. 1– , 1963– . Genève, Librarie Droz. Semi-annual.
Special issues published occasionally. In English, French, German, Italian or Spanish.
Indexed: Int. Bibl. Soc.; Int. Pol. Sc. Abstr.; SSCI; Soc. Abstr.

307 CAHIERS ZAIROÏS D'ÉTUDES POLITIQUES ET SOCIALES. v.1– , Apr. 1973 . Lubumbashi, Presses Universitaires du Zaire. Annual.
Issued by the Centre d'Études Socio-Politiques, Université Nationale du Zaire.
Indexed: Int. Bibl. Soc.; Int. Pol. Sc. Abstr.

308 Cairo. Al-Markaz al-Qawmi lil-Buhuth al-Ijtima'yah Wa'l-Tima'ujah. AL-MAJALLAT AL-IJTIMA'IYAH AL-QAWMIYAH. v.1– , Jan. 1964– . Cairo. Three issues a year.
Issued by the National Centre for Sociological and Criminological Research. Title in English: *The National Review of Social Sciences.* In Arabic.

309 CAIRO PAPERS IN SOCIAL SCIENCE. 1– , Dec. 1977– . Cairo.
Issued by the American University in Cairo. Added title: *Buḥut al-Qahirah fi al'ulum al-ijtima'iyah.*

310 Calcutta. Institute of Social Studies. Research Division. SOCIOLOGY OF FERTILITY SERIES. no.1– , 1971– . Calcutta. Irreg.
Monograph series.

311 California. University. UNIVERSITY OF CALIFORNIA PUBLICATIONS IN CULTURE AND SOCIETY. v.1–8, 1945–1962. Berkeley, University of California Press. Irreg.
Superseded by: *University of California Publications in Sociology.*
Monograph series.

312 California. University. UNIVERSITY OF CALIFORNIA PUBLICATIONS IN SOCIOLOGY. v.1–2, 1964–1966. Berkeley, University of California Press. Irreg.
Supersedes: California. University. *University of California Publications in Culture and Society.*
Monograph series.

313 California. University. UNIVERSITY OF CALIFORNIA PUBLICATIONS IN SOCIOLOGY AND SOCIAL INSTITUTIONS. 1–3, 1951–1956. Berkeley, California University Press. Irreg.
Monograph series.

314 California. University. Institute of Social Sciences. Center for the Study of Law and Society. REPORT. 1961/1962– . Berkeley. Irreg.

315 California. University. Survey Research Center. [MONOGRAPH] SRC. no. 1–30, 1961–1968. Berkeley. Irreg.
Monograph series.

316 California. University. University at Los Angeles. Chicano Studies Center. MONOGRAPH. 1– , 1970– . Los Angeles. Irreg.
Monograph series.

317 California. University. University at Los Angeles. Chicano Studies Center. OCCASIONAL PAPER. 1– , 1978– . Los Angeles. Irreg.
Series of papers.

318 California. University. University at Los Angeles. Institute of Industrial Relations.

MONOGRAPH SERIES. 1– , 1958– . Los Angeles. Irreg.
Title varies: no.2–4, 1958–59, *Industrial Relations Monographs*.

319 California. University. University at Los Angeles. Institute of Urban and Regional Development. WORKING PAPER. 1– , Feb. 1964– . Berkeley. Irreg.
Series of papers.

320 CALIFORNIA SOCIOLOGIST. 1– , winter 1978– . Los Angeles. Calif. Semi-annual.
Issued by the Department of Sociology, California State University. Subtitle reads: 'A journal of sociology and social work'.
Indexed: Soc. Abstr.

321 Cambridge Group for the History of Population and Social Structure. PUBLICATIONS. 1– , 1966– . London, Cambridge University Press. Irreg.
Monograph series.

322 CAMBRIDGE PAPERS IN SOCIOLOGY. 1– , 1970– . London, Cambridge University Press. Irreg.
Monograph series.

323 CAMBRIDGE STUDIES IN CULTURAL SYSTEMS. 1– , 1977– . London, Cambridge University Press. Irreg.
Monograph series.

324 CAMBRIDGE STUDIES IN SOCIAL ANTHROPOLOGY. 1– , 1967– . London, Cambridge University Press. Irreg.
Monograph series.

325 CAMBRIDGE STUDIES IN SOCIOLOGY. 1– , 1969– . London, Cambridge University Press. Irreg.
Monograph series.

326 Canada. Census and Household Surveys Field. Population Estimates and Projections Division. ESTIMATES OF POPULATION BY SEX AND AGE FOR CANADA AND THE PROVINCES. ESTIMATION DE LA POPULATION SELON DE SEXE ET L'AGE, CANADA ET PROVINCES. 1977– . Ottawa.
Continues: Canada. Census Field. Estimates and Projections Division. *Population of Canada and the Provinces by Sex and Age Group, Estimated. Population du Canada et Provinces selon le Sexe et par Groupe d'Age, Estimée.*

327 Canada. Census Field. Population Estimates and Projections Division. POPULATION OF CANADA AND THE PROVINCES BY SEX AND AGE GROUP, ESTIMATED. POPULATION DU CANADA ET DES PROVINCES SELON LE SEXE ET PAR GROUPE D'AGE, ESTIMÉE. 1973/1974–1975/1976. Ottawa. Annual.
Continues: Canada. Census Field. Research Section. Population Estimates and Projections Division. *Sex and Age Group, Estimated Population of Canada and the Provinces.* Continued by: Canada. Census and Household Surveys Field. Population Estimates and Projections Division. *Estimates of Population by Sex and Age for Canada and the Provinces. Estimation de la Population selon le Sexe et l'Age, Canada et Provinces.*

328 Canada. Department of Citizenship and Immigration. Economic and Social Research Division. CITIZENSHIP. IMMIGRATION AND ETHNIC GROUPS IN CANADA. A BIBLIOGRAPHY OF RESEARCH. 1920/1958– . Ottawa. Irreg.

329 Canada. Department of Indian Affairs and Northern Development. Northern Science Research Group. SOCIAL SCIENCE NOTES. no.1–5, 1970–1975. Ottawa.
Monograph series. Processed.

330 Canada. Royal Commission on Bilingualism and Biculturalism. DOCUMENTS. 1–13, 1969–1972. Ottawa, The Queen's Printer.
In English.
Monograph series.

331 Canada. Royal Commission on Bilingualism and Biculturalism. REPORT. 1–5/6, 1967–1970. Ottawa, The Queen's Printer.
In English.

332 Canada. Royal Commission on Bilingualism and Biculturalism. STUDIES. ÉTUDES. no.1–10, 1969–1971. Ottawa, The Queen's Printer. Irreg.
In English.
Monograph series.

333 Canadian Consultative Council on Multiculturalism. ANNUAL REPORT. 1– , 1973/1974– . Ottawa.
Title in French: *Rapport Annuelle du Conseil Consultatif Canadienne du Multiculturalisme.* In English and French.

334 Canadian Council on Urban and Regional Research. URBAN AND REGIONAL REFERENCES. [REFERENCES] URBAINES & RÉGIONALES. 1963/1964– . Ottawa. Irreg.
First issue includes works through 1962; second, through 1964, published 1966; third issue, for 1965/66, published 1968, etc. In English and French.

335 CANADIAN ETHNIC STUDIES. 1– , 1969– . Calgary. Two issues a year.
Issued by the Research Centre for Canadian Ethnic Studies, University of Calgary. Sponsored by the Canadian Ethnic Studies Association. Title in French: *Études Ethniques au Canada.*

336 Canadian Ethnic Studies Association. BULLETIN. 1– , June 1974– . Toronto. Quarterly.
Edited by the Department of Sociology, University of Toronto.

337 CANADIAN JEWISH POPULATION STUDIES. CANADIAN JEWISH COMMUNITY SERIES. v.1– , 1951– . Montréal. Annual.
Issued by the Bureau of Social and Economic Research, Canadian Jewish Congress. Title varies: v.1, no.2–4, 1951, *Jewish Community Series.*

CANADIAN JOURNAL OF AFRICAN STUDIES
See REVUE CANADIENNE DES ÉTUDES AFRICAINES

338 CANADIAN JOURNAL OF BEHAVIORAL SCIENCE. REVUE CANADIENNE DES SCIENCES DU COMPORTEMENT. v.1– , Jan. 1969– . Ottawa, University of Toronto Press. Quarterly.
Issued by the Canadian Psychological Association.
Indexed: LLBA; Soc. Abstr. Urb. Aff. Abstr.

339 CANADIAN JOURNAL OF POLITICAL AND SOCIAL THEORY. REVUE CANADIENNE DE LA THEORIE POLITIQUE SOCIALE. 1– , winter 1977– . Winnipeg. Three issues a year.
Issued by the Department of Political Science, University of Winnipeg.
Indexed: Soc. Abstr.

340 CANADIAN JOURNAL OF POLITICAL SCIENCE. REVUE CANADIENNE DE SCIENCE POLITIQUE. v.1– , 1968– . Waterloo, Ont., Wilfred Laurier University Press. Quarterly.
Issued by the Canadian Political Science Association.
Indexed: Int. Pol. Sc. Abstr.; SSCI; Soc. Abstr.

341 THE CANADIAN JOURNAL OF SOCIOLOGY. CAHIERS CANADIENNE DE SOCIOLOGIE. v.1– , spring 1975– . Edmonton, Alb. Quarterly.
Issued by the Department of Sociology, University of Alberta.
Indexed: Soc. Abstr.

342 CANADIAN PUBLIC POLICY. ANALYSE DE POLITIQUES. 1– , winter 1975– . Toronto, Toronto University Press. Quarterly.
Issued by the Canadian Economics Association, The Canadian Association of Law Teachers, the Canadian Political Science Association, and the Canadian Sociology and Anthropology Association.

343 THE CANADIAN REVIEW OF SOCIOLOGY AND ANTHROPOLOGY. LA REVUE CANADIENNE DE SOCIOLOGIE ET D'ANTHROPOLOGIE. v.1– , Feb. 1964– . Toronto, Toronto University Press. Quarterly.
Sponsored by the Canadian Sociology and Anthropology Association. In English and French.
Indexed: Abstr. Anth.; Int. Bibl. Soc.; Int. Pol. Sc. Abstr.; SSCI; Soc. Abstr.; Wom. Stud. Abstr.

344 CANADIAN REVIEW OF STUDIES IN NATIONALISM. REVUE CANADIENNE DES ÉTUDES SUR LE NATIONALISME. 1– , fall 1973– . Charlottetown, P.E.I. Two issues a year.
Issued by the University of Prince Edward Island in cooperation with the Canadian Council. In English, French, German or Spanish.

345 CANADIAN REVIEW OF STUDIES IN NATIONALISM. BIBLIOGRAPHY. REVUE CANADIENNE DES ÉTUDES SUR LE NATIONALISME. BIBLIOGRAPHIE. 1– , 1974– . Charlottetown, P.E.I. Irreg.
Issued by the University of Prince Edward Island.

Canadian Sociology and Anthropology Association.
See Société Canadienne de Sociologie et d'Anthropologie.

346 No entry.

347 CANADIAN STUDIES IN POPULATION. 1– , 1974– . Edmonton. Annual.
Issued by the Population Research Laboratories, Department of Sociology, University of Alberta.

348 CANADIAN STUDIES IN SOCIOLOGY. v.1–2, 1964–1967. Toronto, Toronto University Press. Irreg.
Issued by the Social Science Research Council of Canada.
Monograph series.

349 Canterbury, N.Z. University. Department of Psychology and Sociology. RESEARCH PROJECTS. 1962– . Christchurch. Two issues a year. (Irreg.)
Indexed: Psych. Abstr.

350 CARAVELLE. 1– , 1963– . Toulouse. Irreg.
Issued by the Institut d'Études Hispaniques, Hispano-Américaines et Luso-Brésilliennes, Université de Toulouse. Subtitle reads: 'Cahiers du Monde Hispanique et Luso-Brésillien'.
Indexed: Int. Bibl. Soc.

351 Carnegie Institution of Washington. Eugenics Record Office, Cold Spring Harbor, N.Y. BULLETIN. 1–27, 1911–1933. Cold Spring Harbor, N.Y.
Contains reprints from journals.

352 LES CARNETS DE L'ENFANCE. ASSIGNMENT CHILDREN. 1– , 1964– . Geneva. Quarterly.
Issued by the Office Européen, Fonds des Nations Unies pour l'Enfance. Title varies: 1964–66, *Assignment Children*. Vols. for 1964–66 in English; 1967– in English, French and Spanish.
Indexed: Bull. sig. soc. eth.; Int. Bibl. Soc.; Soc. Abstr.; Soc. Work Res. Abstr.

353 CASE WESTERN JOURNAL OF SOCIOLOGY. v.1– , 1969– . Cleveland. Annual.
Issued by the Department of Sociology, Case Western Reserve University. Subtitle reads: 'A journal for graduate students of Case Western Reserve University'.
Indexed: Soc. Abstr.

354 CATALYST. no.1– , summer 1965– . Buffalo, N.Y., subsequently Peterborough, Ont. Two issues a year (irreg.).
Issued by the Sociology Club, State University of New York at Buffalo, subsequently Otonabee College, Trent University, Ont.
Indexed: ABC Pol. Sc.; Abstr. Anth.; Soc. Abstr.

355 Catholic University of America. STUDIES IN SOCIOLOGY. 1–72, 1940–1967. Washington, D.C. Irreg.
Monograph series of doctoral dissertations.

CENTENNIAL STUDY AND TRAINING PROGRAMME ON METROPOLITAN PROBLEMS. PAPER
See Toronto. Bureau of Municipal Research. CENTENNIAL STUDY AND TRAINING PROGRAMME ON METROPOLITAN PROBLEMS. PAPER

356 Center for Intergroup Studies. ANNUAL REPORT. v.6– , 1973– . Cape Town.
Continues: *Annual Report. Jaarsverslag*, issued by the Center under its earlier name, Abe Bailey Institute of Interracial Studies. In English and Afrikaans.

357 Centre d'Études Sociologiques. TRAVAUX ET DOCUMENTS. Paris. Irreg.
Monograph series.

358 Centre des Sciences Sociales d'Athens. PUBLICATIONS. 1– , 1962– . The Hague, Paris, Mouton. Irreg.
The Centre known also under its English name, Social Sciences Centre, and in Greek, Kentron Koinōnikon Epistemon Athenon.
Monograph series.

359 Centre for Environmental Studies. CES RESEARCH PAPER. 1–22, 197 –1977. London. Irreg.
Continued by its *Research Series*.

360 Centre for Environmental Studies. CES REVIEW. no.1– , July 1977– . London. Three issues a year.

361 Centre for Environmental Studies. CENTRE FOR ENVIRONMENTAL STUDIES SERIES. 1–2, 1973. Beverly Hills, Calif., Sage Publications. Irreg.
Monograph series. Continued as an unnumbered series.

362 Centre for Environmental Studies. OCCASIONAL PAPERS. no.1– , 1978– . London. Irreg.
Title varies: no.1, *CES OCCASIONAL PAPER*.

363 Centre for Environmental Studies. RESEARCH SERIES. 23– , Aug. 1977– . London. Irreg.
Continues its *CES Research Paper*.

364 Centre for the Study of Developing Societies. MONOGRAPHS. 1– , 1974– . New Delhi, Allied Publishers. Irreg.
Monograph series.

365 Centre Haitien d'Investigation en Sciences Sociales. LES CAHIERS. 1956– . Port-au-Prince. Three issues a year.

366 Centre International d'Études des Problemes Humains. BULLETINS. Monte Carlo. Irreg.
No more information available.

367 Centro Colombiano de Investigaciónes Psico-Sociológicas. SOCIOLÓGICAS. PUBLICACIÓN. no.1– , 1968– . Bogotá. Irreg.
In Spanish.
Monograph series.

368 Centro de Estudios Familiares y de Población. Departamento de Investigaciónes Interdisciplinarias. [PUBLICACIÓN]. 1– , 1970– . Bogatá, SELAP-CEF, Instituto de Desarrollo de la Comunidad. Irreg.
In Spanish.
Monograph series.

369 Centro de Estudios Urbanos y Regionales. CEUR [CUADERNOS]. 1967– . Buenos Aires.
In Spanish. No more information available.

370 Centro Latinoamericano de Pesquisas de Ciências Sociais. BIBLIOGRAFIA. 1– , Sep/Oct. 1962– . Rio de Janeiro.
In Portuguese.

371 Centro Paraguayo de Estudios Sociologicos. COLLECCIÓN DE REIMPRESIONES. 1– , 1967– . Asunción, Centro Paraguayo de Estudios Sociologicos. Irreg.
In Spanish.
Monograph series of reprints.

372 CERCETĂRI SOCIOLOGICE. 1– , 1934?–1939. Iaşi, Rumania.
In Rumanian.

373 THE CEYLON JOURNAL OF HISTORICAL AND SOCIAL STUDIES. v.1–10, no.1/2, Jan. 1958–1967. Paradeniya. Two issues a year.
Issued by the Ceylon Historical and Social Studies Publications Board. Continued by a publication of the same title. Indexes: v.1–5, 1958–62, in v.5.
Indexed: Soc. Abstr.

374 THE CEYLON JOURNAL OF HISTORICAL AND SOCIAL STUDIES. n.s. v.1– , 1971– . Paradeniya, Ceylon Historical and Social Studies Publications Board. Two issues a year.
Issued by the Department of Sociology, University of Ceylon. Continues a publication of the same title.
Indexed: Soc. Abstr.

CHARACTER AND PERSONALITY
See JOURNAL OF PERSONALITY

375 Chicago. University. Center for Health Administration Studies. AN INVENTORY OF SOCIAL AND ECONOMIC RESEARCH. 1st–14th, 1952–1965. New York, subsequently Chicago. Annual.

376 Chicago. University. Committee on Education, Training and Research in Race Relations. INVENTORY OF RESEARCH IN RACIAL AND CULTURAL RELATIONS. BULLETIN. v.1–5, no.2/3, 1945–1953. Chicago.

377 Chile. Instituto Nacional de Estadisticas. DEMOGRAFIA. 1952–1972. Santiago. Annual.
Title varies: 1968, *Anuario Demografia*; 1969, *Anuario de Demografia*. Supersedes, in part, Chile. Servicio Nacional de Estadisticas y Censos. *Demografia y Asistencia Social*. Early volumes issued under the Instituto's previous name, Dirección de Estadisticas y Censos. In Spanish.

378 Chile. Universidad, Santiago. Instituto de Sociologia. BOLETIN. v.1– , Oct. 1964– . Santiago. Semi-annual.
In Spanish. No more information available.

379 Chile. Universidad, Santiago. Instituto de Sociologia. INFORMACIÓNES. no.1– , 196?– . Santiago. Irreg.
In Spanish. Mimeographed. No more information available.

380 CHINDAN HAKPO. v.1– , 1940– . Seoul. Annual.
Issued by the Chindan Hak-Hoe (Chindan Society). Table of contents and summaries also in English. Subtitle reads: 'Scholarly journal devoted to the studies of Korea and her neighboring countries'. In Korean.

381 China (Republic of China — Nei Cheng Pu). CHUNG-HUA MIN KUO T'AI-WAN JEN K'OU T'UNG CHI CHI K'AN. TAIWAN DEMOGRAPHIC QUARTERLY. 1– , Jan. 1975– . Taipei.
In Chinese.

382 CHINA QUARTERLY. v.1– , 1960– . London. Quarterly.
Issued by the Congress for Cultural Freedom.
Indexed: Int. Bibl. Soc.; Int. Pol. Sc. Abstr.; PAIS; Peace Res. Abstr. J.; Soc. Sc. Ind.; Soc. Abstr.; Wom. Stud. Abstr.

383 CHINA REPORT. POLITICAL, SOCIOLOGICAL, AND HISTORY AFFAIRS. no.1– , July 18, 1979– . Arlington, Va. Irreg.
Issued by the Joint Publications Research Service. Subseries of U.S.A., JPRS. On cover: FBIS, Foreign Broadcasting Information Services. Supersedes U.S.A., JPRS's *Translations on People's Republic of China*.

CHINESE JOURNAL OF SOCIOLOGY
See CHUNG-KUO SHE HUI HSUEH KAN

384 THE CHINESE SOCIAL AND POLITICAL SCIENCE REVIEW. v.1–24, no.4, Apr. 1916–Nov. 1941. Peking. Quarterly.
Indexes: v.1–5, 1916–20, in v.5; v.1–20, 1916–Jan. 1937 in v.20.

385 CHINESE SOCIOLOGY AND ANTHROPOLOGY. v.1– , fall 1968– . White Plains. N.Y., International Arts and Sciences Press. Four issues a year.
Indexed: Curr. Cont.; SSCI; Soc. Abstr.

386 Christian Institute for the Study of Religion and Society. SOCIAL RESEARCH SERIES. no.1– , 1964?– . Bangalore, India. Irreg.
Each issue bears also a distinctive title.

CHUNG-HUA MIN KUO T'AI-WAN JEN K'OU T'UNG CHI CHI K'AN
See China (Republic of China = Nei Cheng Pu). CHUNG-HUA MIN KUO T'AI-WAN JEN K'OU T'UNG CHI CHI K'AN

387 CHRISTIANISME SOCIAL; REVUE DE CULTURE SOCIAL ET INTERNATIONALE. 1887–1914; n.s. v.1–79, 1920–1971. Paris. Bimonthly.
Issued by the Mouvement du Christianisme Social. Subtitle varies: v.1–8, 1887–1908, 'Revue de Christianisme Social'. Continued by: *Parole + Societé*.
Indexed: Int. Bibl. Soc.; Peace Res. Abstr. J.

388 CHRISTUS REX; AN IRISH QUARTERLY OF SOCIOLOGY. v.1–25, no.4, Jan. 1947–Oct. 1971. Dublin.
Superseded by: *Social Studies; Irish Journal of Sociology*.
Indexed: Cath. Per. Ind.

389 CHUNG-KUO SHE HUI HSÜEH KAN. 1978– . Taipei, Chung-kuo she hui hsueh she. Annual.
Title in English: *Chinese Journal of Sociology*. In Chinese and English.

390 CIÊNCIA E SOCIEDADE: TEMAS E DEBATES. 1963–1975. Rio de Janeiro. Irreg.
Issued by the Centro Brasileiro de Pesquisas Fisicas. In Portuguese.

391 CIENCIA SOCIAL. 1– , 1971– . Huancayo, Peru.
Issued by the Departamento de Ciencias Sociales, Universidad Nacional del Centro del Peru. In Spanish.

392 CIENCIAS POLITICAS Y SOCIALES. v.1–13 (no.1–50), July/Sep. 1955–Oct/Dec. 1967. Mexico, D.F. Quarterly.
Issued by the Escuela Nacional de Ciencias Politicas y Sociales, Universidad Autonoma de Mexico. Continued by: *Revista Mexicana de Ciencia Politica*. In Spanish.
Indexed: Soc. Abstr.

393 CIENCAS SOCIALES. v.1– , Mar. 1958– . Medellin. Irreg.
Issued by the Instituto Colombiano de Investigaciónes Sociales, Subtitle reads: 'Economia, Sociologia, Derecho'. In Spanish.

394 CIENCAS SOCIALES. v.1– , Dec. 1963– . Cumaná, Venezuela. Semi-annual.
Issued by the Escuela de Ciencias Sociales, Universidad de Oriente. In Spanish.
Indexed: Soc. Abstr.

395 CIENCIAS SOCIALES. 1– , Oct. 1975– . La Paz, Bolivia.
Issued by the Faculdad de Ciencias Sociales, Universidad Boliviana, and Universidad Mayor de San Andres. In Spanish.

396 CIENCIAS SOCIALES CONTEMPORANEAS. Aug. 1965–1971. Habana, Cuba. Irreg.
Issued by the Academia de Ciencias. In Spanish.

397 Cincinnati. University. Department of Sociology. PUBLICATIONS. v.1, 1927. Cincinnati. One volume published.

CIRCULAIRE. SÉRIE A.
See Musée Social, Paris. CIRCULAIRE. SÉRIE A.

CIRCULAIRE. SÉRIE B.
See Musée Social, Paris. CIRCULAIRE. SÉRIE B.

CITIZENSHIP, IMMIGRATION AND ETHNIC GROUPS IN CANADA: A BIBLIOGRAPHY OF RESEARCH
See Canada. Department of Citizenship and Immigration. Economic and Social Division. CITIZENSHIP, IMMIGRATION AND ETHNIC GROUPS IN CANADA: A BIBLIOGRAPHY OF RESEARCH

398 CITTÀ E SOCIETÀ; STUDI E ANALISE SUI PROBLEMI DELLE COMMUNITÀ URBANE. v.1– , 1966– . Milano, Scuola Tipografica San Benedetto. Bimonthly. In Italian.
Indexed: Int. Bibl. Soc. Cult. Anth.

399 THE CITY & SOCIETY. v.1– , 1977– . Beverly Hills, Calif., London, Sage Publications. Irreg.
Monograph series.

400 CITY NOTES. 1– , Feb. 1971– . New Haven, Conn. Irreg.
Issued by the Institute for Social and Policy Studies, Yale University; earlier name, Center for the Study of City and its Environment.

401 CIUDAD Y TERRITORIO. v.1– , 1970– . Madrid. Quarterly.
Issued by the Centro de Estudios Urbanos, Instituto de Estudios de Administración Local. In Spanish.

402 CIVILISATIONS. v.1– , Jan. 1951– . The Hague, Mouton. Quarterly.
Issued by the International Institute of Political and Social Sciences Concerning Countries of Different Civilizations. In English and French; summaries in French or English.
Indexed: Int. Bibl. Soc.; Int. Pol. Sc. Abstr.; Soc. Abstr.

403 CIVILISATIONS ET SOCIÉTÉS. v.1– , 1965– . Paris, The Hague, Mouton. Irreg.
Issued by the 6e Section des Sciences Économiques et Sociales, École Pratique des Hautes Études.
Monograph series.

404 CIVITAS. v.1– , 1919– . Roma, Edizioni Civitas. Monthly.
In Italian.
Indexed: Int. Bibl. Soc.; Int. Pol. Sc. Abstr.; Soc. Abstr.

405 CIVITAS; JAHRBUCH FÜR CHRISTLICHE GESELLSCHAFTSORDNUNG. 1– , 1962– . Mannheim, Pesch-Hause. Annual.
Indexed: Int. Bibl. Soc.; Int. Pol. Sc. Abstr.; Soc. Abstr.

406 CLASE; CITAS LATINOAMERICANAS EN SOCIOLOGIA Y ECONOMIA. 1– , 1976– Mexico, D.F.
Issued by the Centro de Información Cientifica y Humanistica, Universidad Nacional Autonoma de Mexico. In Spanish.

407 CLASSE E STATO. v.1–5, 1965–1968. Bologna. Semi-annual.
In Italian.

408 CLEVELAND COLLEGE SERIES ON URBAN AFFAIRS. REPORT. no.1– , fall 1967– . Cleveland. Irreg.
Issued by the Cleveland College, Western Reserve University.
Monograph series.

409 Cluj. Universitatea Babes-Bolyai. Biblioteca Centrala Universitara. STUDIA UNIVERSITATIS BABES-BOLYAI. SOCIOLOGIA. no.1– , 1970– . Cluj. Annual.
In Rumanian, English, French, German, and Russian; summaries in English, French and Russian.
Indexed: Bull. sig. soc. eth.

410 CO-EXISTENCE. 1– , May 1964– . Pickering, Ont., subsequently Oxford; currently Glasgow. Semi-annual.
Subtitle reads: 'A journal for the comparative study of economics, sociology and politics in a changing world'.
Indexed: Bull, sig. soc. eth.; Int. Bibl. Soc.; Soc. Abstr.

411 COLEÇÃO LITERATURA E SOCIEDADE. 1– , 1973– . Lisboa. Irreg.
In Portuguese. No more information available.
Monograph series.

412 COLEÇÃO PORTUGALIA. 5: CIÊNCIAS SOCIOLOGICAS E PSICOLOGICAS. 1– , 1964– . Lisboa, Portugalia Editoria. Irreg. Ceased?
In Portuguese.
Monograph series.

413 COLEÇÃO SOCIOLOGIA BRASILEIRA. 1– , 1975– . Petrópolis, Voxes. Irreg.
Other title: *Sociologia Brasileira*. In Portuguese.
Monograph series; some works in second editions.

COLECCIÓN DE REIMPRESIONES
See Centro Paraguayo de Estudios Sociológicos. COLECCIÓN DE REIMPRESIONES

COLECCIÓN MONOGRAFIAS DIAGNOSTICAS
See Instituto Centroamericano de Población y Familia. COLECCIÓN MONOGRAFIAS DIAGNOSTICAS

COLLANA DELL'ISTITUTO DI SOCIOLOGIA DELL'UNIVERSITÀ DI PARMA
See Parma. Università, Istituto di Sociologia. COLLANA DELL'ISTITUTO DELL'UNIVERSITÀ DI PARMA

COLLANA DELL'ISTITUTO NAZIONALE DI SOCIOLOGIA RURALE
See Istituto Nazionale di Sociologia Rurale. COLLANA DELL'ISTITUTO DI SOCIOLOGIA RURALE

COLLANA DI SOCIOLOGIA URBANA E RURALE
See SOCIOLOGIA URBANA E RURALE

COLLANA DI STUDI DEMOGRAFICI
See Palermo. Università. Istituto di Scienze Demografiche. COLLANA DI STUDI DEMOGRAFICI

414 COLLANA SOCIOLOGIA E VITA. 196?– . Roma, Idea. Irreg. Ceased publications?
In Italian
Monograph series.

COLLECTION D'ÉTUDES SOCIOLOGIQUES
See Kinshasa, Zaire. Université Lovanium. Institut de Recherches Économiques et Sociales. COLLECTION D'ÉTUDES SOCIOLOGIQUES

COLLECTION DE SOCIOLOGIE GÉNÉRALE ET DE PHILOSOPHIE SOCIALE
See Brussels. Université Libre. Institut de Sociologie. COLLECTION DE SOCIOLOGIE GÉNÉRALE ET DE PHILOSOPHIE SOCIALE

415 COLLECTION "DÉMOGRAPHIE CANADIENNE". 1– , 1972– . Montréal, Les Presses de l'Université de Montréal. Irreg.
Monograph series.

416 COLLECTION LA FAMILLE À TRAVERSE LE MONDE: THE FAMILY THROUGHOUT THE WORLD. 1– , 1967?– . Paris, Fédération Internationale des Écoles de Parents et d'Éducation. Irreg.
Monograph series.

COLLECTION: SÉRIE HISTOIRE INSTITUTIONELLE
See Grenoble. Université des Sciences Sociales. Centre de Recherche d'Histoire Économique, Sociale et Institutionelle. COLLECTION: SÉRIE HISTOIRE INSTITUTIONELLE

417 COLLECTIVE BEHAVIOR IN SPORT SITUATIONS. 1975– . Waterloo, Ont. Three issues a year.
Issued by the SIRLS, Faculty of Kinetics and Leisure Studies, University of Waterloo.

COLLOQUE URBAIN
See URBAN FORUM

418 COLLOQUIUM INTERNATIONALE. July 1976– . St. Saphorin, Switzerland, Georgi Publishing Co. Bimonthly.
Issued by the Society for Human Ecology. In English, French and German; summaries in two of these languages.

419 Cologne. Forschungsinstitut für Sozial- und Verwaltungswissenschaften. Soziologische Abteilung. SCHRIFTEN. 1–2, 1951. Köln.

420 Cologne. Universität. ZENTRALARCHIV FÜR EMPIRISCHE SOZIALFORSCHUNG. 1968– . München, Verlag Dokumentation. Early volumes have added title, *Empirical Social Research.*

421 Colombia. Departamento Administrativo Nacional de Estadistica. ANUARIO DEMOGRAFICO. 1968/1969– . Bogotá. Annual.
In Spanish.

422 Colombia. Universidad Nacional. Faculdad de Sociologia. SERIE LATINOAMERICANA. v.1–5, 1956–1964. Bogotá. Irreg.
In Spanish.
Monograph series.

423 Colorado. University. STUDIES. SERIES D. STUDIES IN SOCIOLOGY. 1–3, 1949–1957. Boulder, Col.

424 Columbia University. Center for Advanced Research in Urban and Environmental Affairs. WORKING PAPER. 1– , 1976– . New York. Irreg.

425 Columbia University. Institute for the Study of Science in Human Affairs. ISHA BULLETIN. no.1–9, 1968–1970. New York. Irreg.
Monograph series.

426 Columbia University. Institute for the Study of Science in Human Affairs. REPORT OF THE DIRECTOR ON THE ACTIVITIES. 1st– , 1966/1968– . New York.
Report ends March 31. Each volume bears also a distintive title.

427 COMENTARIO SOCIOLÓGICO. 1– , 1972– . Barcelona. Quarterly.
Issued by the Servicio de Estudios Sociológicos, Confederación Española de Cajas de Ahorro. Subtitle reads: 'Estructure social de España'. In Spanish.

428 Commission of the European Communities. EURO-BAROMETRE. EURO-BAROMETER. no.1– , June 1974– . Bruxelles. Irreg.
In English and French. Subtitle reads: 'The public opinion in the European Community'.

429 Committee for International Coordination of National Research in Demography. CICRED BULLETIN. no.1– , July 1973– . Paris. Semi-annual.

COMMUNAUTÉS
See ARCHIVES DES SCIENCES SOCIALES DE LA COOPÉRATION ET DU DÉVELOPPEMENT

COMMUNICATIE EN COGNITIE
See COMMUNICATION & COGNITION

430 COMMUNICATIO SOCIALIS. v.1– , Jan/Mar. 1968– . Paderborn, München, Wien, Verlag Ferdinand Schönningh. Quarterly.
Subtitle reads: 'Zeitschrift für Publizistik in Kirch und Welt'.

431 COMMUNICATION. June 1974– . New York, London, Gordon and Breach. Semi-annual.
Some issues are thematic.
Indexed: Soc. Abstr.

COMMUNICATION
See Zambia. University. Institute for Social Research. COMMUNICATION.

432 COMMUNICATION & COGNITION. v.1– , 1968– . Ghent, Belgium.
Issued by the Werkgroep voor de Studie van Communicatieve en Cognitieve Processen aan de R.U.G. Title varies: v.1–3, 1968–70, *Communicatie en cognitie*. In English, Flemish and French.
Indexed: Psych. Abstr.; SSCI; Soc. Abstr.

433 COMMUNICATION BIBLIOGRAPHIES. 1– , 1973– . Singapore.
Issued by the Asian Mass Communication Research and Information Centre.

COMMUNICATION DE DÉMOGRAPHIE HISTORIQUE
See HISTORISCH-DEMOGRAPHISCHE MITTEILUNGEN

434 COMMUNICATION RESEARCH. v.1– , Jan. 1974– . Beverly Hills, Calif., Sage Publications. Quarterly.
Indexed: Soc. Abstr.

435 COMMUNICATION, THE MEDIA, SPORT AND LEISURE. 1975– . Waterloo, Ont. Three issues a year.
Issued by the SIRLS. Faculty of Human Kinetics and Leisure, University of Waterloo.

436 COMMUNICATION YEARBOOK. 1977– . New Brunswick, N.J., Transaction Books. Annual.
Issued by the International Communication Association.

437 COMMUNICATIONS. v.1– , 1961– . Paris, Éditions du Seuil. Semi-annual.
Issued by the 6 e Section des Sciences Économiques et Sociales, École Pratique des Hautes Études. Each issue is thematic.
Indexed: Bull. sig. soc. eth.; Int. Bibl. Soc.; Int. Pol. Sc. Abstr.; Soc. Abstr.

COMMUNICATIONS
See Leiden. Rijksuniversiteit. Afrika-Studiecentrum. COMMUNICATIONS

COMMUNICATIONS
See Rhodes-Livingstone Institute, Lusaka, Zambia. COMMUNICATIONS

COMMUNICATIONS
See University of Cape Town. Centre for African Studies. COMMUNICATIONS

COMMUNICATIONS
See University of Cape Town. School of African Studies. COMMUNICATIONS

438 COMMUNICATIONS AND DEVELOPMENT. v.1– , spring 1977– . Teheran. Quarterly.
Issued by the Iran Communications and Development Institute.
No more information available.

439 COMMUNICATIONS. INTERNATIONALE ZEITSCHRIFT FÜR KOMMUNIKATIONSFORSCHUNG. REVUE INTERNATIONALE DE LA RECHERCHE DE COMMUNICATION. 1975– . Sankt Augustin, Hans Richarz. Three issues a year.
In English, French and German; summaries in these three languages.

440 COMMUNICATIONS ET LANGAGES. 1969– . Paris. Quarterly.
Issued by the Centre d'Études et de Promotion de la Lecture.
Indexed: Bull. sig. soc. eth.

441 COMMUNITY. July 1924–Aug. 1938; v.14– , Sep. 1938– . New York. Monthly, except July and September.
Issued by the United Community Funds and Councils of America (earlier called Community Chests and Councils). Title varies: 1925–June 1938, *New Bulletin*.

442 COMMUNITY. v.1– , Apr. 1954– . Colombo, Sri Lanka. Semi-annual.
Suspended: Dec. 1955–Mar. 1958.

443 COMMUNITY. v.1–2, no. 2, Jan. 1970–Apr. 1971. London. Quarterly.
Issued by the Community Relations Commission. Superseded by: *New Community*.
Indexed: Brit. Hum. Ind.

COMMUNITY ANALYSIS AND ACTION SERIES
See Boston College, Boston, Mass., Bureau of Public Affairs. COMMUNITY ANALYSIS AND ACTION SERIES

444 COMMUNITY DEVELOPMENT. no.1– , 1958– . Roma. Semi-annual.
Issued by the Federation of Settlements and Neighborhood Centers. Running title: *International Review of Community Development*. In English, French and Italian.

Indexed: Abstr. Soc. Work; Afr. Abstr.; Bull. sig. soc. eth.; Int. Bibl. Soc.; Int. Pol. Sc. Abstr.; Soc. Abstr.; Urb. Aff. Abstr.

COMMUNITY DEVELOPMENT BULLETIN
See COMMUNITY DEVELOPMENT REVIEW

445 COMMUNITY DEVELOPMENT DIGEST. v.1–5, Jan/June 1963–1965. Delhi, Manager Publications. Semi-annual.
Issued by the National Institute of Community Development, Mussooree, India.

446 COMMUNITY DEVELOPMENT JOURNAL no.1– , Jan. 1966– . London, Oxford University Press. Quarterly.
Issued by the Community Development Clearinghouse, University of London. Supersedes: *Community Development Bulletin*.
Indexed: Brit. Hum. Ind.; Int. Bibl. Soc.; Int. Pol. Sc. Abstr.; SSCI; Soc. Sc. Ind.; Soc. Abstr.

447 COMMUNITY DEVELOPMENT JOURNAL 1– , Feb. 1971– . Midland, Mich., Pendell Co. Quarterly. No more information available.

448 COMMUNITY DEVELOPMENT REVIEW. [v.1]–8, no.2, Jan. 1956–1963. Washington, D.C. Quarterly.
Issued by the Community Development Division, International Cooperation Administration. Title varies: Jan. 1956–Sep. 1956, *Community Development Bulletin*. Issues for 1956–58, called no.1–11, constitute v.1–3.

449 Community Development Society. JOURNAL. v.1– , spring 1970– . Columbia, Mo. Quarterly.
Indexed: PAIS; Soc. Abstr.

450 COMMUNITY FORUM. v.1– , spring 1971– . Belfast. Quarterly.
Issued by the Northern Ireland Community Relations Commission. For private circulation.

451 COMMUNITY ISSUES. v.1– , 1968– . Queens, N.Y.
Issued by the Queens College, City University of New York. Each issue bears a distinctive title.

452 COMMUNITY PLANNING REVIEW. REVUE CANADIENNE D'URBANISME. v.1–27, no.9, Feb. 1951–Sep. 1977. Ottawa. Quarterly.
Issued by the Community Planning Association of Canada. Supersedes: *Layout for Living and Urbanism*. In French or English; summaries in English or French.
Indexed: Can. Per. Ind.

453 COMMUNITY PRIORITIES & EVALUATIONS. 1– , 197 – . Louisville, Ky.
Issued by the Urban Studies Center, University of Louisville.

454 COMMUNITY PSYCHOLOGY SERIES. no.1– , 1972– . New York, Behavioral Publications. Irreg.
Issued by the American Psychological Association.
Monograph series.

455 COMMUNITY SOCIAL ANALYSIS SERIES. no.1– , 1965– . Atlanta, Ga. Annual.
Issued by the Department of Public Health, Georgia.

COMMUNITY STRUCTURE SERIES
See CONNECTICUT URBAN RESEARCH REPORT

456 COMPARATIVE EVENTS. 5– , 1974– . East Lansing, Mich. Quarterly.
Issued by the Institute for Comparative Sociology, State University of Michigan.

457 COMPARATIVE GROUP STUDIES. 1–3, 1970–1972. Beverly Hills, Calif., Sage Publications. Quarterly.
Continued by: *Small Group Behavior*.

458 COMPARATIVE SOCIAL RESEARCH. v.2– , 1979– . Greenwich, Conn., JAI Press. Annual.
Continues: *Comparative Studies in Sociology*.
Indexed: Soc. Abstr.

459 COMPARATIVE STUDIES IN SOCIETY AND HISTORY. v.1– , Oct. 1958– . London, Cambridge University Press. Quarterly.
Issued by the Society for Comparative Study of Society and History, and the Department of History, University of Michigan. Indexes: v.1–5, 1958–63, in v.5; v.1–10, 1958–68, in v.11, 1969; v.11–15, 1969–73, in v.15, 1973; v.16–30, 1974–78, in v.20, 1978.
Indexed: Bull. sig. soc. eth.; Int. Bibl. Soc.; Int. Pol. Sc. Abstr.; PHRA; Soc. Sc. Hum. Ind.; SSCI; Soc. Abstr.

460 COMPARATIVE STUDIES IN SOCIETY AND HISTORY. SUPPLEMENT. 1–3, 1961–1968. The Hague, Mouton. Irreg.
Monograph series.

461 COMPARATIVE STUDIES IN SOCIOLOGY. 1, 1978. Greenwich, Conn., JAI Press. One issue published.
Continued by: *Comparative Social Research*.

462 COMPARATIVE URBAN RESEARCH. 1– , spring 1972– . New York, subsequently New Brunswick, N.J., Transaction Periodicals Consortium. Three issues a year.
Sponsored by the Committee for Community Research, International Sociological Association, and the Comparative Urban Studies Committee, American Society for Public Administration. Supersedes: International Sociological Association. Comparative Urban Studies Committee. *Newsletter*. Includes bibliographic articles.
Indexed: Int. Bibl. Soc.; Int. Pol. Sc. Abstr.; Urb. Aff. Abstr.

463 COMPARATIVE URBAN STUDIES. 1– , 1974– . Chapel Hill, N.C. Irreg.
Issued by the Institute for Research in Social Science, University of North Carolina.

COMPAS SOCIAL
See SOCIAL COMPASS

COMPONENT STUDY
See Toronto. University. Centre for Urban and Community Studies. RESEARCH PAPERS

COMPREHENSIVE URBAN STUDIES
See SOGO TOSHI KENKYU

COMPTES RENDU STATISTIQUES
See Intergovernmental Committee for European Migration. STATISTICAL REPORT

464 COMPUTER APPLICATIONS. v.5– , 1978– . Nottingham, England. Quarterly.
Issued by the Department of Geography, University of Nottingham. Continues: *Computer Applications in the Natural and Social Sciences*.

465 COMPUTER APPLICATIONS IN THE NATURAL AND SOCIAL SCIENCES. no.1–4, 1969–1976. Nottingham, England, Computer Applications. Irreg.
Continued by: *Computer Applications*.

466 COMPUTERS & SOCIETY. v.1– , 1970– . Trenton, N.J. Quarterly.
Issued by the Special Interest Group on Computers and Society, The Association for Computing Machinery (ACM).

467 COMPUTERS AND URBAN SOCIETY. v.1, Jan–Dec. 1975. New York, Pergamon Press. Quarterly.
Continued by: *Urban Systems*.

468 COMUNICACIÓN. 1– , 1975– . Caracas. Bimonthly.
Issued by the Centro de Comunicación Social Jesus Maria Pellin. In Spanish.

469 COMUNICACIÓN Y CULTURA. no.1– , July 1973– . Buenos Aires, Editorial Galerna. Quarterly.
In Spanish.

470 COMUNIDADES. v.1– , Jan/Feb. 1966– . Madrid. Three issues a year.
Issued by the Instituto de Estudios Sindicales, Sociales y Corporativos. In Spanish.
Indexed: Int. Bibl. Soc.

471 COMUNITÀ. no.1– , Jan. 1946– . Milano. Three issues a year.
In Italian.
Indexed: Int. Bibl. Soc. Cult. Anth.; Int. Pol. Sc. Abstr.; Soc. Abstr.

472 Concepción, Chile. Universidad. Instituto Central de Sociologia. CUADERNOS DE INVESTIGACIÓN. SERIE HISTORIA SOCIAL. 1– , 1971– . Concepción.
In Spanish.

473 CONCERNED DEMOGRAPHY. v.1– , 1971– . Ithaca, N.Y. Irreg.
Issued by the Department of Sociology, Ithaca College. Each issue is thematic.

CONFERENCE
See ÉLITES ET RESPONSIBILITÉS. SÉRIE GÉNÉRALE

474 Conference on Social Issues. PROCEEDINGS. v.1, 1966. Eugene, Oreg.
Issued by the Associated Students of the University of Oregon.

CONFLICT RESOLUTION
See THE JOURNAL OF CONFLICT RESOLUTION

475 CONFLUENCE. v.1–14, 1960–1968. Paris, The Hague, Mouton. Irreg.
Issued by the International Committee for Social Sciences Documentation in cooperation with the International Social Science Council, and with the support of Unesco. In French and English. Subtitle reads: 'Surveys of research in the social sciences. Etats des recherches en sciences sociales'.

476 Congreso de Sociologia Ecuatoriana. MEMORIA. 1– , 1957– . Cuenca.
Issued by the Faculdad de Jurisprudencia y Ciencias Sociales, Universidad de Cuenca. Vol.2, 1957 prepared by Junta Nacional de Planificación y Coordinación Economica. In Spanish.

477 Congreso Latinoamericano de Sociologia. MEMORIA. 6– , 1961– . Caracas.

Issued by the Asociación Latinoamericana de Sociologia. Vols. from the 6th Congress, 1961, published by the Asociación Venezolana de Sociologia. In Spanish.

478 Congreso Nacional de Sociologia, Mexico. ESTUDIOS SOCIOLOGICOS. 1st–14th, 1950–1963. Mexico, D.F.
Issued by the Instituto Investigaciónes Sociales, Universidad Nacional Autonoma de Mexico. In Spanish.
Indexed: Soc. Abstr.

479 Connecticut. Community Development Division. Urban Renewal Section. URBAN RENEWAL IN CONNECTICUT. REPORT. 1964–1965. Hartford, Conn.

480 Connecticut. Community Development Division. Urban Renewal Section. URBAN RENEWAL IN CONNECTICUT. STATISTICAL REPORT. 1964–1967. Hartford, Conn.

481 CONNECTICUT URBAN RESEARCH REPORT. no.1– , Dec. 1963– . Storrs, Conn.
Issued by the Institute of Urban Research, University of Connecticut. Includes subseries: *Community Structure Series*, no.1–13, 1966.

482 CONNEXIONS. no.1–2, 1972– . Paris, Epi S.A. Editeurs. Three issues a year.
Issued by the Association pour la Recherche et l'Intervention Psychosociologiques'. Called also *Revue Connexions. Psychologie, Sciences Humaines*. Subtitle reads: 'Psychosociologie, Sciences Humaines'.
Indexed: Int. Bibl. Soc.; Int. Pol. Sc. Abstr.

483 CONSUMPTION OF LEISURE AND SPORT. 1975– . Waterloo, Ont. Three issues a year.
Issued by the SIRLS, Faculty of Human Kinetics and Leisure Studies, University of Waterloo.

484 CONTEMPORARY CRISES. v.1– , 1977– . Amsterdam, Elsevier Scientific Publications Co. Quarterly.
Indexed: Soc. Abstr.

485 CONTEMPORARY SOCIOLOGY. 1– , Jan. 1972– . Washington, D.C. Bimonthly.
Issued by the American Sociological Association. Continues the book review section of *American Sociological Review*.
Indexed: Soc. Abstr.; Wom. Stud. Abstr.

486 CONTRADICTION. 1971–197?. Clayton, Vic. Annual. Publication ceased.
Issued by the Anthropology and Sociology Society, Monash University.

487 CONTREPOINT. v.1– , 1970– . Paris. Quarterly.
Indexed: Bull. sig. soc. eth.; Int. Bibl. Soc.

488 CONTRIBUTI DI SOCIOLOGIA. no.1– , 1974– . Naples, Franco Ferrotti. Irreg.
In Italian.

489 CONTRIBUTI DI SOCIOLOGIA. READINGS. no.1– , 1974– . Naples, Franco Ferrotti. Irreg.
In Italian.

490 CONTRIBUTII LA SOCIOLOGIA CULTURII DE MASA. 1– , 1970– . Bucureşti, Editura Academiei Republicii Socialiste România. Annual.
In Rumanian.

491 CONTRIBUTIONS. 1– , May 1975– . Blacksburg, Va.
Issued by the Epsilon Chapter, Alpha Kappa Delta, Virginia Polytechnic Institute, and the Department of Sociology, State University. Subtitle reads: 'A journal of student papers in sociology'.

492 CONTRIBUTIONS A L'ÉTUDE DES SCIENCES DE L'HOMME. no.1– , 1952– . Montréal, Éditions du Lévrier.
Issued by the Centre de Recherche en Relations Humaines, Université de Montréal. In English and French.

CONTRIBUTIONS A L'HISTOIRE ÉCONOMIQUE ET SOCIALE
See Brussels. Université Libre. Institut de Sociologie. Centre d'Histoire Économique et Sociale. CONTRIBUTIONS A L'HISTOIRE ÉCONOMIQUE ET SOCIALE

CONTRIBUTIONS À LA SOCIOLOGIE DE LA CONNAISSANCE
See Paris. École Pratique des Hautes Études. 6e Section des Sciences Économiques et Sociales. Laboratoire de la Connaissance. CAHIERS

493 CONTRIBUTIONS IN FAMILY STUDIES. 1– , 1977– . Westport, Conn., Greenwood Press. Irreg.
Monograph series.

494 CONTRIBUTIONS IN SOCIOLOGY. 1– , 1969– . Westport, Conn. Greenwood Press. Irreg.
Monograph series.

495 CONTRIBUTIONS TO ASIAN STUDIES. v.1– , Jan. 1971– . Leiden, E. J. Brill. Semiannual.
Some issues are monographs.

496 CONTRIBUTIONS TO INDIAN SOCIOLOGY. no.1–9, 1957–1966; n.s. no.1– , Dec. 1967– . Paris, 1957–1965, Bombay, New York, Asia Publishing Co. Semi-annual.
Issued by the Institute of Economic Growth, University of Delhi. In English and French.
Indexed: Bull. sig. soc. eth.; Soc. Abstr.

CONTRIBUTIONS TO MILITARY SOCIOLOGY
See CONTRIBUTIONS TO STUDIES ON MILITARY SOCIOLOGY

497 CONTRIBUTIONS TO STUDIES ON MILITARY SOCIOLOGY. v.1– , 1971– . Rotterdam, Rotterdam University Press. Irreg.
Title varies: v.1–2, *Contributions to Military Sociology*.
Monograph series.

CONTRIBUTIONS TO THE SOCIOLOGY OF KNOWLEDGE
See BEITRÄGE ZUR WISSENSSOZIOLOGIE. BEITRÄGE ZUR RELIGIONSSOZIOLOGIE

498 CONTRIBUTIONS TO THE SOCIOLOGY OF LANGUAGE. no.1– , 1971– . The Hague, Mouton. Irreg.
Other title: *Advances in the Sociology of Language*.
Monograph series.

CONTRIBUTIONS TO THE SOCIOLOGY OF RELIGION
See BEITRÄGE ZUR WISSENSSOZIOLOGIE. BEITRÄGE ZUR RELIGIONSSOZIOLOGIE

499 CONTROVERSIES IN SOCIOLOGY. 1– , 1975– . London, George Allen & Unwin. Irreg.
Monograph series.

500 COOPERATION AND CONFLICT. NORDIC STUDIES IN INTERNATIONAL POLITICS. 1– , 1965– . Jahanneshaw, University Book Centre. Two issues a year.
Issued by the Nordic Committee for the Study of International Politics. In English; occasionally in one of the Scandinavian languages.
Indexed: Int. Bibl. Soc.; Int. Pol. Sc. Abstr.; Soc. Abstr.

THE COORDINATOR
See THE FAMILY LIFE COORDINATOR

501 Cordóba, Argentina. Universidad Nacional. Faculdad de Derecho y Ciencias Sociales. BOLETIN. 1937– . Cordóba, Dirección General de Publicaciónes Universitarias. Five issues a year.
In Spanish.
Indexed: Int. Bibl. Soc.

502 THE CORNELL JOURNAL OF SOCIAL RELATIONS. 1– , spring 1966– . Ithaca, N.Y. Semi-annual.
Issued by the Department of Sociology, Cornell University.
Indexed: Int. Pol. Sc. Abstr.; Psych. Abstr.; SSCI; Soc. Abstr.

503 CORNELL STUDIES IN INDUSTRIAL AND LABOR RELATIONS. v.1–22, 1951–1952. Ithaca, N.Y. Irreg.

504 Cornell University. Agricultural Experiment Station. SOCIAL SCIENCES. RURAL SOCIOLOGY. no.1– , July 1973– . Ithaca, N.Y. Irreg.
Monograph series.

505 Cornell University. Department of Rural Sociology. BULLETIN. no.1– , Dec. 1929– . Ithaca, N.Y. Irreg.
Title varies: *Mimeograph Bulletin*.
Series of papers.

506 Cornell University. Program in Urban Development Research. REGIONAL SCIENCE. DISSERTATIONS & MONOGRAPH SERIES. 1– , 1971– . Ithaca, N.Y. Irreg.
Monograph series.

507 Cornell University. Western Societies Program. OCCASIONAL PAPERS. no.1– , 1974– . Ithaca, N.Y. Irreg.
Series of papers.

508 CORSO DI SOCIOLOGIA. 1974– . Milan, Centro Studi Terzo Mondo. Monthly.
In Italian.

509 COUNTRY DEMOGRAPHIC PROFILES. ISP-30. no.1– , 1973– . Washington, D.C. Irreg.
Issued by the Social and Economic Statistics Administration, Department of Commerce and Bureau of the Census.
Monograph series, some in updated editions.

COUNTRY LIFE BULLETIN
See RURAL AMERICA

COUNTRY PROFILES
See Population Council, New York. COUNTRY PROFILES

COUNTRY PROSPECTS
See Population Council, New York. COUNTRY PROSPECTS

510 COURRIER DE L'EXTRÊME ORIENT. BERICHTEN UIT HET VERNE OOSTEN. v.1– , 1966– . Bruxelles. Monthly.
Issued by the Centre d'Etude du Sud-Est Asiatique et de l'Extrême-Orient, Institut de Sociologie, Université Libre.

511 CRIME AND DELINQUENCY. v.1– , July 1955– . New York. Quarterly.
Issued by the National Council on Crime and Delinquency. Title varies: 1955–Apr. 1960, *NPPA Journal.*
Indexed: Psych. Abstr.; SSCI; Soc. Sc. Ind.; Soc. Work Res. Abstr.; Soc. Abstr.

512 CRIME AND DELINQUENCY ABSTRACTS. v.1–8, no.6, Jan. 1963–1972. Bethesda, Md. Monthly.
Issued by the National Institutes of Health, National Institute of Mental Health, Department of Health, Education and Welfare. Title varies: 1963–June 1966, *International Bibliography on Crime and Delinquency.* Absorbed: *Current Projects in the Prevention, Control and Treatment of Crime and Delinquency.*

513 CRIME AND DELINQUENCY LITERATURE. v.1– , Feb. 1970– . New York.
Issued by the National Council on Crime and Delinquency. Supersedes: *Information Review on Crime and Delinquency,* and *Selected Highlights of Crime and Delinquency Literature,* and continues their volume numbering.
Indexed: Soc. Abstr.

514 CRIME AND SOCIAL JUSTICE. 1– , spring/summer 1974– . Berkeley, Calif., Semiannual.
Issued by the School of Criminology, University of California at Berkeley. Title on cover: *Crime and Social Justice. Issues in Criminology.*
Indexed: Soc. Abstr.

CRIME AND SOCIAL JUSTICE. ISSUES IN CRIMINOLOGY
See CRIME AND SOCIAL JUSTICE

515 CRIME IN EAST AFRICA. 1– , 1970– . Uppsala. Irreg.
Issues by the Scandinavian Institute of African Studies.
Monograph series.

516 CRIMINAL JUSTICE AND BEHAVIOR. v.1– , Mar. 1974– . Beverly Hills, Calif., Sage Publications. Quarterly.
Issued by the American Association of Correctional Psychologists.
Indexed: PHRA; PAIS; Psych. Abstr.; Soc. Abstr.

CRIMINOLOGICA
See CRIMINOLOGY

517 CRIMINOLOGY. v.1– , May 1963– . [Place of publication varies, 1963–70] Beverly Hills, Calif., Sage Publications, 1971– . Quarterly.
Issued by the American Society of Criminology. Title varies: v.1–7, 1963–70, *Criminologica.*
Indexed: PAIS; SSCI; Soc. Sc. Ind.; Soc. Abstr.; Soc. Work Res. Abstr.

518 CRIMINOLOGY AND PENOLOGY ABSTRACTS. v.20– , Jan-Feb. 1980– . Amsterdam, Kugler Publications. Bimonthly.
Issued by the Criminologica Foundation in cooperation with the University of Leiden, Ministry of Justics, The Hague, and Joint Borcaus for Dutch Child Welfare. Continues: *Abstracts on Criminology and Penology*. In English.

519 CRISIS AND CHANGE. v.1– , Oct. 1965– . London. Monthly.
Oct–Nov/Dec. 1965 unnumbered, constitute v.1, no.1, 2.

520 CRITICA MARXISTA. 1963–1973. Roma, Editori Riuniti (Sezione Periodici).
In Italian.
Indexed: Bull. sig. soc. eth.; Int. Bibl. Soc.; Int. Pol. Sc. Abstr.; Soc. Abstr.

521 LA CRITICA SOCIOLOGICA. 1– , spring 1967– . Roma. Quarterly.
Issued by the Istituto de Sociologia. In Italian; summaries in English.
Indexed: Bull. sig. soc. eth.; Int. Bibl. Soc.; Int. Pol. Sc. Abstr.; Soc. Abstr.

522 CRITICAL INQUIRY. v.1– , Sep. 1974– . Chicago, The University of Chicago Press. Quarterly.
Indexed: Soc. Abstr.

523 CRITIQUE RÉGIONALES: CAHIERS DE SOCIOLOGIE ET D'ÉCONOMIE RÉGIONALES. 1– , 1979– . Brussels. Four issues a year.
Issued by the Institut de Sociologie, Université Libre in cooperation with the Comite pour l'Étude des Problèmes de l'Emploi et du Chômage.

CRITIQUES OF RESEARCH IN THE SOCIAL SCIENCES
See Social Science Research Council. BULLETIN

524 Cross-Cultural Southwest Ethnic Study Center. NEWSLETTER. – , May 1976– . El Paso, Tex.

[CUADERNO]
See Centro de Estudios Urbanos y Regionales. CEUR [CUADERNOS]

525 CUADERNO DE SOCIOLOGIA. 1– , 1965?– . La Plata. Irreg.
Issued by the Faculdad de Humanidades y Ciencias de la Educación, Universidad Nacional de la Plata. In Spanish.
Monograph series.

526 CUADERNOS AMERICANOS; LA REVISTA DEL MUNDO NUEVO. v.1– , Jan/Feb. 1942– . Mexico, D.F., Editorial Libros de Mexico.
In Spanish.
Indexed: Int. Bibl. Soc.; Int. Pol. Sc. Abstr.; Soc. Abstr.

CUADERNOS DE CIENCIAS SOCIALES
See Honduras. Universidad Nacional Autonoma, Tegucigalpa. Departamento de Ciencias Sociales. CUADERNOS DE CIENCIAS SOCIALES

CUADERNOS DE CIENCIAS SOCIALES
See Montevideo. Universidad. Instituto de Ciencias Sociales. CUADERNOS DE CIENCIAS SOCIALES

CUADERNOS DE INVESTIGACIÓN. SERIE HISTORIA SOCIAL
See Concepción, Chile. Universidad. Instituto Central de Sociologia. CUADERNOS DE INVESTIGACIÓN. SERIE HISTORIA SOCIAL

527 CUADERNOS DE SOCIEDAD Y POLITICA. 1– , 1976– . Lima, Peru, Cuadernos de Sociedad y Cultura. Irreg.
In Spanish.

528 CUADERNOS DE SOCIOGRAFIA. 1– , 1948– . Tucumán. Irreg.
Issued by the Instituto de Sociografia, Colegio Libre de Estudios Superiores. In Spanish.

CUADERNOS DE SOCIOGRAFIA Y PLANEACIÓN
See Tucumán, Argentina. Universidad. Instituto de Sociografia y Planeación. CUADERNOS DE SOCIOGRAFIA Y PLANEACIÓN

529 CUADERNOS DE SOCIOLOGIA. 1– , 1962– . La Plata, Argentina. Irreg.
Issued by the Faculdad de Humanidades y Ciencias de la Educación, Universidad Nacional de la Plata. In Spanish.

CUADERNOS DE SOCIOLOGIA
See Buenos Aires. Universidad Nacional. Instituto de Sociologia. BOLETIN.

CUADERNOS DEL BOLETIN
See Buenos Aires. Universidad. Instituto de Sociologia. BOLETIN

530 CULTURA E SOCIETÀ. v.1, no.1–4, Oct. 1959–July 1960. Bologna, G. Malipiero. Quarterly.
In Italian.

531 Cultural Research Institute. BULLETIN. v.1– , 1962– . Calcutta, Temple Press. Quarterly.

CULTURE AND SOCIETY
See BUNKA TO SHAKAI

532 CULTURE, MEDICINE AND PSYCHIATRY. 1– , 1977– . Dordrecht, Reidel Publishing Co. Four issues a year.
Subtitle reads: 'An international journal of comparative cross-cultural research'.
Indexed: Soc. Abstr.

533 CULTURES ET DÉVELOPPEMENT. v.1– , 1968– . Louvain, Belgium. Quarterly.
Issued by the Institut d'Étude des Pays en Développement, Université Catholique. Supersedes: *Zaire; Revue Congolaise*. Subtitle reads: 'Revue internationale des sciences du développement'. In French and English.
Indexed: Int. Bibl. Soc.

534 CURRENT AFRICANIST RESEARCH; INTERNATIONAL BULLETIN. LA RECHERCHE AFRICANISTE EN COURS; BULLETIN INTERNATIONAL. no.1– , Nov. 1971– . London.
Issued by the Information Liaison Unit, International African Institute.

535 CURRENT ANTHROPOLOGY. v.1– , Jan. 1960– . Chicago, Ill. Five issues a year.
Sponsored by the Wenner-Gren Foundation for Anthropological Research. Vol. for Dec. 1965, pt.2, includes 3rd *International Directory of Anthropological Institutions;* Dec. 1966, pt. 2, includes 4th *International Directory of Anthropological Institutions;* Dec. 1967 includes 4th *International Directory of Anthropologists*.
Indexed: Soc. Sc. Ind.; Soc. Abstr.

CURRENT CONTENTS. BEHAVIORAL, SOCIAL AND EDUCATIONAL SCIENCES
See CURRENT CONTENTS. SOCIAL & BEHAVIORAL SCIENCES

536 CURRENT CONTENTS. SOCIAL & BEHAVIORAL SCIENCES. v.1– , 1969– . Philadelphia, Pa. Weekly.
Issued by the Institute of Scientific Information. Title varies: *Current Contents. Behavioral, Social and Educational Sciences.*

537 CURRENT OPINION. v.1–6, no.1, 1973–1978. Williamstown, Mass.
Issued by the Roper Public Opinion Research Center, Williams College. Superseded by: *Public Opinion*.

538 CURRENT PROJECTS IN THE PREVENTION, CONTROL AND TREATMENT OF CRIME AND DELINQUENCY. v.1–6, spring 1962–winter 1964/1965. Bethesda, Md. Two issues a year.
Issued by the Institute of Mental Health, National Institutes of Health, Public Health Service, Department of Health, Education and Welfare. Absorbed by: *International Bibliography on Crime and Delinquency*. Issues for summer 1964–winter 1964/1965 published as: Public Health Service: *Publication,* no.1296.

CURRENT PROJECTS ON ECONOMIC AND SOCIAL IMPLICATIONS OF SCIENCE AND TECHNOLOGY
See United States. National Science Foundation. Office of Special Studies. CURRENT PROJECTS ON ECONOMIC AND SOCIAL IMPLICATIONS OF SCIENCE AND TECHNOLOGY

539 CURRENT PUBLICATIONS IN POPULATION/FAMILY PLANNING. no.1– , Apr. 1969– . New York. Irreg.
Issued by the Population Council and the International Institute for the Study of Human Reproduction, Columbia University.

540 CURRENT RESEARCH ON PEACE AND VIOLENCE. v.1– , 1978– . Tampere. Quarterly.
Issued by the Tampere Peace Research Institute. Supersedes: *Instant Research on Peace and Violence.*
Indexed: Soc. Abstr.

CURRENT RESEARCH REPORT SERIES
See Ghana. University. Department of Sociology. CURRENT RESEARCH REPORT SERIES

541 CURRENT SOCIOLOGY. v.1, no.1, Jan. 1966. Milwaukee, Wis., Clearinghouse for Sociological Literature. One issue published.
Issued by the Clearinghouse for Sociological Literature, Department of Sociology, University of Wisconsin, Milwaukee. Absorbed by: *Sociological Abstracts*. Includes abstracts of articles deposited with the Clearinghouse.

542 CURRENT SOCIOLOGY. LA SOCIOLOGIE CONTEMPORAINE. v.1– , 1952– . The Hague, Mouton, subsequently Beverly Hills, Calif., Sage Publications. Four issues a year.
Issued by the International Sociological Association. Includes, as supplement, first four volumes of *International Bibliography of Sociology*.
Indexed: Int. Bibl. Soc.; Psych Abstr.; SSCI; Soc. Abstr.; Urb. Aff. Abstr.

543 CURRENT SOCIOLOGY. LA SOCIOLOGIE CONTEMPORAINE. SUPPLEMENT. v.1, 1974. The Hague, Mouton. One issue published.

544 DADOS. no.1– , 1966– . Rio de Janeiro, Editora Campus. Semi-annual.
Issued by the Instituto Universitario de Pesquisas do Rio de Janeiro. In Portuguese; summaries in English and French.

545 DAEDALUS. v.1– , May 1846– . Brookline, Mass. Quarterly.
Issued by the Academy of Arts and Sciences. Title varies: v.1–85, *Proceedings of the American Academy of Arts and Sciences.* Vols. 9–31 numbered also n.s. v.1–23.
Indexed: Int. Bibl. Soc.; Int. Pol. Sc. Abstr.; PHRA; Psych. Abstr.; Soc. Sc. Hum. Ind.; SSCI; Soc. Abstr.; Soc. Work Res. Abstr.

A DANISH SOCIOLOGICAL JOURNAL
See SOCIOLOGISKE MEDDELELSER; A DANISH SOCIOLOGICAL JOURNAL

546 DE HOMINE. 1– , Mar. 1962– . Roma. Quarterly.
Issued by the Centro di Richerca per le Scienze Morali e Sociali, Università di Roma. Includes supplement: Bolletino Bibliografico per le Scienze Morali e Sociali. In Italian.
Indexed: Soc. Abstr.

547 DEATH EDUCATION. v.1– , spring 1977– . Washington, D.C., Hemisphere Publishing Co. Quarterly.
Subtitle reads: 'Pedagogy, counseling, care; an international quarterly'.
Indexed: Soc. Abstr.

548 DEBATES EN SOCIOLOGIA. 1– , Feb. 1977– . Lima, Peru. Monthly.
Issued by the Departamento de Ciencias Sociales, Pontificia Universidad del Peru. In Spanish.

DELINQUENCY AND SOCIETY
See 'AVARYANUT VE-HEVRAH

DELINQUENCY PROFILE OF SYRACUSE AND ONONDAGA COUNTY
See Syracuse. University. Youth Development Center. DELINQUENCY PROFILE OF SYRACUSE AND ONONDAGA COUNTY

549 DEMOGRÁFIA. 1– , 1958– . Budapest, Statisztikai Kiadó Vállalat. Quarterly.
Issued by the Központi Statisztikai Hivatal, 1958–60; Demográfiai Elnökségi Bizottság, Magyar Tudományos Akadémia and Központi Statisztikai Hivatal, 1961– . In Hungarian; summaries in English and Russian.
Indexed: Bull. sig. soc. eth.; Int. Bibl. Soc.; SSCI; Soc. Abstr.

DEMOGRAFIA
See Bolivia. Dirección Nacional de Estadistica y Censos. ANUARIO DEMOGRAFICO

DEMOGRAFIA
See Chile. Instituto Nacional de Estadisticas. DEMOGRAFIA

DEMOGRAFIA
See Panama. Dirección de Estadistica y Censos. ESTADISTICA PANAMENA. SERIA A: DEMOGRAFIA

550 DEMOGRAFIA Y ECONOMIA. v.1– , 1967– . Mexico, D.F. Three issues a year.
Issued by the El Colegio de Mexico. In Spanish.
Indexed: Int. Bibl. Soc.; Soc. Abstr.

551 DEMOGRAFICHNI DOSLIDZHENIA. Kiev.
Issued by the Institut ekonomiky, Akademiia nauk U.S.S.R. In Ukrainian; summaries in English and Russian.

552 DEMOGRAFICKÝ SBORNIK. 1959– . Praha.
Issued by the Státni Úřad Statistický. In Czech; table of contents and summaries also in English and Russian.
Indexed: Int. Bibl. Soc.; Soc. Abstr.

553 DEMOGRAFIE. v.1– , 1959– . Praha, Ustředni komise lidové kontroly a statistiky. Four issues a year.
In Czech; summaries and table of contents also in English and Russian.

DEMOGRAFSKA STATISTIKA
See Bulgaria. Tsentralno statisticheski upravlenie. DEMOGRAFSKA STATISTIKA

DEMOGRAFSKA STATISTIKA
See Yugoslavia. Savezni zavod za statistiku. DEMOGRAFSKA STATISTIKA

554 LE DÉMOGRAPHE. no.1– , Apr. 1955– . Grivegnee, Belgium. Semi-annual, 1955–57; annual, 1958– .
Issued by the International Union for the Scientific Study of Population. In English and French; occasionally also in Spanish.

555 DEMOGRAPHIC REPORTS FOR FOREIGN COUNTRIES. SERIES P–96. no.1— , 1969– . Washington, D.C., Government Printing Office.
Issued by the U.S. Bureau of the Census.

556 Demographic Research Centre, Kerala (India). STUDIES IN DEMOGRAPHY. v.1– , Mar. 1963– . Trivandrum.

557 DEMOGRAPHIC REVIEW OF THE MALTESE ISLANDS. no.1– , 1959– Valletta, Malta. Annual.
Issued by the Office of Statistics.

DEMOGRAPHIC SERIES
See Wyoming. University. Division of Business and Economic Research. DEMOGRAPHIC SERIES

558 DEMOGRAPHIC STATISTICS OF THE JEWISH POPULATION IN ISRAEL. 1969 [covering 1965–67]– . Jerusalem. Triennial.
Issued by the Central Bureau of Statistics, Israel.

559 DEMOGRAPHIC YEARBOOK. 1948– . New York. Annual.
Issued by the Statistical Central Office of the United Nations, in cooperation with its Department of Social Affairs. In English and French.

DÉMOGRAPHIE ET SOCIÉTÉS
See Paris. École Pratique des Hautes Études. Centre de Recherches Historiques. DÉMOGRAPHIE ET SOCIÉTÉS

560 DEMOGRAPHISCHES JAHRBUCH ÖSTERREICHS. 1975– . Wien. Annual.
Issued by the Statistisches Zentralamt. Continues: Austria. Statistisches Zentralamt. *Natürliche Bevölkerungsbewegung*.

561 DEMOGRAPHY. v.1– , 1964– . Chicago, subsequently Washington, D.C. Annual.
Issued by the Population Association of America. Summaries in Spanish. Index to v.1–10, 1964–73.
Indexed: Int. Bibl. Soc.; PAIS; SSCI; Soc. Sc. Ind., Wom. Stud. Abstr.

DEMOGRAPHY AND DEVELOPMENT DIGEST
See Lucknow. University. Demographic Research Centre. DEMOGRAPHY & DEVELOPMENT DIGEST

DEMOGRAPHY. BULLETIN
See Australia. Bureau of Census and Statistics. DEMOGRAPHY. BULLETIN

562 DEMOSTA. v.1– , 1968– . Praha. Quarterly.
Issued by the Federalni statistický uřad, and Institut demografie. Subtitle reads: 'Bulletin for demography and statistics'. In English, French, Rumanian, Russian and Spanish.
Indexed: Bull. sig. soc. eth.; Int. Bibl. Soc.; PAIS.

563 Denver. University. Center for International Race Relations. RACE AND NATIONS. MONOGRAPH SERIES. 1– , 1969–70– . Denver. Irreg.
Monograph series.

DEPARTMENTAL TECHNICAL REPORT *See* Texas. Agricultural and Mechanical University. Department of Agricultural Economics and Sociology. DEPARTMENTAL TECHNICAL REPORT

564 DERECHO Y SOCIOLOGIA, JURISPRUDENCIA, ANTROPOLOGIA, HISTORIA, FILOSOFIA, ETICA, ECONOMIA, POLITICA ET SOCIAL, SOCIOLOGIA. v.1, no.1–9, 1906. Habana, Cuba.
In Spanish.

565 DESARROLLO. no.1– , 1965– . Mexico, D.F. Irreg.
Issued by the Instituto Mexicano de Estudios Sociales. Subtitle reads: 'Estudios sobre estructuración social'. In Spanish.

566 DESARROLLÓ RURAL EN LAS AMERICAS. v.1– , 1969– . Bogotá. Three issues a year.
Issued by the Instituto Interamericano de Ciencias Agricolas, Centro Interamericano de Desarrollo Rural y Reforma Agraria. In Spanish; summaries in English, Portuguese and Spanish.
Indexed: Int. Bibl. Soc.; Soc. Abstr.

567 Deutsche Gesellschaft für Soziologie. SCHRIFTENREIHE. 1. SER. VERHANDLUNGEN DES DEUTSCHEN SOZIOLOGENTAGES. 1–9, 1910–1949. Tübingen, Mohr.

568 Deutscher Soziologentag. VERHANDLUNGEN. VORTRÄGE UND DISKUSIONEN IN DER VERSAMMLUNG UND IN DEN SITZUNGEN DER UNTERGRUPPEN. 1– , 1910– . Tübingen, Mohr.

569 DEVELOPING ECONOMIES. 1– , Jan/June 1963– . Tokyo. Quarterly.
Issued by the Institute of Developing Economies. Vol.1 preceded by preliminary issues 1–2, Mar/Aug. and Sep/Dec. 1962.
Indexed: Int. Bibl. Soc.; SSCI; Soc. Abstr.

570 DEVELOPMENT AND CHANGE. v.1– , 1969– . The Hague, Mouton; subsequently Beverly Hills, Calif., Sage Publications. Three issues a year.
Issued by the Institute of Social Studies, The Hague.
Indexed: Int. Bibl. Soc.; Int. Pol. Sc. Abstr.; SSCI.

571 DEVELOPMENT RESEARCH DIGEST; SUMMARIES OF CURRENT BRITISH RESEARCH ON DEVELOPMENT. no.1– , spring 1978– . Brighton, England. Semiannual.
Issued by the Institute of Development Studies, University of Sussex.

572 DÉVELOPPEMENT & CIVILISATIONS. no.1– , Mar. 1960– . Paris. Quarterly.
Issued by the Institut de Recherche de Formation en Vue du Développement Harmonisée. Supplements accompany some issues. In French; occasionally in English or Spanish. Cumulative index every two years.
Indexed: Bull. sig. soc. eth.; Int. Bibl. Soc.

573 DÉVIANCE ET SOCIÉTÉ. 1– , May 1977– . Genéve, Éditions Médecine et Hygiene. Quarterly.
Issued by the Faculte du Droit, Université de Genève.

574 DEVIANT BEHAVIOR. v.1– , Oct. 1979– . Washington, D.C., Hemisphere Publishing Co. Quarterly.
Title on cover: *An Interdisciplianry Journal on Human Behavior.*
Indexed: Soc. Abstr.

575 DIALECTICAL ANTHROPOLOGY. v.1– , Nov. 1975– . Amsterdam, Elsevier Scientific Publishing Co.
Indexed: Soc. Abstr.

576 DIALOGO SOCIAL; LA REVISTA DE INQUIETUD SOCIAL. 1– , Feb/Mar. 1967– . Panama City. Monthly, except January.
Issued by the Centro de Capacitación Social. In Spanish.

577 Dibrugarh, India. University. Centre for Sociological Studies of the Frontier Region. NORTH EASTERN RESEARCH BULLETIN. no.1– , 1970– . Dibrugarh. Annual.

578 DIDAKOMETRY AND SOCIOMETRY. 1– , 1969– . Malmö. Sweden.
Issued by the School of Education, Department of Education and Sociological Research.

DIFFUSION OF INNOVATIONS IN RURAL SOCIETIES. REPORT
See Michigan. State University, East Lansing. Department of Communication. DIFFUSION OF INNOVATIONS IN RURAL SOCIETIES. TECHNICAL REPORT

DIRECTORY
See American Sociological Association. DIRECTORY

579 DIRECTORY OF DEPARTMENTS OF SOCIOLOGY. 1978– . Washington, D.C. Irreg.
Issued by the American Sociological Association.

580 DIRECTORY OF PUBLISHED PROCEEDINGS. SERIES SSH: SOCIAL SCIENCES AND HUMANITIES. 1/4– , 1968/1971– . Harrison, N.Y., Interdok Co.
Covers proceedings from 1964– . Annual cumulative index in last issue of the year; cumulation, vols. 5–8, 1972–75, published in 1976.

A DIRECTORY OF SOCIOLOGISTS AND ANTHROPOLOGISTS IN CANADA AND THEIR CURRENT RESEARCH
See ANNUAIRE DES SOCIOLOGUES ET ANTHROPOLOGUES ET LEUR RECHERCHE COURANTE

581 DIRITTO E SOCIETÀ. 1973–1975. Florence, Sansoni. Quarterly.
In Italian. Continued by: *Diritto e Società*, n.s.

582 DIRITTO E SOCIETÀ. n.s. Jan/Mar. 1978– . Padua, CEDAM. Quarterly.
In Italian. Continues: *Diritto e Società*.

DISCUSSION PAPER
See Michigan. University. Institute of Public Policy Studies. DISCUSSION PAPER.

DISCUSSION PAPERS. C. SOCIOLOGY AND POLITICS
See Birmingham. University. Faculty of Commerce and Social Science. DISCUSSION PAPERS. C. SOCIOLOGY AND POLITICS

DISCUSSION PAPERS. SERIES F. BIRMINGHAM SOCIETY AND POLITICS
See Birmingham. University. Faculty of Commerce and Social Science. DISCUSSION PAPERS. SERIES F. BIRMINGHAM SOCIETY AND POLITICS

DISCUSSION PAPERS. SERIES RC/C. SOCIOLOGY AND POLITICS
See Birmingham. University. Faculty of Commerce and Social Science, DISCUSSION PAPERS. C. SOCIOLOGY AND POLITICS

DISCUSSION SERIES
See Fabian Society, London. DISCUSSION SERIES

583 DISSERTATION ABSTRACTS: A GUIDE TO DISSERTATIONS AND MONOGRAPHS AVAILABLE ON MICROFILM. v.1–26, 1938–1966. Ann Arbor, Mich. University Microfilms.
Title varies: v.1–11, 1938–51, *Microfilm Abstracts: A Collection of Abstracts of Doctoral Dissertations and Monographs available in Complete Form on Microfilm*. Superseded, in part, by: *Dissertation Abstracts. Section A: The Humanities and Social Sciences*.

584 DISSERTATION ABSTRACTS. SECTION A: THE HUMANITIES AND SOCIAL SCIENCES. v.27– , July 1966– . Ann Arbor, Mich., University Microfilms. Monthly.
Continues, in part, *Dissertation Abstracts; A Guide to Dissertations and Monographs available on Microfilm*.

DISSERTATIONEN AUS AGRARÖKONOMIK UND AGRARSOZIOLOGIE
See Forschungsgesellschaft für Agrarpolitik und Agrarsoziologie. DISSERTATIONEN AUS AGRARÖKONOMIK UND AGRARSOZIOLOGIE

DOC PAL RESUMENES DE POBLACIÓN EN AMERICA LATINA
See RESUMENES DE POBLACIÓN EN AMERICA LATINA. LATIN AMERICAN POPULATION ABSTRACTS

585 DOCTORAL DISSERTATIONS ACCEPTED BY AMERICAN UNIVERSITIES. no.1–22, 1934/1935–1954/1955. New York, Wilson. Annual.
Continued by: 'Index to American Doctoral Dissertations', published in *Dissertation Abstracts*, commencing with v.16.

586 DOCUMENTATION TOURISTIQUE; BIBLIOGRAPHIE INTERNATIONALE. v.1– , 1969– . Marseilles. Annual.
Issued by the Centre d'Études du Tourisme, Université d'Aix-Marseilles.

DOCUMENTOS DE TRABAJO
See Fundación Bariloche. Departamento de Sociologia. DOCUMENTOS DE TRABAJO

DOCUMENTOS DE TRABAJO
See Instituto Torcuato di Tella. Centro de Investigaciónes Sociales. DOCUMENTOS DE TRABAJO

DOCUMENTS
See Canada. Royal Commission on Bilingualism and Biculturalism. DOCUMENTS

587 DOCUMENTS DE SOCIOLOGIE POLITIQUE DU PHÉNOMÉNE RELIGIEUX. 1, 1973. Bruxelles.
Issued by the Institut Belge de Science Politique.

588 DOCUMENTS OF SOCIOLOGY. 1–2, 1971. New York, Essay Press. Irreg.
Monograph series.

LE DOMAINE HUMAINE
See THE HUMAN CONTEXT

589 Dominican Republic. Dirección General de Estadistica y Censos. ESTADISTICA DEMOGRAFICA. 1943/1946– . Ciudad Trujillo.

590 Duke University, Durham, N.C. SOCIOLOGICAL SERIES. no.1–10, 1939–1958. Durham, N.C. Irreg.
Monograph series.

591 Duke University, Durham, N.C. Center for Commonwealth and Comparative Studies. MONOGRAPH AND OCCASIONAL PAPERS SERIES. no.1– , 1966– . Durham, N.C. Irreg.
Issues no.1–42 issued by the Center under its previous name, Commonwealth Studies Center.

592 DUQUESNE REVIEW. v.1–18, no.2, spring 1956–1973. Pittsburgh, Pa.
Issued by the Departments of Economics, Political Science and Sociology, Duquesne University.
Indexed: Cath. Per. Ind.; Soc. Abstr.

ERS. ETHNIC AND RACIAL STUDIES
See ETHNIC AND RACIAL STUDIES

ESPR
See Ohio. State University. Agricultural Economics and Rural Sociology Department. ESPR [ECONOMIC AND SOCIOLOGIC PEER REVIEW]

ESS
See Ohio. State University. Agricultural Economics and Rural Sociology Department. ESS [ECONOMIC AND SOCIOLOGIC SERIES]

593 EASTERN ANTHROPOLOGIST. v.1– , Sep. 1947– . Lucknow. India. Quarterly.
Issued by the Ethnographic and Folk Culture Society.
Indexed: Abstr. Anth.; Soc. Abstr.

594 ECONOMIA Y CIENCIAS SOCIALES. Sep. 1958–Oct. 1969. Caracas. Quarterly.
Issued by the Instituto Investigaciónes de Ciencias Económicas y Sociales, and Faculdad de Economia, Universidad Central de Venezuela. In Spanish.
Indexed: Bull. sig. soc. eth.; Int. Bibl. Soc.; Int. Pol. Sc. Abstr.; Soc. Abstr.

ECONOMIC AND SOCIAL PAPERS
See CAHIERS ÉCONOMIQUES ET SOCIAUX

ECONOMICS AND SOCIOLOGIC OCCASIONAL PAPERS
See Ohio. State University. Agricultural Economics and Rural Sociology Department. ECONOMICS AND SOCIOLOGIC OCCASIONAL PAPERS

ECONOMIC AND SOCIOLOGY MIMEOGRAPHS
See Ohio. State University. Agricultural Economics and Rural Sociology Department. ESS [ECONOMIC AND SOCIOLOGIC SERIES]

595 ECONOMIC DEVELOPMENT AND CULTURAL CHANGE. v.1– , Mar. 1952– . Chicago. Quarterly.
Issued by the Research Center in Economic Development and Cultural Change, The University of Chicago. Index to v.1–15, 1952–67, in v.16, no.2, pt.2.
Indexed: Afr. Abstr.; Bull. sig. soc. eth.; Int. Bibl. Soc.; Int. Pol. Sc. Abstr.; SSCI; Soc. Sc. Ind.; Soc. Abstr.

596 ECONOMIC GEOGRAPHY. v.1– , Mar. 1925– . Worcester, Mass.
Issued by the Clark University.
Indexed: Int. Bibl. Soc.; Int. Pol. Sc. Abstr.; PAIS; Soc. Sc. Hum. Ind.; Soc. Abstr.; Urb. Aff. Abstr.

597 ECONOMICS AND SOCIETY. SERIES B. 1975– . Manila. Monthly.
Issued by the Center for Research and Communication. Supersedes, in part, *Economics and Society*.

598 ECONOMICS AND SOCIOLOGY. OCCASIONAL PAPERS,. no.1– , Nov. 1969– . Columbus, Ohio. Irreg.
Issued by the Department of Agricultural Economics and Rural Sociology, Ohio State University.
Series of papers.

599 ÉCONOMIE ET HUMANISME. v.1–7 (no.1–40), Apr/May 1941–Nov/Dec. 1948; v.11 (no.71–)– , Jan/Feb. 1952– . Lyons, Bimonthly.

Issued by Le Centre d'Économie et Humanisme. Jan/Feb. 1952 issue continues earlier numbering, increased by that of *Diagnostique Économique et Social* and *Idées et Forces* during 1949–51. Absorbed these two publications 1952. Supplement, titled 'Lettre de la Tourette', included 1946–48, later published separately.
Indexed: Bull. sig. soc. eth.; Int. Bibl. Soc.; Int. Pol. Sc. Abstr.; Soc. Abstr.

ECONOMISCH-GEOGRAFISCHE WERELD REVUE
See TIJDSCHRIFT VOOR ECONOMISCHE EN SOCIALE GEOGRAFIE

600 ÉCONOMISTE HAITIEN. v.1–2, no.6, Oct/Nov. 1939–Oct/Dec. 1941. Port-au-Prince.
Title varies: v.1, no.1–2, Oct/Nov. 1939–40, *Sociologie Haitienne*.

601 ECONOMY AND SOCIETY. v.1– , Feb. 1972– . London, Routledge & Kegan Paul. Quarterly.
Indexed: Int. Bibl. Soc.; Int. Pol. Sc. Abstr.; SSCI; Soc. Abstr.; Urb. Aff. Abstr.

602 Edinburgh. University. EDINBURGH UNIVERSITY PUBLICATIONS. GEOGRAPHY AND SOCIOLOGY. 1–2, 1952–1955. Edinburgh. Irreg.

EDINBURGH UNIVERSITY PUBLICATIONS. GEOGRAPHY AND SOCIOLOGY
See Edinburgh. University. EDINBURGH UNIVERSITY PUBLICATIONS. GEOGRAPHY AND SOCIOLOGY

603 EDUCATION AND URBAN SOCIETY. v.1– , Nov. 1968– . Beverly Hills, Calif., Sage Publications. Quarterly.
Issued by the Department of Political Science, Case Western Reserve University.
Indexed: PAIS; PHRA; SSCI; Soc. Abstr.; Urb. Aff. Abstr.

604 EKISTICS. v.1– , Oct. 1955– . Athens, Doxiadis Associates. Monthly.
Issued by the Athens Center of Ekistics, Athens Technological Organization. Title varies: v.1, no.1, Oct. 1955, *Tropical Housing and Planning Monthly Bulletin*. Indexes: v.1–10 (no.1–62), 1955–60, issued as no.63. Subtitle reads: 'Reviews on the problems and science of human settlements'.
Indexed: Bull. sig. soc. eth.; Int. Bibl. Soc.; PHRA; Soc. Sc. Ind.

605 ÉLITES ET RESPONSIBILITÉS. SÉRIE GÉNÉRALE. 1952/1953–1970. Paris. Three issues a year.
Issued by the Fédération Nationale des Syndicats d'Ingénieurs et de Cadres. Title varies: 1952/53–1954/55, *Conférence*.

606 EMERGING SOCIOLOGY. v.1– , Jan. 1979– . Meerut, India. Annual.
Issued by the Meerut Society. Subtitle reads: 'Journal of Sociology Workers Sangam'.

607 Emory University, Atlanta. Center for Research in Social Change. STUDIES IN URBAN CHANGE. REPORT. 1–?, 1970–?. Atlanta, Ga. Irreg. Ceased publication.

EMPIRICAL SOCIAL RESEARCH
See Cologne. Universität. ZENTRALARCHIV FÜR EMPIRISCHE SOZIALFORSCHUNG

ENCUESTA DE INMIGRACIÓN DE LIMA METROPOLITANA
See Peru. Dirección Nacionale de Estadistica y Censos. ENCUESTA DE INMIGRACIÓN DE LIMA METROPOLITANA

608 ENFANCE. 1948– . Paris. Five issues a year.
Issued by the Laboratoire de Psychobiologie de l'Enfant. Subtitle reads: 'Psychologie, Pedagogie — Neuro-Psychiatrie, Sociologie'.
Indexed: Bull. sig. soc. eth.; Psych. Abstr.; Soc. Abstr.

609 ENSAYOS. no.1– , Mar. 1962– . Quito.
Issued by the Instituto Ecuatoriano de Sociologia y Technica, Transculturación e Investigación Social. In Spanish.

610 ENVIRONMENT AND BEHAVIOR. v.1– , June 1969– . Beverly Hills, Calif., Sage Publications. Quarterly.
Issued by the Environmental Psychology Program, City University of New York.
Indexed: PAIS; Psych. Abstr.; SSCI; Soc. Abstr.; Urb. Aff. Abstr.

611 ENVIRONMENT AND CHANGE. v.2, Sep. 1973–Feb. 1974. London, Maddox Editorial, Ltd.
Continues: *Environment this Month*, 1972–73.

612 ENVIRONMENTAL PERIODICALS BIBLIOGRAPHY. v.1– , 1972– . Santa Barbara, Calif. Bimonthly.
Issued by the International Academy at Santa Barbara. Title varies: v.1, 1972, *Environmental Periodicals; Indexed Article Titles*.

ENVIRONMENTAL PERIODICALS; INDEXED ARTICLE TITLES
See ENVIRONMENTAL PERIODICALS BIBLIOGRAPHY

613 ENVIRONMENTAL POLICIES AND URBAN DEVELOPMENT THESIS SERIES. no.1– , 1964– . Chapel Hill, N.C. Irreg.
Issued by the University of North Carolina.
Monograph series of M.A. papers and Ph.D. theses.

614 ÉPISTEMOLOGIE SOCIOLOGIQUE. v.1– , 1954– . Paris. Annual.
Issued by the Groupe d'Épistemologie Sociologique, Centre d'Études Sociologiques.
Indexed: Bull. sig. soc. eth.; Soc. Abstr.

615 EPITHEORÉSIS KOINONIKON EREUNON. no.1– , 1969– . Athens, Greece. Quarterly.
Issued by the Centre National de Recherche Sociales (EKKE), called in English, National Centre of Social Research. Title in English: *Greek Review of Social Research*. Continues: *Koinōlogiké Skepse*. In Greek, English and French; occasionally in German and Italian.
Indexed: Soc. Abstr.

616 EQUALS. Apr. 1975–77? London. Bimonthly.
Issued by the Race Relations Board. Supersedes: *Race Relations*. Superseded by: *New Equals*.

617 Erasmus Universiteit, Rotterdam. Sociologisch Instituut. MEDEDELINGEN. INFORMATION BULLETIN. v.1– , 1970– . Rotterdam. Irreg.
In Dutch.

618 Erivan. Armianskii gosudarstvennyi pedagogicheskii institut. NUCHNYE TRUDY. SERIIA OBSHCHESTVENNYKH NAUK. no.1– , 1966– . Erivan.
Title varies: *Sbornik nauchnykh trudov. Seriia obshchestvennykh nauk*. In Russian.

619 Erivan. Universitet. VESTNIK; OBSHCHESTVENNYE NAUKI. 1– , 1968– . Erivan.
In Russian.
Indexed: Bull. sig. soc. eth.

620 Escuela Latinoamericana de Sociologia. BOLETIN DE ELAS. v.1–6, Jan. 1968–1970. Santiago, Chile.
In Spanish.

ESTADISTICA DEMOGRAFICA
See Dominican Republic. Dirección General de Estadistica. ESTADISTICA DEMOGRAFICA

ESTADISTICA PANAMENA. SERIA A: DEMOGRAFIA
See Panama. Dirección de Estadistica y Censos. ESTADISTICA PANAMENA. SERIA A: DEMOGRAFIA

ESTADISTICAS DEMOGRAFICAS
See Portugal. Instituto Nacional de Estadistica. STATISTIQUES DÉMOGRAPHIQUES

ESTIMATED INTERNAL MIGRATION BULLETIN
See Trinidad and Tobago. Central Statistical Office. ESTIMATED INTERNAL MIGRATION BULLETIN.

ESTIMATES OF POPULATION BY SEX AND AGE FOR CANADA AND THE PROVINCES
See Canada. Census and Household Surveys Field. Population Estimates and Projections Division. ESTIMATES OF POPULATION BY SEX AND AGE FOR CANADA AND THE PROVINCES

ESTIMATION DE LA POPULATION SELON LE SEXE ET L'AGE, CANADA ET PROVINCES
See Canada. Census and Household Surveys Field. Population Estimates and Projections Division. ESTIMATES OF POPULATION BY SEX AND AGE FOR CANADA AND THE PROVINCES

621 ESTUDIOS CENTRO AMERICANOS. no.1– , 1965– . Guatemala City.
Issued by the Seminario de Integración Social Guatemalteca and the Institute of Latin American Studies of the University of Texas.
In Spanish.

622 ESTUDIOS DE HISTORIA SOCIAL. v.1– , Oct. 1965– . Buenos Aires. Quarterly.
Issued by the Centro de Estudios de Historia Social, Universidad de Buenos Aires. In Spanish.

623 ESTUDIOS DE POBLACIÓN. 1– , Jan. 1976– . Bogotá. Monthly.
Issued by the Asociación Colombiana para el Estudio de la Población. In Spanish.

624 ESTUDIOS DE SOCIOLOGIA EMPIRICA. 1–4, 1957–1959. Madrid.
Issued by the Instituto Balmes de Sociologia. In Spanish.

625 ESTUDIOS DE SOCIOLOGIA FAMILIAR. 1– , 1975– . La Paz, Bolivia. Irreg.
Issued by the Centro de Investigaciónes Sociales. In Spanish.

626 ESTUDIOS DE SOCIOLOGIA. STUDIES IN SOCIOLOGY. v.1– , 1961– . Buenos Aires, Bibliografica Omeba. Annual.
In Spanish and English.
Indexed: Soc. Abstr.

ESTUDIOS DEMOGRAFICOS
See Havana. Universidad. Centro de Información Cientifica y Technica. ESTUDIOS DEMOGRAFICOS

ESTUDIOS DEMOGRAFICOS
See Spain. Consejo Superior de Investigaciónes Cientificas. Instituto Balmes de Sociologia. ESTUDIOS DEMOGRAFICOS

627 ESTUDIOS SOCIALES. 1– , Jan/Mar. 1968– . Santo Domingo. Quarterly.
Issued by the Centro de Investigación y Acción de la Companha de Jesus. In Spanish.

628 ESTUDIOS SOCIALES. no.1– , July 1970– . Guatemala City. Quarterly.
Issued by the Instituto de Ciencias Politico-Sociales, Universidad Rafael Landivar. Subtitle reads: 'Revista de ciencias sociales'. In Spanish.

629 ESTUDIOS SOCIALES. no.1– , Mar. 1973– . Santiago, Chile.
Issued by the Corporación de Promoción Universitaria. In Spanish.

ESTUDIOS SOCIALES
See Instituto Torcuato di Tella. Centro de Estudios de Estado y Sociedad. ESTUDIOS SOCIALES

630 ESTUDIOS SOCIALES CENTRO-AMERICANOS. v.1– , Jan/Apr. 1972– . San José, Costa Rica. Three issues a year.
Issued by the Confederación Universitaria Centroamericana. In Spanish.
Indexed: Int. Bibl. Soc.

631 ESTUDIOS SOCIO-RELIGIOSOS LATINO-AMERICANOS. 1–?, 1961–?. Madrid. Irreg. Ceased publication.
Issued by the Oficina Internacional de Investigaciónes Sociales de Feres. In Spanish.
Monograph series.

ESTUDIOS SOCIOLOGICOS
See Congreso Nacional de Sociologia, Mexico. ESTUDIOS SOCIOLOGICOS

ESTUDIOS SOCIOLOGICOS INTER-NACIONALES
See Spain. Consejo Superior de Investigaciónes Cientificas. Instituto Balmes de Sociologia. ESTUDIOS SOCIOLOGICOS INTER-NACIONALES

632 ESTUDIOS SOCIOLOGICOS LATINO-AMERICANOS. v.1– , 1961– . Freiburg, Madrid. Irreg.
Issued by the Oficina Internacional de Investigaciónes Sociales de Feres. Cover title reads: *America Latina. Estudios Sociologicos.* In Spanish.

633 ESTUDIOS SOCIOLOGICOS SOBRE LA SITUACIÓN SOCIAL DE ESPAÑA. 1975– . Madrid.
Issued by the Fundación Foessa. Subseries of *Colección Fundación Foessa. Serie Informes.* Continues: *Informe Sociologico sobre la Situación Social de España.* In Spanish.

ESTUDOS E ANALISES
See Brazil. Centro Brasileiro de Estudios Demograficos. ESTUDOS E ANALISES

634 ESTUDOS POLITICOS E SOCIAIS. v.1– , 1963– . Lisboa. Quarterly.
Issued by the Instituto Superior de Ciências e Politica Ultramarina. Supersedes: *Estudos Ultramarinos,* 1959–62. In Portuguese.
Indexed: Int. Bibl. Soc.; Int. Pol. Sc. Abstr.; Soc. Abstr.

635 ETHICS IN SCIENCE AND MEDICINE. v.1– , Apr. 1973– . New York, Pergamon Press. Quarterly.
Title varies: 1973–Apr. 1975, *Science, Medicine and Man.*

636 ETHNIC & MINORITY SCENE IN WISCONSIN. Sept.–Oct. 1972. Stevens Point, Wis.
Issued by the Ethnic System and Minority Studies Center, University of Wisconsin at Stevens Point.

637 ETHNIC & MINORITY STUDIES REVIEW. 1– , fall/winter 1972/1973– . Stevens Point, Wis.
Issued by the Ethnic System and Minority Studies Center, University of Wisconsin.

638 ETHNIC AND RACIAL STUDIES. 1– , Jan. 1978– . London, Routledge & Kegan Paul. Quarterly.
Other title: *ERS, Ethnic and Racial Studies.*
Indexed: Int. Bibl. Soc.; Soc. Abstr.

639 ETHNIC GROUPS. v.1– , June 1976– . New York, London, Gordon and Breach. Quarterly.
Subtitle reads: 'An international periodical of ethnic studies.' Absorbed: *Afro-American Studies.*
Indexed: Soc. Abstr.

640 ETHNIC STUDIES. 1– , 1977– . Melbourne, Australia, International Press and Publications.

641 ETHNIC STUDIES BIBLIOGRAPHY. 1– , 1977– . Pittsburgh, Pa. Annual.
Issued by the Center for International Studies, University of Pittsburgh, published in conjunction with the Pennsylvania Ethnic Heritage Studies Center. The first issue covers literature through 1975.

642 ETHNICITY. 1– , Apr. 1974– . New York, Academic Press. Quarterly.
Subtitle reads: 'An indisciplinary journal of the study of ethnic relations'.
Indexed: Soc. Abstr.

643 ETHNIES. 1968–1973. Paris, The Hague, Mouton.
Issued by the Centre for Multiracial Studies and Centre d'Études et de Recherches Interethniques et Interculturelles. Subtitle reads: 'Anglo-French Conference on Race Relations in France and Great Britain'. In English and French; summaries in French and English.

644 ETHNOLOGY. 1– , Jan. 1962– . Pittsburgh, Pa. Quarterly.
Issued by the Department of Anthropology, University of Pittsburgh. Subtitle reads: 'An international journal of social anthropology'.
Indexed: Afr. Abstr.; Bull. sig. soc. eth.; Int. Bibl. Soc.; Int. Pol. Sc. Abstr.; Soc. Sc. Hum. Ind.; Soc. Sc. Ind.; Soc. Abstr.

645 ETHNOPSYCHOLOGIE. v.1– , May 1946– . Le Havre. Quarterly.
Issued by the Centre de Recherches et d'Études de Psychologie des Peuples et de Sociologie Économique, 1961– ; Institut Havrais de Sociologie Économique et de Psychologie des Peuples, 1946–60. Subtitle reads: 'Revue de psychologie des peuples'. Title varies: v.1–25, 1946–Sep. 1970, *Revue de Psychologie des Peuples*.
Indexed: Int. Bibl. Soc.; Psych. Abstr.; Soc. Abstr.

ÉTUDE SUR LA POPULATION ET LA TECHNOLOGIE. PERCEPTIONS
See Science Council of Canada. STUDY ON POPULATION AND TECHNOLOGY. PERCEPTIONS

ÉTUDES
See Canada. Royal Commission on Bilingualism and Biculturalism. STUDIES. ÉTUDES

ÉTUDES AFRICAINES
See Brussels. Université Libre. Institut de Sociologie. ÉTUDES AFRICAINES

ÉTUDES COLONIALES
See Brussels. Université Libre. Institut de Sociologie. ÉTUDES AFRICAINES

646 ÉTUDES CONGOLAISES. no.1–12, Mar. 1961–Oct/Dec. 1969. Bruxelles, Éditions Remarques Congolaises.
Issued by the Institut National d'Études Politiques, 1961–67 (called Institut Politiques Congolais, 1961–Feb. 1963) and Centre de Recherche et d'Information Socio-Politiques, 1962–Aug/Sep. 1963. Superseded by: *Études Zaïroïses*. Some contents in revised editions.
Indexed: Int. Pol. Sc. Abstr.; Soc. Abstr.

ÉTUDES D'AGGLOMÉRATIONS
See Brussels. Université Libre. Institut de Sociologie. ÉTUDES D'AGGLOMÉRATIONS

ÉTUDES DE LA COMMISSION ROYALE D'ENQUÊTE SUR LA BILINGUALISME
See Canada. Royal Commission on Bilingualism and Biculturalism. STUDIES

647 ÉTUDES DE SOCIOLOGIE ET D'ETHNOLOGIE JURIDIQUES. v.1–34, 1930–1942. Paris, Les Éditions Domat-Montchrestien.

648 ÉTUDES DE SOCIOLOGIE TUNISIENNE. v.1– , 1968– . Tunis. Annual.
Issued by the Bureau de Recherches Sociologiques.
Indexed: Soc. Abstr.

ÉTUDES DES MIGRATIONS
See STUDI EMIGRAZIONE. ÉTUDES DES MIGRATIONS

ÉTUDES ET CHRONIQUES DE DÉMOGRAPHIE HISTORIQUE
See ANNALES DE DÉMOGRAPHIE HISTORIQUE

ÉTUDES ETHNIQUES AU CANADA
See CANADIAN ETHNIC STUDIES

ÉTUDES HOMMES ET MIGRATIONS
See HOMMES ET MIGRATIONS; ÉTUDES

649 ÉTUDES INTERNATIONALES DE PSYCHO-SOCIOLOGIE CRIMINELLE. 1– , July/Sep. 1956– . Paris. Irreg.
Issued by the Société Internationale de la Prophylaxe Criminelle.

650 ÉTUDES RURALES. no.1– , Apr/June 1961– . Paris, The Hague, Mouton. Quarterly.
Issued by the 6e Section des Sciences Économiques et Sociales, École Pratique des Hautes Études, in cooperation with Centre National de Recherche Scientifique. In English and French.
Indexed: Bull. sig. soc. eth.; Int. Bibl. Soc.; Soc. Abstr.

651 ÉTUDES SOCIALES. Jan. 15, 1881–1935. Paris. Frequency varies.
Issued by the Société d'Économie et des Sciences Sociales, Société Internationale de Science Sociale, Unions de la Paix Sociale. Vols. 11–20 called ser.2; t.1–10, and each ten volumes thereafter numbered in series, e.g. v.21–30 called also ser.3, t.1–10. Title varies: v.1–90, 1886–1930, *La Réforme Sociale;* v.91–95, no.3,

1931–Mar. 1935, *Revue d'Économie Sociale et Rurale*. Supersedes the Société's *Bulletin*. Superseded by a publication of the same title.

652 LES ÉTUDES SOCIALES. 1–49, 1936–1960; n.s. 50/51– , 1961– . Paris. Quarterly.
Issued by the Société d'Économie et des Sciences Sociales, École de la Play. Formed by the merger of *Études Sociales* and *La Science Sociale*.
Indexed: Int. Bibl. Soc.

ÉTUDES SOCIALES
See Instituts Solvay. Institut de Sociologie. ÉTUDES SOCIALES

653 ÉTUDES SOCIOLOGIQUES SUR LE MAROC. [1], Nov. 1971. Rabat.
Issued by the Société d'Études Économiques, Sociales et Statistiques. Subseries of: *Bulletin Économique et Social du Maroc. Série Sociologie.*

654 ÉTUDES SUR L'ÉCONOMIE ET LA SOCIOLOGIE DES PAYS SLAVES. v.1–16, 1956–1974. Paris. Irreg.
Issued by the Centre d'Études Économiques, École Pratique des Hautes Études.
Monograph series.

ÉTUDES SUR LA CONDUITE ANTI-SOCIALE
See ACTA CRIMINOLOGICA

655 ÉTUDES TSIGANES. 1– , Apr. 15, 1955– . n.s. v.1– , 1971– . Paris. Four issues a year.
Issued by the Association des Études Tsiganes.
Indexed: Bull. sig. soc. eth.

656 EUGENICAL NEWS. v.1–8. Jan. 1916–Dec. 1953. New York. Monthly, 1916–31; bi-monthly, 1932–38; quarterly, 1939–53.
Issued by the Eugenics Research Association, 1916–37; American Eugenics Society, 1938–53. Superseded by: *Social Biology*.

657 EUGENICS; A JOURNAL OF RACE BETTERMENT. v.1–4, no.2, Oct. 1928–Feb. 1931. New Haven, Conn.
Issued by the American Eugenics Society. Superseded by: *People*.

EUGENICS LABORATORY LECTURE SERIES
See London. University. University College. Francis Galton Laboratory for Eugenics. EUGENICS LABORATORY LECTURE SERIES

EUGENICS LABORATORY MEMOIRS
See London. University. University College. Francis Galton Laboratory for Eugenics. EUGENICS LABORATORY MEMOIRS

EUGENICS QUARTERLY
See SOCIAL BIOLOGY

658 Eugenics Research Association. MONOGRAPH SERIES. v.1–10, 1929–Oct. 1935. Cold Spring Harbor, Long Island, N.Y. Irreg.

659 THE EUGENICS REVIEW. v.1–60, Apr. 1909–1968. London. Quarterly.
Issued by the Eugenics Education Society. Superseded, in part, by the Eugenics Society, London. *Bulletin,* and *Journal of Biosocial Science*. Index to v.1–60, in v.60, no.4.
Indexed: Int. Bibl. Soc. Cult. Anth.

660 Eugenics Society, London. ANNUAL REPORT. 1–16, 1908–1924. London, The Eugenics Educational Society.

661 Eugenics Society, London. BULLETIN. 1– , Mar. 1969– . London. Quarterly.
Supersedes, in part, *The Eugenics Review*.

662 Eugenics Society, London. PROCEEDINGS. 1971– , London, New York, Academic Press. Irreg.
Each issue has also a distinctive title.

663 EURE. v.1– , 1970– . Santiago, Chile. Three issues a year.
Issued by the Centro Interdisciplinario de Desarrollo Urbano y Regional (CIDU), Universidad Catolica de Chile. Subtitle reads: 'Revista latinoamericana de estudios urbano-regionales'. In Spanish.

EURO-BAROMETER
See Commission of the European Communities. EURO-BAROMETRE

EURO-BAROMETRE
See Commission of the European Communities. EURO-BAROMETRE

EUROPA DES CAPITALES
See Union of Capitals of the European Community. EUROPA DES CAPITALES

EUROPÄISCHES ARCHIV FÜR SOZIOLOGIE
See ARCHIVES EUROPÉENNES DE SOCIOLOGIE

664 European Centre for Leisure and Education. BIBLIOGRAPHIC SERIES. ANNOTATED BIBLIOGRAPHY ON LEISURE. 1– , 1970– . Praha. Irreg.

665 EUROPEAN DEMOGRAPHIC INFORMATION BULLETIN. v.1– , 1970– . The Hague, Nijhoff. Quarterly.
Issued by the European Centre for Population (Centre Europeen d'Études de Population).
Indexed: Int. Bibl. Soc.; PAIS; Urb. Aff. Abstr.

666 EUROPEAN JOURNAL OF SOCIAL PSYCHOLOGY. v.1– , 1971– . The Hague, Mouton. Quarterly.
Summaries in French, German and Russian.
Indexed: Int. Bibl. Soc.; Psych. Abstr.; Soc. Abstr.; Urb. Aff. Abstr.

EUROPEAN JOURNAL OF SOCIOLOGY
See ARCHIVES EUROPÉENNES DE SOCIOLOGIE

667 EUROPEAN MONOGRAPHS IN SOCIAL PSYCHOLOGY. 1– , 1971– . London, Academic Press. Irreg.
Issued by the European Association of Experimental Social Psychology.
Monograph series.

668 European Research Institute for Regional and Urban Planning. REPORT OF ACTIVITIES. 1973– . The Hague.

669 European Society for Rural Sociology. PUBLICATIONS. 1– , 1977– . Assen, Van Gorcum. Irreg.
Monograph series.

670 EUROPEAN YEARBOOK IN LAW AND SOCIOLOGY. 1977– . The Hague, Nijhoff.
In English and French.

671 EVALUATION QUARTERLY. v.1–3, Feb. 1977–1979. Beverly Hills, Calif., Sage Publications.
Subtitle reads: 'A journal of applied social research, social policy, social planning, public service'. Continued by: *Evaluation Review*.
Indexed: Soc. Abstr.

672 EVALUATION REVIEW. v.4– , Feb. 1980– . Beverly Hills, Calif., Sage Publications. Quarterly.
Subtitle reads: 'A journal of applied social research'. Continues: *Evaluation Quarterly*.

EVENTS AND TRENDS IN RACE RELATIONS
See RACE RELATIONS

EXCERPTA CRIMINOLOGICA
See ABSTRACTS ON CRIMINOLOGY AND PENOLOGY

673 EXPLORATIONS IN ETHNIC STUDIES. 1– , Jan. 1978– . La Crosse, Wis., National Association of Interdisciplinary Ethnic Studies.
Issued by the University of Wisconsin.

674 EXPLORATIONS IN SOCIOLOGY. v.1– , 1970– . London, Tavistock Publications. Irreg.
Issued by the British Sociological Association.
Monograph series.

675 EXPLORATIONS IN URBAN ANALYSIS. 1978– . London, Edward Arnold (Publishers). Irreg.

FS FEMINIST STUDIES
See FEMINIST STUDIES

676 Fabian Society, London. DISCUSSION SERIES. no.1–4, 1946–1947? London.

677 Fabian Society, London. RESEARCH SERIES. 1– , 1932– . London.
Title varies: 1–42, 1932–39, *Research Pamphlets; N.F.R.B. Publications*.

A FACT PAPER
See South African Institute of Race Relations. A FACT PAPER

FAMILIE-STATISTIKK
See Norway. Statistisk Sentralbyrå. FAMILIE-STATISTIKK. FAMILY STATISTICS

678 FAMILLE ET HABITATION. 1–2, 1959–1960. Paris.
Issued by the Centre National de la Recherche Scientifique. Called also *Travaux du Groupe d'Ethnologie Sociale*.

679 FAMILLES DANS LE MONDE. 1– , Apr/May, 1948– . Paris. Quarterly.
Issued by the Union Internationale des Organismes Familiaux. Title varies: 1948, *Union's Liaison and Information Bulletin*.

THE FAMILY
See CASEWORK

FAMILY ADJUSTMENT IN SELECTED LOW INCOME AREAS. PRELIMINARY REPORT
See Wisconsin. University. Department of Rural Sociology. Applied Population Laboratory. PRELIMINARY REPORT. FAMILY ADJUSTMENT IN SELECTED LOW INCOME AREAS

680 FAMILY-COMMUNITY DIGEST. v.1, no.1–6, Feb. 1943–June 1944. Poughkeepsie, N.Y.
Issued by the National Council of Parent Education, Inc.

FAMILY JOURNAL OF SOCIAL CASEWORK
See SOCIAL CASEWORK

681 FAMILY LIFE COORDINATOR. v.1–28, 1952–1979. Eugene, Oreg. Irreg., 1952–54; quarterly.
Issued originally by the Oregon Coordinating Council on Social Hygiene and Family, subsequently by the National Council on Family Relations. Title varies: v.1–7, 1952–June 1959, *The Coordinator*. Continued by: *Family Relations*. Indexes quinquennially and decennially.
Indexed: Soc. Work Res. Abstr.

682 FAMILY LIFE DEVELOPMENT. 1– , June 1975– . Ithaca, N.Y.
Issued by the Family Life Development Center, Cornell University.

683 FAMILY PROCESS. v.1– , Mar. 1962– . Baltimore, Md. Semi-annual.
Issued by the Mental Research Institute, Palo Alto Medical Research Foundation.
Indexed: Int. Bibl. Soc.; Soc. Abstr.; Soc. Work Res. Abstr.

684 FAMILY RELATIONS. v.29– , Jan. 1980– . Minneapolis, Minn. Quarterly.
Issued by the National Council on Family Relations. Continues: *Family Life Coordinator*.

FAMILY STATISTICS
See Norway. Statistisk Sentralbyrå. FAMILIESTATISTIKK

THE FAMILY THROUGHOUT THE WORLD
See COLLECTION LA FAMILLE À TRAVERSE LE MONDE

THE FAR EASTERN QUARTERLY
See JOURNAL OF ASIAN STUDIES

685 Fédération des Groupes d'Études et de Recherches Institutionelles. CAHIERS. v.1– , 1966– . Paris. Quarterly.
Title varies: 1966–67, *Recherches*. Other title: *The F.D.G.R.I. Report*.

686 FEMINIST REVIEW. no.1– , 1979– . London, Publications Distribution Co. Three issues a year.

687 FEMINIST STUDIES. v.1– , summer 1972– . New York, Feminist Studies, Inc. Quarterly.
Supported by the Women's Studies Program, University of Maryland. Other title: *F.S. Feminist Studies*.
Indexed: Soc. Abstr.; Wom. Stud. Abstr.

FEMMES ET SOCIOLOGIE CANADIENNE. BULLETIN
See WOMEN IN CANADIAN SOCIOLOGY. BULLETIN

688 FILOZOFIJA. 1–3, 1957–1959. Beograd. Quarterly.
Issued by the Jugoslovensko udruzenje za filozofiju i sociologiju. Title varies: v.1–2, 1957–58, *Filozofija, Sociologija; Jugoslovenski casopis za filozofiju i sociologiju, socijalnu psihologiju i socijalnu antropologiju*. Superseded, in part, by *Sociologija*. In Serbo-Croatian.
Indexed: Soc. Abstr.

FILOZOFIJA, SOCIOLOGIJA; JUGOSLOVENSKI CASOPIS ZA FILOZOFIJU I SOCIOLOGIJU, SOCIJALNU PSIHOLOGIJU I SOCIJALNU ANTROPOLOGIJU
See FILOZOFIJA

689 Florence. Università. Istituto di Sociologia. Gruppo di Studi Audiovisi. PUBBLICAZIONI. no.1– , 1971– . Urbania, Stabilimento Tipografico Bramante. Irreg.
In Italian.
Monograph series.

690 Florence Crittenton Association of America. UNWED MOTHERS. no.1–3, 1963–1972. Chicago.
Title varies: 1963–65, *Services to and Characteristics of Unwed Mothers*.

691 Florida. State University, Tallahassee. Institute for Social Research. RESEARCH REPORTS IN SOCIAL SCIENCE. v.1– , June 1958– . Tallahassee. Two issues a year.
Issues for June 1958–Feb. 1959 published under the Institute's earlier name, Center for Social Research.
Indexed: Soc. Abstr.

692 Florida. University, Gainesville. Urban and Regional Development Center. WORK PAPER. no.1– , 1973– . Gainesville. Irreg.

693 FLORIDA ENVIRONMENTAL AND URBAN ISSUES. 1– , Oct. 1973– . Fort Lauderdale, Fla. Bimonthly.
Issued by the Joint Center for Environmental and Urban Problems. Supersedes: *Florida Planning and Development*.

FOLKEMENDEN ETTER ALDER OG EKTESKAPELIG STATUS
See Norway. Statistisk Sentralbyrå. FOLKEMENDEN ETTER ALDER OG EXTESKAPELIG STATUS

694 Fondazione Giovanni Agnelli. Progetto Stratificazione e Classi Sociali in Italia. QUADERNI DI RICERCHE DEL PROGETTO STRATIFICAZIONE E CLASSI SOCIALI IN ITALIA DELLA FONDAZIONE GIOVANNI AGNELLI. 1– , 1976– . Torino, Editoriale Valentino. Irreg.
In Italian.

695 Fondazione Luigi Einaudi. ANNALI. 1– , 1967– . Torino. Annual.
Indexed: Int. Bibl. Soc.

FOOTNOTES
See American Sociological Association. FOOTNOTES

FOREIGN LANGUAGE INDEX
See Public Affairs Information Service. FOREIGN LANGUAGE INDEX

FORSCHUNGSBERICHTE DES INSTITUTS FÜR SOZIOLOGIE
See Institut für Soziologie, Linz, Donau. FORSCHUNGSBERICHTE DES INSTITUTS FÜR SOZIOLOGIE

696 Forschungsgesellschaft für Agrarpolitik und Agrarsoziologie. DISSERTATIONEN AUS AGRARÖKONOMIK UND AGRARSOZIOLOGIE. v.1– , 1945/1955– . Bonn. Irreg.
Subseries of its *Veröffentlichungen.*

FORSKNINGSRAPPORT
See Göthenborg. Universitet. Sociologiska Institutionen. FORSKNINGSRAPPORT

EIN FORUM JUNGER SOZIALWISSENSCHAFTLICHER
See ARBEITSPAPIERE ZUR POLITISCHEN SOZIOLOGIE

697 France. Centre National de la Recherche Scientifique. BULLETIN SIGNALÉTIQUE. 521: SOCIOLOGIE — ETHNOLOGIE. v.24– , 1970– . Paris. Quarterly.
Supersedes, in part, *Bulletin Signalétique. 521: Sociologie, Ethnologie, Préhistoire et Archéologie.*

698 France. Centre National de la Recherche Scientifique. BULLETIN SIGNALÉTIQUE. 521: SOCIOLOGIE, ETHNOLOGIE, PRÉHISTOIRE ET ARCHÉOLOGIE. v.15–23, 1961–1969. Paris. Quarterly.
Continues: *Bulletin Signalétique. Sciences Humaines. Philosophie.* Continued by: *Bulletin Signalétique. 521: Sociologie — Ethnologie.* Author index included quarterly.

699 France. Centre National de la Recherche Scientifique. Centre d'Études Sociologiques. TRAVAUX ET DOCUMENTS. 1– , 1969– . Paris. Irreg.
Monograph series.

700 France. Centre National de la Recherche Scientifique. Institut d'Aménagement et d'Urbanisme de la Région Parisienne. CAHIERS. v.1– , 1964– . Paris. Quarterly.
Called also *Cahiers de l'I.A.U.R.P.*
Indexed: Bull. sig. soc. eth.; Int. Bibl. Soc.

701 France. Délégation Générale à la Recherche Scientifique et Technique. REPERTOIRE NATIONALE DES CHERCHEURS: SCIENCES SOCIALES ET HUMAINES. TOME I: ETHNOLOGIE, LINGUISTIQUE, PSYCHOLOGIE, SOCIOLOGIE. 1968– . Paris. Irreg.
Issued in cooperation with the Service d'Échange d'Information Scientifique, Maison des Sciences de l'Homme.

702 France. Institut National d'Études Démographiques. TRAVAUX ET DOCUMENTS. CAHIERS. v.1– , 1947– . Paris, Presses Universitaires de France. Irreg.

703 France. Institut National de la Statistique et des Études Économiques. STATISTIQUE DU MOUVEMENT DE LA POPULATION. NOUVELLE SÉRIE. v.1– , 1907– . Paris. Irreg.

FRANCE-ASIE
See FRANCE — ASIE/ASIA

704 FRANCE — ASIE/ASIA. v.1– , 1946– . Tokyo, Koishikawa, Bunkyo-Ku. Monthly (irreg.) 1946–60; bimonthly.
Title varies: v.1–21, 1946–1968/69, *France — Asie.* Vols. 1960– called also 'Nouvelle série'. Subtitle in English: 'Bilingual Review of Asian Culture and Problems'. Absorbed: *Asia* (Saigon), Mar/Apr. 1962. In English and French.
Indexed: Int. Bibl. Soc. Cult. Anth.; Peace Res. Abstr. J.; Soc. Abstr.

705 FRANKFURTER BEITRÄGE ZUR SOZIOLOGIE. v.1– , 1955– . Frankfurt-am-Main, Europäische Verlags-Anstalt. Annual.
Issued on behalf of the Institut für Sozialforschung. Includes monographic supplements.

706 FRANKFURTER BEITRÄGE ZUR SOZIOLOGIE. SONDERHEFT. 1– , 1958– . Frankfurter-am-Main, Europäische Verlags-Anstalt. Irreg.
Monograph series.

707 FRAU UND GESELLSCHAFT. WOMAN AND SOCIETY. 1972–1973. Bonn-Bad Godesberg, Inter Nationes.
Supersedes: *Woman's Forum*. Superseded by: *Sozialpolitische Informationen*.

708 FREE INQUIRY. 1–6. 1972–1978. Tulsa, Okla.
Issued by the Oklahoma Sociological Association, University of Tulsa. Continued by: *Free Inquiry in Creative Sociology*.
Indexed: Soc. Abstr.

709 FREE INQUIRY IN CREATIVE SOCIOLOGY. v.7– , May 1979– . Tulsa, Okla. Semi-annual.
Issued by the Free Oklahoma Sociological Association. Continues: *Free Inquiry*.
Indexed: Soc. Abstr.

710 Frontiers on Urban Planning Conference. PROCEEDINGS. 1st–2nd, 1969–1970. New Brunswick, N.J., 1970–71.
Issued by the Bureau of Government Research and the University Extension, Rutgers University.

711 Fundación Bariloche. Departamento de Sociologia. DOCUMENTOS DE TRABAJO. Buenos Aires. Irreg.
Edited by the Instituto Torcuato de Tella. In Spanish.

712 FUNDAMENTA SCIENTIAE. v.1– , 1980– . Oxford, New York, Pergamon Press. Quarterly.
In English; occasionally in French. Summaries in English and French.

FURTHER PAPERS ON THE SOCIAL SCIENCES
See Institute of Sociology, London. REPORTS OF ANNUAL CONFERENCES

713 FUTURES. v.1– , Sep. 1968– . Guildford, Surrey. Life Science and Technology Publications. Quarterly.
Issued by the Institute for Future, Riverview Center, Middletown, Conn. Subtitle reads: 'The journal of forecasting and planning'.
Indexed: Int. Bibl. Soc.; Soc. Sc. Ind.

714 FUTURIBLES. no.1/2– , winter/spring 1975– . Paris. Quarterly.
Issued by the Société d'Études et de Documentation Économique Industrielles et Sociales (S.E.D.E.I.S.). Supersedes: *Analyse & Prevision; Études, Futuribles, Bibliographie,* and *Prospectives*.
Indexed: Curr. Cont.; Int. Bibl. Soc.; Int. Pol. Sc. Abstr.; Soc. Abstr.

715 GACETA SOCIOLOGICA. no.1– , 1964– . Mexico, D.F.
Issued by the Instituto de Investigaciónes Sociales, Universidad Nacional Autonoma de Mexico. In Spanish.

716 THE GALLUP INTERNATIONAL PUBLIC OPINION POLLS. FRANCE. v.1– , 1939, 1944/1964– . New York, Random House. Irreg.
Vol.2, 1965/75.

717 THE GALLUP INTERNATIONAL PUBLIC OPINION POLLS. GREAT BRITAIN. v.1– , 1937/1964– . New York, Random House, 1976– .
Vol.2, 1965/75.

718 GALLUP OPINION INDEX. REPORT. No.1– , June 1965– . Princeton, N.J., Gallup International, Inc. Monthly.
Title varies: 1965–66, *Gallup Political Index; Report*. Title changed to: *Gallup Report*, 1981.
Indexed: Int. Bibl. Soc.; PAIS.

GALLUP POLITICAL INDEX; REPORT
See GALLUP OPINION INDEX. REPORT

719 THE GALLUP PUBLIC OPINION POLL. 1935/1971– . New York, Random House, 1972–77; Wilmington, SR Scholarly Resources, Inc.

720 GENÈVE — AFRIQUE. GENEVA — AFRICA. 1962–1976. Genève. Semi-annual.
Issued by the Institut Africain de Genève. Title on spine: *Acta Africana*. In French; occasionally in English.
Indexed: Bull. sig. soc. eth.; Int. Bibl. Soc.; Int. Pol. Sc. Abstr.

721 GENUS. v.1– , June 1934– . Roma. Four issues a year.
Issued by the Comitato Italiano per lo Studio dei Problemi della Popolazione.
Indexed: Bull. sig. soc. eth.; Soc. Abstr.

722 GEO-ABSTRACTS. ANNUAL INDEX. v.2– , 1972– . Norwich, England, Geo-Abstracts.
Continues: *Geographical Abstracts. Annual Index*.

723 GEO-ABSTRACTS. D. SOCIAL AND HISTORICAL GEOGRAPHY. 1974– . Norwich, England, Geo-Abstracts. Six issues a year.
Issued by Geo-Abstracts, University of East Anglia. Continues, in part, *Geo-Abstracts. D. Social Geography*.

724 GEO-ABSTRACTS. D. SOCIAL GEOGRAPHY. 1966–1973. Norwich, England, Geo-Abstracts. Six issues a year.

Issued by Geo-Abstracts, University of East Anglia. Continued by: *Geo-Abstracts. D. Social and Historical Geography*.

725 GEO-ABSTRACTS. F. REGIONAL AND COMMUNITY PLANNING. no.1– , 1972– . Norwich, England, Geo-Abstracts. Six issues a year.
Issued by Geo-Abstracts, University of East Anglia.

726 GEOGRAFISKA. ANNALER. SERIES B: HUMAN GEOGRAPHY. v.47– , 1965– . Stockholm, The Almquist & Wiksell Periodical Co. Semi-annual.
Issued by the Svenska Sällskapet för Antropologi och Geografi. Supersedes, in part, and continues the volume numbering of *Geografiska Annaler*. In English, French and German; summaries in these three languages.

727 GEOGRAPHICAL ABSTRACTS ANNUAL INDEX. v.1, 1971. Norwich, England, Geo-Abstracts.
Continued by: *Geo-Abstracts. Annual Index*.

GEOGRAPHY AND SOCIOLOGY
See Edinburgh. University. EDINBURGH UNIVERSITY PUBLICATIONS. GEOGRAPHY AND SOCIOLOGY

728 Georgia. University. Institute of Community and Area Development. SOCIOLOGY SERIES. no.1– , 1968– . Athens, Ga. Irreg.
Series of papers and pamphlets.

729 Germany (Federal Republic). Statistisches Bundesamt. BEVÖLKERUNG UND ERWERBSSTÄTIGKEIT. REIHE 1.1: STAND UND ENTWICKLUNG DER BEVÖLKERUNG. 1976– . Stuttgart, W. Kohlhammer. Annual.
Continues its *Bevölkerung und Kultur. Reihe 1: Gebiet und Bevölkerung. 1. Bevölkerungsstand und Entwicklung*. Subseries of *Fachserie 1*.

730 Germany (Federal Republic). Statistisches Bundesamt. BEVÖLKERUNG UND ERWERBSSTÄTIGKEIT. REIHE 1.2.2: BEVÖLKERUNG DER GEMEINDEN. 1976– . Stuttgart, W. Kohlhammer. Annual.
Continues, in part, its *Bevölkerung und Kultur. Reihe 1: Gebiet und Bevölkerung. IV. Bevölkerung der Gemeinden*. Subseries of *Fachserie 1*.

731 Germany (Federal Republic). Statistisches Bundesamt. BEVÖLKERUNG UND ERWERBSSTÄTIGKEIT. REIHE 1.3: BEVÖLKERUNG NACH ALTER UND FAMILIENSTAND. 1975– . Stuttgart, W. Kohlhammer. Annual.
Continues, in part, its *Bevölkerung und Kultur. Reihe 1: Gebiet und Bevölkerung. II. Alter und Familienstand der Bevölkerung*. Subseries of *Fachserie 1*.

732 Germany (Federal Republic). Statistisches Bundesamt. BEVÖLKERUNG UND FAMILIENSTAND. Stuttgart, W. Kohlhammer.
Continues, in part, its *Bevölkerung und Kultur. Reihe 1: Bevölkerungsstand und Entwicklung*. Continued, in part, by its *Bevölkerung und Erwerbsstätigkeit. Reihe: 1.3: Bevölkerung nach Alter und Familienstand*.

733 Germany (Federal Republic). Statistisches Bundesamt. BEVÖLKERUNG UND KULTUR. REIHE 2: NATURLICHE BEVÖLKERUNGSBEWEGUNG. 1959– . Wiesbaden.

734 Germany (Federal Republic). Statistisches Bundesamt. BEVÖLKERUNG UND KULTUR. REIHE 3: WANDERUNGEN. 1959– . Wiesbaden.

735 Germany (Federal Republic). Statistisches Bundesamt. BEVÖLKERUNG UND KULTUR. REIHE 5: HAUSHALITE UND FAMILIEN. 1957–1976. Wiesbaden, W. Kohlhammer.
Continued by: Germany (Federal Republic). Statistisches Bundesamt. BEVÖLKERUNG UND ERWERBSSTÄTIGKEIT. REIHE 3. HAUSHALTEN. FAMILIEN. 1977– .

736 THE GERONTOLOGIST. v.1– , Mar. 1961– . St. Louis, Mo., subsequently, Philadelphia, Pa. Quarterly, subsequently bimonthly.
Issued by the Gerontological Society.
Indexed: Psych. Abstr.; Soc. Sc. Ind.; Soc. Abstr.; Soc. Work. Res. Abstr.; Wom. Stud. Abstr.

737 GESELLSCHAFT UND ENTWICKLUNG. 1– , June 1972– . Zürich, Thun.

738 GESELLSCHAFT UND WISSENSCHAFT. 1– , 1971– . Tübingen, Mohr (Paul Siebeck). Irreg.
Monograph series.

739 Ghana. Central Bureau of Statistics. MIGRATION STATISTICS. 1953/1957– . Accra. Annual.
Subseries of its *Statistical Reports*.

740 Ghana. University. Department of Sociology. CURRENT RESEARCH REPORT SERIES. no.1– , 1971– . Legon. Irreg.

741 GHANA JOURNAL OF SOCIOLOGY, v.1– , 1964– . Legon. Semi-annual.

Issued by the Ghana Sociological Association and the Sociology Department, University of Ghana.
Indexed: Afr. Abstr.; Soc. Abstr.

742 GHANA POPULATION STUDIES. no.1– , 1969– . Legon. Irreg.
Issued by the Demographic Unit, Department of Sociology, University of Ghana.

743 Glasgow. University of Strathclyde. Department of Sociology. OCCASIONAL PAPERS. no.1–[3], 1968–1977. Glasgow. Irreg.
Each issue has also a distinctive title. Last issue [3] unnumbered.

744 Glasgow. University of Strathclyde. Regional Studies Group. BULLETIN. 1–10, 1965–1970. Glasgow.
Each issue has also a distinctive title.

745 Glasgow. University of Strathclyde. Survey Research Centre. OCCASIONAL PAPER. no. 1– , 1968– . Glasgow. Irreg.
After no.14, temporarily suspended.
Monograph series.

746 Gorky. Universitet. UCHENYE ZAPISKI. SERIIA SOTSOLOGICHESKAIA. SOTSOLOGIIA VYSHSHEI SHKOLY. Gorky. Irreg.
In Russian.

747 GÓRNOŚLĄSKIE STUDIA SOCJOLOGICZNE. v.1– . 1965– . Katowice. Irreg.
Issued by the Sląski Instytut Naukowy in Katowice. In Polish.

748 GOVERNMENT AND OPPOSITION. v.1– , Oct. 1965– . London, The Government and Opposition. Quarterly.
Published with the assistance of the London School of Economics and Political Science.
Indexed: Soc. Sc. Ind.; Soc. Abstr.

749 Götheborg, Sweden. Universitet. Sociologiska Institutionen. FORSKNINGS-RAPPORT. no.1– , 1964– . Götheborg.
In Swedish, summaries in English.

750 Götheborg, Sweden. Universitet. Sociologiska Institutionen. MONOGRAFIER. 1– , 1970– . Götheborg.
Text and summaries in Swedish and English.
Monograph series.

GÖTTINGER ABHANDLUNGEN ZUR SOZIOLOGIE
See GÖTTINGER ABHANDLUNGEN ZUR SOZIOLOGIE UND IHRER GRENZGEBIETE

751 GÖTTINGER ABHANDLUNGEN ZUR SOZIOLOGIE UND IHRER GRENZGEBIETE. 1– , 1957– . Stuttgart.
Title varies: v.1–10, 1957–66, *Göttinger Abhandlungen zur Soziologie*.
Monograph series; some doctoral dissertations.

752 GÖTTINGER BEITRÄGE ZUR GESELLSCHAFTSTHEORIE. no.1– , 1976– . Göttingen. Irreg.
Issued by the Verein zur Förderung Gesellschaftstheoretischen Studien.

753 GRADUATE FACULTY JOURNAL OF SOCIOLOGY. 1– , 1977– . New York.
Issued by the New School for Social Research, New York.
Indexed: Soc. Abstr.

754 Graz. Universität. Institut für Soziologie. SCHRIFTENREIHE. 1– , 1967– . Irreg.
Monograph series.

755 Gt. Britain. Commission for New Towns. REPORT. 1st– , 1962/1963– . London, HMSO. Annual.

756 Gt. Britain. Commission for Racial Equality. REPORT. 1– , 1977– . London, HMSO. Annual.
First report covers the period June–Dec. 1977.

757 Gt. Britain. Office of Population Censuses and Surveys. INTERNATIONAL MIGRATION. no.1– , 1974– . London, HMSO.
Issuing agency called, earlier, Central Statistical Office.

758 Gt. Britain. Office of Population Censuses and Surveys. POPULATION TRENDS. no.1– , 1975– . London. Quarterly.

759 Gt. Britain. Office of Population Censuses and Surveys. REGISTRAR'S GENERAL ANNUAL ESTIMATES OF THE POPULATION OF ENGLAND AND WALES AND OF LOCAL AUTHORITY AREAS. 1973– . London.
Report ends June 30.

760 Gt. Britain. Office of Population Censuses and Surveys. SOCIAL TRENDS. no.1– , 1970– . London, Central Statistical Office. Annual.

761 Gt. Britain. Race Relations Board. REPORT. 1967/1968– . London, HMSO. Annual.

762 GREATER LONDON INTELLIGENCE QUARTERLY. no.1– , 1967– . London, Greater London Council.

Title varies: no.1–25, 1967–73, Greater London Council. *Quarterly Bulletin*. Title on cover: *Greater London Research*.

GREATER LONDON RESEARCH
See GREATER LONDON INTELLIGENCE QUARTERLY

763 Greece. Genike statistike hyperesia. STATISTIQUE DU MOUVEMENT DE LA POPULATION, PENDANT L'ANNÉE. 1926– . Athens. Annual.

GREEK REVIEW OF SOCIAL RESEARCH
See EPITHEORÉSIS KOINONIKON EREUVON

764 GREENWOOD CONTRIBUTIONS TO SOCIOLOGY. 1– , 1970– . Westport, Conn., Greenwood Publications. Irreg.
Monograph series.

765 Grenoble. Université des Sciences Sociales. Centre de Recherche d'Histoire Économique, Social et Institutionelle. COLLECTION. SÉRIE HISTOIRE INSTITUTIONELLE. The Hague, Mouton. Irreg.
Monograph series.

766 GROUP ANALYSIS. 1– , Nov. 1967– . Oxford, New York, Pergamon Press. Three issues a year.
Issued by the Trust for Group Analysis on behalf of the Group Analytic Society (London) and Institute of Group Analysis, in cooperation with *The Human Context*.

767 GROUP AND ORGANIZATION STUDIES. 1– , 1976– . La Jolla, Calif., University Associates, Inc. Quarterly.
Indexed: Soc. Abstr.

768 GROUP PSYCHOTHERAPY AND PSYCHODRAMA. v.1–28, 1947–May, 1976. Beacon, N.Y., Beacon House. Quarterly.
Issued by the American Society of Group Psychotherapy and Psychodrama. Title varies: 1947–Mar. 1949, *Sociatry*. Merged with *Handbook of International Sociometry* to form *Group Psychotherapy, Psychodrama & Sociometry*.
Indexed: Int. Bibl. Soc.; Soc. Abstr.

769 GROUP PSYCHOTHERAPY, PSYCHODRAMA & SOCIOMETRY. v.29– , 1976– . Beacon, N.Y., Beacon House. Annual.
Issued by the American Society of Group Psychotherapy and Psychodrama. Formed by merger of: *Group Psychotherapy and Psychodrama*, and *Handbook of International Sociometry*. Continues the volume numbering of *Group Psychotherapy and Psychodrama*.

770 GRUNDFRAGEN DER SOZIOLOGIE. v.1– , 1970– . Ausburg, Mühlberger. Irreg.
Monograph series; some works in second editions.

771 GRUPPENDYNAMIK; FORSCHUNG UND PRAXIS. 1– , Feb. 1970– . Stuttgart, Ernest Klett Verlag. Quarterly.
Indexed: Psych. Abstr.

772 Guangzhou. Zhongshan Daxue Xuebao. CHUNG-SHAN TA HSÜEH HSÜEH PAO; SHE HUI K'O HSÜEH. JOURNAL OF SUN-YAT-SEN UNIVERSITY; SOCIAL SCIENCES. v.1– , Mar. 1955– . Canton. Quarterly.
The numbering of this series 1955–57 is combined with that of the *Natural Science Edition*. In Chinese; table of contents in Russian and English.

773 GUIDE TO DEPARTMENTS OF SOCIOLOGY AND ANTHROPOLOGY IN CANADIAN UNIVERSITIES. ANNUAIRE DES DÉPARTEMENTS DE SOCIOLOGIE ET D'ANTHROPOLOGIE DU CANADA. 1973/1974–1977. Montréal.
Continued by: *Annuaire des Départements de Sociologie, d'Anthropologie, d'Archéologie des Universités et des Muséums du Canada*.

GUIDE TO DEPARTMENTS OF SOCIOLOGY, ANTHROPOLOGY, ARCHEOLOGY IN UNIVERSITIES AND MUSEUMS IN CANADA
See ANNUAIRE DES DÉPARTEMENTS DE SOCIOLOGIE, D'ANTHROPOLOGIE, D'ARCHÉOLOGIE DES UNIVERSITÉS ET DES MUSÉUMS DU CANADA

774 GUIDE TO INDIAN PERIODICAL LITERATURE (SOCIAL SCIENCES AND HUMANITIES). v.1– , Mar. 1964– . Gurgaon, Prabhu Book Service. Four issues a year.
Issued by the Indian Documentation Service.

775 GUIDE TO THE LITERATURE OF SOCIAL CHANGE. 1– , 1977– . College Park, Md. Urban Information Interpreters. Semi-annual

776 GUIDES TO JEWISH SUBJECTS IN SOCIAL AND HUMANITIES RESEARCH. 1– , 1966– . New York. Irreg.
Issued by the YIVO Institute for Jewish Research.
Monograph series of bibliographies.

777 Gujurat, India (State). ANNUAL ADMINISTRATION REPORT ON SCHEDULED AREAS IN GUJURAT STATE. 1960/1961– . Baroda, Government Press.

778 HACETEPPE BULLETIN OF SOCIAL SCIENCES AND HUMANITIES. v.1– , 1969– . Ankara. Semi-annual.
Issued by the Haceteppe Universitesi. An English edition of *Haceteppe Sosyal ve Beseri Bilimler Dergisi*.
Indexed: Soc. Abstr.

779 Hague. Institute of Social Studies. PUBLICATIONS ON SOCIAL CHANGE. no.1– , 1955– . The Hague. Irreg.
Monograph series.

780 Haifa. Technion-Israel Institute of Technology. Center for Urban and Regional Studies. WORKING PAPER. 1970– . Haifa. Irreg.
Series of papers.

781 HANDBOOK OF INTERNATIONAL SOCIOMETRY. v.1–7, summer 1956–1973. Beacon, N.Y., Beacon Press. Irreg.
Title varies: v.1, no.1, 1956, *International Journal of Sociometry*; v.1, no.2–v.2, no.2, *International Journal of Sociometry and Sociatry*. Merged with *Group Psychotherapy and Psychodrama* to form *Group Psychotherapy, Psychodrama and Sociometry*.
Indexed: Bull. sig. soc. eth.; Psych. Abstr.

782 HANDBOOK OF LATIN AMERICAN STUDIES. [v.1]– , 1935– . Gainesville, Fla., University of Florida Press. Annual.
Issued by the Latin American, Portuguese and Spanish Division, Library of Congress. Since 1964, divided into two sections: Social sciences, and humanities including history, appearing in alternate years. Indexes: no.1–28, 1936–1966, 1 v

783 HANDBUCH DER EMPIRISCHEN SOZIALFORSCHUNG. v.1– , 1973– . Stuttgart, Ferdinand Enke Verlag. Irreg.
Monograph series; some works in second editions.

784 HAN'GUK SAHOEHAK. 1– , 1964– . Seoul.
Title in English: *The Korean Journal of Sociology*. In Korean.

785 HAN'GUK SAHOEHAK YŎN'GU. 1– , 1977– . Seoul. Annual.
Issued by the Seoul Taehakkyo Sahoehak Yŏn'guhoe. Title in English: *Korean Sociological Review*. In Korean.

HAN'GUK YON'GU TOSOGWAN T'ONGBO
See Han'guk Yŏnguwon, Seoul, Korea. BULLETIN OF THE KOREAN RESEARCH CENTER. JOURNAL OF SOCIAL SCIENCES AND HUMANITIES

786 Han'guk Yŏnguwon, Seoul, Korea. BULLETIN OF THE KOREAN RESEARCH CENTER. JOURNAL OF SOCIAL SCIENCES AND HUMANITIES. 1– , June 1956– . Seoul, Korea.
Title varies: no.1–11. 1956–Feb. 1960, *Han'guk Yŏn'gu Tosogwan t'ongbo*. In Korean.

787 HAN'GUK SAHOE KWAHAK NONJIP. THE KOREAN SOCIAL SCIENCE REVIEW. v.1– , 1965– . Seoul, Korea. Irreg.
Issued by the Han'guk Sahoe Kwahak Yŏnguwon (Korean Social Science Research Institute). In Korean. Table of contents also in English.

788 THE HARRIS SURVEY YEARBOOK OF PUBLIC OPINION. 1970– . New York, Louis Harris Associates. Annual (irreg.).

789 HARVARD SOCIOLOGICAL STUDIES. v.1–4, 1935–1947. Cambridge, Mass. Irreg.
Issued by the Department of Sociology, Harvard University.
Monograph series.

790 Harvard University. Program on Technology and Society. ANNUAL REPORT OF THE EXECUTIVE DIRECTOR. 1– , 1965/1966– . Cambridge, Mass. Annual.
Report ends June 30.

791 Harvard University. Program on Technology and Society. RESEARCH REVIEW. no.1–8, fall 1968–1971. Cambridge, Mass. Quarterly.

792 Havana. Universidad. Centro de Información Cientifica y Technica. ESTUDIOS DEMOGRAFICOS. 1– , June 1972– . Habana.
In Spanish.

793 Hawaii. Department of Health. POPULATION CHARACTERISTICS OF HAWAII. 1972– . Honolulu. Annual.
Some volumes issued in cooperation with the Department of Planning and Economic Development. Subseries of its *Population Report*.

794 Hawaii. State Immigration Services Center. IMMIGRANTS IN HAWAII; ANNUAL REPORT. 1– , 1965/1975– . Honolulu. Annual.

795 Hawaii. University, Honolulu. Center for Cultural and Technical Interchange between East and West. REPORT. 1– , 1961– . Honolulu. Annual.
Vol. for 1962 has also the distinctive title: *Blueprint of an Idea*.

796 HEIDELBERGER SOCIOLOGICA. 1– , 1962– . Heidelberg. Irreg.
Issued by the Institut für Soziologie und Ethnologie, Universität Heidelberg. Subseries of: *Veröffentlichungen* des Instituts für Soziologie und Ethnologie der Universität Heidelberg.
Monograph series; includes some doctoral dissertations.

797 Helsinki. Yliopisto. Sociologian Laitos. TUTKIMUKSIA. RESEARCH REPORTS. no.1– , 1959– . Helsinki. Irreg.
Issued by the Research Group for Comparative Sociology, University of Helsinki. In Finnish and English.
Monograph series.

798 HEURISTICS. v.1– , May 1969– . DeKalb, Ill. Two issues a year.
Subtitle reads: 'The graduate journal of sociology, Northern Illinois University'. Mimeographed.

799 HISTOIRE ET SOCIOLOGIE DE L'ÉGLISE. 1– , 1962– . Paris, Sirey.
Monograph series.

800 HISTOIRE ET SOCIOLOGIE DE LA CULTURE. 1– , 1971– . Québec, Presses de l'Université Laval. Irreg.
Monograph series.

801 HISTOIRE SOCIAL. SOCIAL HISTORY. 1– , Apr. 1968– . Ottawa, Les Éditions de l'Université d'Ottawa and Carleton University. Two issues a year.
Issued by the Université d'Ottawa and Carleton University. In English and Franch.
Indexed: Urb. Aff. Abstr.

802 HISTORIA E SOCIOLOGIA DO DESPORTO. 1– , 1970– . Lisboa, Prelo Editora. Irreg.
In Portuguese.
Monograph series; some works in second edition.

803 HISTORICKA DEMOGRAFIE. DÉMOGRAPHIE HISTORIQUE. 1– , 1967– . Praha. Irreg.
Issued by the Komise pro historickou demografii pri Historickem ústavu Československoi akademie věd (Commission for Historical Demography, Institute of History, Czechoslovak Academy of Sciences). Includes subseries: *Z historicko-demografických studii*, published annually. In Czech; summaries in French.

804 HISTORISCH-DEMOGRAPHISCHE MITTEILUNGEN. COMMUNICATION DE DEMOGRAPHIE HISTORIQUE. no.1– , 1971– . Budapest. Annual.
Issued by the Chair of Statistics, University in Budapest. In French and German; summaries in German or French.

805 THE HISTORY OF IDEAS SERIES. no.1–6, 1945–1953. Princeton, N.J., Irreg.
Issued by the Editorial Committee of *Journal of the History of Ideas*.
Monograph series.

806 HOSHAKAIGAKU. no.1–18, Mar. 1951–Apr. 1966; no.19– , Mar. 1967– . Tokyo, Yuhokabu. Irreg.
Issued by the Nihon Ho Shakai Gakkai. In Japanese. Title in English: *Sociology of Law*.

HOMBRE Y SOCIEDAD
See THE HUMAN CONTEXT

807 HOMME. 1950–1957; n.s. no.1– , 1958– . Paris. Irreg.
Issued by the 6e Section des Sciences Économiques et Sociales, École Pratique des Hautes Études. Subtitle reads: 'Cahiers d'ethnologie, de géographie et de linguistique'.
Indexed: Afr. Abstr.; Int. Pol. Sc. Abstr.; Soc. Abstr.

808 L'HOMME ET LA SOCIÉTÉ. no.1– , July/Sep. 1966– . Paris, Éditions Anthropos. Three issues a year.
Subtitle reads: 'Revue internationale de recherches et de syntheses sociologiques'.
Indexed: Afr. Abstr.; Bull. sig. soc. eth.; Int. Bibl. Soc.; Int. Pol. Sc. Abstr.; Soc. Abstr.; Urb. Aff. Abstr.

809 HOMMES ET LES TECHNIQUES NOUVELLES. no.76– , Aug/Sep. 1974– . Paris, Fédération pour le Respect de l'Homme et de l'Humanité.
Continues: Centre d'Étude des Grandes Techniques Nouvelles. *Bulletin*.
Indexed: Bull. sig. soc. eth.; Int. Bibl. Soc.

810 HOMMES ET MIGRATIONS. Jan. 1950–1964. Paris. Études Sociales Nord Africaines. Bimonthly.
Superseded by: *Hommes et Migrations: Documents*, and *Hommes et Migrations: Études*.
Indexed: Int. Bibl. Soc.

811 HOMMES ET MIGRATIONS: DOCUMENTS. 1964– . Paris. Irreg.
Supersedes, in part, *Hommes et Migrations*.
Indexed: Bull. sig. soc. eth.; Int. Bibl. Soc.

812 HOMMES ET MIGRATIONS: ÉTUDES. 1964– . Paris.
Supersedes, in part, and continues the volume numbering of *Hommes et Migrations*. Includes supplements titled *Études Hommes et Migrations*. Processed.

813 HOMMES ET TECHNIQUES. no.1–281, Oct. 1944–1968. Paris.

814 HOMO. v.1– , 1953– . Toulouse, Service des Publications. Annual.
Issued by the Université de Toulouse — Le Mirail. Subseries of *Annales,* Université de Toulouse — Le Mirail. Summaries in English.
Indexed: Int. Bibl. Soc.

815 Honduras. Universidad Nacional Autonoma, Tegucigalpa. Departamento de Ciencias Sociales. CUADERNOS DE CIENCIAS SOCIALES. no.1– , Jan. 1973– . Tegucigalpa.
In Spanish.

816 Hong Kong. Chinese University. JOURNAL. 1973– . Hong Kong, Chinese University Publications Office. Annual.
In Chinese and English; summaries in English and Chinese.

817 HOSPITAL LITERATURE INDEX. 1– , July 1945– . Chicago. Quarterly.
Issued by the American Hospital Association Library. Title varies: v.1–10, 1945–54, *Index of Current Hospital Literature;* v.11–13, no.1, June 1955–June 1957, *Hospital Periodical Literature Index.*

HOSPITAL PERIODICAL LITERATURE INDEX
See HOSPITAL LITERATURE INDEX

818 Howard University, Washington, D.C. Institute for Urban Affairs and Research. OCCASIONAL PAPERS. 1– , 1973– . Washington, D.C. Irreg.
Monograph series.

819 HSIA-MEN TA HSÜEH HSÜEH PAO; SHE HUI K'O HSÜEH PAN. ACTA SCIENTIARUM SOCIALIUM. v.1– , Sep. 1952– . Hsia-Men Shih (Amoy). Two issues a year.
Issued by the Hsia-men ta hsüeh yen chiu pu (Amoy University). In Chinese; summaries in English.

820 HUMAN COMMUNICATION RESEARCH. v.1–5, no.4, fall 1974–summer 1979. New Brunswick, N.J., Transaction Periodical Consortium. Quarterly.
Issued by the International Communication Association.

821 THE HUMAN CONTEXT. v.1–7, Aug. 1968–1975. London, Chaucer Publishing Co., subsequently, Oxford, Blackwell. Three issues a year.
Title in other languages: *Le Domain humain; Hombre y Sociedad; Il Mondo vissuto dell'Uomo,* and *Der Mensch und seine Welt.* In English, French, Spanish, Italian and German.
Indexed: Abstr. Anth.; Bull. sig. soc. eth.; Int. Pol. Sc. Abstr.; Soc. Abstr.

822 HUMAN DEVELOPMENT. v.1– , 1958– . New York, S. Karger. Quarterly.
Title varies: v.1–7, 1958–64, *Vita humana.*
Indexed: Bull. sig. soc. eth.; Psych. Abstr.; Soc. Abstr.; Wom. Stud. Abstr.

823 HUMAN ECOLOGY. v.1– , 1972– . New York, Plenum Publishing Co. Semi-annual.
Issued by the Program in Ecological Anthropology, Columbia University. Subtitle reads: 'An interdisciplinary journal'.
Indexed: Abstr. Anth.; Soc. Abstr.

824 HUMAN ECOLOGY AND EDUCATION SERIES. v.1– , 1971– . Ibadan. Irreg.
Issued by the Institute of Education, University of Ibadan. Subseries of the Institute of Education's *Occasional Publication.*
Monograph series.

825 HUMAN ECOLOGY FORUM. v.1– , summer 1970– . Ithaca, N.Y. Quarterly.
Issued by the New York State College of Human Ecology at Cornell University.
Indexed: Soc. Sc. Ind.; Soc. Abstr.

[HUMAN ECOLOGY] ANNUAL REPORT
See New York State College of Human Ecology. ANNUAL REPORT

826 HUMAN FACTOR; A JOURNAL OF RADICAL SOCIOLOGY. 1– , 1968– . New York. Semi-annual.
Issued by the Graduate Sociology Student Union, Columbia University.
Indexed: Soc. Abstr.

HUMAN GEOGRAPHY
See GEOGRAFISKA ANNALER. SERIES B: HUMAN GEOGRAPHY

HUMAN GEOGRAPHY
See THE JIMBUN CHIRI

HUMAN GEOGRAPHY
See LUND STUDIES IN GEOGRAPHY. SERIES B: HUMAN GEOGRAPHY

HUMAN GEOGRAPHY
See Utrecht. Rijksuniversiteit. Geografisch Instituut. PUBLIKATIES. SERIES A: SOCIALE GEOGRAFIE. HUMAN GEOGRAPHY

827 HUMAN GEOGRAPHY. H.G. 1– , 1969– Canberra. Irreg.
Issued by the Department of Human Geography, Australian National University.
Monograph series.

828 HUMAN MOSAIC. v.1– , spring 1966– . New Orleans. Semi-annual.
Issued by the graduate students of the Department of Anthropology, Tulane University.
Indexed: Soc. Abstr.

829 HUMAN ORGANIZATION. v.1– , Oct/Dec. 1941– . Lexington, Ky. Quarterly.
Issued by the Society for Applied Sociology. Title varies: 1941–fall 1948, *Applied Anthropology*.
Indexed: Bull. sig. soc. eth.; Int. Bibl. Soc.; Int. Pol. Sc. Abstr.; Soc. Sc. Hum. Ind.; Soc. Sc. Ind.; Soc. Abstr.; Soc. Work Res. Abstr.

830 HUMAN ORGANIZATION CLEARINGHOUSE BULLETIN. v.1–3, no.3, summer 1951–June 1955. New York.
Issued by the Society for Applied Anthropology.

831 HUMAN RELATIONS. v.1– , June 1947– . New York, Plenum Press. Quarterly.
Issued by the Tavistock Institute of Human Relations, and the Research Centre for Group Dynamics. Subtitle reads: 'A quarterly journal of studies towards the integration of the social sciences'.
Indexed: Brit. Hum. Ind.; Bull. sig. soc. eth.; Int. Bibl. Soc.; Int. Pol. Sc. Abstr.; PAIS; Psych. Abstr.; Soc. Sc. Ind.; Soc. Work Res. Abstr.; Soc. Abstr.; Urb. Aff. Abstr.; Wom. Stud. Abstr.

832 HUMAN RESOURCES ABSTRACTS. v.1– , Jan/Feb. 1966– . Ann Arbor, Mich., 1966–74; Beverly Hills, Calif., Sage Publications, 1975– . Quarterly.
Issued by the Institute of Labor and Industrial Relations, University of Michigan, 1966–74; by the same Institute and Wayne State University, 1975– . Title varies: v.1–9, 1966–74, *Poverty and Human Resources Abstracts*. Cover title: *PHRA. Poverty & Human Resources Abstracts.*

833 HUMAN SETTLEMENT ISSUES. 1– , 1978– . Vancouver, University of British Columbia Press.
Published in association with the Center for Human Settlement, University of British Columbia.

834 HUMAN STUDIES. v.1– , Jan. 1978– . Norwood, N.J., Ablex Publishing Co. Quarterly.
Issued by the Department of Sociology, Boston University. Subtitle reads: 'A journal for philosophy and the social sciences'.

835 HUMANISMA. 1– , 1971/1972– . Kuala Lumpur, Publications Committee, National University of Malaysia.
Supersedes: *Akademika*. In Malay.

836 HUMANITAS. v.1–15, no.3, spring 1965–Nov. 1979. Pittsburgh, Pa. Three issues a year.
Issued by the Institute of Man, Duquesne University. Superseded by: *Formative Spirituality*.
Indexed: Bull. sig. soc. eth.; Cath. Per. Ind.; Peace Res. Abstr. J.; Psych. Abstr.; Soc. Abstr.; Wom. Stud. Abstr.

HUMANITIES AND SCIENCES
See MULLI NONJIP

837 HUMANITY & SOCIETY. 1– , summer 1977– . Hartford, Conn.
Issued by the Association for Humanistic Sociology.
Indexed: Soc. Abstr.

838 HUMBOLDT JOURNAL OF SOCIAL RELATIONS. 1– , fall 1973– . Arcata, Calif. Three issues a year.
Issued by the Department of Sociology and Social Welfare, Humboldt State University.
Indexed: Soc. Work Res. Abstr.; Psych. Abstr.; Soc. Abstr.

839 Hungary. Központi Statisztikai Hivatal. Demográfiai Elnökségi Bizottság. ANNALS. 1963–1968. Budapest.

IAMCR BULLETIN
See International Association for Mass Communication Research. IAMCR BULLETIN.

ICSSR JOURNAL OF ABSTRACTS AND REVIEWS
See Indian Council of Social Science Research. JOURNAL OF ABSTRACTS AND REVIEWS.

ICSSR JOURNAL OF ABSTRACTS AND REVIEWS; SOCIOLOGY AND SOCIAL ANTHROPOLOGY
See Indian Council of Social Science Research. JOURNAL OF ABSTRACTS AND REVIEWS; SOCIOLOGY AND SOCIAL ANTHROPOLOGY

IEEE TECHNOLOGY AND SOCIETY
See TECHNOLOGY AND SOCIETY

IMP INTERNATIONAL MIGRATION REVIEW
See INTERNATIONAL MIGRATION REVIEW

IPD SOCIOLOGICAL ANALYSES AND SURVEYS; INFORMATION BULLETIN
See ha-Makhon le-Tikhnum U-Fituah. IPD SOCIOLOGICAL ANALYSES AND SURVEYS; INFORMATION BULLETIN

ISA BULLETIN
See International Sociological Association. ISA BULLETIN

ISA NEWSLETTER
See International Sociological Association. ISA BULLETIN

ISHA BULLETIN
See Columbia University. Institute for the Study of Human Affairs. ISHA BULLETIN

ISHI OCCASIONAL PAPERS IN SOCIAL CHANGE
See Institute for the Study of Human Issue. ISHA OCCASIONAL PAPERS IN SOCIAL CHANGE

ISMA PUBLICATION
See Institute for the Study of Man in Africa. ISMA PUBLICATION

ISO BULLETIN
See SOCIAL ORDER

840 IAZYK I OBSHCHESTVO. 1– , 1967– . Saratov, Izd-vo Saratovskogo universiteta. Irreg.
In Russian.

841 IBADAN. v.1– , 1957– . Ibadan, University College Press. Three issues a year.
In English.
Indexed: Afr. Abstr.; Int. Bibl. Soc.

842 Ibadan. University. Institute of African Studies. OCCASIONAL PUBLICATION. 1– , 1964– . Ibadan.
Includes subseries: *Human Ecology,* and *Education Series.*

843 ICONOCLAST. v.1– , 1971– . Kensington, N.S.W. Three issues a year.
Issued by the School of Sociology, University of New South Wales.

844 Ife, Nigeria. University. Demographic Research and Training Unit. REPORT. 1968/1969– . Ife.

845 IKENGA; JOURNAL OF AFRICAN STUDIES. v.1– , Jan. 1972– . Nsukka. Two issues a year.
Issued by the Institute of African Studies, University of Nigeria.

846 Illinois. Northern Illinois University, DeKalb. Center for Black Studies. OCCASIONAL PAPERS. 1– , 1973– . DeKalb, Ill. Irreg.

847 Illinois. University, Urbana. Department of Psychology. RESEARCH IN SOCIAL PSYCHOLOGY. 1–4, 1960–1963. Urbana.

848 IMMIGRANTS IN AUSTRALIA. 1– , 1972– . Canberra, Australian National University Press. Irreg.
Issued by the Academy of the Social Sciences in Australia.
Monograph series.

IMMIGRANTS IN HAWAII. ANNUAL REPORT
See Hawaii. State Immigration Center. IMMIGRANTS IN HAWAII. ANNUAL REPORT

849 IMMIGRATION. v.1–6, no.5, Apr. 1909–Oct. 1914. Springfield, Mass. Monthly.
Issued by the International College.

850 IMPACT. 1– , Oct. 1978– . Syracuse, N.Y. Annual.
Issued by the Institute for Family Research and Education, Syracuse University.

851 IMPACT OF SCIENCE ON SOCIETY. v.1– , Apr/June 1950– . Paris. Four issues a year.
Issued by Unesco. Editions also in French, *Impact; Science et Société,* and Spanish, *Impacto; Ciencia y Sociedad,* 1964– .
Indexed: Int. Bibl. Soc.; Int. Pol. Sc. Abstr.; PAIS; Soc. Sci. Ind.; Soc. Abstr.; Wom. Stud. Abstr.

IMPACT: SCIENCE ET SOCIÉTÉ
See IMPACT OF SCIENCE ON SOCIETY

IMPACTO; CIENCIA Y SOCIEDAD
See IMPACT OF SCIENCE ON SOCIETY

852 IN SUMMARY. 1979– . Edmonton, Alberta. Three issues a year.
Issued by the Population Research Laboratory, Department of Sociology, University of Alberta.

853 INDEX KOMUNALER ZEITSCHRIFTEN. no.1– , Oct. 1970– . Wien, Komunal Wissenschaftliches Dokumentationszentrum. Annual.

854 INDEX KOMUNALWISSENSCHAFTLICHER LITERATUR; BÜCHER. no.1– , May 1970. Wien, Komunal Wissenschaftliches Dokumentationszentrum.

INDEX OF CONFERENCE PROCEEDINGS RECEIVED

See British Library. Lending Division. INDEX OF CONFERENCE PROCEEDINGS RECEIVED.

INDEX OF CURRENT HOSPITAL LITERATURE
See HOSPITAL LITERATURE

855 INDEX TO CURRENT URBAN DOCUMENTS. v.1– , July 1972– . Westport, Conn., Greenwood Press. Quarterly, with annual cumulations.

856 INDEX TO INTERNATIONAL PUBLIC OPINION. 1978/1979– . Westport, Conn., Greenwood Press; subsequently Oxford, Clio Press (1979/1980–). Annual.
Edited by the Survey Research Consultants International, Inc.

INDEX TO LATIN AMERICAN PERIODICALS: HUMANITIES AND SOCIAL SCIENCES
See INDICE GENERAL DE PUBLICACIÓNES LATINOAMERICANAS; HUMANIDADES Y CIENCIAS SOCIALES

857 INDEX TO MEDICAL SOCIOECONOMICS LITERATURE. v.1– , 1962– . Chicago. Annual.
Issued by the Archive-Library Department, American Medical Association. Caption title: *Index to the Literature of Medical Socioeconomics*.

858 INDEX TO SOCIAL SCIENCES AND HUMANITIES PROCEEDINGS. Jan/Mar. 1979– . Philadelphia, Pa. Quarterly.
Issued by the Institute for Social Science Information.

INDEX TO THE LITERATURE OF MEDICAL SOCIOECONOMICS
See INDEX TO MEDICAL SOCIOECONOMICS LITERATURE

859 India (Republic). Census. BIBLIOGRAPHY ON SCHEDULED TRIBES, AND SELECTED MARGINAL COMMUNITIES OF INDIA. PART 1-A-SERIES. 1966– . New Delhi.

860 INDIAN BEHAVIOURAL SCIENCES ABSTRACTS. Jan. 1970–1972? Delhi. Quarterly.
Issued by the Behavioural Sciences Centre.

861 Indian Council of Social Science Research. JOURNAL OF ABSTRACTS AND REVIEWS. v.1–3, Jan. 1972–1974. New Delhi, National Publishing House. Two issues a year.
Vol.1 published in a combined issue. Continued by: Indian Council of Social Science Research. *Journal of Abstracts and Reviews; Sociology and Social Anthropology*.

862 Indian Council of Social Research. JOURNAL OF ABSTRACTS AND REVIEWS: SOCIOLOGY AND SOCIAL ANTHROPOLOGY. v.4– , Jan/June 1975– . New Delhi.
Continues: Indian Council of Social Science Research. *Journal of Abstracts and Reviews*.

863 INDIAN DEMOGRAPHIC BULLETIN. 1– , 1968– . New Delhi.
Issued by the Office of the Registrar General. Supersedes: *Indian Population Bulletin*, Apr. 1960–Jan. 1967.

864 INDIAN JOURNAL OF COMPARATIVE SOCIOLOGY. 1– , Aug. 1974– . Dharwar. Semi-annual.
Issued by the Forum for Sociologists.

865 INDIAN JOURNAL OF SOCIAL RESEARCH. v.1– , 1959– . Baraut, Meerut. Semi-annual.
Issued by the Department of Sociology, Post Graduate Studies, J.V. College.
Indexed: Bull. sig. soc. eth.; Int. Bibl. Soc.; Soc. Abstr.

866 INDIAN JOURNAL OF SOCIAL WORK. 1940– . Bombay, Department of Publications, Tata Institute of Social Sciences. Quarterly.
Issued by the Tata Institute of Social Sciences.
Indexed: Int. Bibl. Soc.; PAIS; Psych. Abstr.; Soc. Abstr.; Wom. Stud. Abstr.

867 INDIAN JOURNAL OF SOCIOLOGY. 1– , Mar. 1970– . New Delhi, Academic Journals of India. Semi-annual.
Issued by the Indian Academy of Social Sciences.
Indexed: Soc. Abstr.

INDIAN SOCIOLOGICAL BULLETIN
See INTERNATIONAL JOURNAL OF CONTEMPORARY SOCIOLOGY

868 INDIAN SOCIOLOGIST. v.1–13, no.2, 1905–Sep. 1922. Paris, London.

869 Indiana. University. International Development Research Center. STUDIES IN DEVELOPMENT. no.1– , 1968– . Bloomington, Ind. Irreg.
Title varies: no.1, 1968, *International Development Research Center Series*.
Monograph series.

INDICADORES ECONOMICO-SOCIAIS
See Portugal. Instituto Nacional de Estatistica. Servicos Centrais. INDICADORES ECONOMICO-SOCIAIS

870 INDICE GENERAL DE PUBLICACIÓNES PERIODICAS LATINOAMERICANAS: HUMANIDADES Y CIENCIAS SOCIALES. INDEX TO LATIN AMERICAN PERIODICALS: HUMANITIES AND SOCIAL SCIENCES. v.1– , Jan/Mar. 1961– . Boston, Mass., G. K. Hall, 1861–62; subsequently Metuchen, N.J., Scarecrow Press. Quarterly, with annual cumulations.
Issued by the New York Public Library and the Columbus Memorial Library, Pan American Union. In Spanish; partly in English. Author, title, and subject indexes included.

INDIKATOR SOSIAL
See Indonesia. Biro Pusat Statistik. INDIKATOR SOCIAL. SOCIAL INDICATORS

INDIKATOR SOCIAL JAVA TENGAH
See Java Tengah, Indonesia. Kantor Sensus dan Statistik. INDIKATOR SOSIAL JAVA TENGAH

871 INDIVIDU EN SAMENLEVING, REEKS "SOCIOLOGIE". 1–6, 1969– . Antwerp, Standaard Wetenschappelijke Uitgewerij. Irreg.
In Flemish.
Monograph series.

872 INDONESIA. no.1– , Apr. 1966– . Ithaca, N.Y. Semi-annual.
Issued by the Cornell Modern Indonesia Project, Cornell University.
Indexed: Int. Bibl. Soc.; Int. Pol. Sc. Abstr.; Soc. Abstr.

873 Indonesia. Biro Pusat Statistik. INDIKATOR SOSIAL. SOCIAL INDICATORS. 1971– . Jakarta.
In English and Indonesian.

874 INDUSTRIAL AND LABOR RELATIONS REVIEW. v.1– , Oct. 1947– . Ithaca, N.Y. Quarterly.
Issued by the New York State School of Industrial and Labor Relations.
Indexed: Bull. sig. soc. eth.; Int. Bibl. Soc.; Int. Pol. Sc. Abstr.; PAIS; PHRA; Soc. Abstr.

875 INDUSTRIAL RELATIONS. v.1– , 1961– . Berkeley, Calif. Three issues a year.
Issued by the Institute of Industrial Relations, University of California at Berkeley. Subtitle reads: 'A journey of economy and society'.
Indexed: Int. Bibl. Soc.; PAIS; Soc. Abstr.; Urb. Aff. Abstr.

INDUSTRIAL RELATIONS
See RELATIONS INDUSTRIELLES

INDUSTRIAL RELATIONS MONOGRAPHS
See California. University. University at Los Angeles. Institute of Industrial Relations. MONOGRAPH SERIES

INDUSTRIAL STUDIES
See British Sociological Association. INDUSTRIAL STUDIES

INFORMACIÓNES
See Chile. Universidad. Instituto de Sociologia. INFORMACIÓNES

INFORMATION BULLETIN
See Erasmus Universiteit, Rotterdam. Centrum voor Maatschappijgeschiedenis. MEDEDELINGEN. INFORMATION BULLETIN

876 INFORMATION REVIEW ON CRIME AND DELINQUENCY. v.1, no.1–10, Sep. 1968–Dec. 1969. Washington, D.C. Bimonthly.
Issued by the National Council on Crime and Delinquency. Superseded by: *Crime and Delinquency Literature.*

877 INFORMATIONEN ZUR SOZIOLOGISCHEN FORSCHUNG IN DER DDR. v.1– , 1965– . Berlin. Six issues a year.
Issued by the Zentralstelle für soziologische Information und Dokumentation, Akademie für Gesellschaftswissenschaften beim Zentral Kommitee der S.E.D. Processed.

INFORME. SER. D. DEMOGRAFIA
See Argentina Republic. Dirección General de Estadistica. INFORME. SER. D. DEMOGRAFIA

878 INGU MUNJE NONJIP. JOURNAL OF POPULATION STUDIES. no.1– , 1965– . Seoul. Irreg.
In Korean.

879 INMIGRACIÓN. v.1– , 1959– . Buenos Aires. Irreg.
Issued by the Dirección Nacional de Migraciónes. In Spanish.

880 INQUIRY. v.1– , spring 1958– . Oslo, Universitetsforlaget. Quarterly.
Subtitle reads: 'An interdisciplinary journal of philosophy and the social sciences'.
Indexed: Abstr. Soc. Work; Int. Bibl. Soc.; Int. Pol. Sc. Abstr.; Soc. Abstr.

881 INSTANT RESEARCH ON PEACE AND VIOLENCE. 1971–1977. Tampere. Quarterly.

Issued by the Tampere Peace Research Institute (TAPRI). Superseded by: *Current Research on Peace and Violence.*
Indexed: Soc. Abstr.

882 No entry.

883 Institut des Sciences Sociales, Brussels. ANNALES. v.1–6, 1894/1895–1900/1901. Bruxelles.

884 Institut Fondamental d'Afrique Noire. BULLETIN. SÉRIE B: SCIENCES HUMAINES. vol.16– , Jan/Apr. 1954– . Dakar. Semi-annual; later quarterly. Some issues combined.
Supersedes, part, and continues the numbering of, its *Bulletin*.
Indexed: Int. Bibl. Soc.

885 Institut für Empirische Soziologie. SCHRIFTENREIHE. no.1, 1956. Köln, Westdeutscher Verlag. Irreg.
Monograph series.

886 Institut für Konfliktforschung. SCHRIFTENREIHE. 1– , 1977– . Basel, S. Karger. Annual.
Indexed: Curr. Cont.

887 Institut für Soziologie. FORSCHUNGSBERICHTE DES INSTITUTS FÜR SOZIOLOGIE. 1– , 1973– . Linz, Donau. Irreg.
The Institut is part of the Hochschule für Sozial- und Wirtschaftswissenshaften.
Monograph series.

888 Institut za kriminološka i sociološka istraživanji. ZBORNIK. 1– , Jan/June 1972– . Beograd. Semi-annual.
In Serbo-Croatian. Summaries in Russian and French.

889 Institute for the Study of Human Issues. ISHI OCCASIONAL PAPERS IN SOCIAL CHANGE. 1– , 1976– . Philadelphia, Pa. Irreg.
Other title: *Institute for the Study of Human Issues Occasional Papers in Social Change.*

INSTITUTE FOR THE STUDY OF HUMAN ISSUES OCCASIONAL PAPERS IN SOCIAL CHANGE
See Institute for the Study of Human Issues, Philadelphia, Pa. ISHI OCCASIONAL PAPERS IN SOCIAL CHANGE

890 Institute for the Study of Man in Africa. ISMA PUBLICATION. 1– , 1963– . Johannesburg. Irreg.
Monograph series.

INSTITUTE MONOGRAPH SERIES
See Purdue University. Institute for the Study of Social Change. INSTITUTE MONOGRAPH SERIES

891 Institute of Applied Social and Economic Research. BIBLIOGRAPHY. 1– , 1977– . Boroko, Papua New Guinea.

892 Institute of Community Studies. REPORTS. 1–8, 1957–1963. London, Routledge & Kegan Paul. Irreg.
Monograph series.

893 Institute of Race Relations. ANNUAL REPORT. 1974/1975– . London.

894 Institute of Race Relations. NEWS LETTER. Mar. 1960–Apr. 1969. London. Monthly.
Supersedes: the Institute's publication of the same title, and *African Press Summary*. Superseded by: *Race Today*. Supplements accompany some issues.

895 Institute of Race Relations. REGISTER OF RESEARCH ON COMMONWEALTH IMMIGRANTS IN BRITAIN. 1st ed.– , May 1966– . London. Irreg.
Title varies: 1, 1966, *Register of Research on Commonwealth Immigrants*. Also called *Newsletter*.

896 Institute of Sociology, London. REPORTS OF ANNUAL CONFERENCES. 1– , 1935– . Westminster, England.
Title varies: 1935, *Social Sciences;* 1936, *Further Papers on the Social Sciences;* 1937, *Papers on the Social Sciences*. The Institute of Sociology called, through 1929, the Sociological Society.

Institute of Sociology, London
See also Sociological Society, London

897 Institute of Student Opinion. INSTITUTE OF STUDENT OPINION POLL. no.1–?, May 1943–?. New York. Ceased publication.
No.1–2 called *Tabulation of Results,* issued by the Scholastic Institute of Student Opinion Poll. Supplements accompany some issues.

INSTITUTE OF STUDENT OPINION POLL
See Institute of Student Opinion. INSTITUTE OF STUDENT OPINION POLL.

898 Instituto Centroamericano de Población y Familia. COLECCION MONOGRAFIAS DIAGNOSTICAS. 1–3, 1968. Guatemala City.
Issued in cooperation with Instituto para el Desarrollo Económico Social de America Central. In Spanish.
Monograph series.

899 Instituto de Ciencias Sociales. REVISTA. v.1– , 1963– . Barcelona. Semi-annual.
In Spanish.
Indexed: Bull. sig. soc. eth.; Int. Pol. Sc. Abstr.; Soc. Abstr.

900 Instituto do Algodão de Moçambique. SERIA ECONOMIA E SOCIOLOGIA 1–3, 1964–1966. Lourenço-Marques. Irreg.
In Portuguese
Monograph series.

901 Instituto Otavaleno de Antropologia. BREVIARIOS DE CULTURA. SERIE: SOCIOLOGIA. v.1– , 1970– . Otavalo, Ecuador.
In Spanish.

902 Instituto Torcuato di Tella. Centro de Estudios de Estado y Sociedad. ESTUDIOS SOCIALES. Córdoba.
Supersedes, in part, Centro de Investigaciónes de Administración Publica. *Documentos.* In Spanish.

903 Instituto Torcuato di Tella. Centro de Investigaciónes Sociales. DOCUMENTOS DE TRABAJO. no.1– , 1964– . Buenos Aires.
In Spanish.
Series of papers. Some issues in revised editions.

904 Instituts Solvay. Institut de Sociologie. BIBLIOTHÈQUE SOCIOLOGIQUE. 1, 1903. Bruxelles.
Superseded by its *Études Sociales.*

905 Instituts Solvay. Institut de Sociologie. BULLETIN. v.1–5 (no.1–33), 1910–July 1914. Bruxelles.
Title varies: 1910–11, *Bulletin Mensuel.* Includes *Archives Sociologiques.* Superseded by its *Revue.*

906 Instituts Solvay. Institut de Sociologie. ÉTUDES SOCIALES. 1–8, 1904–1913; n.s. v.1–5, 1932–1934. Bruxelles
Supersedes its *Bibliothèque Sociologique.* Superseded by its *Travaux.*
Monograph series.

907 Instituts Solvay. Institut de Sociologie. MONOGRAPHIES BIBLIOGRAPHIQUES. 1–2, 1911–1912. Bruxelles.
Monograph series.

908 Instituts Solvay. Institut de Sociologie. NOTES & MÉMOIRES. 1–12, 1905–1914. Bruxelles. Irreg. Vol.10 not published.
Superseded by its *Travaux.*
Monograph series.

909 Instituts Solvay. Institut de Sociologie. SEMAINE SOCIALE UNIVERSITAIRE. Bruxelles. Ceased publication.
Title varies: *Semaine Sociale.* Proceedings of each meeting have distinctive title.

910 Institute Solvay. Institut de Sociologie. TRAVAUX. n.s. 1–2, 1921. Bruxelles.
Supersedes its *Notes et Mémoires,* and *Actualités Sociales.*

911 Instituts Solvay. Institut de Sociologie. TRAVAUX DES GROUPES D'ÉTUDES DE LA RECONSTRUCTION NATIONALE. 1–9, 1919. Bruxelles.
Monograph series.

912 INSURGENT SOCIOLOGIST. 1– , 1971– . Eugene, Oreg. Quarterly.
Issued by the Department of Sociology, University of Oregon.
Indexed: Int. Bibl. Soc.; Soc. Abstr.

913 INTEGRATION. v.1–9, 1954–1962. München. Quarterly.
Issued by the European Association for the Study of Refugee Problems. Supersedes its *Information.* Index to v.1–5 in v.5.

INTEGRATION AND COMMUNITY BUILDING IN EASTERN EUROPE
See JOHNS HOPKINS SERIES IN INTEGRATION AND COMMUNITY BUILDING IN EASTERN EUROPE

914 INTEGRATION OF IMMIGRANTS; A DIGEST OF SOURCE MATERIAL. v.1– , 1964– . New York. Semi-annual.
Issued by the Committee on Integration, American Immigration and Citizenship Conference. Some issues are reports of Seminars on the Integration of Immigrants.

915 Inter-American Indian Institute. SERIE: ANTROPOLOGIA SOCIAL. 1–?, 1964–?. Mexico, D.F. Ceased publication.
Issued by the Instituto Indigenista Interamericano. In Spanish.

916 INTERAÇÃO. 1– , 1964– . Juiz de Fora. Quarterly.
Issued by the Centro de Estudos Sociologicos de Juiz de Fora. In Portuguese.

917 INTERACTION. L'HOMME ET SON ENVIRONMENT. 1–3, 1974–1975. The Hague, Mouton. Irreg.
Monograph series.

918 INTERDISCIPLINE. v.1– , 1964– . Rajhart, Varanasi. Quarterly.

Issued by the Ghandian Institute of Studies. Title varies: 1964–Dec. 1965, *Social Science Abstracts*.
Indexed: Soc. Abstr.

919 Intergovernmental Committee for European Migration. ANNUAL REPORT. 1954–1962. Genève. Annual.

920 Intergovernmental Committee for European Migration. INTERNATIONAL MIGRATION. MIGRATIONS INTERNATIONALES. MIGRACIÓNES INTERNACIONALES. 1– , 1963– . Genève. Quarterly.
Issued in cooperation with the Research Group for European Migration Problems. Title varies: 1963–70, *Migrations Internationales*. Supersedes: *Migration (ICEM)*, and *REMP Bulletin*.
In English; summaries in French and Spanish.
Indexed: Int. Bibl. Soc.

921 Intergovernmental Committee for European Migration. STATISTICAL REPORT. COMPTES RENDU STATISTIQUES. 1952–1961. Geneva. Annual.

922 Intergovernmental Committee for European Migration. Department of Plans and Liaison. RESEARCH DIGEST. 1–?, Oct. 1954–?. Geneva. Ceased publication.

923 INTERGROUP RELATIONS NEWSLETTER. no.1–3, 1974. Berkeley, Calif.
Issued by the Institute for Studies of Social Change, University of California at Berkeley.

924 INTERMET METROPOLITAN STUDIES SERIES. no.1–3, 1970–1973? Toronto, Intermet.
Other title: *Metropolitan Studies Series*.
Monograph series.

INTERNAL MIGRATION
See Australia. Bureau of Census and Statistics. INTERNAL MIGRATION

INTERNATIONAL ANNALS OF CRIMINOLOGY
See ANNALES INTERNATIONALES DE CRIMINOLOGIE

INTERNATIONAL ARCHIVES OF SOCIOLOGY OF COOPERATION
See ARCHIVES INTERNATIONALES DE SOCIOLOGIE DE LA COOPÉRATION

925 International Association for Mass Communication. IAMC BULLETIN. Oct. 1962– . Amsterdam. Quarterly.
Issued in cooperation with *International Journal Gazette*. Supersedes an earlier publication of the same title.

926 INTERNATIONAL BEHAVIORAL SCIENTIST. v.1– , Mar. 1969– . Meerut, India, "Sadhna Prakashan". Quarterly.
Issued by the Delta Tau Kappa.
Indexed: Int. Bibl. Soc.; Int. Pol. Sc. Abstr.; Soc. Abstr.

927 INTERNATIONAL BIBLIOGRAPHY OF ECONOMICS. BIBLIOGRAPHIE INTERNATIONALE DE SCIENCE ÉCONOMIQUE. v.1– , 1957– . Paris, Unesco. Annual.
Issued by the Fondation Nationale des Sciences Politiques, in cooperation with the International Economic Association and the International Committee for Social Studies.

INTERNATIONAL BIBLIOGRAPHY OF PSYCHOLOGY
See BIBLIOGRAPHIE INTERNATIONALE DE PSYCHOLOGIE

INTERNATIONAL BIBLIOGRAPHY OF RESEARCH IN MARRIAGE AND THE FAMILY
See INVENTORY OF MARRIAGE AND FAMILY LITERATURE

928 INTERNATIONAL BIBLIOGRAPHY OF SOCIAL AND CULTURAL ANTHROPOLOGY. BIBLIOGRAPHIE INTERNATIONALE D'ANTHROPOLOGIE SOCIALE ET CULTURELLE. v.1– , 1955– . Paris, Unesco, 1955–59; London, Tavistock Publications; Chicago, Aldine Publications. Annual.
Issued by the International Committee for Social Sciences Documentation, 1955–59, in cooperation with the International Congress of Anthropological and Ethnological Sciences.

929 INTERNATIONAL BIBLIOGRAPHY OF SOCIOLOGY. BIBLIOGRAPHIE INTERNATIONALE DE SOCIOLOGIE. [1]– , 1951– . London, Tavistock Publications. Annual.
Issued by the International Committee for Social Science Information and Documentation. Issues for 1951–54 published as part of *Current Sociology*.

INTERNATIONAL BIBLIOGRAPHY OF THE SOCIAL SCIENCES
See INTERNATIONAL BIBLIOGRAPHY OF ECONOMICS
INTERNATIONAL BIBLIOGRAPHY OF POLITICAL SCIENCE

INTERNATIONAL BIBLIOGRAPHY OF SOCIAL AND CULTURAL ANTHROPOLOGY

INTERNATIONAL BIBLIOGRAPHY OF SOCIOLOGY

INTERNATIONAL BIBLIOGRAPHY ON CRIME AND DELINQUENCY
See CRIME AND DELINQUENCY ABSTRACTS

INTERNATIONAL CENSUS BIBLIOGRAPHY
See Texas. University. Bureau of International Business Research. Population Research Center. INTERNATIONAL CENSUS BIBLIOGRAPHY

930 International Centre for African Economic and Social Documentation. BULLETIN OF INFORMATION ON CURRENT RESEARCH ON HUMAN SCIENCES CONCERNING AFRICA. no.1–, 1963– . Bruxelles. Two volumes a year.

Title varies: 1963–64 (no.1), *Bulletin d'Information sur les Thèses et les Études en Cours ou en Projet. Bulletin of Information on Theses and Studies in Progress or Proposed*. Title in French: *Bulletin d'Information sur les Recherches dans les Sciences Humaines concernant l'Afrique*. Temporarily suspended, 1975.

931 INTERNATIONAL COMPARISONS IN SOCIAL POLICY. 1– , 1972– . London. Irreg.

Issued by the Fabian Society. Subseries of its *Fabian Tract*.

Series of pamphlets.

932 International Conference on Cybernetics and Society. PROCEEDINGS. 1972– . New York.

Issued by the Institute of Electrical and Electronics Engineers.

933 International Congress of Sociology. MEMOIRE. 14– , 1950– . Mexico.

Proceedings of the 1st–10th congresses published in *Annales de l'Institut International de Sociologie*.

INTERNATIONAL DEVELOPMENT RESEARCH CENTER SERIES
See Indiana. University. International Development Center. STUDIES IN DEVELOPMENT

INTERNATIONAL DEVELOPMENT REVIEW
See REVISTA DESARROLLO INTERNACIONAL

INTERNATIONAL INDEX
See SOCIAL SCIENCES & HUMANITIES INDEX

INTERNATIONAL INDEX TO PERIODICALS
See SOCIAL SCIENCES & HUMANITIES INDEX

934 International Institute for Social History, Amsterdam. BULLETIN. v.1–10, 1937–1955. Leiden, E. J. Brill.

935 International Institute of Sociology. ANNALES DE L'INSTITUT INTERNATIONAL DE SOCIOLOGIE. v.1–16, 1894–1932. Paris, V. Gerard & Briere. Publication suspended 1914–27.

Includes transactions of the 1st–10th congresses of the International Institute of Sociology.

936 INTERNATIONAL JOURNAL OF COMPARATIVE SOCIOLOGY. v.1– , 1960– . Dharwar, Mysore; subsequently Leiden, E. J. Brill. Quarterly.

Issued by the Department of Social Anthropology, Karnatak University, through v.5, no.2; subsequently by the Department of Sociology, York University, Canada.

Indexed: Bull. sig. soc. eth.; Int. Bibl. Soc.; Soc. Sc. Hum. Ind.; SSCI; Soc. Sc. Ind.; Soc. Abstr.; Urb. Aff. Abstr.

937 INTERNATIONAL JOURNAL OF CONTEMPORARY SOCIOLOGY. v.1– , Oct. 1963– . Ghaziabad, U.P., J. G. Mohan at Intercontinental Press. Quarterly.

Edited by the Department of Sociology and Anthropology, Auburn University, Auburn, Ala. Title varies: v.1–7, 1963–70, *Indian Sociological Bulletin*.

Indexed: Curr. Cont.; Int. Bibl. Soc.; Int. Pol. Sc. Abstr.; SSCI; Soc. Abstr.

938 INTERNATIONAL JOURNAL OF CRIMINOLOGY AND PENOLOGY. 1–6, 1973–1978. New York, Academic Press. Quarterly.

Continued by: *International Journal of the Sociology of Law*.

Indexed: Psych. Abstr.

939 THE INTERNATIONAL JOURNAL OF CRITICAL SOCIOLOGY. 1– , Sep. 1974– . New Brunswick, N.J., Transaction Periodicals Consortium. Semi-annual.

Issued by the Jaipur Institute of Sociology.

INTERNATIONAL JOURNAL OF ECONOMIC AND SOCIAL HISTORY
See CAHIERS INTERNATIONAUX D'HISTOIRE ÉCONOMIQUE ET SOCIALE

940 THE INTERNATIONAL JOURNAL OF GROUP PSYCHOTHERAPY. v.1– , Apr. 1951– . New York, International Universities Press. Quarterly.
Issued by the American Group Psychotherapy Association.
Indexed: Sage Fam. Stud. Abstr.; Soc. Work Res. Abstr.; Soc. Abstr.

941 INTERNATIONAL JOURNAL OF GROUP TENSIONS. v.1– , Jan/Mar. 1971– . Washington, D.C. Quarterly.
Issued by the International Organization for the Study of Group Tensions.
Indexed: Int. Bibl. Soc.; Int. Pol. Sc. Abstr.

942 INTERNATIONAL JOURNAL OF HUMAN RELATIONS. 1– , June 1976– . Norman, Okla. Annual.
Issued by the Human Relations Association.

943 INTERNATIONAL JOURNAL OF INTERCULTURAL RELATIONS. v.1– , 1977– . New York, Oxford, Pergamon Press; subsequently New Brunswick, Transaction Periodicals Consortium. Quarterly.
Issued by SIETAR, Society for Intercultural Education, Training and Research, and the Department of Sociology, Indiana University.

944 INTERNATIONAL JOURNAL OF OPINION AND ATTITUDE RESEARCH. v.1–5, Mar. 1947–Dec. 1951. Mexico, D.F. Quarterly.

945 INTERNATIONAL JOURNAL OF PSYCHOLOGY. JOURNAL INTERNATIONAL DE PSYCHOLOGIE. v.1– , 1966– . Paris, subsequently Amsterdam, North-Holland Publishing Co. Quarterly.
Issued by the International Union of Psychological Science (Union International de Psychologie). In French or English; summaries in English or French.
Indexed: Soc. Abstr.

946 INTERNATIONAL JOURNAL OF SEXOLOGY. v.1– , 1948– . Bombay. Quarterly.

947 THE INTERNATIONAL JOURNAL OF SOCIAL PSYCHIATRY. v.1– , July 1955– . London, The Avenue Publishing Co. Quarterly, 1955–74; three issues a year, 1977– .
Issued by the Institute of Social Psychiatry.
Indexed: Bull. sig. soc. eth.; Int. Bibl. Soc.; Psych. Abstr.; Soc. Sc. Ind.; Soc. Abstr.; Soc. Work Res. Abstr.; Wom. Stud. Abstr.

948 INTERNATIONAL JOURNAL OF SOCIOLOGY. 1– , spring 1971– . New York, International Arts and Sciences Press. Four issues a year.
Supersedes: *Eastern European Studies in Sociology and Anthropology*. Contains translations of papers published in journals and monographs.
Indexed: Bull. sig. soc. eth.; Int. Bibl. Soc.

949 INTERNATIONAL JOURNAL OF SOCIOLOGY OF THE FAMILY. v.1– , 1971– . Lucknow, subsequently New Dehli, Vicas Publishing House. Semi-annual.
Issued by the Department of Sociology, Northern Illinois University. Subtitle reads: 'Journal of cross-national, cross-cultural and interdisciplinary approach'.
Indexed: Curr. Cont.; SSCI; Soc. Abstr.

INTERNATIONAL JOURNAL OF SOCIOMETRY AND SOCIATRY
See HANDBOOK OF INTERNATIONAL SOCIOMETRY

950 INTERNATIONAL JOURNAL OF THE SOCIOLOGY OF LANGUAGE. 1–14, 1974–1977. The Hague, Mouton. Three issues a year, 1974–76; four issues a year, 1977– .

951 INTERNATIONAL JOURNAL OF THE SOCIOLOGY OF LAW. v. 1– , Feb. 1979– . London, New York, Academic Press. Quarterly.
Continues: *International Journal of Criminology and Penology*.
Indexed: Soc. Abstr.

952 INTERNATIONAL JOURNAL OF URBAN AND REGIONAL RESEARCH. REVUE INTERNATIONALE DE RECHERCHE URBAINE ET RÉGIONALE. v.1– , Mar. 1977– . London, Edward Arnold. Three issues a year.

INTERNATIONAL MIGRATION
See Gt. Britain. Office of Population Censuses and Surveys. INTERNATIONAL MIGRATION

INTERNATIONAL MIGRATION
See Intergovernmental Committee for European Migration. INTERNATIONAL MIGRATION

INTERNATIONAL MIGRATION
See Papua New Guinea. Bureau of Statistics. STATISTICAL BULLETIN. INTERNATIONAL MIGRATION

953 INTERNATIONAL MIGRATION DIGEST. v.1–3, no.1, spring 1964–1966. Staten Island, N.Y.
Issued by the Center of Migration Studies in Staten Island. Superseded by: *International Migration Review*.

954 INTERNATIONAL MIGRATION REVIEW. v.1– , fall 1966– . Staten Island, N.Y. Quarterly.

Issued by the Center of Migration Studies in Staten Island, N.Y., in cooperation with Centro Studi Emigrazione in Rome. Supersedes: *International Migration Digest*. Other title: *IMR. International Migration Review*. Called n.s. in continuation of *International Migration Digest*. Summaries in French, German and Spanish.

Indexed: Bull. sig. soc. eth.; Int. Bibl. Soc.; PHRA; Soc. Abstr.; Urb. Aff. Abstr.

955 INTERNATIONAL MIGRATIONS. v.1– , 1969– . New York, Gordon and Breach. Irreg.

Subseries of: *Demographic Monographs*. Monograph series.

956 INTERNATIONAL POPULATION AND URBAN RESEARCH. PRELIMINARY PAPERS: RESULTS OF CURRENT RESEARCH IN DEMOGRAPHY. 1– , Sep. 1972– . Berkeley, Calif. Irreg.

Issued by the Institute of International Studies, University of California at Berkeley.

957 INTERNATIONAL REGIONAL SCIENCE REVIEW. v.1– , spring 1975– . Philadelphia, Pa. Semi-annual.

Issued by the Regional Science Association and the Department of Regional Sciences, University of Pennsylvania. Supersedes: Regional Science Association. *Papers*. Summaries in French and German.

958 INTERNATIONAL REVIEW FOR SOCIAL HISTORY. v.1–4, 1936–1939. Amsterdam.

Issued by the International Institute for Social Studies. Superseded by: *International Review of Social History*. In various languages.

INTERNATIONAL REVIEW OF COMMUNITY DEVELOPMENT
See COMMUNITY DEVELOPMENT

959 INTERNATIONAL REVIEW OF MODERN SOCIOLOGY. 1— , Mar. 1971– . Lucknow, Lucknow Publishing House; subsequently, New Dehli, Vicas Publishing House. Semi-annual.

Title varies: v.1, 1971–Mar. 1972, *International Review of Sociology*. Subtitle reads: 'Journal of cross-national, cross-cultural and interdisciplinary research'.

Indexed: Curr. Cont.; SSCI; Soc. Abstr.

960 INTERNATIONAL REVIEW OF MUSIC, AESTHETICS AND SOCIOLOGY. v.1, 1971. Zagreb.

Issued by the Institute of Musicology, Zagreb Academy of Music. Continued by: *International Review of the Aesthetics and Sociology of Music*. In English; summaries in Serbo-Croatian.

INTERNATIONAL REVIEW OF PUBLICATIONS IN SOCIOLOGY
See SOCIOLOGICAL ABSTRACTS

961 INTERNATIONAL REVIEW OF SOCIAL HISTORY. v.1– , 1956– . Assen, Van Gorcum. Three issues a year,

Issued by the International Institute for Social History (International Institut voor Sociale Geschiedenis). Supersedes: *International Review for Social History*.

Indexed: Int. Bibl. Soc.; Int. Pol. Sc. Abstr.; Soc. Sc. Hum. Ind.; Soc. Sc. Ind.; Urb. Aff. Abstr.

INTERNATIONAL REVIEW OF SOCIOLOGY
See INTERNATIONAL REVIEW OF MODERN SOCIOLOGY

INTERNATIONAL REVIEW OF SOCIOLOGY
See REVUE INTERNATIONALE DE SOCIOLOGIE

962 INTERNATIONAL REVIEW OF SPORT SOCIOLOGY. v.1– , 1966– . Warsaw, Państowe Wydawnictwo Naukowe. Annual.

Issued by the Committee for Sociology of Sport and Physical Education, Unesco, and International Sociological Association. In English; summaries in French, German and Russian.

Indexed: Bull. sig. soc. eth.; Int. Bibl. Soc.; Soc. Abstr.

963 INTERNATIONAL REVIEW OF THE AESTHETICS AND SOCIOLOGY OF MUSIC. v.2– , June 1971– . Zagreb. Two issues a year.

Issued by the Institute of Musicology, Zagreb Academy of Music with the support of the International Committee of Music. Continues: *International Review of Music, Aesthetics and Sociology*. Includes section 'Bibliography. Sociology of Music'. In English, French, German and Italian; summaries in Serbo-Croatian.

964 INTERNATIONAL SELECTIVE BIBLIOGRAPHY ON LEISURE; EUROPE. 1959/1973– , Prague.

Issued by the European Centre for Leisure and Education.

965 International Seminar on Family Research. RECHERCHES SUR LA FAMILLE. STUDIES ON THE FAMILY. v.1–3, 1954–1958. Tübingen, Mohr.
In English, French and German. In *Schriftenreihe*, Unesco's Institut für Sozialwissenschaften, Köln.

966 INTERNATIONAL SOCIAL DEVELOPMENT REVIEW. no.1– , 1968– . New York. Irreg.
Issued by the Social Development Division, Department of Economic and Social Affairs, United Nations. Supersedes the Department's *Housing, Building & Planning*, and its *Population Bulletin of the United Nations*; also *International Social Service Review*. Subseries of: U.N.(Document/St/SOA/ser.X).
Indexed: Urb. Aff. Abstr.

INTERNATIONAL SOCIAL SCIENCE BULLETIN
See INTERNATIONAL SOCIAL SCIENCE JOURNAL

967 International Social Science Council. SOCIAL SCIENCE INFORMATION. no.1–29, May 1954–Dec. 1961; n.s. v.1– , Apr. 1962– . Paris, Mouton, 1962–73; London, Beverly Hills, Calif., Sage Publications, 1974– . Bimonthly; subsequently quarterly.
Nos. for Oct. 1959–July 1960 issued by the Council's Office on Social Implication of Technological Change. Title varies: 1954/61, *Information*. Title in French: *Information sur les Sciences Sociales*. In English and French.
Indexed: Int. Bibl. Soc.; Soc. Abstr.

968 INTERNATIONAL SOCIAL SCIENCE JOURNAL. v.1– , 1949– . Paris, Unesco. Quarterly.
Title varies: 1949–58, *International Social Science Bulletin*. Issues for 1949 have also title in French. In English. Includes two supplements annually, listing new periodicals that have appeared since the latest editions of *Liste mondiale des périodiques spécialises dans les sciences sociales. World List of Social Science Periodicals* (5th ed. 1980), and *World Index of Social Science Institutions. Répertoire mondiale des institutions des sciences sociales*. Published also in French, *Revue Internationale des Sciences Sociales*, and in Spanish, *Revista Internacional de Ciencias Sociales* whose no.1 is a translation of the *Journal*'s no.3 of 1976. Some articles are translated into Arabic and published under the title *al-Majallah al-duwalīyah lil-'ulūm al-ijtimā'īyah*.
Indexed: Int. Pol. Sc. Abstr.; PAIS; Psych. Abstr.; Sage Fam. Stud. Abstr.; Soc. Sc. Hum. Ind.; Soc. Work Res. Abstr.; Soc. Abstr.; Urb. Aff. Abstr.

International Society for the Sociology of Knowledge. NEWSLETTER
See SOCIOLOGICAL ABSTRACTS

969 International Sociological Association. ISA Bulletin. 1– , 1972– . Montréal. Irreg.
Title varies: 1, 1972, *ISA Newsletter*; 2–9, 1972–75, *Bulletin Newsletter*. Published as a supplement to *Sociological Abstracts*.

INTERNATIONAL STATISTICAL YEARBOOK OF LARGE TOWNS
See ANNUAIRE DE STATISTIQUE INTERNATIONALE DES GRANDES VILLES

INTERNATIONAL STATISTICS OF LARGE TOWNS
See ANNUAIRE DE STATISTIQUE INTERNATIONALE DES GRANDES VILLES

970 INTERNATIONAL STUDIES IN SOCIOLOGY AND SOCIAL ANTHROPOLOGY. 1– , 1963– . Leiden, E. J. Brill. Irreg.
Monograph series; some works are reprints.

971 International Union for the Scientific Study of Population. WORKING PAPER. 1– , 1975– . Liège, Ordina Editions. Irreg.

INTERNATIONAL YEARBOOK FOR THE SOCIOLOGY OF KNOWLEDGE AND RELIGION
See INTERNATIONALES JAHRBUCH FÜR WISSEN- UND RELIGIONSSOZIOLOGIE

972 INTERNATIONAL YEARBOOK OF ORGANIZATION STUDIES. 1979– . London, Routledge & Kegan Paul.

INTERNATIONALE ZEITSCHRIFT FUR KOMUNIKATIONSFORSCHUNG
See COMMUNICATIONS

INTERNATIONALE ZEITSCHRIFT FÜR SOZIOLOGIE UND SOZIALPSYCHOLOGIE
See SOCIOLOGIA INTERNATIONALIS

973 INTERNATIONALES JAHRBUCH FÜR INTERDISZIPLINARE FORSCHUNG. 1– , 1974– . Berlin, New York, W. de Gruyter.
Issued by the Interdisziplinare Forschungsstelle für Anthropologie und Sozialkulturelle Probleme der Wissenschaften an der Universität München. In English, French and German; summaries in these languages.

974 INTERNATIONALES JAHRBUCH FÜR RELIGIONSSOZIOLOGIE. INTERNATIONAL YEARBOOK FOR SOCIOLOGY OF KNOWLEDGE AND RELIGION. v.1–8, 1965–1974. Opladen, Westdeutscher Verlag. Annual.
Continued by: *Internationales Jahrbuch für Wissen- und Religionssoziologie*.
Indexed: Int. Bibl. Soc. Cult. Anth.

975 INTERNATIONALES JAHRBUCH FÜR WISSEN- UND RELIGIONSSOZIOLOGIE. INTERNATIONAL YEARBOOK FOR THE SOCIOLOGY OF KNOWLEDGE AND RELIGION. v.9– , 1975– . Opladen, Westdeutscher Verlag. Annual.
Continues: *Internationales Jahrbuch für Religionssoziologie. International Yearbook for Sociology of Knowledge and Religion*. Includes subseries: *Beiträge zur Wissenssoziologie, Beiträge zur Religionssoziologie (Contributions to the Sociology of Knowledge, Contributions to the Sociology of Religion)*.

976 INTERPERSONAL DEVELOPMENT. v.1– , 1970– . Basel, New York, S. Karger. Quarterly.
Indexed: Soc. Abstr.

977 INTERRACIAL REVIEW. v.1–40, Mar. 1928–spring 1971. New York. Monthly.
Issued by the National Catholic Interracial Federation, called, until Sep. 1932, Federated Colored Catholics of the US; Oct. 1932–June 1933, National Catholic Federation for the Promotion of Better Race Relations. Title varies: 1928–Sep. 1929, *St. Elizabeth Chronicle*. Subtitle reads: 'A journal for Christian democracy'.
Indexed: Cath. Per. Ind.

978 INTISARI. v.1– , 1962– . Singapore. Quarterly.
Issued by the Malaysian Sociological Research Institute. In English.
Indexed: Anth. Ind.

979 INVANDRARE OCH MINORITETER. SCANDINAVIAN MIGRATION AND ETHNIC MINORITY REVIEW. v.3– , 1976– . Stockholm. Bimonthly.
Continues: *Nordisk Minoritetsforskning*.

INVENTORY AND ANALYSIS OF FEDERAL POPULATION RESEARCH
See United States. Interagency Committee on Population Research. INVENTORY AND ANALYSIS OF FEDERAL POPULATION RESEARCH

INVENTORY OF FEDERAL POPULATION RESEARCH
See United States. Interagency Committee on Population Research. INVENTORY AND ANALYSIS OF FEDERAL POPULATION RESEARCH

980 INVENTORY OF MARRIAGE AND FAMILY LITERATURE. v.1– , 1900/1964– . St. Paul, Minn. (publ. 1967), subsequently Beverly Hills, Calif., Sage Publications, beginning with v.3. Annual, beginning with v.6.
Issued by the Inventory of Marriage and Family Project, University of Minnesota. Title varies: v.1–2, 1900/1964–1965/1972, *International Bibliography of Research in Marriage and the Family*. Vol.3 covers 1973/74; v.4 covers 1975/76; v.5, 1977/78; v.6, 1979.

981 INVENTORY OF POPULATION PROJECTS IN DEVELOPING COUNTRIES AROUND THE WORLD. 1973/1974– . New York. Annual.
Issued by the Fund for Population Activities, United Nations.

INVENTORY OF RESEARCH IN RACIAL AND CULTURAL RELATIONS. BULLETIN
See Chicago. University. Commitee on Education, Training and Research in Race Relations. INVENTORY OF RESEARCH IN RACIAL AND CULTURAL RELATIONS. BULLETIN

AN INVENTORY OF SOCIAL AND ECONOMIC RESEARCH
See Chicago. University. Center for Health Administration Studies. AN INVENTORY OF SOCIAL AND ECONOMIC RESEARCH

982 INVESTIGACIÓNES EN SOCIOLOGIA. v.1–4, Jan/June 1962–1965. Mendoza. Semiannual.
Issued by the Instituto de Sociologia, Universidad de Cuyo. In Spanish; summaries in English, French and Spanish.

983 Iowa. State University of Science and Technology, Ames. Department of Economics and Sociology. RURAL SOCIOLOGY REPORT. no.1–59, 1958–1967. Ames. Irreg.
Series of papers.

984 Iowa University. STUDIES IN THE SOCIAL SCIENCES. v.1–11, 1899–1943. Iowa City, University Press. Irreg.
Title varies: v.1–4, *Studies in Sociology, Economics, Politics and History*.

985 IPARGAZDASÁG. 1947– . Budapest. Müszaki es Könyvkiadó. Monthly.
Issued by the Müszaki es Természettudományi Egyesületek Szövetsége.
In Hungarian.

986 IRANIAN STUDIES. v.1– , 1968– . Chestnut Hill, Boston College, Mass. Quarterly.
Issued by the Society for Iranian Studies.

IRISH JOURNAL OF SOCIOLOGY
See SOCIAL STUDIES; IRISH JOURNAL OF SOCIOLOGY

987 Irkutsk, Siberia. Irkutskii gosudarstvennyi pedagogicheskii Institut innostrannykh iazykov. Kafedra istorii KPSS i politicheskoi ekonomii. UCHENYE ZAPISKI. Irkutsk.
In Russian.

988 IŞ VE DÜSÜNCE. v.1– , 1959– . Istanbul. Monthly.
Issued by the Société des Recherches Sociologiques et Culturelles de la Turquie. In Turkish.

989 ISSUES AND TRENDS IN SOCIOLOGY. 1972– . New York. Irreg.
Issued by the American Sociological Association.

990 ISSUES IN CANADIAN SOCIAL POLICY. no.1–3, 1974. Ottawa.
Issued by the Science Council of Canada.

991 ISSUES IN CRIMINOLOGY. v.1–10, no.1, fall 1965–spring 1975. Berkeley, Calif. Two issues a year.
Issued by the School of Criminology, University of California, Berkeley.
Indexed: Crime Del. Lit.; Soc. Sc. Ind.; Soc. Abstr.

992 ISSUES IN INDUSTRIAL SOCIETY. v.1–2, no.1, 1969–1970. Ithaca, N.Y. Three issues a year.
Issued by the New York School of Industrial Relations. Supersedes: *ILR Research*.

993 Istituto Luigi Sturzo. BOLLETINO DI SOCIOLOGIA. v.1–12?, May/June 1956–1967. Milano, Giuffré. Quarterly.
Superseded by: *Sociologia*. In Italian.

994 Istituto Nazionale di Sociologia Rurale. COLLANA DELL'ISTITUTO DI SOCIOLOGIA RURALE. 1– , 1974– . Milano, F. Angeli. Irreg.
Includes subseries *Collana Insor*. In Italian.
Monograph series.

995 Italy. Istituto Centrale di Statistica. POPOLAZIONE E MOVIMENTO ANAGRAFICO DEI COMUNI. 1966– . Roma. Annual.
In Italian.

IZVESTIIA
See Akademiia nauk Tadziskoi S.S.R. Otdelenie obshchestvennykh nauk. IZVESTIIA

IZVESTIIA. VI SERIIA. OTDELENIE HUMANITARNYKH NAUK
See Akademiia nauk S.S.S.R. IZVESTIIA. OTDELENIE OBSHCHESTVENNYKH NAUK

IZVESTIIA. VII SERIIA. OTDELENIE OBSHCHESTVENNYKH NAUK
See Akademiia nauk S.S.S.R. IZVESTIIA. OTDELENIE OBSHCHESTVENNYKH NAUK

IZVESTIIA. OTDELENIE OBSHCHESTVENNYKH NAUK
See Akademiia nauk S.S.S.R. IZVESTIIA. OTDELENIE OBSHCHESTVENNYKH NAUK

IZVESTIIA. SERIIA ISTORII, ARKHEOLOGII I ETNOGRAFII
See Akademiia nauk Kazakhskoi S.S.R. IZVESTIIA. SERIIA OBSHCHESTVENNYKH NAUK

IZVESTIIA. SERIIA ISTORII, EKONOMIKI, PRAVA
See Akademiia nauk Kazakhskoi S.S.R. IZVESTIIA. SERIIA OBSHCHESTVENNYKH NAUK

IZVESTIIA. SERIIA OBSHCHESTVENNYKH NAUK
See Akademiia nauk Armianskoi S.S.R. IZVESTIIA. SERIIA OBSHCHESTVENNYKH NAUK

IZVESTIIA. SERIIA OBSHCHESTVENNYKH NAUK
See Akademiia nauk Estonskoi S.S.R. IZVESTIIA. SERIIA OBSHCHESTVENNYKH NAUK

IZVESTIIA. SERIIA OBSHCHESTVENNYKH NAUK
See Akademiia nauk Kazakhskoi S.S.R. IZVESTIIA. SERIIA OBSHCHESTVENNYKH NAUK

IZVESTIIA. SERIIA OBSHCHESTVENNYKH NAUK
See Akademiia nauk Kirgizskoi S.S.R. IZVESTIIA. SERIIA OBSHCHESTVENNYKH NAUK

IZVESTIIA. SERIIA OBSHCHESTVENNYKH NAUK
See Akademiia nauk Moldavskoi S.S.R. IZVESTIIA. SERIIA OBSHCHESTVENNYKH NAUK

IZVESTIIA. SERIIA OBSHCHESTVENNYKH NAUK
See Akademiia nauk S.S.S.R. Sibirskoe otdelenie. IZVESTIIA. SERIIA OBSHCHESTVENNYKH NAUK

IZVESTIIA. SERIIA OBSHCHESTVENNYKH NAUK
See Severo-Kavkazskii nauchnyi tsentr vyshshei shkoly. IZVESTIIA. SERIIA OBSHCHESTVENNYKH NAUK

IZVESTIIA AKADEMII NAUK TURKMENSKOI SSR
See Akademiia nauk Turkmenskoi S.S.R. IZVESTIIA. SERIIA OBSHCHESTVENNYKH NAUK

IZVESTIIA TURKMENSKOGO FILIALA AKADEMII NAUK SSSR
See Akademiia nauk Turkmenskoi S.S.R. IZVESTIIA. SERIIA OBSHCHESTVENNYKH NAUK

JPMS JOURNAL OF POLITICAL & MILITARY SOCIOLOGY
See JOURNAL OF POLITICAL & MILITARY SOCIOLOGY

JPSS JOURNAL OF PERSONALITY AND SOCIAL SYSTEMS
See JOURNAL OF PERSONALITY AND SOCIAL SYSTEMS

JAARSVERSLAG
See Center for Intergroup Studies. ANNUAL REPORT

JAHRBUCH
See Österreichische Gesellschaft für Soziologie. JAHRBUCH

JAHRBUCH DER ÖFFENTLICHEN MEINUNG
See ALLENSBACHER JAHRBUCH DER DEMOSKOPIE

JAHRBUCH DER SOZIALSTATISTIK
See SOZIALSTATISTIKS JAHRBUCH. STATISTIQUES SOCIALES; ANNUAIRE

996 JAHRBUCH FÜR RECHTSSOZIOLOGIE UND RECHTSTHEORIE. 1– , 1970– . Bielefeld, Bertelsmann Universitäts Verlag. Irreg.
Monograph series.

997 JAHRBUCH FÜR SOZIALWISSENSCHAFT UND SOZIALPOLITIK. 1–2, 1879–1881. Zürich-Oberstrasse, F. Kolber.

998 JAHRBUCH FÜR SOZIOLOGIE: EINE INTERNATIONALE SAMMLUNG. v.1–3, 1925–1927. Karlsruhe, G. Braun.

999 JAHRBUCH FÜR SOZIOLOGIE UND SOZIALPOLITIK. 1980– . Berlin, Akademie Verlag. Annual.
Issued by the Institut für Soziologie und Sozialpolitik, Akademie der Wissenschaften der DDR. Summaries in English, French and Russian.

1000 Japan. Kōseishō. Daijin Kambō. Tōkai Jōhūbu. SAIKIN NO JINKO DOTAI. no.10, 1972– . Tokyo. Annual.
Continues: Japan. Kōseishō. Daijin Kambō. *Tōkei Chōsubu.* In Japanese.

1001 Japan. Naikaku Tōkeikyoku. MOUVEMENT DE LA POPULATION DE L'EMPIRE DU JAPON. 1899–1918. Tokyo.
Superseded by its *Résumé Statistique du Mouvement de la Population de l'Empire du Japon.* In Japanese and French.

1002 Japan. Naikaku Tōkeikyoku. RÉSUMÉ STATISTIQUE DU MOUVEMENT DE LA POPULATION DE L'EMPIRE DU JAPON. 1–?, 1919–?. Tokyo. Annual.
Supersedes its *Mouvement de la Population de l'Empire du Japon.* In Japanese and French. Ceased publication.

JAPAN JOURNAL OF EDUCATIONAL SOCIOLOGY
See KYOIKU SHAKAI-GAKU KENKYU

JAPANESE PERIODICAL INDEX. HUMANITIES AND SOCIAL SCIENCES SECTION
See ZASSHI KIJI SAKUIN. JIMBUN SHAKAIHEN

JAPANESE SOCIOLOGICAL REVIEW
See SHAKAIGAKU HYORON

1003 JAPANESE WOMEN. v.1–3, Jan. 1938–1940. Tokyo. Bimonthly.
Issued by the Woman's Suffrage League of Japan.

1004 Java Tengah, Indonesia. Kantor Sensus dan Statistik. INDIKATOR SOSIAL JAVA TENGAH. 1973?– . Semarang.

1005 JEN YÜ SHE HUI. MAN & SOCIETY. 1– , Apr. 1973– . Taipei, Shih Chien Wen Wu Kung Ying She Tsung Ching Hsiao. Bimonthly.
In Chinese.

1006 JERNAL ANTROPOLOJI DAN SOSIOLOJI. no.1– , 1971/1972– . Kuala Lumpur. Annual.
Issued by the Persatuan Kajimanusia dan Kajimasharakat, Universiti Kebangsaan Malaysia. In Malay and English.

1007 Jerusalem. Hebrew University. Department of Sociology. RESEARCH REPORT. 1st–3rd, 1949–1959/1963. Jerusalem. Irreg.
Superseded by the University's *Research Report; Humanities, Social Sciences and Law*.

1008 Jerusalem. Hebrew University. Institute of Urban and Regional Studies. PAPERS IN SOCIOLOGY. 1972– . Jerusalem. Irreg.
Continues: *Jerusalem Urban Studies*.
Monograph series.

1009 JERUSALEM STUDIES ON ASIA. MODERNIZATION SERIES. 1, 1973. Jerusalem.
Issued by the Institute of Asian and African Studies.

1010 JERUSALEM URBAN STUDIES. 1966–1977?. Jerusalem. Irreg.
Issued by the Institute of Urban and Regional Studies, Hebrew University. Continued by the Institute's *Papers in Sociology*. Some issues are monographs.

1011 JEWISH AFFAIRS. v.1– , 1946– . Johannesburg, Sheffield House. Monthly.
Issued by the South African Jewish Board of Deputies.

JEWISH COMMUNITY SERIES
See CANADIAN JEWISH POPULATION STUDIES. CANADIAN JEWISH COMMUNITY SERIES

1012 THE JEWISH JOURNAL OF SOCIOLOGY. v.1– , Apr. 1959– . London, Heineman. Semi-annual.
Published on behalf of the World Jewish Congress. Summaries in French and Hebrew.
Indexed: Bull. sig. soc. eth.; Int. Bibl. Soc.; Int. Pol. Sc. Abstr.; PAIS; SSCI; Soc. Abstr.

1013 JEWISH POPULATION STUDIES. 1971– . Jerusalem. Irreg.
Issued by the Institute of Contemporary Jewry, Hebrew University.
Monograph series.

1014 JEWISH SOCIAL STUDIES. v.1– , Jan. 1939– . New York. Quarterly.
Issued by the Conference on Jewish Social Studies. Summaries in French and Hebrew. Subtitle reads: 'Quarterly journal devoted to contemporary and historical aspects of Jewish life'. Indexes: v.1–15, 1939–53, in v.15.
Indexed: Int. Bibl. Soc.; PAIS; SSCI; Soc. Sc. Hum. Ind.; Soc. Sc. Ind.; Soc. Abstr.

1015 JIMBUN-CHIRI. THE HUMAN GEOGRAPHY. v.1– , 1948– . Kyoto, Japan Publications Trading Co. Bimonthly.
Issued by the Jimbun-Chiri Gakkai (Society of Human Geography) and Kyoto Daigaku Bungaku (Institute of Geography, Kyoto University). In Japanese; summaries in English. Table of contents in Japanese and English.

1016 JOHNS HOPKINS SERIES IN INTEGRATION AND COMMUNITY BUILDING IN EASTERN EUROPE. 1, 1968–1973. Baltimore, Md., Johns Hopkins University Press. Irreg. Monograph series; some volumes not numbered.

JOINT NEWSLETTER ON INTERGROUP RELATIONS
See RESEARCH ANNUAL ON INTERGROUP RELATIONS

1017 JORNAL BRASILEIRO DE SOCIOLOGIA. 1– , 1958– . Recife.
Issued by the Sociedade Brasileira de Sociologia, Faculdade de Filosofia, Universidade Federal de Pernambuco. Supersedes: *Revista Pernambucana de Sociologia*.

JOURNAL
See American Planning Association. JOURNAL

JOURNAL
See Australian Planning Institute. JOURNAL

JOURNAL
See Community Development Society. JOURNAL

JOURNAL
See Hong Kong. Chinese University. JOURNAL

JOURNAL
See Hong Kong. Institute of Social Research. JOURNAL

JOURNAL
See Papua and New Guinea Society. JOURNAL

JOURNAL
See Royal Asiatic Society. Ceylon Branch. JOURNAL

JOURNAL
See Singapore. University. Social Science Society. JOURNAL

LE JOURNAL CANADIEN DES ÉTUDES AFRICAINES
See REVUE CANADIENNE DES ÉTUDES AFRICAINES

A JOURNAL FOR EMPIRICAL SOCIOLOGY, SOCIAL ANTHROPOLOGY, AND ETHNIC RESEARCH
See SOCIOLOGUS; ZEITSCHRIFT FÜR EMPIRISCHE SOZIOLOGIE, SOZIALPSYCHOLOGIE UND ETHNOPSYCHOLOGISCHE FORSCHUNG

JOURNAL FOR SOCIAL RESEARCH
See TYDSKRIF VIR MAATSKAPLIKE NOVORSING.

1018 JOURNAL FOR THE THEORY OF SOCIAL BEHAVIOUR. v.1– , 1971– . Oxford, Blackwell. Semi-annual; beginning with v.8, three issues a year.
Indexed: Int. Pol. Sc. Abstr.; Soc. Abstr.; Urb. Aff. Abstr.

JOURNAL INTERNATIONAL DE PSYCHOLOGIE
See INTERNATIONAL JOURNAL OF PSYCHOLOGY

1019 JOURNAL OF AFRICAN AND ASIAN STUDIES. v.1– , 1967– . Delhi, Om Prakash Goel et Kay-Kay Printers. Semi-annual.
Issued by the Department of African Studies, University of Delhi and the Association for the Study of African and Asian Affairs.
Indexed: Int. Bibl. Soc.

1020 JOURNAL OF AFRICAN STUDIES. 1— , spring 1974– . Los Angeles, Calif., California University Press. Quarterly.
Issued by the African Studies Center, University of California at Los Angeles.

1021 THE JOURNAL OF AFRO-AMERICAN ISSUES. v.1–5, no.3, summer 1972–1977. Columbus, Ohio. Quarterly.
Issued by the Educational and Community Associates. Superseded by: *Journal of African-Afro-American Affairs.*

1022 JOURNAL OF APPLIED BEHAVIORAL SCIENCE. v.1– , Jan/Mar. 1965– . Washington, D.C., Scripts Publications Co. Quarterly, 1965–70; bimonthly.
Issued by the National Training Laboratories and National Education Association.
Indexed: Bull. sig. soc. eth.; Crime Del. Lit.; Int. Bibl. Soc.; Int. Pol. Sc. Abstr.; PHRA; Psych. Abstr.; Soc. Sc. Ind.; Soc. Abstr.; Soc. Work. Res. Abstr.

1023 JOURNAL OF APPLIED COMMUNICATIONS RESEARCH. v.1– , winter/spring 1973– . Mississippi State, Miss. Semi-annual.
Indexes: v.1–6, in v.7, no.1.
Indexed: Soc. Abstr.

JOURNAL OF APPLIED SOCIOLOGY
See SOCIOLOGY AND SOCIAL RESEARCH

1024 JOURNAL OF ASIAN AND AFRICAN STUDIES. v.1– , Jan. 1966– . Leiden, E. J. Brill. Quarterly; some combined issues.
Issued by the Department of Sociology, York University, Toronto.
Indexed: Abstr. Anth.; Bull. sig. soc. eth.; Int. Bibl. Soc.; Int. Pol. Sc. Abstr.; SSCI; Soc. Sc. Ind.; Soc. Abstr.

1025 JOURNAL OF ASIAN STUDIES. v.1– , Nov. 1941– . Ann Arbor, Mich. Quarterly, 1941–54; five times a year.
Issued by the Association for Asian Studies (Called Far Eastern Association 1941–Feb. 1957). Title varies: 1941—May 1956, *The Far Eastern Quarterly*. Includes 'Bibliography of Asian Studies', formerly 'Far Eastern Bibliography'.
Indexed: Bull. sig. soc. eth.; Int. Pol. Sc. Abstr.; PAIS; Soc. Sc. Hum. Ind.; Soc. Abstr.

1026 JOURNAL OF BIOSOCIAL SCIENCE. v.1– . Jan. 1969– . Oxford, Blackwell Scientific Publications. Four issues a year.
Issued by the Galton Foundation. Supersedes: *The Eugenics Review*. Includes *Supplement*, listed separately.
Indexed: Int. Bibl. Soc.; PAIS; Soc. Abstr.; Urb. Aff. Abstr.

1027 JOURNAL OF BIOSOCIAL SCIENCE. SUPPLEMENT. no.1– , July 1969– . Oxford, Blackwell Scientific Publications. Irreg.

1028 JOURNAL OF BLACK PSYCHOLOGY. 1– , Aug. 1974– . Cincinnati, Ohio. Semi-annual.
Issued by the National Association of Black Psychologists.
Indexed: Soc. Abstr.

1029 JOURNAL OF BLACK STUDIES. v.1– , Sep. 1970– . Beverly Hills, Calif., Sage Publications. Quarterly.
Issued by the Afro-American Center, University of California at Los Angeles.

Indexed: Curr. Cont.; Int. Bibl. Soc.; Int. Pol. Sc. Abstr.; PAIS; PHRA; SSCI; Sage Fam. Stud. Abstr.; Sage Urb. Abstr.; Soc. Sc. Ind.; Soc. Work Res. Abstr.; Soc. Abstr.; Urb. Aff. Abstr.

1030 JOURNAL OF CLINICAL PSYCHOLOGY. v.1– , 1945– . Brandon, Vt., Clinical Psychology Publishing Co. Quarterly.

Some issues are thematic, numbered as regular issues and also as monographs, titled *Monograph Supplement* and also, beginning with no.44, *Archives of the Behavioral Sciences*.

Indexed: Soc. Abstr.; Soc. Work Res. Abstr.

1031 THE JOURNAL OF COMMUNICATION. v.1– , May 1951– . Jacksonville, Fla., subsequently Lawrence, Kansas, Allen Press. Semiannual, 1951–53; quarterly.

Issued by the National Society for the Study of Communication, 1951–73; The Annenberg School of Communications, University of Pennsylvania, 1974– . Subtitle reads: 'A publication devoted to the interdisciplinary approach to the study of communication in human relations'.

Indexed: Int. Bibl. Soc.; Sage Fam. Stud. Abstr.; Soc. Abstr.

1032 JOURNAL OF COMPARATIVE ADMINISTRATION. v.1–5, May 1969–1974. Beverly Hills, Calif., Sage Publications. Quarterly.

Issued in cooperation with the Comparative Administration Group, American Society for Public Administration. Continued by: *Administration and Society*.

Indexed: Int. Bibl. Soc.; Soc. Abstr.

1033 THE JOURNAL OF COMPARATIVE CULTURES. v.1– , fall 1972– . Cypress, Calif. Quarterly.

Issued by the National Bilingual Education Association.

1034 JOURNAL OF COMPARATIVE FAMILY STUDIES. v.1– , autumn 1970– . Calgary, Canada. Three issues a year.

Issued by the Department of Sociology and Anthropology, The University of Calgary.

Indexed: Abstr. Anth.; Int. Bibl. Soc.; Psych. Abstr.; Sage Fam. Stud. Abstr.; Soc. Abstr.

1035 JOURNAL OF COMPARATIVE SOCIOLOGY. no.1– , 1973– . Ottawa. Annual.

Issued by the Sociological Research Centre, sponsored by the MRW Management Training and Productivity Motivation, Ltd.

Indexed: Soc. Abstr.

1036 THE JOURNAL OF CONFLICT RESOLUTION. v.1– , Mar. 1957– . Lawrence, Kansas, Allen Press. Quarterly.

Issued by the Department of Journalism, University of Michigan, 1957–63, and the Center for Research on Conflict Resolution, University of Michigan, 1964– . Title varies: Mar–June, 1957, *Conflict Resolution*. Subtitle reads: 'A quarterly for research related to war and peace'.

Indexed: Int. Bibl. Soc.; Int. Pol. Sc. Abstr.; PAIS; Soc. Sc. Ind.; Soc. Abstr.; Soc. Work Res. Abstr.

1037 JOURNAL OF CROSS-CULTURAL PSYCHOLOGY. v.1– , Mar. 1970– . Bellingham, Wash. Quarterly.

Issued by the Center for Cross-Cultural Research, Department of Psychology, Western Washington State College. Summaries in English, French and German.

Indexed: Int. Bibl. Soc.; Soc. Abstr.; Urb. Aff. Abstr.

1038 JOURNAL OF DEVELOPING AREAS. v.1– , Oct. 1966– . Macomb, Ill., Western Illinois University Press. Quarterly.

Includes 'Bibliography of Periodicals and Monographs'. In English and French.

Indexed: Int. Bibl. Soc.; Int. Pol. Sc. Abstr.; PAIS; SSCI; Soc. Sc. Ind.; Soc. Abstr.

1039 THE JOURNAL OF DEVELOPMENT STUDIES. v.1– , Oct. 1964– . London, F. Cass. Quarterly.

Issued by the School of Oriental and African Studies, University of London.

Indexed: Afr. Abstr.; Brit. Hum. Ind.; Int. Bibl. Soc.; Int. Pol. Sc. Abstr.; PAIS; SSCI; Sage Fam. Stud. Abstr.; Soc. Sc. Ind.; Soc. Abstr.

1040 JOURNAL OF DIVORCE. v.1– , fall 1977– . New York, Haworth Press. Quarterly.

Indexed: Sage Fam. Stud. Abstr.; Soc. Abstr.

1041 JOURNAL OF EAST ASIATIC STUDIES. v.1– , 1951– . Manila. Quarterly.

Issued by the University of Manila.

Indexed: Anth. Ind.; Soc. Abstr.

1042 THE JOURNAL OF ECONOMIC ABSTRACTS. v.1– , Jan. 1963– . Cambridge, Mass. Quarterly.

Issued by the American Economic Association.

JOURNAL OF ECONOMIC AND SOCIAL GEOGRAPHY
See TIJDSCJRIFT VOOR ECONOMISCH EN SOCIALE GEOGRAFIE

THE JOURNAL OF EDUCATIONAL SOCIOLOGY
See SOCIOLOGY OF EDUCATION

1043 THE JOURNAL OF ETHNIC STUDIES. v.1– , spring 1973– . Bellingham, Wash. Quarterly.
Issued by the College of Ethnic Studies, Western Washington University. Subtitle reads: 'A publication of interdisciplinary scholarship, opinion, and creative expression'.
Indexed: Eth. Stud. Bibl.; Soc. Abstr.

JOURNAL OF EWHA SOCIOLOGY
See SAHOEHAK YON'GU

1044 JOURNAL OF EXPERIMENTAL SOCIAL PSYCHOLOGY. v.1– , Jan. 1965– . New York, Academic Press. Four issues a year.
Issued by the Department of Psychology, University of North Carolina.
Indexed: Int. Bibl. Soc.; Int. Pol. Sc. Abstr.; Soc. Sc. Ind.; Soc. Abstr.

1045 JOURNAL OF EXPERIMENTAL SOCIAL PSYCHOLOGY. SUPPLEMENT. no.1– , Sep. 1966– . New York, Academic Press. Irreg.

1046 JOURNAL OF FAMILY HISTORY. v.1– , 1976– . Minneapolis, Minn. quarterly.
Issued by the National Council on Family Relations. Supersedes: *Family in Historical Perspective*. Subtitle reads: 'Studies of family, kinship and demography'.
Indexed: Sage Fam. Stud. Abstr.; Soc. Abstr.

1047 JOURNAL OF FAMILY ISSUES. v.1– , Mar. 1980– . Beverly Hills, Calif., Sage Publications. Quarterly.
Sponsored by the National Council on Family Relations. Two issues a year are thematic.
Indexed: Sage Fam. Stud. Abstr.

1048 JOURNAL OF FAMILY WELFARE: PERSONAL, MARITAL AND SOCIOLOGICAL. v.1– , Nov. 1954– . Bombay. Quarterly.
Issued by the Family Planning Association of India.
Indexed: Soc. Abstr.

JOURNAL OF HEALTH AND HUMAN BEHAVIOR
See JOURNAL OF HEALTH AND SOCIAL BEHAVIOR

1049 JOURNAL OF HEALTH AND SOCIAL BEHAVIOR. v.1– , 1960– . Fort Worth, subsequently Washington, D.C. Originally quarterly; presently annual.
Issued originally by the Leo Potishman Foundation at Texas, later by the American Sociological Association, and Heller Graduate School, Brandeis University. Title varies: v.1–7, 1960–66, *Journal of Health and Human Behavior*.
Indexed: Bull. sig. soc. eth.; Int. Bibl. Soc.; Psych. Abstr.; SSCI; Sage Fam. Stud. Abstr.; Soc. Sc. Ind.; Soc. Abstr.; Soc. Work Res. Abstr.; Wom. Stud. Abstr.

1050 JOURNAL OF HISTORY AND THE SOCIAL SCIENCES. v.1–3, no.1, 1967–1970. Portland, Oreg. Irreg.
Issued by the Division of History and Social Sciences, Reed College.
Indexed: Soc. Abstr.

1051 JOURNAL OF HUMAN ECOLOGY. v.1–3, no.1, Mar. 1951–1953. Crystal Lane, Ill., Weather Forecasts. Quarterly.
Issued by the Weather Science Foundation.

1052 JOURNAL OF HUMAN RELATIONS. v.1–21, spring 1952–1973. Wilberforce, Ohio. Quarterly.
Issued by the Central State College.
Indexed: Abstr. Soc. Work; Curr. Cont.; Peace Res. Abstr. J.; Psych. Abstr.; SSCI; Soc. Abstr.

1053 THE JOURNAL OF INDUSTRIAL RELATIONS. v.1– , Apr. 1959– . Sydney, Sydney University Press. Semi-annual, 1959–63; three issues a year, 1964– .
Issued by the Industrial Relations Society, 1959–July 1964; Industrial Relations Society of Australia, 1964–. Author index to v.3–4, 1961–62, in v.3–4.
Indexed: Int. Bibl. Soc.; Soc. Abstr.

1054 JOURNAL OF INTERDISCIPLINARY HISTORY. v.1– , autumn 1970– . Cambridge, Mass., M.I.T. Press. Four issues a year.
Issued by the School of Humanities and Social Science, Massachusetts Institute of Technology.
Indexed: Int. Bibl. Soc.; Soc. Abstr.

1055 JOURNAL OF INTERDISCIPLINARY MODELING AND SIMULATION. 1978– . New York, Marcel Dekker. Quarterly.
Issued by the University of Pittsburgh.

1056 THE JOURNAL OF INTERGROUP RELATIONS. v.1–5, no.1, 1959/1960–1966; [n.s.] v.1– , fall 1970– . New York. Quarterly.
Supersedes a publication with the same title. v.1, no.6, Feb. 1960 called *Special Report*. Not published, fall 1966–fall 1970.
Indexed: Soc. Abstr.

1057 JOURNAL OF LEGAL AND POLITICAL SOCIOLOGY. v.1–4, no.3/4, Oct. 1942–summer 1946/winter 1946. New York, International University Press. Semi-annual.

1058 JOURNAL OF MARRIAGE AND THE FAMILY. v.1– , Jan. 1939– . Menasha, Wis. Quarterly.

Issued by the National Council on Family Relations. Title varies: 1939–Nov. 1941, *Living*; Feb. 1942–Nov. 1963, *Marriage and Family Living*. Index to v.1–14, 1939–52 in v.14.

Indexed: APAIS; Bull. sig. soc. eth.; Curr. Cont.; Int. Bibl. Soc.; Psych. Abstr.; Sage Fam. Stud. Abstr.; Soc. Sc. Hum. Ind.; Soc. Sc. Ind.; Soc. Abstr.; Soc. Work Res. Abstr.; Wom. Stud. Abstr.

1059 JOURNAL OF MATHEMATICAL SOCIOLOGY. v.1– , Jan. 1971– . New York, Gordon and Breach Science Publishers. Semiannual.

Issued by the Department of Sociology, University of Pittsburgh.

Indexed: Int. Bibl. Soc.; Psych. Abstr.; SSCI; Soc. Abstr.

JOURNAL OF MENTAL HEALTH
See BRITISH JOURNAL OF PSYCHIATRY

1060 THE JOURNAL OF MODERN AFRICAN STUDIES. v.1– , 1963– . London, New York, Cambridge University Press. Quarterly.

Issued by the University College, Dar-es-Salaam. Subtitle reads: 'A quarterly survey of politics, economics and related topics in contemporary Africa'.

Indexed: Afr. Abstr.; Brit. Hum. Ind.; Bull. sig. soc. eth.; Int. Bibl. Soc.; Sage Fam. Stud. Abstr.; Soc. Sc. Hum. Ind.; Soc. Sc. Ind.; Soc. Abstr.; Wom. Stud. Abstr.

1061 JOURNAL OF PALESTINE STUDIES. v.1– , 1971– . Beirut, Quarterly.

Issued by the Institute of Palestine Studies, and Kuwait University. Subtitle reads: 'A quarterly on Palestinian affairs and the Arab-Israeli conflict'.

Indexed: Int. Bibl. Soc.; Int. Pol. Sc. Abstr.; Soc. Abstr.

1062 JOURNAL OF PEACE RESEARCH. v.1– , 1964– . Oslo, Universitetsforlaget. Monthly.

Issued by the Peace Research Institute, Institute for Social Research, Oslo. Summaries in English and Russian.

Indexed: Int. Bibl. Soc.; Peace Res. Abstr. J.; Psych. Abstr.; Soc. Sc. Ind.; Soc. Abstr.; Wom. Stud. Abstr.

1063 JOURNAL OF PERSONALITY. v.1– , Sep. Oct. 1973– . London, F. Cass. Quarterly.

Issued by the Centre of International Area Studies, University of London.

Indexed: Int. Bibl. Soc.; Int. Pol. Sc. Abstr.

1064 JOURNAL OF PERSONALITY. v.1– , Sep. 1932– . Durham, N.C., Duke University Press. Quarterly.

Title varies: 1932–Mar/June 1945, *Character and Personality*.

Indexed: Bull. sig. soc. eth.; Psych. Abstr.; Soc. Abstr.; Soc. Work Res. Abstr.; Wom. Stud. Abstr.

1065 JOURNAL OF PERSONALITY AND SOCIAL PSYCHOLOGY. v.1– , Jan. 1965– . Washington, D.C. Monthly, forming two volumes a year.

Issued by the American Psychological Association. Supersedes: *Journal of Abnormal and Social Psychology*. Includes *Monograph Supplement*.

Indexed: Bull. sig. soc. eth.; Int. Pol. Sc. Abstr.; PAIS; SSCI; Psych. Abstr.; Sage Fam. Stud. Abstr.; Soc. Sc. Ind.; Soc. Abstr.; Soc. Work Res. Abstr.; Wom. Stud. Abstr.

1066 JOURNAL OF PERSONALITY AND SOCIAL SYSTEMS. 1– , Jan. 1977– . Washington, D.C.

Issued by the A. K. Rice Institute. Other title: *JPSS Journal of Personality and Social Systems*.

1067 JOURNAL OF POLITICAL AND MILITARY SOCIOLOGY. v.1–2, 1973–1974. DeKalb, Ill. Semi-annual.

Issued by the Department of Sociology, Northern Illinois University. Other title: *JPMS Journal of Political and Military Sociology*.

Indexed: Int. Bibl. Soc.; Int. Pol. Sc. Abstr.; PAIS; Soc. Sc. Hum. Ind.; SSCI; Soc. Abstr.

1068 JOURNAL OF POLITICS. v.1– , Feb. 1939– . Gainesville, Fla. Quarterly.

Issued by the Southern Political Science Association, and the University of Florida.

Indexed: Int. Bibl. Soc.; Int. Pol. Sc. Abstr.; Soc. Sc. Hum. Ind.; Soc. Sc. Ind.; Soc. Abstr.

1069 JOURNAL OF POPULATION. v.1–2, spring 1978–1979. New York, Human Sciences Press. Quarterly.

Issued by the Division of Population and Environmental Psychology, American Psychological Association. Subtitle reads: 'Behavioral, social and environmental issues'. Continued by: *Population and Environment*.

Indexed: Soc. Abstr.

1070 JOURNAL OF POPULATION RESEARCH. 1– , July/Dec. 1974– . New Dehli.

Issued by the National Institute of Family Planning.

1071 JOURNAL OF POPULATION STUDIES. 1– , spring 1976– . Islamabad. Quarterly.
Issued by the Pakistan Population Planning Council.

JOURNAL OF POPULATION STUDIES
See IN'GU MUNJE NONJIP

JOURNAL OF RACIAL AFFAIRS
See TYDSKRIF VIR RASSE; AANGELEENTHEDE

A JOURNAL OF RADICAL SOCIOLOGY
See HUMAN FACTOR; A JOURNAL OF RADICAL SOCIOLOGY

1072 JOURNAL OF REGIONAL SCIENCE. v.1– , 1958– . Philadelphia, Pa. Semi-annual.
Issued by the Regional Science Research Institute, and the Department of Regional Science, Wharton School, University of Pennsylvania.
Indexed: Int. Bibl. Soc.; PHRA; Soc. Abstr.

1073 JOURNAL OF RELIGIOUS PSYCHOLOGY, INCLUDING ITS ANTHROPOLOGICAL AND SOCIOLOGICAL ASPECTS. v.1–7, May 1904–Dec. 1915. Worcester, Mass., L.N. Wilson. Three issues a year, 1904–11; quarterly, 1912–15.
Title varies: 1904–July 1911, *The American Journal of Religious Psychology and Education*.

1074 JOURNAL OF RESEARCH IN CRIME AND DELINQUENCY. v.1– , Jan. 1964– . New York; subsequently Hackensack, N.J. Semi-annual.
Issued by the National Council on Crime and Delinquency, and the Center for Youth and Community Studies, Harvard University.
Indexed: Crime Del. Abstr.; Soc. Sc. Ind.; Soc. Abstr.; Soc. Work Res. Abstr.; Urb. Aff. Abstr.

1075 JOURNAL OF SEX RESEARCH. v.1– , Mar. 1965– . New York. Three issues a year, 1965–66; quarterly, 1967– .
Issued by the Society for the Scientific Study of Sex. Supersedes: *Advances in Sex Research*. Cumulative index to vols. 1965–77 in v.14, no.3.
Indexed: Soc. Abstr.

1076 JOURNAL OF SOCIAL AND BEHAVIORAL SCIENCES. v.1– , 1954– . Washington, D.C. Quarterly.
Issued by the Association of Social and Behavioral Scientists.

1077 JOURNAL OF SOCIAL AND BIOLOGICAL STRUCTURES. v.1– , Jan. 1978– . New York, London, Academic Press. Quarterly.
Issued by the Institute of Higher Studies. Subtitle reads: 'Studies in human sociobiology'.

JOURNAL OF SOCIAL AND POLITICAL AFFAIRS
See JOURNAL OF SOCIAL AND POLITICAL STUDIES

1078 JOURNAL OF SOCIAL AND POLITICAL STUDIES. v.1–15, Jan. 1976–winter 1980. Washington, D.C.
Issued by the Council on American Affairs. Title varies: v.1, 1976, *Journal of Social and Political Affairs*. Continued by *Journal of Social and Political Affairs*.
Indexed: Soc. Abstr.

JOURNAL OF SOCIAL CASEWORK
See SOCIAL CASEWORK

THE JOURNAL OF SOCIAL FORCES
See SOCIAL FORCES

1079 JOURNAL OF SOCIAL HISTORY. v.1– , fall 1967– . Berkeley, Calif., University of California Press. Quarterly.
Issued by the Rutgers University.
Indexed: APAIS; Curr. Cont.; Soc. Sc. Ind.; SSCI; Soc. Abstr.; Wom. Stud. Abstr.

1080 JOURNAL OF SOCIAL HYGIENE. v.1–10, Dec. 1914–Dec. 1954; n.s. 1955– . Albany, N.Y. Quarterly, 1914–Oct. 1922; monthly (except July–Sep.) 1923–54; annual 1955– .
Issued by the American Social Hygiene Association. Title varies: 1914–Oct. 1921, *Social Hygiene*. Supplements accompany some issues.

1081 THE JOURNAL OF SOCIAL ISSUES. v.1– , Feb. 1945– . Worcester, Mass., Efferman Press. Quarterly.
Issued by the Society for the Psychological Study of Social Issues. Cumulative index every three years.
Indexed: Bull. sig. soc. eth.; Int. Bibl. Soc.; Int. Pol. Sc. Abstr.; PHRA; Sage Fam. Stud. Abstr.; Soc. Sc. Hum. Ind.; Soc. Abstr.; Soc. Work Res. Abstr.; Urb. Aff. Abstr.; Wom. Stud. Abstr.

1082 THE JOURNAL OF SOCIAL ISSUES. SUPPLEMENT SERIES. no.1–13, Dec. 1948–1959. New York. Irreg.
Issued by the Society for the Study of Social Issues.

1083 JOURNAL OF SOCIAL POLICY. 1– , Jan. 1972– . London, Cambridge University Press. Quarterly.
Issued by the Social Administration Association.
Indexed: Int. Bibl. Soc.; PAIS; PHRA; SSCI; Soc. Abstr.; Urb. Aff. Abstr.

1084 THE JOURNAL OF SOCIAL PSYCHOLOGY. v.1– , Feb. 1930– . Worcester, Mass., Journal Press. Bimonthly.
Summaries in French and German.
Indexed: Afr. Abstr.; Bull. sig. soc. eth.; Int. Pol. Sc. Abstr.; Psych. Abstr.; Soc. Sc. Ind.; Soc. Abstr.; Soc. Work Res. Abstr.; Wom. Stud. Abstr.

1085 JOURNAL OF SOCIAL RESEARCH. v.1– , Sep. 1958– . Ranchi. Biannual.
Indexed: Soc. Abstr.

1086 JOURNAL OF SOCIAL RESEARCH. 1– , 1965– . Seoul, Korea.
Issued by the Research Institute of Korean Society.

1087 JOURNAL OF SOCIAL SCIENCE. v.1–46, June 1869–Dec. 1909. New York.
Suspended 1908. Superseded by: National Institute of Social Sciences. *Journal.*

1088 JOURNAL OF SOCIAL SCIENCE. v.1– , 1972– . Limbe, Malawi. Annual.
Issued by the Social Science Group Board, Chancellor College, University of Malawi.

1089 JOURNAL OF SOCIAL SCIENCE. 1973– . Kuwait. Quarterly.
Issued by the Kuwait University College of Commerce and Economics.

JOURNAL OF SOCIAL SCIENCE
See SHE HUI K'O HSÜEH LUN TS'UNG

1090 JOURNAL OF SOCIAL SCIENCE CONTAINING THE PROCEEDINGS OF THE AMERICAN ASSOCIATION. no.1–46, June 1869–Dec. 1909. New York.
Title varies: no.1–35, 1869–Dec. 1909, *Journal of Social Science Containing the Transactions of the American Association.* Subtitles vary: nos. 12–22, 'Saratoga Papers of 1880–99'; nos. 38–40, 'Washington Papers of 1900–02'; nos. 41–43, 'Boston Papers of 1903–05'; no.44 'New York Papers of 1906'; no. 45, 'Buffalo Papers of 1907'; no. 46, 'New York Papers of 1908'. Nos. 6–7 have continuous pagination. Superseded by: National Institute of Social Science. *Journal.*

JOURNAL OF SOCIAL SCIENCE CONTAINING THE TRANSACTIONS OF THE AMERICAN ASSOCIATION
See JOURNAL OF SOCIAL SCIENCE CONTAINING THE PROCEEDINGS OF THE AMERICAN ASSOCIATION

1091 JOURNAL OF SOCIAL SCIENCE REVIEW. 1– , Mar. 1976– . Bangkok, Thailand, Social Science Press.
Issued by the Social Science Association of Thailand. Mar. 1976 issue called *English Edition* and *Special English Issue.*

1092 JOURNAL OF SOCIAL SCIENCES. v.1– , Jan. 1958– . Agra, U.P. Semi-annual.
Issued by the Institute of Social Sciences, Agra University.

JOURNAL OF SOCIAL SCIENCES AND HUMANITIES
See Han'guk Yon'guwon, Seoul, Korea. BULLETIN OF THE KOREAN RESEARCH CENTER; JOURNAL OF SOCIAL SCIENCES AND HUMANITIES

1093 JOURNAL OF SOCIETAL ISSUES. v.1– , 1965– . Melbourne, Australia. Semi-annual.
Issued by the Cairnmillar Institute.
Indexed: APAIS; Soc. Abstr.

1094 JOURNAL OF SOCIOLOGIC MEDICINE. v.1–20, no.3, Feb. 1891–June 1919. Easton, Pa.
Issued by the American Academy of Medicine. Title varies: v.1–5, *Bulletin of the Academy of Medicine.*

JOURNAL OF SOCIOLOGY
See Washington (State). University. Department of Sociology. UNIVERSITY OF WASHINGTON JOURNAL OF SOCIOLOGY

THE JOURNAL OF SOCIOLOGY AND ANTHROPOLOGY
See WARSAN SANGKHOMWITTHAYA-MANUTWITTHAYA

1095 JOURNAL OF SOCIOLOGY AND PSYCHOLOGY. v.1– , 1978– . Singapore.
Issued by the University of Singapore Sociology Society, and Nanyang University Sociology & Psychology Society.

1096 JOURNAL OF SOCIOLOGY AND SOCIAL WELFARE. 1– , fall 1973– . West Hartford, Conn. Quarterly.
Issued by the Division on Sociology and Social Welfare, Society for the Study of Social Problems.
Indexed: Soc. Abstr.; Soc. Work Res. Abstr.

JOURNAL OF SOUTHEAST ASIA
See REVUE DU SUD-EST ASIATIQUE ET DE L'EXTRÊME-ORIENT. JOURNAL OF SOUTHEAST ASIA AND THE FAR EAST

JOURNAL OF SOUTHEAST ASIA AND THE FAR EAST
See REVUE DU SUD-EST ASIATIQUE ET DE L'EXTRÊME ORIENT. JOURNAL OF SOUTHEAST ASIA AND THE FAR EAST

1097 JOURNAL OF SOUTHERN AFRICAN STUDIES. v.1– , Oct. 1974– . London, Oxford University Press.
Issued by the Faculty of Social Sciences at Chancellor College.
Indexed: Int. Bibl. Soc.; Int. Pol. Sc. Abstr.; Soc. Abstr.

1098 JOURNAL OF SPORT AND SOCIAL ISSUES. 1– , 1976– . Norfolk, Va. Two issues a year.
Issued by the ARENA, the Institute for Sport and Social Analysis, Virginia Wesleyan College.

1099 JOURNAL OF SPORT BEHAVIOR. v.1– , Feb. 1978– . Park Forest South, Ill. Quarterly.
Issued by the Governor's State University and sponsored by the United States Sports Academy at the University of South Alabama.

1100 JOURNAL OF STUDENT PAPERS IN ANTHROPOLOGY AND SOCIOLOGY. 1973. Victoria, B.C. Irreg.
Issued by the University of Victoria. Continued by: *Kumtuks Review*.

1101 JOURNAL OF STUDIES ON ALCOHOL. v.36– , Jan. 1975– . New Brunswick, N.J., Journal of Studies on Alcohol, Inc. Monthly.
Issued by the Center of Alcohol Studies, Rutger's University. Continues: *Quarterly Journal of Studies on Alcohol*. Odd-numbered issues contain original articles and are paged continuously; even-numbered issues, paged continuously, are called 'Current Literature' and contain abstracts and subject and author indexes.
Indexed: Soc. Sc. Ind.; Soc. Abstr.; Soc. Work Res. Abstr.

JOURNAL OF SUN YAT-SEN UNIVERSITY: SOCIAL SCIENCES
See Guangshou. Zhongshan Daxue Xuebao. CHUNG-SHAN TA HSÜEH HSÜEH PAO; SHE HUI K'O HSÜEH

1102 JOURNAL OF THE EXPERIMENTAL ANALYSIS OF BEHAVIOR. 1– , Jan. 1958– . Bloomington, Ind. Bimonthly.
Issued by the Society of Experimental Analysis of Behavior; edited by the Department of Psychology, University of Indiana.
Indexed: Soc. Abstr.

1103 JOURNAL OF THE HISTORY OF SOCIOLOGY. v.1– , fall 1978– . Brookline, Mass., J. N. Potter. Semi-annual.
Issued by the Department of Sociology, University of Massachusetts, Campus at Boston.
Indexed: Soc. Abstr.

1104 JOURNAL OF THE THEORY OF SOCIAL BEHAVIOUR. v.1– , Apr. 1971– . Oxford, Blackwell. Semi-annual 1971–77; three issues a year 1978– .
Indexed: Soc. Abstr.

1105 THE JOURNAL OF URBAN ANALYSIS. v.1–6, no.1, Oct. 1972–Oct. 1979. New York, London, Gordon and Breach. Two issues a year.
Indexed: Soc. Abstr.

A JOURNAL OF URBAN AND RURAL PLANNING THOUGHT
See URBAN AND RURAL PLANNING THOUGHT

1106 JOURNAL OF URBAN HISTORY. v.1– , 1974– . Beverly Hills, Calif., London, Sage Publications. Three issues a year.
Indexed: Soc. Abstr.

1107 JOURNAL OF WOMEN'S STUDIES. 1– , 1979– . Montreal, Eden Press. Quarterly.

JOURNAL; SOCIAL SCIENCES
See Guangzhou. Zhongshan Daxue Xuebao. CHUNG-SHAN TA HSÜEH HSÜEH PAO; SHE HUI K'O HSÜEH

JUGOSLOVENSKI CASOPIS ZA FILOZOFIJU I SOCIOLOGIJU, SOCIJALNU PSIHOLOGIJU I SOCIJALNU ANTROPOLOGIJU
See FILOZOFIJA

1108 KABUL. Kabul, Pakistan. Monthly.
Issued by the Academy Pohand Reshthecu. No more information available.

1109 Kampala. Makerere University. Department of Sociology. Social Psychology Section. OCCASIONAL PAPERS. no.1– , 1971– . Kampala. Irreg.
Series of papers. Mimeographed.

1110 Kansas. Fort Hays State College, Hays. STUDIES. SOCIOLOGY SERIES. no.1, 1941. Topeka. One volume published.
Subseries of its *Studies. General Series* and *Bulletin*.

1111 Kansas. State University of Agriculture and Applied Science, Manhattan. Department of Sociology and Anthropology. REPORT. 1– , 1965– . Manhattan. Irreg.

1112 KANSAS JOURNAL OF SOCIOLOGY. v.1–11, no.1, winter 1964–spring 1975. Lawrence, Kansas. Semi-annual.
Issued by the Graduate Students, Department of Sociology, University of Kansas. Superseded by: *Mid-American Review of Sociology*.
Indexed: Psych. Abstr.; Soc. Abstr.

1113 KANSEI GAKUIN DAIGAKU SHAKAIGAKUBU KIYO. no.1–14, Nov. 1960–Dec. 1965; no.15– , Dec. 1967– . Nishinomiya, Hyogo. Two issues a year.
Issued by the Kansei Gakuin Daigaku-in Shakai Kenkyu-shitsu. Title in English: *Kansei Gakuin Journal of Sociology*. In Japanese.

KANSEI GAKUIN JOURNAL OF SOCIOLOGY
See KANSEI GAKUIN DAIGAKU SHAKAIGAKUBU KIYO

1114 KEIO GIJUKU DAIGAKU-IN SHAKAIGAKU KENKYUKA KIYO. no.1–7, June 1962–Dec. 1966; no.8– , Mar. 1968– . Tokyo.
Issued by the Keio Gijuku Daigaku-in Shakaigaku Kenkyu. Title in English: *Keio Journal of Sociology*. In Japanese.

KEIO JOURNAL OF SOCIOLOGY
See KEIO GIJUKU DAIGAKU-IN SHAKAIGAKU KENKYUKA KIYO

1115 Kentron Epistemonikon Ereumon. EPETERIS. 1967/1968– . Leukosia. Annual.
Issued by the Cyprus Research Center. In Greek, English and French.

1116 Kenya. Department of Community Development. ANNUAL REPORT. Nairobi.
Issued in cooperation with Kenya's Department of Social Services.

1117 THE KIBBUTZ. 1– , 1973– . Tel-Aviv. Annual.
Issued by the Federation of Kibbutz Movements. Text in Hebrew and English.
Indexed: Soc. Abstr.

1118 Kinshasa, Zaire. Université Lovanium. Institut de Recherches Économiques et Sociales. COLLECTION D'ÉTUDES SOCIOLOGIQUES. no.1– , 1965– . Kinshasa. Irreg.
University renamed Université nationale du Zaire, Campus de Kinshasa.

1119 KNOWLEDGE; CREATION, DIFFUSION, UTILIZATION. 1– , Sep. 1979– . Beverly Hills, Calif., Sage Publications. Quarterly.

1120 KÖLNER BEITRÄGE ZUR SOZIALFORSCHUNG UND ANGEWANDTEN SOZIOLOGIE. v.1–?, 1966–197?. Meisenheim am Glan, Verlag A. Hain. Irreg.
Monograph series.

KÖLNER VIERTELJAHRESHEFTE FÜR SOZIALWISSENSCHAFTEN
See KÖLNER VIERTELJAHRESHEFTE FÜR SOZIOLOGIE

1121 KÖLNER VIERTELJAHRESHEFTE FÜR SOZIOLOGIE. v.1–12, 1921–1934. München. Quarterly.
Issued by the Forschungsinstitut für Sozialwissenschaften in Köln. Title varies: v.1–2, 1921–22, *Kölner Zeitschrift für Soziologie und Sozialpsychologie*. vol. 3–12 called also 'Neue Folge' of *Kölner Vierteljahreshefte für Sozialwissenschaften.*

1122 KÖLNER VIERTELJAHRESHEFTE FÜR SOZIOLOGIE. ERGÄNZUNGSHEFTE. BEITRÄGE ZUR BEZIEHUNGSLEHRE. 1–3, 1928–30. Leipzig.

KÖLNER ZEITSCHRIFT FÜR SOZIOLOGIE
See KÖLNER ZEITSCHRIFT FÜR SOZIOLOGIE UND SOZIALPSYCHOLOGIE

1123 KÖLNER ZEITSCHRIFT FÜR SOZIOLOGIE UND SOZIALPSYCHOLOGIE. 1– , 1948/1949– . Köln, Westdeutscher Verlag. Quarterly.
Issued by the Forschungsinstitut für Sozial- und Verwaltungswissenschaften in Köln. Title varies: 1948/49–1953/54, *Kölner Zeitschrift für Soziologie.* Vol.1 also numbered 13 in continuation of *Kölner Vierteljahreshefte für Soziologie.*
Indexed: Int. Bibl. Soc.; Int. Pol. Sc. Abstr.; Psych. Abstr.; SSCI; Soc. Abstr.

KÖLNER ZEITSCHRIFT FÜR SOZIOLOGIE UND SOZIALPSYCHOLOGIE
See KÖLNER VIERTELJAHRESHEFTE FÜR SOZIOLOGIE

1124 KÖLNER ZEITSCHRIFT FÜR SOZIOLOGIE UND SOZIALPSYCHOLOGIE. SONDERHEFT. 1– , 1956– . Köln, Westdeutscher Verlag. Irreg.
Monograph series.

THE KOREAN JOURNAL OF SOCIOLOGY
See HAN'GUK SAHOENAK

THE KOREAN SOCIAL SCIENCE REVIEW
See HAN'GUK SAHOE KWAHAK NONJIP. THE KOREAN SOCIAL SCIENCE REVIEW

KOREAN SOCIOLOGICAL REVIEW
See HAN'GUK SAHOENAK YON'GU

1125 KÖRÖS NÉPE. v.1– , 1957– . Békéscsaba, Békéscsaba Város Tanácsa. Irreg.
In Hungarian.

1126 Kraków. Uniwersytet Jagielloński. PRACE SOCJOLOGICZNE. 1– , 1973– . Kraków. Irreg.

Subseries of its *Zeszyty Naukowe*. Includes subseries: *Studia z Socjologii Mlodziezy i Wychowania*. In Polish.

1127 KRIMINALSOZIOLOGISCHE BIBLIOGRAPHIE. no.1– , 1973– . Wien. Quarterly.
Issued by the Ludwig Boltzmann-Institut für Kriminalsoziologie. No.11/13, 1976 called also v.4.

1128 KRIMINALOGISCHE ABHANDLUNGEN. 1–9, 1926–1933; n.s. 1– , 1946– . Wien, Spryer. Irreg.

1129 KRONIEK VAN AFRIKA. 1961–1965. Leiden, Universitaire Pers. Quarterly.
Issued by the Afrika-Studiecentrum. Continued by: *African Perspectives*. In Dutch; occasionally in English.
Indexed: Afr. Abstr.

1130 KULTURA I SPOŁECZEŃSTWO. v.1– , 1957– . Warszawa, Państwowe Wydawnictwo Naukowe. Quarterly.
Issued by the Komitet Nauk Socjologicznych, Polska Akademia Nauk. In Polish.
Indexed: Int. Bibl. Soc.; Soc. Abstr.

1131 KUMTUKS REVIEW. spring 1974– . Victoria, B.C., Alma Mater Society. Semi-annual; subsequently annual.
Issued by the University of Victoria, B.C. Continues: *Journal of Student Papers in Anthropology and Sociology*.

1132 KURUKSHETRA. v.1– , Aug. 1952– . New Delhi. Monthly (irreg.).
Issued by the Community Projects Association, Ministry of Community Development, Panchayati Raj and Cooperation.
Indexed: Soc. Abstr.

1133 KYOIKU SHAKAIGAKU KENKYU. ser. 1–20, May 1951–Oct. 1965; ser. 22– , Oct. 1967–
Issued by the Nihon Kyoiku Shakai Gakkai. Title in English: *Japan Journal of Educational Sociology*.

1134 LLBA. LANGUAGE AND LANGUAGE BEHAVIOR ABSTRACTS. v.1– , Jan. 1967– . New York. Appleton-Century-Crofts. Quarterly.
Issued by the Center for Research on Language amd Language Behavior, University of Michigan. Jan. 1967 issue preceded by 'Trial issue' v.0, no.1.

1135 LSU [Louisiana State University] JOURNAL OF SOCIOLOGY. v.1–3, Mar. 1971–1973. Baton Rouge, La.
Issued by the Department of Sociology and Rural Sociology, Louisiana State University.
Indexed: Soc. Abstr.

1136 LA TROBE SOCIOLOGY PAPERS. no.1– , 1975– . Bundoora, Australia. Irreg.
Issued by the Department of Sociology, La Trobe University.

1137 LABOR HISTORY. v.1– , 1960– . New York. Quarterly.
Issued by the Tamiment Institute.
Indexed: Int. Bibl. Soc.; Soc. Sc. Hum. Ind.; Wom. Stud. Abstr.

1138 LABOUR AND SOCIETY. v.1– , Jan. 1976– . Geneva, Switzerland. Quarterly.
Issued by the International Institute of Labour Studies.
Indexed: Sage Fam. Stud. Abstr.; Soc. Abstr.

1139 LANGAGE ET SOCIÉTÉ. 1977– . Paris. Quarterly.
Issued by the Service de Mathématiques Appliquées et de Calcul, Maison de l'Homme.

1140 LANGUAGE IN SOCIETY. 1– , Apr. 1972– . London, New York, Cambridge University Press. Semi-annual.
Issued by the Center for Urban Ethnography, University of Pennsylvania.
Indexed: Abstr. Anth.; Brit. Hum. Ind.

1141 LANGUE. 1– , 1973– . Anvers-sur-Oise. Irreg.
Issued by the Centre d'Analyse et de Sociologie des Langages.

LATIN AMERICAN POPULATION ABSTRACTS
See RESUMENES DE POBLACIÓN EN AMERICA LATINA. LATIN AMERICAN POPULATION ABSTRACTS

1142 LATIN AMERICAN RESEARCH REVIEW. v.1– , 1965– . Washington, D.C. Three issues a year.
Issued by the Latin American Studies Association. In English, Portuguese and Spanish.
Indexed: Int. Bibl. Soc.; Int. Pol. Sc. Abstr.; SSCI; Soc. Abstr.

1143 LATIN AMERICAN URBAN RESEARCH. v.1–6, 1970–1978. Beverly Hills, Calif., Sage Publications. Annual.

1144 LAW AND HUMAN BEHAVIOR. 1– , Mar. 1977– . New York, Plenum Press. Quarterly.

Issued in association with the American Psychology-Law Society, and with the assistance of students at the Law School, University of Virginia.
Indexed: Soc. Abstr.

1145 LAW AND SOCIETY IN THE CARIBBEAN. 1– , 1972– . St. Augustine.
Issued by the Institute of Social and Economic Research, University of the West Indies.

LAW AND SOCIETY NEWSLETTER
See LAW AND SOCIETY QUARTERLY

1146 LAW AND SOCIETY QUARTERLY. 1– , 1971– . New Delhi.
Issued by the Centre for the Study of Law & Society, Institute of Constitutional and Parliamentary Studies. Title varies: v.1, 1971, *Law and Society Newsletter.*

1147 LAW & SOCIETY REVIEW. v.1– , Nov. 1966– . Beverly Hills, Calif., subsequently Denver, Colo. Quarterly.
Issued by the Law and Society Association and the College of Law, University of Denver.
Indexed: Int. Bibl. Soc.; Int. Pol. Sc. Abstr.; Soc. Sc. Ind.; Soc. Abstr.

1148 Leiden. Rijksuniversiteit. Afrika-Studiecentrum. COMMUNICATIONS. 1– , 1970– . The Hague, Mouton. Irreg.
In Dutch.

1149 Leiden. Rijksuniversiteit. Sociologisch Instituut. PUBLIKATIES. 1–9, 1953–1963. Leiden, H. E. Stenfert Kroese. Irreg.
In Dutch.

1150 LEISURE AND SOCIAL STRATIFICATION. 1975– . Waterloo, Ont. Three issues a year.
Issued by the SIRLS, Faculty of Human Kinetics and Leisure Studies, University of Waterloo.

1151 LEISURE AND SPORT IN A CROSS-NATIONAL AND CROSS-CULTURAL PERSPECTIVE. 1975– . Waterloo, Ont. Three issues a year.
Issued by the SIRLS, Faculty of Human Kinetics and Leisure Studies, University of Waterloo.

1152 LEISURE SCIENCES. Feb. 1977– . New York, Crane, Russak & Co. Quarterly.

LEISURE STUDIES AND RESEARCH PROGRAMME PUBLICATIONS
See Salford. University. Department of Sociology. LEISURE STUDIES AND RESEARCH PROGRAMME PUBLICATIONS

1153 LEMMING. 1– , May/June 1967– . Los Angeles, Calif.
Issued by the Department of Sociology, University of California at Los Angeles.

1154 LENGAS. 1– , 1977– . Montpellier. Semi-annual.
Issued by the Centre d'Études Occitanes, Université Paul-Valéry.

1155 LENGUAJE Y CIENCIAS. v.1– , 1961– . Trujillo. Quarterly.
Issued by the Departamento de Idiomas y Linguistica, Universidad Nacional de Trujillo. In English, French, German, Portuguese and Spanish.

1156 Leningrad. Universitet. Nauchno-issledovatel'skii institut kompleksnykh sotsialnykh issledovanii. UCHENYE ZAPISKI. 1966– . Leningrad. Irreg.
In Russian.

1157 LEO M. FRANKLIN MEMORIAL LECTURES IN HUMAN RELATIONS. v.1–20, 1951–1972. Detroit, Mich., Wayne State University Press. Annual.

Leopoldville, Congo
See Kinshasa, Zaire

1158 LIBERIAN STUDIES JOURNAL. v.1– , Oct. 1968– . Greencastle, Ind., 1968–69; Newark, Del., 1970– . Biennial.
Issued by the Department of Anthropology, University of Delaware, v.1; the Liberian Studies Association, v.2–7; African Studies Center, De Pauw University, v.8– .
Indexed: Int. Bibl. Soc.

1159 LIBERIAN STUDIES MONOGRAPH SERIES. no.1– , 1972– . Newark, Del., Liberian Studies Association. Irreg.
Issued by the Department of Anthropology, University of Delaware.
Monograph series.

1160 LIBERIAN STUDIES RESEARCH WORKING PAPER. no.1– , 1971– . Newark, Del., Liberian Studies Association. Irreg.
Issued by the Department of Anthropology, University of Delaware. Processed.
Series of papers.

1161 LIBRE. v.1– , 1971– . Paris, Éditions libres. Quarterly.

1162 Liège. Université. Institut de Sociologie. TRAVAUX. 1– , 1949– . Liège. Irreg.
Monograph series.

1163 Lietuvos TSR Mokslu Akademija, Vilnius. TRUDY. SERIIA A. OBSHCHESTVENNYE NAUKI. Vilnius.
Text in Lithuanian and Russian; summaries in Lithuanian, Russian, English, French and German.

1164 LIFE-STYLE, LEISURE AND SPORT. 1975– . Waterloo, Ont. Three issues a year.
Issued by the SIRLS, Faculty of Human Kinetics and Leisure Studies, University of Waterloo.

LIFE-THREATENING BEHAVIOR
See SUICIDE AND LIFE-THREATENING BEHAVIOR

1165 LIPUNAN. v.1– , 1965– . Quezon City. Semi-annual.
Issued by the Institute of Asian Studies, University of the Philippines.

1166 A LIST OF AMERICAN LEARNED JOURNALS DEVOTED TO HUMANISTIC AND SOCIAL STUDIES. no.1–5, 1925–1945. Washington, D.C., American Council of Learned Societies.
Nos. 1–2 issued in the Council's *Bulletin;* nos. 4 and 8 comprise the Council's Bulletin nos. 21, 30 and 37. Cover title 1940–45, *American Learned Journals.*

1167 LITERATURSOZIOLOGIE. 1– , 1974– . Stuttgart, Berlin. Irreg.

1168 Liverpool. University. Department of Geography. African Population Mobility Project. WORKING PAPER. no.1– , 1973– . Liverpool. Irreg.
Series of papers; mimeographed.

LIVING
See JOURNAL OF MARRIAGE AND THE FAMILY

1169 LOCAL POPULATION STUDIES; MAGAZINE AND NEWSLETTER. no.1– , autumn 1968– . Matlock, England. Semi-annual.
Issued by the Cambridge Group for the History of Population, in cooperation with the Department of Adult Education, Nottingham University.
Indexed: Brit. Hum. Ind.; Urb. Aff. Abstr.

LOCAL STUDIES SERIES
See Morija, Lesotho. University of Botswana, Lesotho and Swaziland. LOCAL STUDIES SERIES

1170 LOISIR ET SOCIÉTÉ. SOCIETY AND LEISURE. v.1– , 1978– . Montréal, Presses de l'Université du Québec. Semi-annual.
Sponsored by the International Sociological Association. In French and English.
Indexed: Soc. Abstr.

1171 London. University. University College. Francis Galton Laboratory for Eugenics. EUGENICS LABORATORY LECTURE SERIES. 1–14, 1909–1927. London.

1172 London. University. University College. Francis Galton Laboratory for Eugenics. EUGENICS LABORATORY MEMOIRS. 1–29, 1907–1935. London. Irreg.

1173 London. University. University College. School of Environmental Studies. RESEARCH BULLETIN. v.1– , 1971– . London.

1174 London. University. University College. School of Environmental Studies. Planning Methodology Research Unit. WORKING PAPER. no.1– , 1972– . London. Irreg.

1175 Louisiana. State University, New Orleans. Division of Business and Economic Research. POPULATION STUDY. no.1– , 1968– . New Orleans. Irreg.
Subseries of its *Research Study.*
Monograph series.

1176 Louvain. Université Catholique. Sociologisch Onderzoeksinstituut. VREEMDE ARBEIDERS. no.1– , 1972– . Leuven. Irreg.
In French and Flemish. Processed.
Monograph series.

1177 Lublin. Uniwersytet. ANNALES. SECTIO I. PHILOSOPHIA — SOCIOLOGIA. v.1– , 1976– . Lublin. Irreg.
In Polish.

1178 Lucknow. University. Demographic Research Centre. DEMOGRAPHY & DEVELOPMENT DIGEST. v.1– , Jan. 1967– . Lucknow, India. Semi-annual.

1179 Lucknow. University. Demographic Research Centre. OCCASIONAL PAPER. no.1– , 1967– . Lucknow, India. Irreg.
Monograph series.

1180 LUDNOŚĆ POLSKI WSPÓŁCZESNEJ. v.1–2, 1967–1968. Warszawa. Irreg.
Issued by the Komitet Przestrzennego Zagospodarowania Kraju, Polska Akademia Nauk, in cooperation with Międzyuczelniany Zaklad Podstawowych Problemów Architektury, Urbanistyki i Budownictwa. In Polish.
Monograph series.

1181 LUND STUDIES IN GEOGRAPHY. SERIES B: HUMAN GEOGRAPHY. no.1– , 1949– . Lund, Sweden, Gleerup. Irreg.

Issued by the Department of Geography, The Royal University of Lund.
Monograph series.

1182 Lvov. Universytet. VISNIK. SERIIA SUSPIL'NYKH NAUK. 1965– . Lviv, Vyd. L'vivskogo universitetu.
In Ukrainian; summaries in Russian.

1183 McMaster University. Sociology of Women Program. OCCASIONAL PAPERS. vo.1– , 1977– . Hamilton, Ont. Irreg.

MADJALAH HUKUM ADAT
See SOSIOGRAFI INDONESIA DAN HUKUM ADAT

1184 A Magyar Tudományos Akadémia. Társadalmitörténeti. TUDOMÁNUOK OSZTALYANAK KÖZLEMÉNYEI. 1950– . Budapest, Akadémiai Kiadó. Quarterly.
In Hungarian.

1185 Maharaja Sayajirao University of Baroda. Department of Sociology. PUBLICATION. no.1– , 1960– . Baroda. Irreg.
Monograph series.

1186 MAIN CURRENTS IN INDIAN SOCIOLOGY. 1–2, 1976. Chapel Hill, N.C., Carolina Academic Press.

1187 Maison des Sciences de l'Homme. Service d'Échange d'Informations Scientifiques. MÉTHODES DE LA SOCIOLOGIE. 1– , 1965– . Paris. Mouton. Irreg.
Monograph series; some works in revised editions.

1188 MAJALAH DEMOGRAFI INDONESIA. 1– , June 1974– . Jakarta. Semi-annual.
Issued by the Lembaga Demografi, Fakultas Ekonomi, Universitas Indonesia. In English and Indonesian.

1189 AL-MAJALLAH AL-'ARABIYAH LIL-DIFA' AL-IJTIMA'I. 1969– . Cairo, Egypt. Annual.
Title in English: *Arab Journal for Sociological Defence*. In Arabic.

1190 AL-MAJALLAH AL-DUWALIYAH LIL-'ULUM AL IJTIMA'IYAH. Cairo. Egypt, Unesco Publications Centre. Quarterly.
Selections from *International Social Science Journal (Revue Internationale des Sciences Sociales)* translated into Arabic.

1191 AL MAJALLAH AL-QAWMIYAH. v.1– , 1926– . Beirut. Monthly.
In Arabic.

AL-MAJALLAH AL-TUNISIYAH LIL-'ULUM AL-IJTIMA'IYAH
See REVUE TUNISIENNE DES SCIENCES SOCIALES

1192 MAJALLAT AL-'AMAL WA-AL-SHU'UN AL-IJTIMA'IYAH. 1950– . Damascus. Bimonthly.
Issued by the Direction du Travail et des Affaires Sociales. In Arabic.

AL-MAJALLAT AL-IJTIMA'IYAH AL-QAWMIYAH
See Cairo. Al-Markaz al-Qawmī lil-Buḥūth al-Ijtimā'īyah wa-al-Tima'ījah. AL-MAJALLAT AL-IJTIMA'IYAH AL-QAWMIYAH

1193 MAJALLAT KULLIYAT AL-TARBIYAH. 1955– . Damascus. Three Issues a year.
Issued by the Faculté de Pedagogie, Université Syrienne. In Arabic.

1194 Makerere Institute of Social Research. ABSTRACTS AND NEWSLETTER. v.1– , 1970– . Kampala. Irreg.
Supersedes its *Policy Abstracts and M.I.S.R. Newsletter* (v.1, no.1–3, 1970–73).

1195 MAKERERE SOCIOLOGICAL JOURNAL. 1– , 1966– . Kampala. Three issues a year.
Issued by the Makerere Sociological Society.
Indexed: Soc. Abstr.

1196 Ha-Makhon le-Tikhnum U-Fituah. IPD SOCIOLOGICAL ANALYSES AND SURVEYS: INFORMATION BULLETIN. 1969– . Tel-Aviv. Annual.
In English. Publication suspended.

1197 Malagasy Republic. Service de Statistique et des Études Socio-Économiques. POPULATION DU MADAGASCAR. 1960– . Tananarive.

1198 Malaysian Sociological Institute. REPORT. 1963?– . Singapore.
No more information available.

1199 MALLAJAH-'TULUM-I IQTISADI VA UTIMA'I. 1– , 1958?– . Teheran, Mu'Assah-I 'Ulum-i Uiqtisadi va Utima'i.
Issued by the Institut des Sciences Politiques et Sociales. Title in French: *Revue des Sciences Économiques et Sociales*. No recent information available. In Persian.

1200 MAN. n.s. v.1– , Mar. 1966– . London. Quarterly.
Issued by the Royal Anthropological Institute of Great Britain and Ireland. Supersedes the Institute's *Journal* and *Man* (1901–65).
Indexed: Abstr. Anth.; Afr. Abstr.; Brit. Hum. Ind.; Bull. sig. soc. eth.; Int. Bibl. Soc,; Soc. Sc. Ind.; Soc. Abstr.; Wom. Stud. Abstr.

1201 MAN AND HIS ENVIRONMENT. 1970–. Oxford, Pergamon Press. Irreg.
Monograph series, unnumbered.

MAN AND INDUSTRY
See MENS EN ONDERNEMING

1202 MAN AND SOCIETY. 1961–1975. London. Semi-annual.
Issued by the Albany Trust.

MAN AND SOCIETY
See JEN YÜ SHE HUI

MAN AND SOCIETY
See MANUSIA DAN MASHARAKAT

1203 MAN IN NEW GUINEA. Oct. 1968–1973. Boroko, Papua New Guinea.
Issued by the Department of Anthropology and Sociology, University of Papua New Guinea. Subtitle reads: 'A newsletter of anthropological and sociological research in Papua New Guinea'. Superseded by: *Research in Melanesia*, 1975– .
Indexed: Abstr. Anth.

1204 MAN IN SOUTHEAST ASIA. no.1– , 1968– . Brisbane.
Issued by the Department of Anthropology and Sociology and the Department of Geography, University of Brisbane.

1205 MANAGEMENT OF MINORITY STATUS. 1971– . Oslo. Annual.
Issued by the Ethnographic Museum and the University of Oslo.

1206 Manitoba. University. Center for Settlement Studies. SERIES 1: ANNUAL AND PROGRESS REPORT. no.1–6, 1969–1974. Winnipeg. Annual.

1207 Manitoba. University. Center for Settlement Studies. SERIES 2: RESEARCH REPORTS. 1969–1972. Manitoba. Irreg.
Monograph series.

1208 Manitoba. University. Center for Settlement Studies. SERIES 3: BIBLIOGRAPHY AND INFORMATION. Apr. 1969–1970. Winnipeg.

1209 Manitoba. University. Center for Settlement Studies. SERIES 4: PROCEEDINGS. no.1, 1968. Winnipeg. One volume published.

1210 Manitoba. University. Center for Settlement Studies. SERIES 5: OCCASIONAL PAPERS. 1970–1975. Winnipeg. Irreg.

1211 MANKIND. v.1– , 1931– . Sydney, Sydney University Press. Quarterly.
Issued by the Anthropological Society of New South Wales, for the Anthropological Societies of Australia.

1212 MANKIND. v.1–6, no.7, Aug. 1956–1962. Hyderabad, India, G. Murahari. Monthly.
Indexed: Soc. Abstr.

1213 THE MANKIND QUARTERLY. v.1– , July 1960– . Edinburgh, The Mankind Quarterly. Quarterly.
Subtitle reads: 'An international quarterly journal dealing with race and inheritance in the fields of ethnology, ethno- and human genetics, ethnopsychology, racial history, demography and anthropogeography'.
Indexed: Bull. sig. soc. eth.; Soc. Abstr.

1214 MANUSIA DAN MASHARAKAT. MAN AND SOCIETY. no.1– , 1972– . Kuala Lumpur. Annual.
Title in Malay only, in 1972. Subtitle reads: 'Jernal Persatuan Antropologi & Sosiologi Universiti Malaya'. In English and Malay.

1215 MARBURGER STUDIEN ZUR VERGLEICHENDE ETHNOSOZIOLOGIE. 1– , 1973– . Marburg. Irreg.
Issued by the Arbeitsgruppe für Vergleichende Ethnosoziologie.

MARRIAGE AND FAMILY LIVING
See JOURNAL OF MARRIAGE AND THE FAMILY

1216 MARRIAGE AND FAMILY REVIEW. 1– , Jan/Feb. 1978– . New York, Haworth Press. Bimonthly; subsequently quarterly.
Includes section 'Current abstracts'.
Indexed: Sage Fam. Stud. Abstr.

1217 AL-MASHRIQ. 1898–1942; 1944– . Beirut. Bimonthly.
Issued by the Université St. Joseph. Subtitle reads: 'Revue Catholique Orientale. Sciences — Lettres — Arts'. In Arabic; articles occasionally in a European language; summaries in French. Cumulative indexes: 1898–1907; 1908–22.

1218 Massachusetts Institute of Technology. Migration and Development Study Group. WORKING PAPERS. no.1– , 1975– . Cambridge, Mass. Irreg.

MATERIALSAMMLUNG
See Agrarsoziale Gesellschaft. MATERIALSAMMLUNG

1219 MAWAZO. v.1–4, no.4, June 1967–1975. Kampala.
Issued by the Faculties of Arts and Social Sciences, Makerere University (called Makerere University College, 1967–69). Supersedes: *Makerere Journal.*
Indexed: Afr. Abstr.; Int. Bibl. Soc.

MEDEDELINGEN
See Erasmus Universiteit, Rotterdam. Sociologisch Instituut. MEDEDELINGEN

1220 MEDICAL BEHAVIORAL SCIENCE. no.1– , 1971– . Winston-Salem, N.C. Irreg.
Issued by the Overseas Research Center, Wake Forest University. This publication is 'Series 2' of the University's *Developing Nations Monograph Series*. Each issue is thematic.
Monograph series.

1221 MEDICAL SOCIO-ECONOMIC RESEARCH SOURCES. v.1–9, no.4, Jan. 1971–1979. Chicago. Quarterly, with annual cumulations.
Issued by the Archive Library Department, American Medical Association. Supersedes: *Index to Medical Socio-Economic Literature*.

MEDITERRANEAN PEOPLES
See PEUPLES MÉDITERRANÉES

1222 MEDIZINSOZIOLOGISCHE MITTELUNGEN. 1– , 1975– . Frankfurt-am-Main.
Issued by the Deutsche Gesellschaft für Medizinsiche Soziologie in der Bundesrepublik Deutschland.

1223 MEETING HUMAN NEEDS. 1–2, 1975–1976. Beverly Hills, Calif., Sage Publications. Annual.

1224 MEIJI GAKUIN RONSO KENKYU NENPO SHAKAI GAKU. SHAKAI JIGYO. no.1–3, 1965–1967. Tokyo.
Issued by the Meiji Gakuin Daigaku Bunkei Gakkai.

MÉLANGES D'HISTOIRE SOCIALE
See ANNALES D'HISTOIRE SOCIALE

MEMOIRE
See International Congress of Sociology. MÉMOIRE

MÉMOIRES ET DOCUMENTS (SUPPLEMENTS AUX ANNALES)
See Musée Social, Paris. MÉMOIRES ET DOCUMENTS (SUPPLEMENTS AUX ANNALES)

MEMOIRS
See AMERICAN ANTHROPOLOGIST

MEMOIRS
See Yale University. Center of Alcohol Studies. MEMOIRS

MEMORIA
See Congreso de Sociologia Ecuatoriana. MEMORIA

MEMORIA
See Congreso Latinoamericano de Sociologia. MEMORIA

1225 Mendoza, Argentina (City). Universidad Nacional de Cuyo. Facultad de Ciencias Economicas. SERIE ESTUDIOS. SECCIÓN SOCIOLOGIA. no.1– , 1969– . Mendoza. Irreg.
In Spanish.
Monograph series.

1226 MENS EN GEMEENSKAP. v.1– , Apr. 1960– . Pretoria, S.A., Haum. Quarterly; some double issues.
Issued by the Navorsings- en Publikasie Komitee van die Universiteit van Pretoria (Research and Publication Committee, University of Pretoria). In Afrikaans.

1227 MENS EN MAATSCHAPPIJ. v.1– , 1925– . Rotterdam, Rotterdam University Press; subsequently Deventer, Van Loghum Slaterus. Quarterly.
Issued by the Rotterdam University and Nederlandse Sociologisch Vereninging (Dutch Sociological Association). In Dutch; some articles in English.
Indexed: Bull. sig. soc. eth.; Int. Bibl. Soc.; Soc. Abstr.; Urb. Aff. Abstr.

1228 MENSCH UND GESELLSCHAFT. v.1–9, 1944–1949. Bern, Francke. Irreg.
Monograph series.

DER MENSCH UND SEINE WELT
See THE HUMAN CONTEXT

1229 MENTAL HEALTH AND SOCIETY. v.1–6, 1974–1979. New York, S. Karger. Bimonthly.
Indexed: Soc. Abstr.

MERRILL-PALMER QUARTERLY
See MERRILL-PALMER QUARTERLY OF BEHAVIOR AND DEVELOPMENT

1230 MERRILL-PALMER QUARTERLY OF BEHAVIOR AND DEVELOPMENT. v.1– , fall 1954– . Detroit, Mich. Quarterly.
Issued by the Institute of Human Development and Family Life. Title varies: 1954–58, *Merrill-Palmer Quarterly*.
Indexed: Abstr. Soc. Work; Soc. Abstr.; Soc. Work Res. Abstr.; Wom. Stud. Abstr.

MÉTHODES DE LA SOCIOLOGIE
See Maison des Sciences de l'Homme. MÉTHODES DE LA SOCIOLOGIE

1231 METODOLOGICHESKIE I SOTSIALNYE PROBLEMY TEKHNIKI I TEKHNICHESKIKH NAUK. 1– , 1972– . Leningrad.
Issued by the Institut istorii, estestvoznaniia i tekhniki, Leningradskoe otdelenie, Akademiia nauk S.S.S.R. In Russian.

1232 METODOLOGICHESKIE PROBLEMY OBSHCHESTVENNYKH NAUK. no.1– , 1968– . Leningrad, Izd-tvo Leningradskogo universiteta. Irreg.
Title varies: no.1–4, 1968–75, *Metodologicheskie voprosy obshchestvennykh nauk.* In Russian.

METODOLOGICHESKIE VOPROSY OBSHCHESTVENNYKH NAUK
See METODOLOFICHESKIE PROBLEMY OBSHCHESTVENNYKH NAUK

METROPOLITAN AREA ANNUAL
See New York. State University, Albany. Graduate School of Public Affairs. METROPOLITAN AREA ANNUAL

1233 METROPOLITAN AREA DIGEST. Oct/Nov. 1957–1968. Albany, N.Y. Bimonthly.
Issued by the Graduate School of Public Affairs, State University of New York. Issues for Oct/Nov. 1957–Sep/Oct. 1962 published by the Conference on Metropolitan Area Problems. Title varies: 1957–Jan/Feb. 1966, *Metropolitan Area Problems.* Vols. 1–7 include annual supplement titled *Metropolitan Surveys.*

METROPOLITAN AREA PLANNING
See PLANNING IN NORTH EASTERN ILLINOIS

METROPOLITAN AREA PROBLEMS
See METROPOLITAN AREA DIGEST

METROPOLITAN STUDIES SERIES
See INTERMET METROPOLITAN STUDIES SERIES

1234 METROPOLITAN STUDY. 1– , 1967– . Kingston, R.I. Irreg.
Issued by the Bureau of Government Research, University of Rhode Island.
Monograph series.

METROPOLITAN SURVEY
See METROPOLITAN AREA DIGEST

METROPOLITAN SURVEYS
See New York (State). State University. Graduate School of Public Affairs. METROPOLITAN SURVEYS

1235 METROPOLITAN VIEWPOINTS. v.1–3, no.2, Aug. 1966–May 1968. Albany, N.Y. Quarterly.
Issued by the Graduate School of Public Affairs, State University of New York.

MEXICAN JOURNAL OF BEHAVIOR ANALYSIS
See REVISTA MEXICANA DE ANALISIS DE LA CONDUCTA

1236 Michigan. State University, East Lansing. Department of Communications. DIFFUSION OF INNOVATIONS IN RURAL SOCIETIES. TECHNICAL REPORT. no.1–13, 1967–1972. East Lansing. Irreg.

1237 Michigan. State University, East Lansing. Institute for Community Development and Services. BIBLIOGRAPHY. no.1–16, 1962–1965. East Lansing.
Title varies: *Bibliographic Services.*

1238 Michigan. State University, East Lansing. Institute for Community Development and Services. POPULATION REPORT; COMMUNITY DEVELOPMENT SERIES. 1–3, 1972–1974. East Lansing.
Subseries of its *Technical Bulletin.*

1239 Michigan. State University, East Lansing. Institute for Community Development and Services. TECHNICAL BULLETIN. no.1– , 1972– . East Lansing, Mich. Ceased publication.
Mimeographed.

1240 Michigan. University. Detroit Area Study. A SOCIAL PROFILE OF DETROIT. 1952–1956. Ann Arbor, Mich.
Continued by: *Report to the Respondents.*

1241 Michigan. University. Institute of Public Policy Studies. DISCUSSION PAPER. no.1– , 1968– . Ann Arbor, Mich. Irreg.
Series of papers. Processed.

1242 Michigan. University. Population Studies Center. ANNUAL REPORT. 1959–1962– . Ann Arbor, Mich. Report year-end June 30.

1243 Michigan. University. Research Center for Group Dynamics. RCGDS PUBLICATIONS. no.1–6, 1948–1959. Ann Arbor, Mich.

1244 Michigan. University. Survey Research Center. YOUTH IN TRANSITION. v.1– , 1972– . Ann Arbor, Mich. Irreg.
Monograph series.

1245 THE MICHIGAN INDEX TO LABOR PERIODICALS. Jan/June 1960–1967. Ann Arbor, Mich. Monthly, with semi-annual cumulations in 1960; annual cumulations 1961– .
Issued by the Bureau of Industrial Relations, University of Michigan. Title varies: 1960–66, *The University of Michigan Index to Labor Union Periodicals.*

1246 MID-AMERICAN REVIEW OF SOCIOLOGY. 1– , spring 1976– . Lawrence, Kansas. Semi-annual.
Issued by the Department of Sociology, University of Kansas. Supersedes: *Kansas Journal of Sociology*.
Indexed: Int. Bibl. Soc.; Soc. Abstr.

1247 THE MIDDLE EAST JOURNAL. v.1– , Jan. 1947– . Washington, D.C. Quarterly.
Issued by the Oriental Institute.
Indexed: Afr. Abstr.; Anth. Ind.; Bull. sig. soc. eth.; Int. Bibl. Soc.; Int. Pol. Sc. Abstr.; PAIS; Peace Res. Abstr. J.; Soc. Sc. Hum. Ind.; Soc. Sc. Ind.; Soc. Abstr.

1248 MIDDLE EASTERN STUDIES. v.1– , Oct. 1964– . London, F. Cass. Three issues a year.
Issued by the London School of Economics and Political Science.
Indexed: Abstr. Anth.; Brit. Hum. Ind.; Int. Pol. Sc. Abstr.; Int. Bibl. Soc.; Soc. Sc. Ind.; Soc. Abstr.

1249 THE MIDWEST SOCIOLOGIST. v.1–21, 1939–July 1959. St. Louis, Mo. Semi-annual.
Superseded by: *Sociological Quarterly*.

1250 MIGRACIÓN, POBLACIÓN, TURISMO. v.1–2, no.8, 1940–1941. Mexico, D.F.
In Spanish.

MIGRACIÓNES INTERNACIONALES
See Intergovernmental Committee for European Migration, Geneva. INTERNATIONAL MIGRATION

1251 MIGRATION. v.1, Jan–Dec. 1952. Geneva. Bimonthly.
Issued by the International Labour Office. Superseded by: *Migration,* a supplement to the periodical *Industry and Labour*.

1252 MIGRATION. v.1–2, Jan/Mar. 1961–July/Dec. 1962. Geneva. Quarterly.
Issued by the Intergovernmental Committee for European Migration. Superseded by its *International Migration*.

1253 MIGRATION NEWS. [1]– , Oct. 1952– . Geneva. Monthly. 1952–Dec. 1955; bimonthly, Jan/Feb. 1956– .
Issued by the Commission Internationale Catholique pour les Migrations. Published also in French, with a slightly different content.
Indexed: Soc. Abstr.; Urb. Aff. Abstr.

MIGRATION STATISTICS
See Ghana. Central Bureau of Statistics. MIGRATION STATISTICS

1254 MIGRATION TODAY. 1– , 1973– . Staten Island, N.Y. Bimonthly.
Issued by the Center for Migration Studies of New York.
Indexed: Urb. Aff. Abstr.

MIGRATIONS INTERNATIONALES
See Intergovernmental Committee for European Migration, Geneva. INTERNATIONAL MIGRATION

1255 MIGRATIONS; SERIE INFORMATIVE. Genève.
Issued by the Secretariat Générale, Commission Internationale Catholique pour les Migrations. Published also in English, with a slightly different content.

1256 Milan. Università Cattolica del Sacro Cuore. PUBBLICAZIONI. SERIE TERZA: SOCIOLOGIA. 1– , 1961– . Milano. Irreg.
Continues, in part, its *Pubblicazioni. Serie 2: Nueva Serie*. In Italian.

1257 Milan. Università Commerciale L. Bocconi. Centro per la Ricercha Operativa. BOLLETINO. SERIE SOCIOLOGICA. 1– , Jan/Apr. 1959– . Milano. Irreg.
Supersedes, in part, its *Bolletino*.

1258 MILBANK MEMORIAL FUND QUARTERLY. 1– , 1923– . New York. Quarterly.
Indexed: Bull. sig. soc. eth.; Int. Bibl. Soc.; PAIS; Soc. Abstr.

MIMEOGRAPH BULLETIN
See Cornell University. Department of Rural Sociology. BULLETIN

MIMEOGRAPH BULLETINS
See Ohio. State University. Agricultural Economics and Rural Sociology Department. ESS [ECONOMIC AND SOCIOLOGIC SERIES]

1259 MIN TSU T'UAN-CHIEH. v.1– , Oct. 1957–. Pekin. Monthly.

1260 MINERVA. v.1– , autumn 1962– . London, Macmillan Journals. Quarterly.
Issued by the International Association for Cultural Freedom. Subtitle reads: 'A review of science, learning and policy'.
Indexed: Afr. Abstr.; Int. Bibl. Soc. Cult. Anth.; Int. Pol. Sc. Abstr.; PAIS; Soc. Abstr.; Urb. Aff. Abstr.

1261 Minnesota. Agricultural Experiment Station, St. Anthony Park. SOCIOLOGY OF RURAL LIFE. 1–4, 1959–1963. St. Anthony Park. Irreg.
Continued by a quarterly publication with the same tile, v.1– , Mar. 1978– . Extension Service, Agricultural Experiment Station, University of Minnesota.

1262 Minnesota. University. Center for Population Studies. OCCASIONAL STUDIES. no.1– , 1973– . Minneapolis, Minn. Irreg.

1263 Minnesota. University. Center for Youth Development and Research. SEMINAR SERIES. 1–7, 1970–1976. St. Paul. Minn. Annual.

1264 MINORITY ORGANIZATIONS: A NATIONAL DIRECTORY. 1– , 1978– . Garret Park, Md., Garret Park Press. Irreg.

1265 Minority Rights Group. REPORT. no.1– , 1970– . London. Irreg.
Series of papers.

1266 Mississippi. Agricultural Experiment Station, State College. PROGRESS REPORT IN SOCIOLOGY AND RURAL LIFE. no.1–35, 1954–July 1970. State College, Miss.

1267 Mississippi. Agricultural Experiment Station, State College. SOCIOLOGY AND RURAL LIFE SERIES. 1–30, 1950–June 1975. State College, Miss. Irreg.
Monograph series.

1268 Mississippi. State University. Department of Sociology and Anthropology. SOC[IOLOGY] AND AN[THROPOLOGY] REPORT. no.1–16, Nov. 1966–Oct. 1971. State College, Miss.

1269 Mississippi. University. Bureau of Governmental Research. SOCIOLOGICAL STUDY SERIES. no.1–5, 1947–1955. Lafayette County.
The Bureau earlier called Bureau of Public Administration.

MITTEILUNGEN
See Österreichische Gesellschaft für Soziologie. MITTEILUNGEN

1270 MODERN ASIAN STUDIES. v.1– , 1966– . London, Cambridge University Press. Quarterly.
Issued by the School of Oriental and African Studies, University of London; Centre of South Asian Studies, University of Cambridge; Centre for South East Asian Studies, University of Hull; Department of Chinese Studies, University of Leeds, and Centre of Japanese Studies, University of Sheffield.
Indexed: Int. Bibl. Soc.; Int. Bibl. Soc. Cult. Anth.; Int. Pol. Sc. Abstr.; Soc. Sc. Ind.; Soc. Abstr.; Wom. Stud. Abstr.

1271 MODERN LAW AND SOCIETY. v.1– , 1968– . Tübingen. Semi-annual.
Issued by the Institute for Scientific Cooperation. Subseries of *German Studies, Section 2.* Subtitle reads: 'A review of German language and research contributions on law, political science and sociology'.

1272 MONATSCHRIFT FÜR SOZIOLOGIE. v.1, Jan–Dec. 1909. Leipzig.
Merged with *Archiv für Sozialwissenschaft und Sozialpolitik.*

IL MONDO VISSUTO DELL'UOMO
See THE HUMAN CONTEXT

1273 MONOGRAFIAS DE SOCIOLOGIA FAMILIAR. 1– , 1974– . La Paz, Bolivia. Irreg.
Issued by the Centro de Investigaciónes Sociales.

1274 MONOGRAFIAS SOCIOLOGICAS. no.1–27, 1959–1968. Bogotá. Irreg.
Issued by the Faculdad de Sociologia, Universidad Nacional de Colombia. In Spanish. Some works with summaries in English.
Series of papers.

MONOGRAFIER
See Götheborg, Sweden. Universitet. Sociologiska Institutionen. MONOGRAFIER

MONOGRAPH
See Association of Social Anthropologists. MONOGRAPH

MONOGRAPH
See California. University. University at Los Angeles. Chicano Studies Center. MONOGRAPH

MONOGRAPH
See North Carolina. University. Carolina Population Center. MONOGRAPH

MONOGRAPH
See North Dakota. University. Center for the Study of Cultural and Social Change. MONOGRAPH

MONOGRAPH
See Rural Sociological Society. MONOGRAPH

MONOGRAPH
See Washington (State). Center for Urban and Regional Research. MONOGRAPH

[MONOGRAPH] SRC
See California. University. Survey Research Center. [MONOGRAPH] SRC

[MONOGRAPH] SRC M
See California. University. Survey Research Center. [MONOGRAPH] SRC

MONOGRAPH AND OCCASIONAL PAPER SERIES
See Duke University, Durham, N.C. Commonwealth Studies Center. Program in Comparative Studies on Southern Asia. MONOGRAPH AND OCCASIONAL PAPER SERIES

MONOGRAPH SERIES
See California. University. University at Los Angeles. Institute of Industrial Relations. MONOGRAPH SERIES

MONOGRAPH SERIES
See Eugenics Research Association. MONOGRAPH SERIES

MONOGRAPH SERIES
See South African Institute of Race Relations. MONOGRAPH SERIES

1275 MONOGRAPH SERIES ON SOCIAL AND CULTURAL CHANGE. 1, 1965. Kalamazoo, Mich. Irreg.
Issued by the Institute of International and Area Studies, Western Michigan University.

MONOGRAPH SERIES; SOCIOLOGY
See Société Canadienne de Sociologie et d'Anthropologie. MONOGRAPH SERIES; SOCIOLOGY

MONOGRAPH SUPPLEMENT
See JOURNAL OF PERSONALITY AND SOCIAL PSYCHOLOGY

1276 MONOGRAPHIEN UND STUDIEN ZUR KONFLIKT-PSYCHOLOGIE. ABT.1: KONFLIKT ANALYSE. v.1–6, 1963–1969. München, E. Reinhardt. Irreg.
Monograph series.

MONOGRAPHIEN ZUR SOZIOLOGIE UND GESELLSCHAFTSPOLITIK
See SOCIAL STRATEGIES; MONOGRAPHS ON SOCIOLOGY AND SOCIAL POLICY

MONOGRAPHIES BIBLIOGRAPHIQUES
See Instituts Solvay. Institut de Sociologie. MONOGRAPHIES BIBLIOGRAPHIQUES

MONOGRAPHS
See Centre for the Study of Developing Societies. MONOGRAPHS

MONOGRAPHS
See Rutgers University. Center for Alcohol Studies. MONOGRAPHS

MONOGRAPHS
See Yale University. Center of Alcohol Studies. MONOGRAPHS

MONOGRAPHS IN SOCIAL RESEARCH
See National Opinion Research Center. MONOGRAPHS IN SOCIAL RESEARCH

MONOGRAPHS OF THE RUTGERS CENTER FOR ALCOHOL STUDIES
See Rutgers University. Center for Alcohol Studies. MONOGRAPHS

1277 Montana. State University. Department of Anthropology and Sociology. ANTHROPOLOGY AND SOCIOLOGY PAPERS. no.1–31, 1950–1965. Missoula, Mont.

1278 Montevideo. Universidad. Instituto de Ciencias Sociales. CUADERNOS DE CIENCIAS SOCIALES. 1– , 1970– . Montevideo. Irreg.
In Spanish.
Monograph series.

A MONTHLY SUMMARY OF EVENTS AND TRENDS IN RACE RELATIONS
See RACE RELATIONS

1279 Morija, Lesotho. University of Botswana, Lesotho and Swaziland. LOCAL STUDIES SERIES. 1– , 1971– . Morija. Irreg.
Monograph series.

MOUVEMENT DE LA POPULATION DE l'EMPIRE DU JAPON
See Japan. Naikaku Tokeikyoku. MOUVEMENT DE LA POPULATION DE L'EMPIRE DU JAPON

MOUVEMENT DE LA POPULATION EN SUISSE
See Switzerland Statistisches Amt. BEVÖLKERUNGSBEWEGUNG IN DER SCHWEITZ

MOUVEMENT SOCIOLOGIQUE
See LE MOUVEMENT SOCIOLOGIQUE INTERNATIONAL

1280 LE MOUVEMENT SOCIOLOGIQUE INTERNATIONAL. 1–11, 1900–1911. Bruxelles, Louvain.
Title varies: v.1–7, no.1, 1900–1906, *Mouvement Sociologique,* supplement to *Revue Néo-scholastique de Philosophie.* Merged with *Annales de Sociologie.*

1281 AL-MUJTAMA! 1962– . Khartoum. Irreg.
In Arabic and English.

1282 IL MULINO. 1– , Nov. 1951– . Bologna. Monthly, subsequently bimonthly.
Subtitle reads: 'Rivista bimestrale di culture e di politica'. In Italian.
Indexed: Soc. Abstr.

1283 MULTIVARIATE BEHAVIORAL RESEARCH. v.1– , Jan. 1966– . Fort Worth, Tex. Quarterly.
Issued by the Society for Multivariate Experimental Psychology, University of Colorado, Boulder.
Indexed: Psych. Abstr.; Soc. Abstr.

1284 MULLI NONJIP. HUMANITIES AND SCIENCES. v.1– , 1955– . Seoul, Korea. Annual.
Issued by the Mullikwa-Taehak, Koryŏ-Taehakkyo. Each issue is divided into two sections: Humanities and social sciences, and Natural sciences. In Korean. Table of contents also in English.

1285 Musée Social, Paris. ANNALES. v.7–19, no.7, 1902–Jan. 1914. Paris. Vols. 14–19, 1909–14, misnumbered 16–21.

1286 Musée Social, Paris. BULLETIN MENSUELLE. 4–6, 1899–1901. Paris.

1287 Musée Social, Paris. CAHIERS. 1944–1963? Paris. Supersedes: *Revue Mensuelle*. Superseded by *Vie Sociale*.

1288 Musée Social, Paris. CIRCULAIRE. SÉRIE A. 1896–1898. Paris.

1289 Musée Social, Paris. CIRCULAIRE. SÉRIE B. 1896–1898. Paris.

290 Musée Social, Paris. MÉMOIRES ET DOCUMENTS (SUPPLÉMENTS AUX ANNALES). 1902–[1921]. Paris. Not published Aug. 1914–17. Paris.

1291 Musée Social, Paris. REVUE MENSUELLE. 1896–1939. Paris.
Superseded by its *Cahiers*.

1292 Museo Social Argentino, Buenos Aires. BOLETIN. v.1– , Jan/Feb. 1912– . Buenos Aires. Frequency varies.
Title varies: 1948, *Revista*. Publication suspended Feb/Aug. 1922, 1927, 1949 58. Issues for 1912–48 also called no. 1–317/318. Indexes: v.1–15, 1912–26, in 1 vol. In Spanish.
Indexed: Int. Bibl. Soc.

MUTATION SOCIALE ET RÉVOLUTION
See SOCIALE VERANDERING EN REVOLUTIE

1293 München. Universität. Max Weber Institut. VERÖFFENTLICHUNGEN. 1– , 1967– . Tübingen, J.C.B. Mohr (Paul Siebeck). Irreg.
Monograph series.

N.F.R.B. PUBLICATIONS
See Fabian Society, London. RESEARCH SERIES

NOP BULLETIN
See National Opinion Polls, Ltd. NOP BULLETIN

NORC MONOGRAPHS IN SOCIAL RESEARCH
See National Opinion Research Center. MONOGRAPHS IN SOCIAL RESEARCH

NPPA JOURNAL
See CRIME AND DELINQUENCY

NANYANG QUARTERLY
See REVIEW OF SOUTHEAST ASIAN STUDIES

1294 Nanyang University. Institute of Humanities and Social Sciences. RESEARCH PROJECT SERIES. no.1– , 1976– . Singapore. Irreg.

1295 NARODY AZII I AFRIKI. 1961– . Moskva, 'Nauka'. Bimonthly.
Indexed: Int. Bibl. Soc.

1296 National Council on Family Relations. ANNUAL MEETING PROCEEDINGS. 1966–1970/71. Minneapolis. Annual.
Mimeographed.

1297 NATIONAL DIRECTORY OF SOCIOLOGY OF EDUCATION AND EDUCATIONAL SOCIOLOGY. 1– , 1974– . Lincoln, Nebr. Annual.
Issued by the Teachers College, University of Nebraska.

1298 NATIONAL OPINION POLL. 1– , Jan. 1978– . San Raphael, Calif., National Opinion Poll Co.

1299 National Opinion Polls, Ltd. NOP BULLETIN. 1– , 1963– . London. Monthly.

1300 National Opinion Research Center. MONOGRAPHS IN SOCIAL RESEARCH. no.1– , 1964– . Chicago, Ill. Irreg.
Monograph series.

1301 National Opinion Research Center. NEWSLETTER. no.1– , 1967– . Chicago. Irreg.

1302 National Opinion Research Center. OCCASIONAL REPORTS. SERIES FA. no.1–4, 1953–1957. Chicago.

1303 National Opinion Research Center. REPORT. no.[1]– , Dec. 1941– . Chicago.

NATIONAL REGISTER OF RESEARCH PROJECTS; NATURAL AND HUMAN SCIENCES

See South Africa. Office of the Scientific Adviser to the Prime Minister. NASIONALE REGISTER VAN NAVORSINGSPROJECTE: NATUUR- EN GEESTESWETENSCHAPPE

THE NATIONAL REVIEW OF SOCIAL SCIENCES
See Cairo. al-Markaz al-Qawmi lil-Buḥuth al-Ijtima'iyah. AL-MAJALLAT AL-IJTIMA'IYAH AL-QAWMIYAH

1304 NATIONAL STUDIES. 1– , Jan. 1975– . Belize City. Bimonthly.
Issued by the Belize Institute of Social Research and Action.

NATIONAL TAIWAN UNIVERSITY JOURNAL OF SOCIOLOGY
See T'ai-wan to Hsüeh, Taipei. T'AI-WAN TA HSÜEH SHE HUI HSÜEH K'AN

NATÜRLICHE BEVÖLKERUNGSBEWEGUNG
See Austria. Statistisches Zentralamt. NATÜRLICHE BEVÖLKERUNGSBEWEGUNG

NATÜRLICHE BEVÖLKERUNGSBEWEGUNG IN BERLIN (West)
See Berlin (West). Statistisches Landesamt. NATÜRLICHE BEVÖLKERUNGSBEWEGUNG IN BERLIN (West)

NAUCHNI TRUDOVE
See Akademiia za obshchestveni nauki i sotsialno upravlenie. NAUCHNI TRUDOVE

NAUCHNYE TRUDY. SERIIA OBSHCHESTVENNYKH NAUK
See Erivan. Armianskii gosudarstvennyi pedagogicheskii institut. NAUCHYE TRUDY. SERIIA OBSHCHESTVENNYKH NAUK

1305 Nederlands Interuniversitair Demografisch Instituut (N.I.D.I.). PUBLIKATIES. 1– , 1971– . Assen, Van Gorcum. Irreg.
In Dutch; summaries in English.
Monograph series.

NESELENIE
See Bulgaria. Durzhavno upravlenie za informatsiia. NESELENIE

1306 Netherlands. Centraal Bureau voor de Statistiek. BEVOLKING DER GEMEENTEN VAN NEDERLAND. 1920– . Zeist. Annual.
Title varies: 1920–32, *Bevolking en oppervlakte der Gemeenten van Nederland.*

NETHERLANDS JOURNAL OF ECONOMIC AND SOCIAL GEOGRAPHY
See TIJDSCHRIFT VOOR ECONOMISCHE EN SOCIALE GEOGRAFIE

1307 THE NETHERLANDS JOURNAL OF SOCIOLOGY. v.12– , July 1976– . Amsterdam, Elsevier Scientific Publichers. Semi-annual.
Issued by the Netherlands Sociological and Anthropological Society. Continues: *Sociologia Neerlandica.*
Indexed: SSCI; Soc. Abstr.

1308 NEW APPROACHES TO COMMUNITY IN NEW ZEALAND. MONOGRAPH. 1– , 1972– . Wellington, N.Z. Irreg.
Issued by the Policy Study Group, Labour Party.
Series of papers and monographs.

NEW BULLETIN
See COMMUNITY

1309 NEW COMMUNITY. v.1– , Oct. 1971– . London. Quarterly.
Issued by the Community Relations Commission. Supersedes: *Community.*
Indexed: Brit. Hum. Ind.; Urb. Aff. Abstr.

1310 NEW EQUALS. v.1– , Nov/Dec. 1977– . London. Six issues a year.
Issued by the Commission for Racial Equality. Supersides: *Equals.*

1311 NEW GUINEA RESEARCH BULLETIN. no.1–63, Apr. 1963–1975. Canberra. Six or seven issues a year.
Issued by the New Guinea Research Unit, Research School of Pacific Studies, Australian National University.
Indexed: Int. Bibl. Soc.; Soc. Abstr.

NEW GUINEA RESEARCH UNIT BULLETIN
See NEW GUINEA RESEARCH BULLETIN

1312 NEW LEFT REVIEW. no.1– , 1960– . London, New Left Review, Ltd. Bimonthly.
Supersedes: *Universities and Left Review.*
Indexed: Brit. Hum. Ind.; Bull. sig. soc. eth.; PAIS; Soc. Sc. Ind.; Soc. Abstr.; Urb. Aff. Abstr.

1313 THE NEW SCHOLAR. v.1– , Apr. 1969– . San Diego. Two issues a year.
Issued by the San Diego State College.
Indexed: Psych. Abstr.; Soc. Abstr.

1314 NEW SOCIETY. no.1– , Oct. 1962– . London, New Science Publications. Weekly.
Indexed: Brit. Hum. Ind.; Bull. sig. soc. eth.; Crime Del. Lit.; SSCI; Sage Fam. Stud. Abstr.; Soc. Abstr.; Urb. Aff. Abstr.; Wom. Stud. Abstr.

1315 NEW SOCIOLOGY. v.1– , 1971– . Kingston-upon-Thames.
Issued by the School of Sociology, Kingston Polytechnic.
Indexed: Soc. Abstr.

1316 New South Wales. University, Kensington. School of Sociology. STUDIES IN SOCIOLOGY. no.1–3, 1961–1963. Kensington.
Superseded by: *Studies in Society*.

1317 NEW WOMAN SERIES. 1–?, 1971–?. Toronto, New Press. Irreg. Ceased publication.
Monograph series.

1318 New York (City). University. NEW YORK UNIVERSITY REVIEW OF LAW AND SOCIAL CHANGE. v.1– , 1971– . New York.

1319 New York (State). State College of Human Ecology. REPORT. v.51– , 1975/1976– . Ithaca, N.Y.
Earlier vols. issued in the series: New York (State) Legislature. *Legislative Document*. Report year-end, June 30. Continues its *Annual Report* 1945–49, 1969/70–1973/74; and earlier, New York. State College of Human Economics. *Annual Report*.

1320 New York (State). State University, Albany. Graduate School of Public Affairs. METROPOLITAN AREA ANNUAL. 1966–1969. Albany, N.Y. Annual.
Supersedes: *Metropolitan Surveys; A Digest* (1925–57). Data based on *Metropolitan Surveys*, issued by the Graduate School of Public Affairs.

1321 New York (State). State University. Graduate School of Public Affairs. METROPOLITAN SURVEYS. 1967–1968. Albany, N.Y. Annual.

NEW YORK UNIVERSITY REVIEW OF LAW AND SOCIAL CHANGE
See New York (City). University. NEW YORK UNIVERSITY REVIEW OF LAW AND SOCIAL CHANGE

1322 Newcastle-upon-Tyne. University. Department of Geography. PAPERS ON MIGRATION AND MOBILITY IN NORTHERN ENGLAND. no.1–5, 1965–1969. Newcastle-upon-Tyne. Irreg.
Title varies: no.1–3, *Papers on Migration and Mobility in Northeast England*.

NEWSLETTER
See Institute of Race Relations. NEWS LETTER

NEWSLETTER
See Cross-Cultural Southwest Ethnic Study Center. NEWSLETTER

NEWSLETTER
See International Society for the Sociology of Knowledge. NEWSLETTER

NEWSLETTER
See National Opinion Research Center. NEWSLETTER

NEWSLETTER
See Sociologists for Woman in Society. NEWSLETTER

1323 NEWSLETTER ON HUMAN ECOLOGY. v.1–?, 1958–?. Elsah, Ill. Quarterly (irreg.). Ceased publication.
Issued by the Human Ecological Society. First issues published by the Institute of Human Ecology.

1324 Nicaragua. Dirección General de Estadistica y Censos. BOLETIN DE ESTADISTICA. ESTADISTICAS DEMOGRAFICAS. 1967– . Managua. Annual.

1325 THE NIGERIAN JOURNAL OF SOCIOLOGY AND ANTHROPOLOGY. 1– , Sep. 1974– . Ibadan. Annual.
Issued by the Nigerian Anthropological and Sociological Association.

1326 NIV HA-KEVUTSAH. 1952– . Tel-Aviv. Quarterly.
Issued by the Ihud ha-Kevutsot veha-Kibutsim. In Hebrew.

1327 NORDISK KRIMINALISTIK ÅRSBOK. YEARBOOK OF THE NORTHERN ASSOCIATION OF CRIMINALISTS. 1963– . Oslo; subsequently Stockholm. Annual.
Issued by the Finnish, Icelandic, Danish and Swedish Association of Criminalists. Title varies: 1936–51, *Nordiska Kriminalist Föreningarnas Årsbok*. In Scandinavian, Icelandic and English. Table of contents and summaries in English and French.

1328 NORDISK MINORITETSFORSKNING. v.1–2, 1975–1976. Johanneshov.
Continued by: *Invandrare och Minoriteter. Scandinavian Migration and Ethnic Review*.

1329 NORDISK TIDSSKRIFT FOR KRIMINAL VIDENSKAB. 1913– . København, Gade Vorlag. Quarterly.
Title varies: *Nordisk Tidsskrift for Strafferet*, 1913–1948.
Indexed: Soc. Abstr.

NORDISKA KRIMINALIST FÖRENINGARNAS ÅRSBOK
See NORDISK KRIMINALISTIK ÅRSBOK

1330 NORDISKE STUDIER I SOCIOLOGI. 1–3, 1948–1951? København, GESC.
Title in English: *Scandinavian Studies in Sociology*. In Danish and English.
Monograph series.

1331 North Carolina. University. Carolina Population Center. MONOGRAPH. no.1– , 1969– . Chapel Hill, N.C. Irreg.
Monograph series.

1332 North Dakota. University. Center for the Study of Cultural and Social Change. MONOGRAPH. no.1–5, 1967–1969. Grand Forks, N.Dak. Irreg.
Monograph series.

NORTH EASTERN RESEARCH BULLETIN
See Dibrugarh, India. University. Centre for Sociological Studies of the Frontier Region. NORTH EASTERN RESEARCH BULLETIN

1333 Northern Ireland. Community Relations Commission. ANNUAL REPORT. 1971–1974. Belfast. Annual.
Mimeographed.

1334 Norway. Statistisk Sentralbyraa. FAMILIESTATISTIKK. FAMILY STATISTICS. Oslo.
Subseries of: *Norges Offisielle Statistikk*. In Norwegian and English.

1335 Norway. Statistisk Sentralbyraa. FOLKEMENGDEN ETTER ALDER OG EKTESKAPELIG STATUS. POPULATION BY AGE AND MARITAL STATUS. Oslo. Annual.
Subseries of its *Norges Offisielle Statistikk*. In Norwegian and English.

1336 NOTAS DE POBLACIÓN. 1– , Apr. 1973– . Santiago, Chile.
Issued by the Centro latinoamericano de Demografia (CELADE), United Nations. Supersedes the Centro's *Boletin Informativo*, 1961–72. In Spanish; summaries in English.

1337 NOTES CRITIQUES; SCIENCES SOCIALES. BULLETIN BIBLIOGRAPHIQUE. 1–7, Jan. 1900–Oct. 1906. Paris, Société Nouvelle de Librarie et d'Éditions.

NOTES & MÉMOIRES
See Institute Solvay. Institut de Sociologie.

1338 NOTIZIARIO DI SOCIOLOGIA. 1958– . Genoa. Bimonthly.
In Italian. No more information available.

1339 NOVAIA INOSTRANNAIA LITERATURA PO OBSHCHESTVENNYM NAUKAM. 1976– . Moskva. Monthly.
Issued by the Institut nauchnoi informatsii po obshchestvennym naukam, Adademiia nauk SSSR. Continues: *Novaia inostrannaia literatura po filosofii*. In Russian.

1340 NOVINKY LITERATURY. SOCIOLOGIE. 1971– . Praha, Státni knihovna ČSSR.
Issued by the Ústredni bibliograficke stredisko. Continues: *Novinky literatury. Společenske vědy. Rada X. Filosofie, vědecky komunismus, sociologie*. In Czech.

1341 NOVINKY LITERATURY: SPOLEČENSKE VĚDY. ŘADA X. FILOSOFIE, VĚDECKY KOMUNISMUS, SOCIOLOGIE. 1962–1970. Praha, Státni knihovna ČSSR. Monthly.
Issued by the Bibliograficke stredovisko společenskych věd. Continued by: *Novinky literatury. Sociologie.*

1342 NUEVA SOCIEDAD. REVISTA DE PROBLEMAS SOCIALES, POLITICOS ECONOMICOS Y CULTURALES. 1– , July/Aug. 1972– . San José, Costa Rica. Bimonthly.

1343 NUSANTARA. 1– , Jan. 1972– . Kuala Lumpur, Dewan Bahasa dan Pustaka. Semiannual.
Subtitle reads: 'Journal of the arts and social sciences of Southeast Asia. Majalah sa Sastra dan ILMU2 Kemsharakatan Asia Tenenggara'. In Malay and English.

OBSHCHESTVENNYE NAUKI
See Lietuvos TSR Mosklu Akademija, Vilnius. TRUDY. SERIIA A. OBSHCHESTVENNYE NAUKI

1344 OBSHCHESTVENNYE NAUKI V SSSR. SERIIA 1: PROBLEMY NAUCHNOGO KOMUNIZMA. 1973– . Moskva. Quarterly.
Issued by the Institut nauchnoi informatsii po obshchestvennym naukam, Akademiia nauk S.S.S.R. In Russian.

1345 OBSHCHESTVENNYE NAUKI V TADZHIKISTANE; UKAZATEL' LITERATURY. Dushanbe.
Issued by the Tsentralnaia nauchnaia biblioteka, Akademiia nauk Tadzhiskoi S.S.R. In Russian.

1346 OBSHCHESTVENNYE NAUKI V UZBEKISTANE. Jan. 1961– . Tashkent. Monthly.
Issued by the Akademiia nauk Uzbekskoi S.S.R. Supersedes: Akademiia nauk Uzbekskoi S.S.R. *Izvestiia. Seriia obshchestvennykh nauk.* In Russian.

1347 OBSHCHESTVENNYE NAUKI ZA RUBEZHOM. SERIIA 3: FILOSOFIIA I SOTSIOLOGIIA. 1973– . Moskva. Quarterly.
Issued by the Akademiia nauk S.S.S.R. In Russian.

OCCASIONAL MONOGRAPH
See The Research Centre for Canadian Ethnic Studies. OCCASIONAL MONOGRAPH

OCCASIONAL PAPER
See Birmingham, England. University. Centre for Urban and Regional Studies. OCCASIONAL PAPER

OCCASIONAL PAPER
See California. University. University at Los Angeles. Chicano Studies Center. OCCASIONAL PAPER

OCCASIONAL PAPER
See Centre for Environmental Studies. OCCASIONAL PAPER

OCCASIONAL PAPER
See Glasgow. University of Strathclyde. Survey Research Centre. OCCASIONAL PAPER

OCCASIONAL PAPER
See Kampala. Makerere University. Department of Sociology. Social Psychology Section. OCCASIONAL PAPER

OCCASIONAL PAPER
See Lucknow. University. Demographic Research Centre. OCCASIONAL PAPER

OCCASIONAL PAPERS
See Ahmadu Bello University, Zaria, Nigeria. Sociology Department. OCCASIONAL PAPERS.

OCCASIONAL PAPERS
See Bangor, Wales. University College of North Wales. Department of Social Theory and Institutions. OCCASIONAL PAPERS

OCCASIONAL PAPERS
See Brighton, England. University of Sussex. Research Unit for the Study of the Multi-Racial Societies. OCCASIONAL PAPERS

OCCASIONAL PAPERS
See Cornell University. Western Societies Program. OCCASIONAL PAPERS

OCCASIONAL PAPERS
See Glasgow. University of Strathclyde. Department of Sociology. OCCASIONAL PAPERS

OCCASIONAL PAPERS
See Howard University, Washington, D.C. Institute for Urban Affairs and Research. OCCASIONAL PAPERS

OCCASIONAL PAPERS
See Illinois. Northern Illinois University, DeKalb. Center for Black Studies. OCCASIONAL PAPERS.

OCCASIONAL PAPERS
See McMaster University. Sociology of Women Program. OCCASIONAL PAPERS

OCCASIONAL PAPERS
See Manitoba. University. Center for Settlement Studies. SERIES 5: OCCASIONAL PAPERS

OCCASIONAL PAPERS
See Open University. Urban Research Group. OCCASIONAL PAPERS

OCCASIONAL PAPERS
See Rocky Mountain College, Billings, Mont. Center for Indian Studies. OCCASIONAL PAPERS

OCCASIONAL PAPERS
See Salisbury, Zimbabwe. University. Department of Sociology. OCCASIONAL PAPERS

OCCASIONAL PAPERS
See World Fertility Survey. OCCASIONAL PAPERS

OCCASIONAL PAPERS IN APPLIED POLICY RESEARCH
See Oregon Research Institute. OCCASIONAL PAPERS IN APPLIED POLICY RESEARCH

1348 OCCASIONAL PAPERS IN SURVEY RESEARCH. 1– , 1972– . London. Irreg.
Issued by the Survey Unit, Social Science Research Council.

OCCASIONAL PUBLICATION
See Ibadan, Nigeria. University. Institute of African Studies. OCCASIONAL PUBLICATION

OCCASIONAL PUBLICATIONS
See Ahmadu Bello University, Zaria, Nigeria. Sociology Department. OCCASIONAL PAPERS

OCCASIONAL REPORTS. SERIES FA
See National Opinion Research Center. OCCASIONAL REPORTS. SERIES FA

OCCASIONAL STUDIES
See Minnesota. University. Center for Population Studies. OCCASIONAL STUDIES

1349 OEUVRE SOCIOLOGIQUE. The Hague, Mouton. Irreg.
Subseries of: *Collection Géographique, Historique, Sociologique.* Ceased publication.

1350 Ohio. State University. Agricultural Economics and Rural Sociology Department. ESPR [ECONOMIC AND SOCIOLOGIC PEER REVIEW]. no.1– , Feb. 1980– . Columbus, Ohio. Irreg.

1351 Ohio. State University. Agricultural Economics and Rural Sociology Department. ESS [ECONOMIC AND SOCIOLOGIC SERIES]. no.1– , 1927?– .
Title varies: no.1–215, 1927?–Apr. 1950?, *Rural Sociology Mimeographs,* issued by the Department of Rural Economics; no.216–448, May 1950–May? 1971, *Mimeograph Bulletins,* issued by the Department of Agricultural Economics and Rural Sociology; no. 449–496, June 1971–Oct? 1973, *Economic and Sociology Mimeographs,* issued by Ohio State University Extension Service at Ohio State University; no. 497–582, Nov. 1973–197?, *Economic and Sociology Studies.* Issues no.583–599 not published.

1352 Ohio. State University. Agricultural Economics and Rural Sociology Department. ECONOMICS AND SOCIOLOGY OCCASIONAL PAPERS. no.1– , Nov. 1969– . Columbus, Ohio. Irreg.

1353 OHTANI DAIGAKU SHAKAIGAKU NENPO. no.1–9, Oct. 1947–1965. Kyoto. Irreg. Issued by the Ohtani Daigaku Shakai Gakkai. Title in English: Ohtani University Annual Report on Sociology. In Japanese.

OHTANI UNIVERSITY ANNUAL REPORT ON SOCIOLOGY
See OHTANI DAIGAKU SHAKAIGAKU NENPO

1354 Ontario Conference on Inter-Group Relations. REPORT. v.1– , 1961– . Ontario, Canada. Annual.

1355 Open University. Urban Research Group. OCCASIONAL PAPER. no.1– , 1978– . Milton Keynes, England. Irreg.

1356 OPINION NEWS. v.1–11, no.7, Sep. 13, 1943–Oct. 1948. Denver. Biweekly.
Issued by the National Opinion Research Center, University of Denver. Subtitle reads: 'A fortnightly digest of outstanding polls and surveys'.

1357 Oregon. University. UNIVERSITY OF OREGON MONOGRAPHS. STUDIES IN SOCIOLOGY. no.1, Nov. 1953. Eugene, Oreg., University Press. One volume published.

1358 Oregon Research Institute. OCCASIONAL PAPERS IN APPLIED POLICY RESEARCH. 1– , 1975– . Eugene, Oreg. Irreg.

1359 Oregon Social Hygiene Society. THE BULLETIN. v.1–4, no.10, 1913–Oct. 1917. Portland.

1360 Organisation of Sociologists in Polytechnics and Cognate Institutions. SIP PAPER. no.1– , 1976– . Hatfield, England. Irreg.
Series of papers.

1361 ORGANIZATION STUDIES. 1– , Jan. 1980– . Berlin, New York, Walter de Gruyter. Quarterly.
Issued in cooperation with the European Group for Organizational Studies (EGOS) and the Maison des Sciences de l'Homme. Paris.
Indexed: Soc. Abstr.

1362 Oslo. Universitet. Instituut för Sosiologi. STUDIES IN SOCIETY. no.1– , 1957– . Oslo, Oslo University Press. Irreg.

1363 OSTEUROPA. v.1– , 1951– . Stuttgart, Deutsche Verlags-Anstalt GmbH. Monthly.
Issued by the Deutsche Gesellschaft für Osteuropakunde. Subtitle reads: 'Zeitschrift für Gegenwartsfragen des Ostens'.
Indexed: Soc. Abstr.

OVERSEA MIGRATION
See Papua New Guinea. Bureau of Statistics. STATISTICAL BULLETIN. INTERNATIONAL MIGRATION

1364 OXFORD STUDIES IN SOCIAL MOBILITY: WORKING PAPERS. 1– , 1972– . Oxford, Clarendon Press. Irreg.
Monograph series.

1365 OYO SHAKAI-GAKU KENKYU. ser.1–10, June 1958–Nov. 1966; n.s. 11– , Mar. 1967– . Tokyo. Irreg.
Issued by the Rikkyō Daigaku Shakaigakubu Kenkyūshitsu. Title in English: *Rikkyō Review of Applied Sociology.*

1366 Österreichische Gesellschaft für Soziologie. JAHRBUCH. 1– , 1976– . Wien, Hermann Bohlaus Nachf. Annual.
Continues: *Österreichesches Jahrbuch für Soziologie.*

1367 Österreichische Gesellschaft für Soziologie. MITTEILUNGEN. no.1– , 1968– . Wien. Quarterly.

1368 ÖSTERREICHISCHES JAHRBUCH FÜR SOZIOLOGIE. 1970–1975. Wien, New York, Springer.
Continued by: Österreichische Gesellschaft für Soziologie. *Jahrbuch.*
Indexed: Int. Bibl. Soc.

1369 ØKOLOGISKE UNDERSØGELSER AF DANSK VAELGERADFORD. 1– , 1968– . Århus. Irreg.
Issued by the Sociologisk Afdeling. Institut for Statskundskab, University of Århus. Irreg.
In Danish; summaries in English.
Monograph series.

PHRA. POVERTY AND HUMAN RESOURCES ABSTRACTS
See HUMAN RESOURCES ABSTRACTS

1370 PACIFIC AFFAIRS. v.1– , 1928– . Richmond, Va. Quarterly.
Issued by the University of British Columbia, Vancouver.
Indexed: Int. Bibl. Soc.; Int. Pol. Sc. Abstr.; PAIS; Peace Res. Abstr. J.; Soc. Sc. Hum. Ind.; Soc. Abstr.; Wom. Stud. Abstr.

1371 THE PACIFIC SOCIOLOGICAL REVIEW. v.1– , spring 1958– . Beverly Hills, Calif., Sage Publications. Quarterly.
Issued by the Pacific Sociological Society and the Department of Sociology, Oregon State University, Corvallis.
Indexed: Curr. Cont.; Int Bibl. Soc.; Int. Pol. Sc. Abstr.; PHRA; Soc. Sc. Ind.; SSCI; Soc. Work Res. Abstr.; Soc. Abstr.

1372 PACIFIC VIEWPOINT. v.1– , Mar. 1960– . Wellington, N.Z. Two issues a year.
Issued by the Department of Geography, Victoria University of Wellington. Indexes: 1–5, 1960–64.
Indexed: Curr. Cont.; Int. Bibl. Soc.; Int. Pol. Sc. Abstr.; SSCI; Soc. Abstr.

1373 PAKISTAN JOURNAL OF FAMILY PLANNING. v.1– , July 1967– . Karachi. Semiannual.
Issued by the National Research Institute of Family Planning.

1375 Palermo. Università. Istituto di Scienze Demografiche. COLLANA DI STUDI DEMOGRAFICI. 1– , 1967– . Palermo, Edizioni Ingrana. Irreg.
In Italian.
Monograph series.

1376 Panama. Dirección de Estadistica y Censo. ESTADISTICA PANAMENA. SERIE A: DEMOGRAFIA. ano.18–, 1957/1958– . Panama. Annual.
Cover title: *Demografia.* Supersedes, in part, and continues the volume numbering of its *Estadistica Panamena.* In Spanish.

1377 Panama (City). Universidad. Instituto Investigaciónes Sociales y Económicas. BOLETIN. v.1–2, no.4, Feb. 1944–June 1945. Panama City.
Chiefly in Spanish; title also in English, French and Portuguese.

THE PAPERS AND PROCEEDINGS
See Regional Science Association. PAPERS AND PROCEEDINGS

PAPERS FROM THE CONFERENCE
See Pakistan Sociological Association. PAPERS FROM THE CONFERENCE

PAPERS FROM THE CONGRESS
See Association for Sociologists in Southern Africa. QUEEN'S UNIVERSITY PAPERS FROM THE CONGRESS

PAPERS IN COMPARATIVE SOCIOLOGY
See Auckland, N.Z. University. Department of Sociology. PAPERS IN COMPARATIVE SOCIOLOGY

PAPERS IN SOCIOLOGY
See Jerusalem. Hebrew University. Institute of Urban and Regional Studies. PAPERS IN SOCIOLOGY

1378 PAPERS IN URBAN PROBLEMS. no.1– , 1976– . Philadelphia, Pa. Irreg.
Issued by the Department of City and Regional Planning, University of Pennsylvania.

PAPERS ON MIGRATION AND MOBILITY IN NORTHEASTERN ENGLAND
See Newcastle-upon-Tyne. University. Department of Geography. PAPERS ON MIGRATION AND MOBILITY IN NORTHERN ENGLAND

PAPERS ON MIGRATION AND MOBILITY IN NORTHERN ENGLAND
See Newcastle-upon-Tyne. University. Department of Geography. PAPERS ON MIGRATION AND MOBILITY IN NORTHERN ENGLAND

PAPERS ON NON-MARKET DECISION MAKING
See PUBLIC CHOICE

PAPERS ON THE SOCIAL SCIENCES
See Institute of Sociology, London. REPORTS OF ANNUAL CONFERENCES

1379 Papua New Guinea. Bureau of Statistics. STATISTICAL BULLETIN: INTERNATIONAL MIGRATION. Jan. 1976– . Port Moresby. Quarterly.
Continues: *Oversea Migration*, called also *Migration*. Subseries of its *Statistical Bulletin*.

1380 Papua and New Guinea Society. JOURNAL. v.1– , summer 1966/1967– . Port Moresby. Two issues a year.
Indexed: APAIS.

1381 Paris. École Pratique des Hautes Études. Centre de Psychiatrie Sociale. PUBLICATIONS. 1– , 1962– . Paris, Mouton. Irreg.
Monograph series.

1382 Paris. École Pratique des Hautes Études. Centre de Recherches Historiques. DÉMOGRAPHIE ET SOCIÉTÉS. 1–16, 1960–1972. Paris. Irreg.
Monograph series.

1383 Paris. École Pratique des Hautes Études. Centre de Sociologie Européenne. CAHIERS. SOCIOLOGIE DE L'ÉDUCATION. no.1–9, 1964–1969. Paris, Mouton. Irreg.
Monograph series.

1384 Paris. École Pratique des Hautes Études. 6e Section des Sciences Économiques et Sociales. LES TEXTES SOCIOLOGIQUES. 1– , 1968– . Paris, Mouton & Bordas. Irreg.
Monograph series.

1385 Paris. École Pratique des Hautes Études. 6e Section des Sciences Économiques et Sociales. Laboratoire de Sociologie de la Connaissance. CAHIERS. 1– , 1967– . Paris. Irreg.
This series called also *Contributions à la Sociologie de la Connaissance.*
Monograph series.

1386 Parma. Università. Istituto de Sociologia. COLLANA DELL'ISTITUTO DI SOCIOLOGIA DELL'UNIVERSITÀ DI PARMA. 1–2, 197?–1973. Parma. Irreg.

1387 PARTICIPATION IN SPORT AND LEISURE ACTIVITIES. 1975– . Waterloo, Ont. Three issues a year.
Issued by the SIRLS, Faculty of Human Kinetics and Leisure Studies, University of Waterloo.

1388 PATTERNS OF AMERICAN PREJUDICE SERIES. no.1–7, 1966–1975. New York, Harper & Row Publishers. Irreg.
Monograph series.

1389 PATTERNS OF PREJUDICE. v.1– , Jan/Feb. 1967– . London. Bimonthly.
Issued by the Institute of Jewish Affairs. Early issues subtitled: 'A bimonthly on international anti-semitism, radical right movements and counter activities'.
Indexed: Anth. Ind.; Int. Bibl. Soc. Cult. Anth.

PAYS COMMUNISTES
See REVUE DES PAYS DE L'EST

1390 PEASANT STUDIES. v.1–6, no.3, Jan. 1972–Mar/Apr. 1978. Pittsburgh. Quarterly.
Issued by the Department of History, University of Pittsburgh. Title varies: v.1–4, 1972–76, *Peasant Studies Newsletter.*

PEASANT STUDIES NEWSLETTER
See PEASANT STUDIES

1391 Pennsylvania. State University. Department of Agricultural Economics and Rural Sociology. A.E. & R.S. no.1– , 1956– . University Park, Pa. Irreg.
No.74 not published.

1392 PERSONALITY AND SOCIAL PSYCHOLOGY BULLETIN. 1– , 1974– . St. Louis, Mo.; subsequently Beverly Hills, Calif., Sage Publications. Quarterly.
Issued by the Department of Psychology, University of Missouri; subsequently by the Society for Personality and Social Psychology. Continues *Proceedings* of the Division of Personality and Social Psychology, American Psychological Association.
Indexed: Sage Fam. Stud. Abstr.

1393 PERSOON EN GEMEENSCHAP. v.1– , 1946– . Antwerp, Uitgiverij Ontwickelink Leeuwerikstr. Ten issues a year.
Subtitle reads: 'Tijdschrift voor opvoeding en onderwijs'. In Flemish.

1394 Peru. Dirección Nacional de Estadistica y Censos. BOLETIN DE ANALYSIS DEMOGRAFICO. 1– , Nov. 1964– . Lima, Peru.
Nos.1–5 called also Ano.1–3. In Spanish.

1395 Peru. Dirección Nacional de Estadistica y Censos. ENCUESTA DE INMIGRACIÓN LIMA METROPOLITANA. no.1– , 1966– . Lima, Peru.
In Spanish.

1396 PEUPLES MÉDITERRANÉES. MEDITERRANEAN PEOPLES. 1– , 1977– . Paris, Éditions Anthropos. Quarterly.
Text and summaries in English and French.
Indexed: Soc. Abstr.

1397 PHILIPPINE QUARTERLY OF CULTURE AND SOCIETY. 1– , Mar. 1973– . Cebu City. Quarterly.
Issues by the University of San Carlos. Supersedes: *San Carlos Publications. Series E. Miscellaneous Contributions in the Humanities*.

1398 PHILIPPINE SOCIOLOGICAL REVIEW. v.1– , Aug. 1953– . Quezon City. Quarterly.
Issued by the Philippine Sociological Society. Subject index quinquennially; author/title index: v.1–12, 1953/64, in v.12, no.3/4.
Indexed: Abstr. Anth. (through 1972); SSCI; Soc. Abstr.

1399 Philippine Sociological Society. SPECIAL PAPERS. 1– , 1966– . Manila. Irreg.
Monograph series.

PHILOSOPHIA — SOCIOLOGIA
See Lublin (City). Uniwersytet. ANNALES. SECTIO I. PHILOSOPHIA — SOCIOLOGIA

PHILOSOPHISCHE UND SOZIOLOGISCHE VERÖFFENTLICHUNGEN
See Berlin. Freie Universität. Osteuropa Institut. PHILOSOPHISCHE UND SOZIOLOGISCHE VERÖFFENTLICHUNGEN

1400 PHILOSOPHY AND SOCIAL CRITICISM. 1– , 1978– . Boston, Mass. Quarterly.
Issued by the Department of Philosophy, Boston College. Subtitle reads: 'An international interdisciplinary journal'. Continues: *Cultural Hermeneutics*.
Indexed: Soc. Abstr.

1401 PHILOSOPHY OF THE SOCIAL SCIENCES. v.1– , Jan. 1971– . Aberdeen, Scotland. Aberdeen University Press, v.1–4; Waterloo, Ont., Wilfrid Laurier University Press, v.5– . Quarterly.
Issued by the York University, Ont.
Indexed: Int. Bibl. Soc.; Int. Pol. Sc. Abstr.; Soc. Abstr.

1402 THE PHYLON. v.1– , first quarter 1940– . Atlanta, Ga. Quarterly.
Issued by the Atlanta University. Subtitle reads: 'The Atlanta University review of race and culture'.
Indexed: Bull. sig. soc. eth.; Int. Bibl. Soc.; PHRA; PAIS; SSCI; Soc. Sc. Hum. Ind.; Soc. Sc. Ind.; Soc. Abstr.; Wom. Stud. Abstr.

1403 PIN POINT. 1– , Dec. 1970– . Windsor, Ont. Biennial.
Issued by the Department of Sociology, Ontario University.

1404 Pisa. Università. Istituto di Sociologia. COLLANA DELL'ISTITUTO DI SOCIOLOGIA. 1– , 1973– . Pisa. Irreg.
Monograph series.

1405 PLAN. v.1– , 1959– . Toronto. Three issues a year.
Issued by the Town Planning Institute of Canada. In French and English; summaries in English and French.

THE PLANNER'S JOURNAL
See American Planning Association. JOURNAL

1406 PLANNING & PUBLIC POLICY. 1– , 1974/1975– . Urbana, Ill. Quarterly.
Issued by the Bureau of Urban and Regional Planning Research, Illinois University.

1407 PLANNING IN NORTHEASTERN ILLINOIS. v.1– , May/June 1959– . Chicago. Bimonthly.
Issued by the Northeastern Illinois Metropolitan Area Planning Commission. Title varies: May/June 1959–Mar/Apr. 1963, *Metropolitan Area Planning*.

1408 PLURAL SOCIETIES. 1– , 1970– . The Hague. Quarterly.
Issued by the Stichting Plurale Samenlevingen.

1409 Poland. Glowny Urząd Statystyczny. PRACE STATYSTYCZNO-SOCJOLOGICZNE. 1– , 1969– . Warszawa. Irreg.
In Polish.

1410 Poland. Głowny Urząd Statystyczny. ROCZNIK DEMOGRAFICZNY. 1945/1966– . Warszawa. Annual.
Subseries of *Roczniki Branzowe*. In Polish.

1411 POLICY FOR AUSTRALIA. no.1– , 1966– . Melbourne, Hawthorn Press. Irreg.
Monograph series.

POLICY PAPER SERIES
See Toronto. University. Institute for Quantitative Analysis of Social and Economic Policy. POLICY PAPER SERIES

1412 POLICY RESEARCH CENTERS DIRECTORY. 1978– . Urbana, Ill. Irreg.
Issued by the Policy Studies Organization.

1413 THE POLICY SCIENCES. v.1– , spring 1970– . New York, American Elsevier Publishing Co. Quarterly.
Indexed: PHRA; Soc. Abstr.

1414 POLICY STUDIES JOURNAL. 1– , autumn 1972– . Urbana, Ill. Eight issues a year.
Issued by the Policy Studies Organization.

Indexed: ABC Pol. Sc.; Curr. Cont.; Soc. Sc. Hum. Ind.; PAIS; Sage. Fam. Stud. Abstr.; Sage Urb. Abstr.; SSCI; Soc. Abstr.

1415 POLICY STUDIES REVIEW ANNUAL. 1977– . Beverly Hills, Calif., Sage Publications. Annual.
Indexed: Soc. Abstr.

1416 THE POLISH SOCIOLOGICAL BULLETIN. no.1– , June/Dec. 1961– . Warszawa, Zakład Narodowy im. Ossolińskich. Semi-annual.
Issued by the Polskie Towarzystwo Sociologiczne.
Indexed: Bull. sig. soc. eth.; Int. Bibl. Soc.; Int. Pol. Sc. Abstr.; SSCI; Soc. Abstr.

1417 POLISH SOCIOLOGY. 1– , 1975– . Wroclaw, Zaklad Narodowy im. Ossolińskich. Annual.
Issued by the Polskie Towarzystwo Socjologiczne. A selection of previously published articles. In English.

POLITICAL AND SOCIOLOGICAL REPORT ON ALBANIA
See United States. Joint Publications Research Service. POLITICAL AND SOCIOLOGICAL REPORT ON ALBANIA

POLITICAL RESEARCH ORGANIZATION AND DESIGN
See THE AMERICAN BEHAVIORAL SCIENTIST

1418 POLITICAL SCIENCE QUARTERLY. v.1– , Mar. 1886– . New York. Bimonthly.
Issued by the Academy of Political Science. Subtitle reads: 'A review devoted to the historical, statistical and comparative study of politics, economics, and public law'. vols.4–38, 40–41, Oct. 1, 1888–Dec. 31, 1925 include 'Record of Political Events', issued as separately paged supplements.
Indexed: Int. Bibl. Soc.; Int. Pol. Sc. Abstr.; PHRA; Peace Res. Abstr. J.; Soc. Sc. Hum. Ind.; Soc. Sc. Ind.; Soc. Abstr.; Soc. Work Res. Abstr.

1419 POLITICAL STUDIES. v.1– , Feb. 1953– . London, Oxford University Press; subsequently, Clarendon Press. Quarterly.
Issued by the Political Studies Association of the United Kingdom.
Indexed: Brit. Hum. Ind.; Bull. sig. soc. eth.; Int. Bibl. Soc.; Int. Pol. Sc. Abstr.; PHRA; Peace Res. Abstr. J.; Soc. Sc. Hum. Ind.; Soc. Abstr.

1420 POLITICAL THEORY. v.1– , 1973– . Beverly Hills, Calif.; Sage Publications. Quarterly.
Subtitle reads: 'An international journal of political philosophy'.
Indexed: ABC Pol. Sc.; Curr. Cont.; Int. Pol. Sc. Abstr.; PAIS; Sage Fam. Stud. Abstr.; Sage Urb. Abstr.; SSCI; Soc. Abstr.

1421 POLITICS AND SOCIETY. v.1– , Nov. 1970– . Los Altos, Calif. Geron-X Publishers. Quarterly.
Indexed: Bull. sig. soc. eth.; Int. Bibl. Soc.; Int. Pol. Sc. Abstr.; Soc. Sc. Ind.

POLITISCHE BILDUNG
See POLITISCHE STUDIEN

1422 POLITISCHE STUDIEN. v.1– , 1950– . München, G. Olzog. Bimonthly.
Title varies: 1950–51, *Schriftenreihe der Hochschule für Politische Wissenschaften;* 1951–53, *Politische Bildung*.
Indexed: Int. Bibl. Soc.; Int. Pol. Sc. Abstr.; Peace Res. Abstr. J.; Soc. Abstr.

1423 POLITISCHE VIERTELJAHRESSCHRIFT. v.1– , 1960– . Heidelberg, Westdeutscher Verlag. Quarterly.
Issued by the Deutsche Vereigningung für Politische Wissenschaft.
Indexed: Int. Bibl. Soc. Cult. Anth.; Int. Pol. Sc. Abstr.; Soc. Abstr.

1424 POLLS. v.1– , spring 1965– . Amsterdam, Systemen Keesing.
Indexed: Int. Bibl. Soc. Cult. Anth.; Int. Pol. Sc. Abstr.

1425 Polska Akademia Nauk. Komisja Socjologiczna. PRACE. no.1– , 1963– . Wrocław, Zakład Narodowy im. Ossolińskich. Irreg.
In Polish; summaries in English and Russian. Monograph series.

POPOLAZIONE E MOVIMENTO ANAGRAFICO DEI COMMUNI
See Italy. Istituto di Statistica. POPOLAZIONE E MOVIMENTO ANAFRAFICO DEI COMMUNI

1426 POPULAR MUSIC AND SOCIETY. v.1– , fall 1971– . Bowling Green, Ohio, Quarterly.
Issued by the Department of Sociology, Bowling Green University.

1427 POPULATION. v.1–3, no.1, Jan. 1932–Jan. 1939. London, Allen & Unwin.
Subtitle reads: 'Journal of the International Union for the Scientific Investigation of Population Problems'.

1428 POPULATION. v.1– , Jan/Mar. 1946– . Paris, Presses Universitaires de France. Bimonthly.

Issued by the Institut National d'Études Démographiques.

Indexed: Bull. sig. soc. eth.; Int. Bibl. Soc.; Peace Res. Abstr. J.; Soc. Abstr.; Urb. Aff. Abstr.; Wom. Stud. Abstr.

POPULATION AND CULTURE SERIES
See United Nations Educational, Scientific and Cultural Organization. POPULATION AND CULTURE SERIES

1429 POPULATION AND DEVELOPMENT REVIEW. 1– , Sep. 1975– . New York. Quarterly.

Issued by the Population Council.

1430 POPULATION AND ENVIRONMENT. v.3– , spring 1980– . New York, Human Sciences Press. Quarterly.

Continues: *Journal of Population*. Sponsored by the American Psychological Association's Division of Population and Environmental Psychology.

1431 POPULATION AND REPRODUCTION ABSTRACTS. no.1–3, 1969–1970. Bethesda, Md. Quarterly.

Issued by the National Institutes of Health, U.S. Department of Health, Education & Welfare. Continued by: *Population and Reproduction Research Abstracts*.

1432 POPULATION AND REPRODUCTION RESEARCH ABSTRACTS. no.4– , 1970– . Bethesda, Md. Quarterly.

Issued by the Scientific Information Centers Branch, National Institute of Child Health and Development. Continues: *Population and Reproduction Abstracts*.

1433 POPULATION AND THE POPULATION EXPLOSION: A BIBLIOGRAPHY. 1970– . Troy, N.Y., Whitston Publishing Co. Annual.

Spine title: *Population Bibliography*.

POPULATION AND VITAL STATISTICS
See Australia. Bureau of Census Statistics. DEMOGRAPHY

POPULATION BIBLIOGRAPHY
See POPULATION AND THE POPULATION EXPLOSION; A BIBLIOGRAPHY

POPULATION BULLETIN
See United Nations. Department of Economics and Social Affairs. POPULATION BULLETIN

POPULATION BULLETIN
See United Nations. Economic Commission for Western Asia. POPULATION BULLETIN

POPULATION BY AGE AND MARITAL STATUS
See Norway. Statistisk Sentralbyraa. FOLKEMENDEN ETTER ALDER OG EKTESKAPELIG STATUS

1434 Population Center Foundation. Population Information Division. ABSTRACT — BIBLIOGRAPHY SERIES. 1– , Apr. 1976– . Rizal.

'Prepared by Population Education Research Utilization, and Population Center Foundation Library'.

POPULATION CHARACTERISTICS OF HAWAII
See Hawaii. Department of Health. POPULATION CHARACTERISTICS OF HAWAII

1435 Population Council, New York. COUNTRY PROFILES. [1–20], 1969–May 1978. New York. Irreg.

Each issue is devoted to a single country.

1436 Population Council, New York. COUNTRY PROSPECTS. v.1– , 1974– . New York.

Each issue is a projection for one country.

1437 Population Council, New York. STUDIES IN FAMILY PLANNING. v.1– , 1970– . New York. Monthly.

Indexed: Soc. Abstr.

1438 POPULATION COUNCIL PERIODICAL INDEX. 1972– . New York. Irreg.

Issued by the Population Council. The publication is an index to the Council's publications; *Studies in Family Planning; Reports on Population/Family Planning; Country Profiles*. Second cumulated index: Jan. 1973–Dec. 1975.

POPULATION DE MADAGASCAR
See Malagasy Republic. Service de Statistique et des Études Socioéconomiques. POPULATION DE MADAGASCAR

1439 POPULATION DYNAMICS QUARTERLY. 1– , winter 1973– . Washington, D.C.

Issued by the Interdisciplinary Communications Program, Smithsonian Institution. In English, French and Spanish.

1440 POPULATION ET FAMILLE. no.26/27– , Dec. 1972– . Bruxelles. Three issues a year.

Issued by the Centre d'Étude de la Population et de la Famille, in cooperation with the Department of Demography, University of Montréal, and the Department of Demography, University of Louvain. Continues: *Population et Famille. Bevolking en Gezin*. Summaries in English and French. Includes bibliographies of Belgian works on population.

Indexed: Soc. Abstr.

1441 POPULATION ET FAMILLE. BEVOLKING EN GEZIN. v.1–8, 1963–1971. Bruxelles. Three issues a year.

Issued by the Centre de l'Étude de la Population et de la Famille Ministère de la Santé Publique et de la Famille. In French and Flemish; summaries in Flemish and/or French, English, German, Italian, Spanish. Annual supplementary issue of *Statistical Annexes*. Continued by: *Population et Famille*.

Indexed: Bull. sig. soc. eth.; Int. Bibl. Soc. Cult. Anth.

1442 POPULATION ET SOCIÉTÉS. no.1– , 1968– . Paris. Monthly.

Issued by the Institut National d'Études Démographiques. Subtitle reads: 'Bulletin Mensuelle d'Informations Démographiques, Économiques, Sociales'.

Indexed: Int. Bibl. Soc.

1443 POPULATION INDEX. v.1– , Jan. 1935– . Princeton, N.J. Quarterly.

Issued by the Office of Population Research, Woodrow Wilson School of Public and International Affairs, Princeton University, and the Population Association of America. Title varies: 1935–Oct. 1936, *Population Literature*.

Indexed: PAIS; Soc. Abstr.

POPULATION LITERATURE
See POPULATION INDEX

1444 POPULATION MONOGRAPH SERIES. no.1– , 1967– , Berkeley, Calif. Irreg.
Issued by the Institute of International Studies, University of California at Berkeley.

POPULATION NEWSLETTER
See United Nations. Department of Economic and Social Affairs. Population Division. POPULATION NEWSLETTER

POPULATION NOTES
See Wisconsin. University. Department of Rural Sociology. Applied Population Laboratory. POPULATION NOTES 1960

POPULATION NOTES
See Wisconsin. University. Department of Rural Sociology. Applied Population Laboratory. POPULATION NOTES 1970

POPULATION OF CANADA AND THE PROVINCES BY SEX AND AGE GROUP, ESTIMATED
See Canada. Census Field. Population Estimates and Projections Division. POPULATION OF CANADA AND THE PROVINCES BY SEX AND AGE GROUP, ESTIMATED

POPULATION: PRINCIPAL CITIES AND TOWNS
See Australia. Bureau of Census and Statistics. POPULATION; PRINCIPAL CITIES AND TOWNS

POPULATION PROJECTIONS
See Wisconsin. Department of Administration. Bureau of State Planning. Management and Information Science Section. WISCONSIN POPULATION PROJECTIONS

1445 Population Reference Bureau. SELECCIÓNES DE POBLACIÓN. 1968–Dec. 1974. Washington, D.C. Irreg.

In Spanish.

POPULATION REPORT. COMMUNITY DEVELOPMENT SERIES
See Michigan. State University, East Lansing. Institute for Community Development and Services. POPULATION REPORT. COMMUNITY DEVELOPMENT SERIES

1446 POPULATION REVIEW. v.1– , Jan. 1957– . Madras. Semi-annual.

Issued by the Indian Institute for Population Studies. Subtitle reads: 'A journal of Asian demography'.

Indexed: Int. Bibl. Soc.

POPULATION SCIENCES
See United States. Interagency Committee on Population Research. INVENTORY AND ANALYSIS OF FEDERAL POPULATION RESEARCH

POPULATION SERIES
See Texas. University. Bureau of Business Research. POPULATION SERIES

POPULATION SERIES
See Wisconsin. University. Department of Rural Sociology. POPULATION SERIES — WISCONSIN'S POPULATION

1447 POPULATION STUDIES. v.1– , June 1947– . London, Cambridge University Press. Three issues a year.

Issued by the Population Investigation Committee, London School of Economics and Political Science.

Indexed: Afr. Abstr.; Brit. Hum. Ind.; Int. Bibl. Soc.; PAIS; Peace Res. Abstr. J.; Urb Aff. Abstr.

1448 POPULATION STUDIES. no.1– , 1976– . Strasbourg. Irreg.

Issued by the Council of Europe.

POPULATION STUDY
See Louisiana. State University, New Orleans. Division of Business and Economic Research. POPULATION STUDY

POPULATION TRENDS
See Gt. Britain. Office of Population Censuses and Surveys. POPULATION TRENDS

1449 Portugal. Instituto Nacional de Estatistica. INDICADORES ECONOMICO-SOCIAIS. SOCIAL ECONOMIC INDICATORS. 1973– . Lisboa.
Supplements accompany some issues. In English and Portuguese.

1450 Portugal. Instituto Nacional de Estatistica. STATISTIQUES DÉMOGRAPHIQUES. STATISTICAS DEMOGRAFICAS. 1941– . Lisboa.
Title varies: 1941– , *Anuario Demografico; Annuaire Démographique*. Supersedes: *Anuario Demografico; Estatistica do Movimento Fisiologico de População de Portugal*. In Portuguese.

1451 Posen. Uniwersytet. Wydział Filozoficzno-Historyczny. PRACE. SERIA SOCJOLOGIA. 1– , 1964– . Poznań. Irreg.
In Polish.
Monograph series.

1452 POUNT. v.1– , 1966– . Djibuti. Quarterly.
Issued by the Société d'Etudes de l'Afrique Orientale. In French.

POVERTY AND HUMAN RESOURCES ABSTRACTS
See HUMAN RESOURCES ABSTRACTS

Poznań
See Posen

PRACE
See Polska Akademia Nauk. Komisja Socjologiczna. PRACE

1453 PRACE BADAWCZE I PUBLIKACJE Z ZAKRESU SOCJOLOGII W POLSCE. v.1–6/7. 1969–1974/1975. Wrocław, Zakład Narodowy im. Ossolińskich.
Continued by: *Socjologia w Polsce*. In Polish.

PRACE. SERIA B: GEOGRAFIA SPOŁECZNA I EKONOMICZNA
See Breslau. Uniwersytet. Instytut Geograficzny. PRACE. SERIA B: GEOGRAFIA SPOŁECZNA I EKONOMICZNA

PRACE. SERIA SOCJOLOGIA
See Posen. Uniwersytet. Wydział Filozoficzno-Społeczny. PRACE. SERIA SOCJOLOGIA

PRACE SOCJOLOGICZNE
See Kraków. Universytet Jagielloński. PRACE SOCJOLOGICZNE

PRACE STATYSTYCZNO-SOCJOLOGICZNE
See Poland. Główny Urząd Statystyczny. PRACE STATYSTYCZNO-SOCJOLOGICZNE

1454 PRAXIS; A STUDENT JOURNAL OF SOCIOLOGY. 1–?, 1971–?. Montréal. Ceased publication.
Issued by the Loyola Students' Association.

1455 PREVISIONI DEI MUTAMENTI SOCIALI: DOCUMENTAZIONE. 1970?– . Roma, Edizioni Previsionali. Annual.
Issued by the Istituto Ricerche Applicate, Documentazione i Studi. In Italian.

1456 PRIMARY SOCIALIZATION. LANGUAGE AND EDUCATION. 1–6, 1971–1973. London, Routledge & Kegan Paul; subsequently, Beverly Hills, Calif., Sage Publications. Irreg.
Indexed: Soc. Abstr.

1457 Princeton University. Bureau of Urban Research. THE URBAN REFERENCE. v.1–16, no.3, Jan. 1943–Apr/June 1957. Princeton, N.J. Monthly.
Title varies: 1943–51, *Selected Items from the Urban Reference*. Indexes: 4–5, 1945–60.

1458 Princeton University. Research Center for Urban and Environmental Planning. BIBLIOGRAPHY. 1– , 1973– . Princeton, N.J. Irreg.

1459 Princeton University. Research Center for Urban and Environmental Planning. WORKING PAPER. 1– , 1973– . Princeton, N.J.
Series of papers.

1460 PROBLÉME DER SPORTSOZIOLOGIE. 1– , 1972– . Ahrensburg by Hamburg.

1461 PROBLÉMES SOCIAUX CONGOLAIS. v.1–94/95, 1946–1972. Lubumbashi, Zaire. Quarterly.
Issued by the Centre d'Études des Problémes Sociaux Indigenes. Title vaires: 1946–52, *Bulletin*. Continued by: *Problémes Sociaux Zairoïs*. No.25 contains Catalog of the Centre's library; no.30 has also a distinctive title, *L'Oeuvre de Pierre Romani Desfosses;* nos. 29 and 31 include a separately paged section, 'Revue pedagogique Congolais'.
Indexed: Afr. Abstr.

1462 PROBLÉMES SOCIAUX ZAIROÏS. no.96/97– , May/June 1973– . Bruxelles. Quarterly.

Issued by the Centre d'Exécution des Programmes Sociaux et Économiques. Continues: *Problémes Sociaux Congolais*.
Indexed: Int. Bibl. Soc.

1463 PROBLEMS OF THE SCIENCE OF SCIENCE. v.1–6, 1970–1977/1979. Wrocław, Zakład Narodowy im. Ossolińskich. Irreg.
Issued by the Committee of Science of Science, Polish Academy of Sciences, initially as special issues of the quarterly, *Zagadnienia Naukoznawstwa*. Superseded by: *Science of Science*.
Indexed: Soc. Abstr.

1464 PROBLEMY FILOSOFII I SOTSIOLOGII. 1– , 1969– . Moskva.
Issued by the Filosofskii fakultet, Moskovskii gosudarstvennyi institut imeni M. V. Lomonosova. In Russian.

1465 PROBLEMY SOTSIAL'NEGO ROZVITIIA. 2– , 1973– . Tyumen', Russia.
Issued by the Tyumenskii industrial'nyi institut. Subseries of the Institut's *Trudy*. In Russian.

1466 PROBLEMY SOTSIAL'NYKH ISSLEDOVANII. 1971– . Tomsk.
Issued by the Tomskii universitet. Subseries of the Universitet's *Uchenye zapiski*. In Russian.

PROCEEDINGS
See Conference on Social Issues, University of Oregon. PROCEEDINGS.

PROCEEDINGS
See Eugenics Society, London. PROCEEDINGS

PROCEEDINGS
See Frontiers of Urban Planning Conference. PROCEEDINGS

PROCEEDINGS
See International Conference on Cybernetics and Society. PROCEEDINGS

PROCEEDINGS
See Urban Policy Conference. PROCEEDINGS

PROCEEDINGS
See Vanderbilt Sociology Conference. PROCEEDINGS

PROCEEDINGS
See Washington (State). University. Urban Data Center. PROCEEDINGS

PROCEEDINGS
See Western Association of Sociology and Anthropology. Meeting. PROCEEDINGS

PROCEEDINGS OF THE AMERICAN ACADEMY OF ARTS AND SCIENCES
See DAEDALUS

PROCEEDINGS OF THE AMERICAN COUNTRY LIFE CONFERENCE
See American Country Life Association. PROCEEDINGS OF THE CONFERENCE

PROCEEDINGS OF THE ANNUAL CONFERENCE
See Sociological Association of Ireland. Cuman Sochelaiochta na h Eireann. PROCEEDINGS OF THE ANNUAL CONFERENCE

PROCEEDINGS OF THE CONFERENCE
See American Country Life Association, Inc. PROCEEDINGS OF THE CONFERENCE

PROCEEDINGS OF THE SOUTHWESTERN SOCIOLOGICAL ASSOCIATION
See Southwestern Sociological Association. PROCEEDINGS

PROD
See THE AMERICAN BEHAVIORAL SCIENTIST

PROD TRANSLATIONS
See THE AMERICAN BEHAVIORAL SCIENTIST

1467 PROFILES IN POPULAR CULTURE. no.1– , 1974– . Bowling Green, Ohio, Popular Press.
Issued by the Center for the Study of Popular Culture, State University, Bowling Green.

1468 Programa Avanzado Latinoamericano de Sociologia Rural. BOLETIN INFORMATIVO. no.1– , 1974– . Asunción.

1469 PROGRESS IN SOCIAL PSYCHOLOGY. v.1– , 1979– . Hillsdale, N.J., Lawrence Erlbaum Associates. Annual.

PROGRESS REPORT IN SOCIOLOGY AND RURAL LIFE
See Mississippi. Agricultural Experiment Station, State College. PROGRESS REPORT IN SOCIOLOGY AND RURAL LIFE

1470 PROMETHEUS. v.1– , May 1971– . Washington, D.C. Irreg.
Issued by the Social Innovation Information Service. Subtitle reads: 'A review of the literature of social development and institutional change'.

1471 PROMOVERE. 1969–1975. Bruxelles, Promovere. Quarterly.
Subtitle reads: 'Revue trimestrielle internationale de socio-criminologie clinique'.

1472 PRZEGLAD NAUK HISTORYCZNYCH I SPOLECZNYCH. v.1–7, 1950–1956. Lôdz. Annual.
Issued by the Lôdzkie Towarzystwo Naukowe. Published during the suspension of *Przeglad Socjologizny*.

1473 PRZEGLAD SOCJOLOGICZNY. SOCIOLOGICAL REVIEW. v.1– , 1930– . Wroclaw, Zaklad Narodowy im. Ossolińskich. Semi-annual.
Issued by the Polski Instytut Socjologiczny, 1930–58; Socjologiczny Ośrodek Lôdzki, 1957– . Publication suspended 1940–45, and 1949–56; during its second suspension, *Przeglad Nauk Historycznych i Spolecznych* was published.
Indexed: Bull. sig. soc. eth.; Int. Bibl. Soc.; Soc. Abstr.

1474 PRZESZLOŚĆ DEMOGRAFICZNA POLSKI. MATERIALY I STUDIA. 1– , 1967– . Warszawa, Państwowe Wydawnictwo Naukowe. Irreg.
Issued by the Komitet Nauk Demograficznych, Polska Akademia Nauk. Summaries in English; table of contents in Polish and English.

1475 PSYCHIATRY. v.1– , Feb. 1938– . Baltimore, Md. Quarterly.
Issued by the William Alanson White Psychiatric Foundation. Author indexes: v.1–5, 1938–42, in v.5; v.1–6, 1938–43, in v.6.
Indexed: Abstr. Soc. Work; Bull. sig. soc. eth.; Peace Res. Abstr. J.; Psych. Abstr.; Soc. Sc. Ind.; Soc. Work Res. Abstr.; Soc. Abstr.; Wom. Stud. Abstr.

1476 PSYCHOLOGICAL ABSTRACTS. v.1– , 1927– . Lancaster, Pa. Monthly.
Issued by the American Psychlogical Association. Subtitle reads: 'Non-evaluative summaries of the world's literature in psychology and related disciplines'.

1477 THE PSYCHOLOGICAL INDEX; A BIBLIOGRAPHY OF THE LITERATURE OF PSYCHOLOGY AND COGNATE SUBJECTS. no.1–42, 1894–1935. New York.

1478 PSYCHOLOGIE FRANCAISE. v.1– , Oct. 1956– . Paris. Quarterly.
Issued by the Société Francaise de Psychologie.
Indexed: Bull. sig. soc. eth.; Int. Pol. Sc. Abstr.; Psych. Abstr.; Soc. Abstr.

1479 PSYCHOPATHOLOGIE AFRICAINE. 1– , 1965– . Dakar. Irreg.
Issued by the Société de Psychopathologie et d'Hygiéne Mentale de Dakar. Faculté de Médicine de Dakar, Centre Hôpitalier de Fann, Dakar. Text and summaries in English and French.
Indexed: Bull. sig. soc. eth.; Int. Bibl. Soc.; Cult. Anth.

1480 PSYCHOTHERAPY AND BEHAVIOR CHANGE. v.1–3, 1972–1973. Chicago, Aldine-Atherton. Annual.
Supersedes: *Psychotherapy*, 1955–70. Continued by: *Behavior Change*.

PUBBLICAZIONI
See Florence. Università. Istituto di Sociologia. Gruppo di Studi Audiovisive. PUBBLICAZIONI

PUBBLICAZIONI
See Rome (City). Università. Istituto di Demografia. PUBBLICAZIONI

PUBBLICAZIONI. SERIE TERZA: SOCIOLOGIA
See Milan. Università Cattolica del Sacro Cuore. PUBBLICAZIONI. SERIE TERZA: SOCIOLOGIA

1481 The Public Affairs Information Service. BULLETIN. 1915– . New York. 48 issues a year; quarterly and annual cumulations.

1482 The Public Affairs Information Service. FOREIGN LANGUAGE INDEX. v.1– , 1968/1971– . New York. Quarterly, with annual cumulations.

1483 PUBLIC CHOICE. v.1– , 1966– . Charlottesville, Va., subsequently Leiden, Boston, Mass., Nijhoff Social Sciences Division.
Issued by the Thomas Jefferson Center for Political Economy; subsequently by the Center for the Study of Public Choice, Virginia Polytechnic Institute and State University, Blacksburg. Title varies: v.1–3, 1966–68, *Papers on Non-Market Decision Making*.
Indexed: Int. Bibl. Soc.; Int. Pol. Sc. Abstr.; PAIS; Soc. Abstr.

1484 THE PUBLIC INTEREST. no.1– , fall 1965– . New York. Quarterly.
Issued by the Freedom House; subsequently by National Affairs.
Indexed: Int. Bibl. Soc.; Int. Pol. Sc. Abstr.; PAIS; SSCI; Soc. Sc. Ind.; Soc. Abstr.; Soc. Work Res. Abstr.

1485 PUBLIC OPINION. 1– , Mar-Apr. 1978– . Washington, D.C. Bimonthly.
Issued by the American Enterprise Institute for Public Policy Research. Supersedes *Current Opinion*.

1486 PUBLIC OPINION POLLS. no.1– , June 1960– . Nairobi, Kenya Research Services. Irreg.
No.1–17, 1960–67 issued by Marco Surveys, Ltd.

1487 PUBLIC OPINION QUARTERLY. v.1– , Jan. 1937– . Princeton, N.J., Princeton University Press. Quarterly.
Issued by the American Association for Public Opinion Research, and Princeton University.
Indexed: Bull. sig. soc. eth.; Int. Bibl. Soc.; Int. Pol. Sc. Abstr.; Sage Fam. Stud. Abstr.; Soc. Sc. Hum. Ind.; Soc. Sc. Ind.; Soc. Abstr.; Urb. Aff. Abstr.

1488 PUBLIC POLICY. v.1–29, 1939–fall 1981. New York, Wiley. Quarterly.
Issued by the John Fitzgerald Kennedy School of Government, Harvard University. Continued by *Journal of Policy Analysis and Management*.
Indexed: Int. Bibl. Soc.; Int. Pol. Sc. Abstr.; Soc. Sc. Ind.; Soc. Abstr.

PUBLICACIÓN
See Centro Colombiano de Investigaciónes Psico-Sociológicas. SOCIOLÓGICAS. PUBLICACIÓN

[PUBLICACIÓN]
See Centro de Estudios Familiares de Población. Departamento de Investigaciónes Interdisciplinarias. [PUBLICACIÓN]

PUBLICACIÓN
See Santiago, Chile. Universidad Catolica. Centro de Investigaciónes Sociológicas. PUBLICACIÓN

PUBLICATION
See Maharaja Sayajirao University of Baroda. Department of Sociology. PUBLICATION

PUBLICATIONS
See American Sociological Association. PUBLICATIONS

PUBLICATIONS
See Cambridge Group for the History of Population and Social Structure. PUBLICATIONS

PUBLICATIONS
See Centre des Sciences Sociales d'Athens. PUBLICATIONS

PUBLICATIONS
See Cincinnati. University. Department of Sociology. PUBLICATIONS

PUBLICATIONS
See European Society for Rural Sociology. PUBLICATIONS

PUBLICATIONS
See Paris. École Pratique des Hautes Études. Centre de Psychiatrie Sociale. PUBLICATIONS

PUBLICATIONS
See Research Group on European Migration Problems. PUBLICATIONS

PUBLICATIONS IN SOCIOLOGY
See California. University. UNIVERSITY OF CALIFORNIA PUBLICATIONS IN SOCIOLOGY

PUBLICATIONS IN SOCIOLOGY AND SOCIAL INSTITUTIONS
See California. University. UNIVERSITY OF CALIFORNIA PUBLICATIONS IN SOCIOLOGY AND SOCIAL INSTITUTIONS

PUBLICATIONS ON SOCIAL CHANGE
See The Hague. Institute of Social Studies. PUBLICATIONS ON SOCIAL CHANGE

PUBLIKATIES
See Belgium. Ministère de la Santé Publique et de la Famille. Centre d'Étude de la Population et de la Famille. CAHIERS. PUBLIKATIES

PUBLIKATIES
See Centre d'Étude de la Population et de la Famille, Brussels. CAHIERS

PUBLIKATIES
See Leiden Rijksuniversiteit. Sociologisch Instituut. PUBLIKATIES

PUBLIKATIES
See Nederlands Interuniversitaire Demografisch Instituut (N.I.D.I.) PUBLIKATIES

PUBLIKATIES. SERIES A. [SOCIALE GEOGRAFIE. HUMAN GEOGRAPHY]
See Utrecht. Rijksuniversiteit. Geografisch Instituut. PUBLIKATIES. SERIES A. SOCIALE GEOGRAFIE. HUMAN GEOGRAPHY

1489 PUBLIZISTIK. 1– , Jan/Feb. 1956– . Bremen, B.C. Heye. Six issues a year.
Subtitle reads: 'Zeitschrift für die Wissenschaft von Presse, Runkfunk, Film, Rhetorik, Werbung und Meinungsbildung'.
Indexed: Bull. sig. soc. eth.; Int. Bibl. Soc.; Int. Pol. Sc. Abstr.; Peace Res. Abstr. J.; Soc. Abstr.

1490 Purdue University. Institute for the Study of Social Change. INSTITUTE MONOGRAPH SERIES. no.1– , 1968– . Lafayette, Ind. Irreg.
Monograph series. Processed.

1491 Purdue University. Purdue Opinion Panel, Measurement & Research Center. REPORT. v.1–33 (no.1–101), 1941–June 1975. Lafayette, Ind. Annual.

1492 QUADERNI DE LA CRITICA SOCIOLOGICA. 1– , 1975– . Roma.
Issued by the Istituto di Sociologia, Università di Roma. In Italian.

1493 QUADERNI DELLA "RASSEGNA ITALIANA DI SOCIOLOGIA". 1– , 1970– . Bologna, Società Editrice Il Mulino. Irreg.
In Italian.
Monograph series.

QUADERNI DI RICERCHE DEL PROGETTO STRATIFICAZIONE E CLASSI SOCIALI IN ITALIA DELLA FONDAZIONE GIOVANNI AGNELLI
See Fondazione Giovanni Agnelli. Progetto Stratificazione e Classi Sociali in Italia. QUADERNI DI RICERCHE DEL PROGETTO STRATIFICAZIONE E CLASSI SOCIALI IN ITALIA

1494 QUADERNI DI SCIENZE SOCIALI. Aug. 1962–1969. Milano, A. Giuffré. Three issues a year.
Issued by the Istituto di Scienze Sociali di Genoa. In Italian.
Indexed: Bull. sig. soc. eth.; Int. Bibl. Soc.; Int. Pol. Sc. Abstr.; Soc. Abstr.

1495 QUADERNI DI SOCIOLOGIA. v.1– , estate 1951–1964; n.s. 1965– . Torino, Casa Editrice Taylor, now Einaudi. Quarterly.
Issued by the Istituto di Sociologia, Università di Torino. In Italian; summaries in English.
Indexed: Int. Bibl. Soc.; Int. Pol. Sc. Abstr.; Soc. Abstr.

1496 QUADERNI DI SOCIOLOGIA RURALE. v.1–3, 1961–1963. Roma, Feltrinelli. Three issues a year.
Issued by the Società Italiana di Sociologia Rurale. Superseded by *Società Rurale*. In Italian.

QUADERNI INTERNAZIONALI DI STORIA ECONOMICA E SOCIALE
See CAHIERS INTERNATIONAUX D'HISTOIRE ÉCONOMIQUE ET SOCIALE

1497 QUALITATIVE SOCIOLOGY. v.1– , May 1978– . Baltimore, Md., subsequently New York, Human Sciences Press. Three issues a year; subsequently quarterly.
Issued by the Department of Sociology, Syracuse University.
Indexed: Psych. Abstr.; Soc. Abstr.

1498 QUALITATIVE SOCIOLOGY NEWSLETTER. London. Irreg.
Issued by the Qualitative Sociology Group, British Sociological Association. Processed.

1499 QUALITY AND QUANTITY. v.1– , Jan. 1967– . Padua, Marsilio Editore; subsequently Amsterdam, Elsevier Publishing Co. Quarterly; some double issues.
Subtitle reads: 'European journal of methodology. Revue Européenne de methodologie'. In English and French.
Indexed: Int. Bibl. Soc.; Int. Pol. Sc. Abstr.; Psych. Abstr.; Soc. Abstr.

1500 QUANTITATIVE SOCIOLOGY NEWSLETTER. no.1– , Feb. 1970– . London. Two issues a year.
Issued by the Computing and Statistical Group, British Sociological Association.

QUARTERLY BULLETIN
See GREATER LONDON INTELLIGENCE QUARTERLY

1501 QUARTERLY CHECK-LIST OF ETHNOLOGY & SOCIOLOGY. v.1–18, Mar. 1958–1975. Darien, Conn. Quarterly.
Title varies: 1964–73, *ABS Quarterly Check-List of Ethnology & Sociology*.

1502 QUARTERLY DIGEST OF URBAN AND REGIONAL RESEARCH. v.1–17, no.4, 1954–1970. Urbana, Ill. Two issues a year.
Issued by the Bureau of Community Planning, University of Illinois. Title varies: 1954–67, *Research Digest*.

1503 QUARTERLY JOURNAL OF STUDIES ON ALCOHOL. v.1–35, 1940–1974. New Brunswick, N.J. Quarterly.
Issued by the Rutgers Center on Alcohol Studies. Continued by: *Journal of Studies on Alcohol*.
Indexed: Soc. Abstr.

QUEEN'S UNIVERSITY PAPERS IN SOCIAL ANTHROPOLOGY
See Belfast. Queen's University. Department of Social Anthropology. QUEEN'S UNIVERSITY PAPERS IN SOCIAL ANTHROPOLOGY

RCGDS PUBLICATIONS
See Michigan. University. Research Center for Group Dynamics. RCGDS PUBLICATIONS

REMP BULLETIN
See Research Group on European Migration Problems. REMP BULLETIN

RIIE BIBLIOGRAPHIC STUDIES
See Smithsonian Institution. Research Institute on Immigration and Ethnic Studies. RIIE BIBLIOGRAPHIC STUDIES

RIIE RESEARCH NOTES
See Smithsonian Institution. Research Institute on Immigration and Ethnic Studies. RIIE RESEARCH NOTES

1504 R.S. CUADERNOS DE REALIDADES SOCIALES. v.1– , 1973– . Madrid. Three issues a year.
Issued by the Instituto de Sociologia Aplicada de Madrid. In Spanish.

RSRI ABSTRACTS
See Regional Science Research Institute. RSRI ABSTRACTS

RACE
See RACE & CLASS

1505 RACE & CLASS. v.1– , Oct. 1959– . London, Oxford University Press. Quarterly.
Issued by the Institute of Race Relations and the Transnational Institute. Title varies: v.1–16, no.1, 1959–July/Sep. 1974, *Race*.
Indexed: Brit. Hum. Ind.; Bull. sig. soc. eth.; Int. Bibl. Soc.; PAIS; Psych. Abstr.; SSCI; Soc. Abstr.; Soc. Work Res. Abstr.

RACE AND NATIONS MONOGRAPH SERIES
See Denver. University. Center for International Race Relations. RACE AND NATIONS MONOGRAPH SERIES

1506 RACE RELATIONS. v.1–5, no.9/12, Aug. 1943–June/Dec. 1948. Nashville, Tenn. Monthly.
Issued by the Social Science Institute, Fisk University. Title varies. v.1–4, *A Monthly Summary of Events and Trends in Race Relations;* Jan.–June 1947, *Events and Trends in Race Relations*. Not published July and Oct/Nov. 1947.

1507 RACE RELATIONS. 1967–1972; n.s. 1–21, 1973–winter 1974/1975. London
Issued by the Race Relations Board. Superseded by *Equals*.

RACE RELATIONS
See RACE RELATIONS JOURNAL

1508 RACE RELATIONS ABSTRACTS. v.1–2, no.3, winter 1968–1970. London, Research Publications. Quarterly.
Issued by the Institute of Race Relations.

1509 RACE RELATIONS ABSTRACTS. 1–2, 1967–1970; n.s. 1973–1974. London, Runnymede Trust.

1510 RACE RELATIONS ABSTRACTS. v.1– , 1975/1976– . Beverly Hills, Calif., Sage Publications. Three issues a year.
Issued by the Institute of Race Relations in London. Cumulative indexes published annually.

1511 RACE RELATIONS JOURNAL. v.1–29, no.1, Nov/Dec. 1933–Jan/Mar. 1962. Johannesburg. Bimonthly, 1933–34; quarterly, 1935–56; Semi-annual, 1957–58.
Issued by the Suid Afrikaanse Instituut vir Rassenverhouldings. Title varies: v.1–17, no.1–2, 1933–50, *Race Relations*. Some issues have title also in Afrikaans, *Rasse Verhouldings*. Indexes: v.1–4, 1933–Nov. 1937.

1512 RACE RELATIONS LAW REPORTER. v.1–12, no.4, Feb. 1956–winter 1967. Nashville, Tenn. Bimonthly.
Issued by the School of Law, Vanderbilt University.

1513 RACE RELATIONS NEWS. [1]– , July 1938– . Johannesburg. Monthly.
Issued by the South African Institute of Race Relations (Suid Afrikaanse Institut vir Rassenverhouldings).

1514 RACE RELATIONS REPORTER. [1]– , 1970– . Nashville, Tenn.
Issued by the Race Relations Information Center. Issues for 1970 constitute v.1.
Indexed: PHRA.

1515 THE RACIAL POLICIES OF AMERICAN INDUSTRY: REPORT. no.1–31, 1968–1974. Philadelphia, Pa. Irreg.
Issued by the Industrial Research Unit, Wharton School of Finance and Commerce, University of Pennsylvania.
Monograph series.

1516 RACIAL RELATIONS: STUDIES IN CONFLICT AND COOPERATION. no.1–5, 1945–1947. Ledbury, Herefordshire, Le Play House Press.
Issued by the Racial Relations Group, London.

1517 RADICAL AMERICA. v.1– , 1967– . Somerville, Mass. Bimonthly.
Issued by the Alternative Education Project
Indexed: Soc. Abstr.

[RADOVI]
See Akademija nauka i umjetnosti Bosne i Hercegovine. Odjeljenje drustvenih nauka. [RADOVI]

1518 RANDOM HOUSE STUDIES IN SOCIOLOGY. 10[First numbered issue]– , 1970– . New York, Random House. Irreg.
Other title: *Studies in Sociology*. Some works in revised editions.
Monograph series.

RAPPORT ANNUEL [AFFAIRES URBAINES]
See Canada. Ministry of State for Urban Affairs. RAPPORT ANNUEL [AFFAIRES URBAINES]

RAPPORT ANNUEL DU CONSEIL CONSULTATIF CANADIEN DU MULTICULTURALISME
See Canadian Consultative Council on Multiculturalism. ANNUAL REPORT

RAPPORT ANNUEL ET PROGRAMME DES TRAVAUX
See Brussels. Université Libre. Institut de Sociologie. RAPPORT ANNUEL ET PROGRAMME DES TRAVAUX

RASSE VERHOULDINGS
See RACE RELATIONS JOURNAL

1519 RASSEGNA ITALIANA DI SOCIOLOGIA. 1– , Jan/Mar. 1960– . Roma, Il Mulino. Quarterly; subsequently three issues a year.
Vol.6 called also 3rd series. In Italian; summaries in English.
Indexed: Bull. sig. soc. eth.; Int. Bibl. Soc.; Int. Pol. Sc. Abstr.; Psych. Abstr.; Soc. Abstr.

1520 LA RAZA. 1967–1970. Los Angeles, Calif., El Bario Communications Project.
Superseded by a publication of the same title. In Spanish.

1521 LA RAZA. v.1–2, no.4, 1971–1975. Los Angeles, Calif., El Bario Communications Project.
Supersedes a publication of the same title. In Spanish; occasionally in English.

READERS' GUIDE TO PERIODICAL LITERATURE. SUPPLEMENT
See SOCIAL SCIENCES & HUMANITIES INDEX

1522 RECENT PUBLICATIONS IN THE BEHAVIORAL SCIENCES. 1966–1975. New York, subsequently Beverly Hills, Calif., Sage Publications. Annual.
Supplement to: *ABC Guide to Recent Publications in the Social and Behavioral Sciences.*

RECENT SOCIAL CHANGES IN THE UNITED STATES SINCE THE WAR AND PARTICULARLY SINCE 1927
See SOCIAL CHANGES

1523 RECENT SOCIOLOGY. no.1– , 1969– . London, New York, Macmillan. Irreg.
Includes chiefly reprints.

LA RECHERCHE AFRICANISTE EN COURS; BULLETIN INTERNATIONAL
See CURRENT AFRICAN RESEARCH; INTERNATIONAL BULLETIN

1524 RECHERCHE URBAINE. 1– , Feb. 1974– . Montréal. Irreg.
Issued by the Centre de Recherche et Innovation Urbaines, Université de Montréal. In French. Processed.
Monograph series.

RECHERCHES. THE F.D.G.R.I. REPORT
See Fédération des Groupes d'Études et de Recherches Institutionelles. CAHIERS

1525 RECHERCHES D'ÉCONOMIE ET DE SOCIOLOGIE RURALES. v.1–2, no.2, 1967–1971? Paris, Service des Publications, I.N.R.A. Four issues a year. Irreg.
Issued by the Institut National de la Recherche Agronomique. Superseded by: *Annales d'Économie et de Sociologie Rurales.*

1526 RECHERCHES OUBAGUIENNES. 1– , 1969– . Paris, Librarie C. Klincksieck. Irreg.
Issued by the Laboratoire d'Ethnologie et de Sociologie Comparative, Université de Paris X.
Monograph series.

1527 RECHERCHES SOCIOGRAPHIQUES. v.1– , Jan/Mar. 1961– . Québec, Presses Universitaires Laval. Three issues a year.
Issued by the Département de Sociologie et d'Anthropologie, in cooperation with the Centre de Recherches Sociales, Université Laval. Indexes: 1961–64.
Indexed: Bull. sig. soc. eth.; Int. Bibl. Soc.; Int. Pol. Sc. Abstr.; Soc. Abstr.; Urb. Aff. Abstr.

1528 RECHERCHES SOCIOLOGIQUES. v.1– , June 1970– . Louvain. Two issues a year.
Issued by the Centre de Recherches Sociologiques, Université Catholique de Louvain.
Indexed: Bull. sig. soc. eth.; Int. Bibl. Soc.; Soc. Abstr.

RECHERCHES SUR LA FAMILLE
See International Seminar on Family Research. RECHERCHES SUR LA FAMILLE

1529 RECUEIL D'ABSTRACTS SUR L'URBANISME. no.1– , 1970?– . Paris. Irreg.
Issued by the Centre de Documentation sur l'Urbanisme.

RECUEILS
See Société Jean Bodin pour l'Histoire Comparative des Institutions. RECUEILS

REEKS SOCIOLOGISCHE MONOGRAFIEËN
See SOCIOLOGISCHE MONOGRAFIEËN

1530 REFERATEBLATT SOZIOLOGIE. REIHE A. 1969– . Berlin (East).
Issued by the Akademie für Gesellschaftswissenschaften of the Zentral Komitee of the SED.

[REFERENCES] URBAN AND REGIONAL
See Canadian Council on Urban and Regional Research. [REFERENCES] URBAN AND REGIONAL

LA REFORMA SOCIAL
See ÉTUDES SOCIALES

REGIONAL SCIENCE. DISSERTATIONS & MONOGRAPH SERIES
See Cornell University. Program in Urban Development Research. REGIONAL SCIENCE. DISSERTATIONS & MONOGRAPH SERIES

1531 Regional Science Association. PAPERS AND PROCEEDINGS [OF THE] ANNUAL MEETING. v.1–22–1975. Cambridge, Mass.
Superseded by: *International Regional Science Review.*

1532 Regional Science Research Institute. RSRI ABSTRACTS. 1– , June 1976– . Philadelphia, Pa. Three issues a year.

REGISTER OF RESEARCH ON COMMONWEALTH IMMIGRANTS
See Institute of Race Relations, London. REGISTER OF RESEARCH ON COMMONWEALTH IMMIGRANTS

REGISTRAR'S GENERAL ANNUAL ESTIMATES OF THE POPULATION OF ENGLAND AND WALES AND OF LOCAL AUTHORITY AREAS
See Gt. Britain. Office of Population Censuses and Surveys. REGISTRAR'S GENERAL ANNUAL ESTIMATES OF ENGLAND AND WALES AND OF LOCAL AUTHORITY AREAS

1533 REIHE POLITOLOGIE, SOZIOLOGIE. 1– , 1976– . München. Irreg.
Monograph series.

REIHE SOZIOLOGIE IN DER SCHWEITZ
See SOZIOLOGIE IN DER SCHWEITZ

1534 REIHE STRUKTUR- UND ENTWICKLUNGSPOLITIK. 1– , 1979– . Bonn, Verlag Neue Gesellschaft. Irreg.
Issued by the Forschungsinstitut der Friedrich-Ebert-Stiftung.

REIS
See REVISTA ESPAÑOLA DE INVESTIGACIONES SOCIOLOGICAS

1535 RELACIÓN CRIMINOLOGICA. v.1– , 1968– . Valencia. Semi-annual.
Issued by the Centro de Investigaciónes Penales y Criminologicas, Universidad de Carabobo. In Spanish.

1536 RELAÇÕES HUMANAS. Apr. 1958–1965? São Paulo. Three issues a year.
Issued by the Instituto de Relações Sociais e Industriais. In Portuguese.

1537 RELATIONS INDUSTRIELLES. INDUSTRIAL RELATIONS. 1945– . Québec. Quarterly.
Issued by the Département des Relations Industrielles, Université Laval. Title varies: 1945–50, *Bulletin des Relations Industrielles.* In French and English.
Indexed: Can. Per. Ind.; Int. Bibl. Soc.

RELEVE OFFICIEL DU CHIFFRE DE LA POPULATION DU ROYAUME
See Belgium. Institut National de Statistique. RELEVE OFFICIEL DU CHIFFRE DE LA POPULATION DU ROYAUME

1538 RELIGION AND SOCIETY. v.1– , Sep. 1954– . Bangalore. Quarterly.
Issued by the Christian Institute for the Study of Religion and Society. Title varies: Sep. 1954, *Bulletin.*

1539 RELIGIONSSOZIOLOGISCHE SCHRIFTEN. v.1– , 1971– . Berlin, Morus-Verlag. Irreg.
Monograph series.

RÉPERTOIRE DES DONNÉES EN SCIENCES SOCIALES
See SOCIAL SCIENCE DATA INVENTORY

RÉPERTOIRE MONDIALE DES INSTITUTIONS DES SCIENCES SOCIALES
See INTERNATIONAL SOCIAL SCIENCE JOURNAL

REPERTOIRE NATIONAL DES CHERCHEURS SCIENCES SOCIALES ET HUMAINES. TOME I: ETHNOLOGIE, LINGUISTIQUE, PSYCHOLOGIE, PSYCHOLOGIE SOCIALE, SOCIOLOGIE

See France. Délégation Générale a la Recherche Scientifique et Technique. RÉPERTOIRE NATIONAL DES CHERCHEURS SCIENCES SOCIALES ET HUMAINES. TOME I: ETHNOLOGIE, LINGUISTIQUE, PSYCHOLOGIE, PSYCHOLOGIE SOCIALE, SOCIOLOGIE

1540 REPLICATIONS IN SOCIAL PSYCHOLOGY. 1– , fall 1979– . Hays, Kans. Quarterly.

Issued by the Fort Hays State University. Subtitle reads: 'A journal for the development of empirical foundations'.

REPORT
See Boston University. School of Public Relations and Communications. Communications Research Center. REPORT

REPORT
See California University. Institute of Social Sciences. Center for the Study of Law and Society. REPORT

REPORT
See Canada. Royal Commission on Bilingualism and Biculturalism. REPORT

REPORT
See Emory University, Atlanta. Center for Research in Social Change. STUDIES IN URBAN CHANGE. REPORT

REPORT
See Gt. Britain. Commission for Racial Equality. REPORT

REPORT
See Gt. Britain. Commission for the New Towns. REPORT

REPORT
See Gt. Britain. Race Relations Board. REPORT

REPORT
See Hawaii. University, Honolulu. Center for Cultural and Technical Intercourse between East and West. REPORT

REPORT
See Ife. University. Demographic Research and Training Unit. REPORT

REPORT
See Kansas. State University of Agriculture and Applied Science, Manhattan. Department of Sociology and Anthropology. REPORT

REPORT
See Malaysian Sociological Institute. REPORT

REPORT
See Minority Rights Group. REPORT

REPORT
See National Opinion Research Center. REPORT

REPORT
See Ontario Conference on Intergroup Relations. REPORT

REPORT
See Purdue University. Purdue Opinion Panel, Measurement & Research Center. REPORT

REPORT
See Sagamore Sociological Conference. REPORT

REPORT
See Social Science Research Council of Canada. REPORT

[REPORT]
See World Fertility Survey. REPORT

REPORT OF ACTIVITIES
See European Research Institute for Regional and Urban Planning. REPORT OF ACTIVITIES

REPORT OF THE COMMISSION FOR RACIAL EQUALITY
See Gt. Britain. Commission for Racial Equality. REPORT

REPORT OF THE DIRECTOR ON THE ACTIVITIES
See Columbia University. Institute for the Study of Science in Human Affairs. REPORT OF THE DIRECTOR ON THE ACTIVITIES

REPORT OF THE ROYAL COMMISSION ON BILINGUALISM AND BICULTURALISM
See Canada. Royal Commission on Bilingualism and Biculturalism. REPORT

REPORT ON MARRIAGES AND DIVORCES, SOUTH AFRICA
See South Africa. Department of Statistics. VERSLAG VOOR HUWELIKE EN EGSKEIDINGS, SUID AFRIKA

REPORTS
See Institute of Community Studies. REPORTS

REPORTS OF ANNUAL CONFERENCES
See Institute of Sociology, London. REPORTS OF ANNUAL CONFERENCES

REPORTS ON THE POPULATION OF TRUST TERRITORIES
See United Nations. Department of Economic and Social Affairs. POPULATION STUDIES

1541 REPRESENTATIVE RESEARCH IN SOCIAL PSYCHOLOGY. v.1– , 1970– . Chapel Hill, N.C. Two issues a year.
Issued by the Department of Psychology, University of North Carolina.
Indexed: Psych. Abstr.

RESEARCH ABSTRACTS AND NEWSLETTER
See Makerere Institute of Social Research. RESEARCH ABSTRACTS AND NEWSLETTER

RESEARCH AND DEVELOPMENT ABSTRACTS
See United States. Agency for International Development. RESEARCH AND DEVELOPMENT ABSTRACTS

1542 RESEARCH ANNUAL ON INTERGROUP RELATIONS. 1962–1972. New York, Praeger.
Issued by the Committee on Desegregation and Integration, Society for the Psychological Study of Social Issues, and the Committee on Intergroup Relations, Society for the Study of Social Problems, in cooperation with the Anti-Defamation League of B'nai B'rith and other societies. Title varies: 1962–65, *Research Bulletin on Intergroup Relations*. Supersedes: *Joint Newsletter on Intergroup Relations*. Not published 1967–69.

RESEARCH BULLETIN
See London. University. University College. School of Environmental Studies. RESEARCH BULLETIN

RESEARCH BULLETIN ON INTERGROUP RELATIONS
See RESEARCH ANNUAL ON INTERGROUP RELATIONS

1543 The Research Centre for Canadian Ethnic Studies. OCCASIONAL MONOGRAPH. no.1– , 1973– . Calgary, Canada. Irreg.

RESEARCH DIGEST
See Intergovernmental Committee for European Migration. Department of Planning and Liaison. RESEARCH DIGEST

RESEARCH DIGEST
See QUARTERLY DIGEST OF URBAN AND REGIONAL RESEARCH

1544 Research Group on European Migration Problems. PUBLICATIONS. 1–6, 1951–1952. The Hague, Nijhoff. Irreg.
Monograph series.

1545 Research Group on European Migration Problems. REMP BULLETIN. v.1–10, Apr. 1952–Dec. 1962. The Hague. Four issues a year; subsequently quarterly.
Superseded by: *International Migration*.

1546 RESEARCH IN LAW AND SOCIOLOGY. 1–3, 1979–1980. Greenwich, Conn., JAI Press. Annual.
Continued by: *Research in Law, Deviance and Social Control*, 1981– .

1547 RESEARCH IN MELANESIA. 1– , Apr. 1975– . Port Moresby, Papua New Guinea.
Issued by the Department of Anthropology and Sociology, University of Papua New Guinea.

1548 RESEARCH IN RACE AND ETHNIC RELATIONS. 1– , 1979– . Greenwich, Conn. JAI Press. Annual.

1549 RESEARCH IN SOCIAL MOVEMENTS, CONFLICTS AND CHANGE. 1– , 1978– . Greenwich, Conn., JAI Press. Annual.
Subtitle reads: 'An annual compilation of research'.

1550 RESEARCH IN SOCIAL PROBLEMS AND PUBLIC POLICY. 1– , 1979– . Greenwich, Conn. JAI Press. Annual.

RESEARCH IN SOCIAL PSYCHOLOGY
See Illinois. University, Urbana. Department of Psychology. RESEARCH IN SOCIAL PSYCHOLOGY

1551 RESEARCH IN SOCIOLOGY OF EDUCATION AND SOCIALIZATION. v.1– , 1980– . Greenwich, Conn. JAI Press. Annual.

1552 RESEARCH IN SOCIOLOGY OF KNOWLEDGE, SCIENCES AND ART. 1–2, 1978–1980. Greenwich, Conn., JAI Press. Annual.
Continued by: *Knowledge and Society; Studies in Sociology of Culture Past and Present*.

1553 RESEARCH IN THE INTERWEAVE OF SOCIAL ROLES: WOMEN AND MEN. 1, 1980. Greenwich, Conn., JAI Press. Annual.
Continued by: *Research in the Interweave of Social Roles; Friendship*.
Indexed: Soc. Abstr.

1554 RESEARCH IN THE SOCIOLOGY OF HEALTH CARE. v.1– , 1980– . Greenwich, Conn., JAI Press. Annual.
Includes *Supplement*.

RESEARCH PAMPHLETS. N.F.R.B. PUBLICATIONS

See Fabian Society, London. RESEARCH SERIES

RESEARCH PAPER
See Toronto. University. Centre for Urban and Community Studies. RESEARCH PAPER

1555 RESEARCH PREVIEWS. v.1–21, no.2, 1953–Nov. 1974. Chapel Hill, N.C. Irreg.

Issued by the Institute for Research in Social Science, University of North Carolina. Continued by its *Newsletter*.

Indexed: Soc. Abstr.

RESEARCH PROJECT SERIES
See Nanyang University. Institute of Humanities and Social Sciences. RESEARCH PROJECT SERIES

RESEARCH PROJECTS
See Canterbury, N.Z. University. Department of Psychology and Sociology. RESEARCH PROJECTS

RESEARCH REPORT
See Jerusalem. Hebrew University. Department of Sociology. RESEARCH REPORT

RESEARCH REPORT
See Washington (State). University. Urban Data Center. RESEARCH REPORT

RESEARCH REPORTS
See Helsinki. Yliopisto. Sociologian Laitos. TUTKIMUKSIA

RESEARCH REPORTS AND TECHNICAL NOTES
See Boston University. Center for Applied Social Science. RESEARCH REPORTS AND TECHNICAL NOTES

RESEARCH REPORTS IN SOCIAL SCIENCE
See Florida. State University, Tallahassee. Institute for Social Research. RESEARCH REPORTS IN SOCIAL SCIENCE

RESEARCH REPORTS OF THE DEPARTMENT OF SOCIOLOGY
See Uppsala. Universitet. Sociologiska Institutionen. RESEARCH REPORTS OF THE DEPARTMENT OF SOCIOLOGY

RESEARCH REVIEW
See Harvard University. Program on Technology and Society. RESEARCH REVIEW

RESEARCH SERIES
See Centre for Environmental Studies. RESEARCH SERIES

RESEARCH SERIES
See Fabian Society, London. RESEARCH SERIES

RESEARCH SUPPORTED BY THE SSRC
See Social Science Research Council (Gt. Britain). RESEARCH SUPPORTED BY THE SSRC

RÉSUMÉ STATISTIQUE DU MOUVEMENT DE LA POPULATION DE L'EMPIRE DU JAPON
See Japan. Naikaku Tokeikyoku. RÉSUMÉ STATISTIQUE DU MOUVEMENT DE LA POPULATION DE L'EMPIRE DU JAPON

1556 RESUMENES DE POBLACIÓN EN AMERICA LATINA. LATIN AMERICAN POPULATION ABSTRACTS. 1– , June 1977– . Santiago, Chile. Semi-annual.

Issued by the Centro Latinoamericano de Demografia. At head of title: DOC PAL. No. for June 1977 called also *Numero Experimental*. Other title: *DOC PAL Resumenes de Población en America Latina*. In Spanish.

REUNION DE ESTUDIOS
See Asociación Española de Economia y Sociologia Agrarias. REUNIÓN DE ESTUDIOS

REVIEW (Institute of Human Sciences)
See URBAN AND SOCIAL CHANGE REVIEW

1557 REVIEW OF APPLIED URBAN RESEARCH. 1– , Aug. 1973– . Omaha, Nebr. Monthly.

Issued by the Center for Applied Urban Research, University of Nebraska.

REVIEW OF DATA ON RESEARCH AND DEVELOPMENT
See United States. National Science Foundation. REVIEW OF DATA ON RESEARCH AND DEVELOPMENT

REVIEW OF DATA ON SCIENCE RESOURCES
See United States. National Science Foundation. Office of Economic and Power Studies. REVIEWS OF DATA ON SCIENCE RESOURCES

1558 REVIEW OF PUBLIC DATA USE. v.1– , Dec. 1972– . Arlington, Va. Bimonthly.

Issued by the Clearinghouse and Laboratory for Census Data. Author/title index every three years.

Indexed: Soc. Abstr.

1559 THE REVIEW OF SOCIAL SCIENCE. v.1– , Mar. 1976– . Bangkok.
Issued by the Social Science Association of Thailand.

1560 REVIEW OF SOCIAL THEORY. 1– , Sep. 1972– . Columbia, Mo. Semi-annual.
Issued by the Department of Sociology and Rural Sociology, University of Missouri. 'A student edited journal'.
Indexed: Int. Bibl. Soc.; Int. Pol. Sc. Abstr.; Soc. Abstr.

REVIEW OF SOCIOLOGY
See SHAKAIGAKU HYORON

REVIEW OF SOCIOLOGY AND SOCIAL CHANGE
See New York (City). University. NEW YORK UNIVERSITY REVIEW OF LAW AND SOCIAL CHANGE

1561 REVIEW OF SOUTHEAST ASIAN STUDIES. 1– . 1971– . Singapore. Quarterly.
Issued by the South Seas Society. Title varies: 1–3, 1971–73, *Nanyang Quarterly*.

1562 REVIEWING SOCIOLOGY. Issue no.1– , autumn 1979– . Birmingham. Three issues a year.
Issued by the School of Sociological Studies, Department of Sociology & Applied Social Studies, City of Birmingham Polytechnic. Cumulative index in each issue, beginning with Issue no.2.

REVIEWS OF CURRENT RESEARCH
See Social Science Research Council (Gt. Britain). REVIEWS OF CURRENT RESEARCH

REVIEWS ON THE PROBLEMS AND SCIENCE OF HUMAN SETTLEMENTS
See EKISTICS; REVIEWS ON THE PROBLEMS AND SCIENCE OF HUMAN SETTLEMENTS

1563 REVIJA ZA SOCIOLOGIJU. SOCIOLOGICAL REVIEW. v.1– , 1971– . Zagreb. Quarterly.
Issued by the Sociološko drustvo hrvatske. In Serbo-Croatian; summaries in English.
Indexed: Soc. Abstr.

REVISTA
See Instituto de Ciencias Sociales. REVISTA

REVISTA
See Museo Social Argentino, Buenos Aires. BOLETIN

1564 REVISTA BRASILEIRA DE CIÊNCIAS SOCIAIS. v.1– , Mar/June 1961– . Belo Horizonte. Three issues a year.
Issued by the Faculdade de Ciências Economicas, Universidad de Minas Gerais. In Portuguese.
Indexed: Soc. Abstr.

1565 LA REVISTA DE CIENCIAS ECONÓMICAS Y SOCIALES. v.1– , Mar/June 1972– . Santo Domingo. Quarterly.
Issued by the Universidad Autonoma de Santo Domingo. In Spanish.

REVISTA DE CIENCIAS JURIDICAS, POLITICAS Y SOCIALES
See REVISTA DE DERECHO, CIENCIAS POLITICAS Y SOCIALES

1566 REVISTA DE CIÊNCIAS SOCIAIS. 1– , 2nd quarter 1970– . Fortaleza, Brazil. Semi-annual.
Issued by the Departamento de Sociologia, Universidade Federal do Ceará. In English, French and Portuguese.

1567 REVISTA DE CIENCIAS SOCIALES. v.1– , Mar. 1957– . Rio Piedras, P.R. Quarterly.
Issued by the Colegio de Ciencias Sociales; subsequently by El Centro de Investigaciónes Sociales. Universidad de Puerto Rico. In Spanish.
Indexed: Int. Bibl. Soc.; Soc. Abstr.

1568 REVISTA DE CIENCIAS SOCIALES. v.1– , 1963– . Cumaná. Semi-annual.
Issued by the Universidad de Costa Rica, called earlier Universidad Nacional. Supersedes a publication of the same title. In Spanish.

1569 REVISTA DE CIENCIAS SOCIALES. v.1– , 1970– . San José. Semi-annual.
Issued by the Universidad de Costa Rica. In Spanish.

1570 REVISTA DE COMUNICAÇÃO SOCIAL. 1– , 1971– . Ceará, Brazil. Semi-annual.
Issued by the Departamento de Comunicação Social, Universidade Federal. In Portuguese.

1571 REVISTA DE DERECHO, CIENCIAS POLITICAS Y SOCIALES. v.1– , Oct. 1957– . Oruro, Bolivia. Ceased publication?
Issued by the Faculdad de Ciencias Juridicas, Politicas y Sociales, Universidad Tecnica. Title varies: v.1–3, no.1, 1957–Jan. 1960, *Revista de Ciencias Juridicas, Politicas y Sociales*. Supersedes: *Revista de Estudios Juridicos, Politicos y Sociales*, 1952–56. In Spanish.

1572 REVISTA DE DERECHO Y DE SOCIOLOGIA. v.1, 1895. Madrid. One volume published. In Spanish.

1573 REVISTA DE ESTUDIOS AGROSOCIALES. v.1– , Oct/Dec. 1952– . Madrid. Quarterly.
Issued by the Instituto de Estudios Agro-Sociales. Indexes: no.1–9, 1952–54, 1 v. In Spanish.

1574 REVISTA DE ESTUDIOS JURIDICOS, POLITICOS Y SOCIALES. no.1–25, July 1940–1967. Sucre, Bolivia. Annual.
Issued by the Faculdad de Derecho, Ciencias Politicas y Sociales, Universidad Mayor de San Francisco Xavier. In Spanish.

1575 REVISTA DE REFERATI ȘI RECENZII. 1964– . București. Bimonthly.
Issued by the Centrul de Documentáre Științifica, Academia Republicii Socialiste România. In Rumanian.

1576 REVISTA DE SOCIOLOGIA. v.1–3, July/Dec. 1964–1966. Lima, Peru. Semi-annual.
Issued by the Departamento de Sociologia, Universidad Nacional Mayor de San Marcos. In Spanish.
Indexed: Soc. Abstr.

1577 REVISTA DE SOCIOLOGIA. 1– , Jan/June 1968– . Medellin. Two issues a year.
Issued by the Instituto de Sociologia, Faculdad de Ciencias Sociales, Universidad Pontificia Bolivariana. In Spanish.

1578 REVISTA DE SOCIOLOGIA. no.1– , 1972– . Santiago, Chile.
Issued by the Departamento de Sociologia, Universidad de Chile. In Spanish.

1579 REVISTA DE SOCIOLOGIE. v.1, no.1–7, Jan/July 1931. Cluj, România.
In Rumanian.

1580 REVISTA DEL DESARROLLO INTERNACIONAL. REVUE DU DÉVELOPPEMENT INTERNATIONAL. INTERNATIONAL DEVELOPMENT REVIEW. v.1– , 1959– . Washington, D.C. Quarterly.
Issued by the Society for International Development. Title varies: 1959–69, *International Development Review*. In English.
Indexed: Int. Bibl. Soc.; PAIS; Soc. Abstr.

REVISTA DEL INSTITUTO DE CIENCIAS SOCIALES
See Instituto de Ciencias Sociales. REVISTA

REVISTA DEL INSTITUTO DE SOCIOLOGIA BOLIVIANA
See Sucre, Bolivia. Universidad Mayor de San Francisco Xavier. Instituto de Sociologia Boliviana. REVISTA

1581 REVISTA ESPAÑOLA DE INVESTIGACIÓNES SOCIOLOGICAS. no.1– , Jan-Mar. 1978– . Madrid, Itaca Distribuciónes Editoriales. Quarterly.
Issued by the Centro de Investigaciónes Sociologicas. Other title: *Reis*. In Spanish.

1582 REVISTA ESPAÑOLA DE LA OPINIÓN PÚBLICA. no.1– , May/Aug. 1965– . Madrid. Four issues a year.
Issued by the Instituto de la Opinión Pública. In Spanish.
Indexed: Int. Bibl. Soc.; Int. Pol. Sc. Abstr.; Psych. Abstr.; Soc. Abstr.

REVISTA HOLLANDESE DE GEOGRAFIA ECONÓMICA Y SOCIAL
See TIJDSCHRIFT VOOR ECONOMISCHE EN SOCIALE GEOGRAFIE

1583 REVISTA INTERAMERICANA DE CIENCIAS SOCIALES. v.1–4, no.2, 1961–1967. Washington, D.C. Irreg.
Issued by the Departamento de Asuntos Sociales, Unión Panamericana. Supersedes: *Ciencias Sociales; Notas e Informaciónes*. Called '2. epoca'. In Portuguese and Spanish.
Indexed: Int. Bibl. Soc. Cult. Anth.; Soc. Abstr.

1584 REVISTA INTERAMERICANA DE CIENCIAS SOCIALES. no.1– , Dec. 1976– . Buenos Aires, Huemul. Four issues a year.
Issued by the United Nations Educational, Scientific and Cultural Organization. A Spanish edition of *International Social Science Journal*, beginning with the latter's issue no.4, 1976.

1585 REVISTA INTERNACIONAL DE SOCIOLOGIA. [1]– , Jan/Mar. 1943– . Madrid. Quarterly.
Issued by the Instituto Sancho de Moucada, 1943–44; subsequently by the Instituto Balmes de Sociologia. Early volumes include 'Boletin Bibliografico de Revistas'. In Spanish.
Indexed: Bull. sig. soc. eth.; Int. Pol. Sc. Abstr.; Soc. Abstr.; Wom. Stud. Abstr.

1586 REVISTA LATINOMERICANA DE CIENCIAS SOCIALES. no.1/2–4, June/Dec. 1971–1972. Santiago, Chile. Semi-annual.
Issued by the Flacso (Faculdad Latinoamericana de Ciencias Sociales), Escuela Latinoamericana de Sociologia, and Instituto Coordinado de Investigaciónes Sociales. Supersedes: *Boletin ELAS,* 1968–70. In Spanish.
Indexed: Soc. Abstr.

1587 REVISTA LATINOAMERICANA DE SOCIOLOGIA. INVESTIGACIÓNES SOCIALES. Mar. 1965–1975. Buenos Aires. Four issues a year.
Issued by the Instituto Torcuato di Tella. In Spanish; summaries in English.
Indexed: Bull. sig. soc. eth.; Int. Bibl. Soc.; Int. Pol. Sc. Abstr.; Soc. Abstr.

1588 REVISTA MEXICANA DE ANALISIS DE LA CONDUCTA. MEXICAN JOURNAL OF BEHAVIOR ANALYSIS. 1– , 1975– . Mexico, D.F. Semi-annual.
Issued by the Universidad Nacional Autonoma de Mexico. In Spanish and English.

1589 REVISTA MEXICANA DE SOCIOLOGIA. v.1– , Mar/Apr. 1939– . Mexico, D.F. Bimonthly, 1939; quarterly, 1940– .
Issued by the Instituto de Investigaciónes Sociales, Universidad Nacional Autonoma de Mexico. In Spanish and English.
Indexed: Bull. sig. soc. eth.; Int. Bibl. Soc.; Int. Pol. Sc. Abstr.; Psych. Abstr.; Soc. Abstr.

1590 REVISTA PARAGUAYA DE SOCIOLOGIA. v.1– , Sep/Dec. 1964– . Asunción. Three issues a year; some double issues.
Issued by the Centro Paraguayo de Estudios Sociologicos. In Spanish.
Indexed: Bull. sig. soc. eth.; Int. Bibl. Soc.; Psych. Abstr.; Soc. Abstr.

1591 REVISTA PERNAMBUCANA DE SOCIOLOGIA. v.1–3, no.3, 1954–1956. Recife, Brazil.
Issued by the Universidade Federal de Pernambuco, and Sociedade Brasileira de Sociologia. In Portuguese. Superseded by: *Jornal Brasileiro de Sociologia*.

1592 REVISTA PERUANA DE CIENCIAS JURIDICAS Y SOCIALES. v.1– , 1954– . Lima, Peru. Quarterly.
In Spanish.

1593 REVISTA URUGUAYA DE SOCIOLOGIA. no.1– , 1972– . Montevideo.
Issued by the Centro de Investigación Social, and Instituto de Ciencias Sociales. In Spanish.

1594 REVISTA VENEZOLANA DE SOCIOLOGIA Y ANTROPOLOGIA. 1– , 1960– . Caracas.
In Spanish.
Indexed: Soc. Abstr.

REVUE
See Action Populaire, Rheims. REVUE

REVUE
See Brussels, Belgium. Université Libre. Institut de Sociologie. REVUE

REVUE CANADIENNE D'URBANISME
See COMMUNITY PLANNING REVIEW

LA REVUE CANADIENNE DE LA SOCIOLOGIE ET D'ANTHROPOLOGIE
See THE CANADIAN REVUE OF SOCIOLOGY AND ANTHROPOLOGY

REVUE CANADIENNE DE LA THÉORIE POLITIQUE ET SOCIALE
See CANADIAN JOURNAL OF SOCIAL AND POLITICAL THEORY

REVUE CANADIENNE DE SCIENCE POLITIQUE
See CANADIAN JOURNAL OF POLITICAL SCIENCE

1595 REVUE CANADIENNE DES ÉTUDES AFRICAINES. CANADIAN JOURNAL OF AFRICAN STUDIES. v.1– , Mar. 1967– . Montréal; subsequently Ottawa. Three issues a year.
Issued by the Canadian Association of African Studies. Title varies: *Journal Canadien des Études Africaines*. Title inverted on cover: *Canadian Journal of African Studies. Revue Canadienne des Études Africaines*.
Indexed: Int. Bibl. Soc.; SSCI; Soc. Abstr.; Wom. Stud. Abstr.

REVUE CANADIENNE DES ÉTUDES SUR LE NATIONALISME
See CANADIAN REVIEW OF STUDIES IN NATIONALISM

REVUE CANADIENNE DES ÉTUDES SUR LE NATIONALISME: BIBLIOGRAPHIE
See CANADIAN REVIEW OF STUDIES IN NATIONALISM. BIBLIOGRAPHY

REVUE CANADIENNE DES SCIENCES DU COMPORTEMENT
See CANADIAN JOURNAL OF BEHAVIORAL SCIENCE

1596 REVUE CATHOLIQUE SOCIALE ET JURIDIQUE. 1–29, 1897–1925. Bruxelles.
Formed by merger of *Revue Sociale Catholique* and *Revue Catholique du Droit*. Issued by the Université Catholique. Title varies: 1–24, 1897–Mar. 1920, *Revue Sociale Catholique*. Not published Nov.19–23, 1914–Mar. 1919.

REVUE CONNECTIONS. PSYCHOLOGIE. SCIENCES HUMAINES
See CONNECTIONS

REVUE D'ÉCONOMIE SOCIALE ET RURALE
See ÉTUDES SOCIALES

1597 REVUE D'ETHNOGRAPHIE ET DE SOCIOLOGIE. v.1–5, no.3/4, 1910–Mar/Apr. 1914. Paris.
Issued by the Institut Ethnographique. Supersedes: *Revue des Études Ethnographiques et Sociologiques*.

1598 REVUE D'ÉTUDES SUD-EST EUROPÉENNES. v.1– , 1963– . Bucureşti. Quarterly.
Issued by the Institut d'Études Sud-Est Européennes, Academia Republicii Socialiste de Roumanie. In English, French, German and Russian.
Indexed: Int. Bibl. Soc.; Soc. Abstr.

REVUE DE L'INSTITUT DE SOCIOLOGIE
See Brussels, Belgium. Université Libre. Institut de Sociologie. REVUE

REVUE DE PSYCHOLOGIE
See VIE CONTEMPORAINE; REVUE DE PSYCHOLOGIE SOCIALE

REVUE DE PSYCHOLOGIE DES PEUPLES
See ETHNOPSYCHOLOGIE

REVUE DE PSYCHOLOGIE SOCIALE
See VIE CONTEMPORAINE; REVUE DE PSYCHOLOGIE SOCIALE

REVUE DE SOCIOLOGIE
See RIVISTA DI SOCIOLOGIA

REVUE DE SOCIOLOGIE
See SOCIOLOGICKÁ REVUE

REVUE DE SOCIOLOGIE
See SOSYOLOJI DERGISI

1599 REVUE DES ÉTUDES ETHNOGRAPHIQUES ET SOCIOLOGIQUES. 1–2, 1908–1909. Paris.
Superseded by: *Revue d'Ethnographie et de Sociologie*.

1600 REVUE DES PAYS DE L'EST. v.1– , 1960– . Bruxelles, Éditions de l'Université Libre de Bruxelles. Semi-annual.
Issued by the Centre d'Étude des Pays de l'Est, Institut de Sociologie, Université Libre, and Centre National pour l'Étude des Etats de l'Est. Title varies: v.1–3, 1960–63, *Pays Communistes;* v.4–8, 1963–67, *Bulletin de Centre d'Étude des Pays de l'Est et du Centre National pour l'Étude des Etats de l'Est;* v.9–12, *Revue du Centre d'Étude des Pays de l'Est et du Centre National pour l'Étude des Etats de l'Est.*
Indexed: Int. Bibl. Soc.; Int. Pol. Sc. Abstr.; Soc. Abstr.

REVUE DES SCIENCES ÉCONOMIQUES ET SOCIALES
See MALLAJAH-'TULUM-I IQTISADI VA ISTIMAI

REVUE DES SCIENCES SOCIALES
See REVUE ROUMAINE DES SCIENCES SOCIALES. PHILOSOPHIE — PSYCHOLOGIE

1601 REVUE DES SCIENCES SOCIALES DE LA FRANCE DE L'EST. v.1– , 1972– . Strasbourg. Annual.
Issued by the Université des Sciences Humaines.
Indexed: Int. Bibl. Soc.

REVUE DU CENTRE D'ÉTUDE DES PAYS DE l'EST ET DU CENTRE NATIONALE POUR L'ÉTUDE DES ETATS DE L'EST
See REVUE DES PAYS DE L'EST

REVUE DE CHRISTIANISME SOCIAL
See CHRISTIANISME SOCIAL; REVUE DE CULTURE SOCIAL ET INTERNATIONAL

REVUE DU DÉVELOPPEMENT INTERNATIONAL
See REVISTA DEL DESARROLLO INTERNACIONAL

REVUE DU SUD-EST ASIATIQUE
See REVUE DU SUD-EST ASIATIQUE ET DE L'EXTRÊME-ORIENT

1602 REVUE DU SUD-EST ASIATIQUE ET DE L'EXTRÊME-ORIENT. JOURNAL OF SOUTHEAST ASIA AND THE FAR EAST. 1961–1970. Bruxelles, Éditions de l'Institut de Sociologie.
Issued by the Institut de Sociologie, Université Libre. Title varies: 1961–67, *Revue du Sud-Est Asiatique. Journal of Southeast Asia.* Superseded by: *Asia Quarterly; A Journal from Europe.*
Indexed: Int. Bibl. Soc.; Soc. Abstr.

REVUE EUROPÉENNE D'HISTOIRE DES SCIENCES SOCIALES
See CAHIERS VILFREDO PARETO: REVUE EUROPÉENNE D'HISTOIRE DES SCIENCES SOCIALES

1603 REVUE FRANCAISE DE SOCIOLOGIE. v.1– , Jan/Mar. 1960– . Paris. Quarterly.
Issued by the Centre d'Études Sociologiques. Supersedes: *Recherches Sociologiques,* 1954–57. Summaries in English, German, Russian and Spanish.

Indexed: Bull. sig. soc. eth.; Int. Bibl. Soc.; Int. Pol. Sc. Abstr.; Peace Res. Abstr. J.; Psych. Abstr.; Soc. Abstr.

1604 REVUE FRANCAISE DES AFFAIRES SOCIALES. v.1– , 1947– . Paris. Documentation Francaise. Quarterly.

Issued by the Ministère de la Santé et de Sécurité Sociale du Travail et le Ministère des Affaires Sociales. Title varies: 1947–66, *Revue Francaise du Travail.*

Indexed: Bull. sig. soc. eth.; Int. Bibl. Soc.; Soc. Abstr.

REVUE FRANCAISE DU TRAVAIL
See REVUE FRANCAISE DES AFFAIRES SOCIALES

REVUE INTERNATIONALE DE LA RECHERCHE DE COMMUNICATION
See COMMUNICATIONS

REVUE INTERNATIONALE DE RECHERCHE URBAINE ET RÉGIONALE
See INTERNATIONAL JOURNAL OF URBAN AND REGIONAL RESEARCH

1605 REVUE INTERNATIONALE DE SOCIOLOGIE. INTERNATIONAL REVIEW OF SOCIOLOGY. v.1–47, Jan/Feb. 1893–Sep/Dec. 1939; n.s. 2, v.1–7, 1954/1957–1971. Roma. Three issues a year.

Issued by the École de Perfectionment en Sociologie et en Sciences Sociales, Università di Roma, International Association for the Advancement of Ethnology and Eugenics, Comité Italien pour l'Étude des Problémes de la Population, Istituto di Statistica, Faculta di Scienze Statistiche, Demografia e Affuriali, Università di Roma. In English, French, German, Italian and Spanish. Indexes: 1893–1902, v.10, pp.946–960; 1913–22, 1 v.

Indexed: Int. Bibl. Soc.; Int. Pol. Sc. Abstr.; Soc. Abstr.

1606 REVUE INTERNATIONALE DES SCIENCES SOCIALES. v.1– , 1949– . Paris, Unesco. Quarterly.

A French-language edition of *International Social Science Journal.*

REVUE MENSUELLE
See Musée Social, Paris. REVUE MENSUELLE

REVUE NEDERLANDAISE DE GEOGRAPHIE ÉCONOMIQUE ET SOCIALE
See TIJDSCHRIFT VOOR ECONOMISCHE EN SOCIALE GEOGRAFIE

1607 REVUE ROUMAINE DES SCIENCES SOCIALES. PHILOSOPHIE — PSYCHOLOGIE. 1956–1965/1966. Bucureşti, Éditions de l'Académie République Socialiste de Roumaine. Annual.

Issued by the Académie République Socialiste de Roumaine. Title varies: 1956–58, *Revue Roumaine des Sciences Sociales.* Supersedes: *La Science dans la République Populaire Roumaine.* Continued by: *Revue Roumaine des Sciences Sociales. Série de Sociologie.*

Indexed: Int. Bibl. Soc.

1608 REVUE ROUMAINE DES SCIENCES SOCIALES. SÉRIE DE SOCIOLOGIE. v.10/11– , 1966/1967– . Bucureşti, Éditions de l'Académie République Socialiste Roumaine. Annual.

Continues, in part, *Revue Roumaine des Sciences Sociales. Série Philosophie — Psychologie.*

Indexed: Int. Bibl. Soc.

REVUE SCANDINAVE DE SOCIOLOGIE
See ACTA SOCIOLOGICA. SCANDINAVIAN REVIEW OF SOCIOLOGY

REVUE SUISSE DE SOCIOLOGIE
See SCHWEIZERISCHE ZEITSCHRIFT FÜR SOZIOLOGIE

REVUE TIERS-MONDE
See TIERS-MONDE

1609 REVUE TUNISIENNE DES SCIENCES SOCIALES. 1– , Sep. 1964– . Tunis. Semiannual; subsequently quarterly.

Issued by the Centre d'Études et de Recherches Économiques et Sociales, Université de Tunis. Title in Arabic: *al-Majallah al-Tūnisīyah alil-'ulūm al-ijtimā'īyah.*

Indexed: Bull. sig. soc. eth.; Int. Bibl. Soc.; LLBA; Soc. Abstr.

1610 Rhodes-Livingstone Institute, Lusaka, Zambia. COMMUNICATIONS. no.1–29, 1943–1965. Lusaka.

Superseded by: Zambia. University. Institute for Social Research. *Communication.*

1611 RHODES-LIVINGSTONE JOURNAL; HUMAN RELATIONS IN BRITISH CENTRAL AFRICA. no.1–38, June 1944–1965. Cape Town, Oxford University Press.

No. 1–4 published by the Rhodes-Livingstone Institute in Livingstone. Superseded by: *African Social Research.*

1612 RICERCA SOCIALE. no.1– , 1972– . Bologna. Three issues a year.

Issued by the Centro di Studi sul Problemi della Città e del Territorio, Istituto di Sociologia, Università di Bologna. Subtitle reads: 'Quadrimestrielle di sociologia urbana, rurale et cooperazione'. In English, French and Italian.

1613 RICERCHE DI SOCIOLOGIA DELL'EDUCAZIONE E PEDAGOGIA COMPARATA. 1– , 1973?– . Messina, Poloritana. Irreg.
Issued by the Istituto di Pedagogia, Università di Messina. In Italian.

1614 RICERCHE DI SOCIOLOGIA SPERIMENTALE. 1– , 1970– . Milano, F. Angeli. Issued by the Istituto di Sociologia, Università di Parma. In Italian.

1615 RICERCHE SOCIOLOGICHE. 1– , 196?– . Pádova, Marsilio Editore. Irreg. Ceased publication.
In Italian
Monograph series.

RIKKYŌ REVIEW OF APPLIED SOCIOLOGY
See ŌYŌ SHAKAI-GAKU KENKYŪ

1616 Rio de Janeiro. Universidad do Brasil. Instituto de Ciências Sociais. TEXTOS DO SOCIOLOGIA. 1–?, 1963–?. Rio de Janeiro. Irreg.
In Portuguese. Ceased publication.
Monograph series

1617 RIOT DATA REVIEW. no.1–3, May 1968–Feb. 1969. Waltham, Mass.
Issued by the Lemberg Center for the Study of Violence, Brandeis University. Mimeographed.

1618 RIVISTA DE ECONOMIA AGRARIA. v.1– , Mar. 1946– . Roma. Quarterly.
Issued by the Istituto Nazionale di Economia Agraria. Absorbed, in 1965, *Società Rurale; Rivista di Sociologia Agraria, di Economia et Politica Agraria.* Subtitle reads: 'Studi di economia agraria, politica agraria, sociologia rurale'.
Indexed: Int. Bibl. Soc.; Soc. Abstr.

1619 RIVISTA DI SOCIOLOGIA. v.1–4, 1894–June 1898. Roma.
In Italian. Suspended in 1897.

1620 RIVISTA DI SOCIOLOGIA. v.1–10, no. 2/3/4, July/Aug. 1927–June/Dec. 1940. Milano. Quarterly (irreg.).
Title varies: Mar/Apr. 1933, *Rivista di Sociologia e Archives di Sociologia;* 1–9, 1927–39 also as series 2; v.6–7, no.1, 1932–34 also with secondary title *Revue de Sociologie*. Series 2, no.3–5/6 have cover title *Rivista di Sociologia et Archives de Sociologie*. v.8, 1938 as series 3. Suspended: Apr. 1934–Dec. 1937. In English, French and Italian.
Indexed: Afr. Abstr.; Bull. sig. soc. eth.; Int. Bibl. Soc.; Int. Pol. Sc. Abstr.

1621 RIVISTA DI SOCIOLOGIA. v.1–16, 1963–1978. Roma. Quarterly.
Issued by the Istituto di Sociologia, Libera Università Internazionale degli Studi Sociali pro Deo. In English, French and Italian. Indexes: 1963–66.
Indexed: Afr. Abstr.; Int. Bibl. Soc.; Int. Pol. Sc. Abstr.; Soc. Abstr.

RIVISTA DI SOCIOLOGIA ET ARCHIVES DE SOCIOLOGIE
See RIVISTA DI SOCIOLOGIA (Milano)

1622 RIVISTA DI SOCIOLOGIA HELLENISTA. v.1–3, no.2, Apr. 1921–Mar. 1923. Roma.
In Italian.

1623 RIVISTA INTERNAZIONALE DI SCIENZE SOCIALI. 1–106, 1893–Dec. 1926; n.s. 1927–1929, ser.3, v.1– , 1930– . Roma, Milano. Bimonthly.
Issued by the Università Cattolica del Sacro Cuore, and Societa Cattolica Italiana per gli Studi Scientifici. Title varies: 1–ser.3, v.4, 1893–1933, *Rivista Internazionale di Scienze Sociali e Discipline Ausiliare*. In English, French and Italian.
Indexed: Bull. sig. soc. eth.; Int. Bibl. Soc.; Int. Pol. Sc. Abstr.; Soc. Abstr.

RIVISTA INTERNAZIONALE DI SCIENZE SOCIALI E DISCIPLINE AUSILIARE
See RIVISTA INTERNAZIONALE DI SCIENZE SOCIALI

1624 RIVISTA ITALIANA DI SOCIOLOGIA. v.1–25, no.2, July 1897–Jan/June 1921. Roma.
In Italian.

1625 RIV'ON LE-MEḤKAR ḤEVRATI. no.1– , Jan. 1972– . Haifa. Quarterly.
Issued by the Department of Sociology and the Department of Political Science, University. In Hebrew; summaries in English. Added title: *Social Science Review*.

1626 Rocky Mountain College, Billings, Mont. Center for Indian Studies. OCCASIONAL PAPERS. no.1– , 1968– . Billings, Mont. Irreg.
Series of papers.
Indexed: Soc. Abstr.

ROCZNIK DEMOGRAFICZNY
See Poland. Główny Urząd Statystyczny. ROCZNIK DEMOGRAFICZNY

1627 ROCZNIKI SOCJOLOGII WSI. v.1–3, 1936–1938. Warszawa.

1628 ROCZNIKI SOCJOLOGII WSI; STUDIA I MATERIAŁY. v.1– , 1963– . Warszawa, Państwowe Wydawnictwo Naukowe. Annual.
Issued by the Zakład Socjologii Wsi, Instytut Filozofii i Socjologii, Polska Akademia Nauk. Title in English: *Annals of Rural Sociology — Studies and Materials*. In Polish; table of contents and summaries in English and Russian.
Indexed: Int. Bibl. Soc.

1629 THE ROMANIAN JOURNAL OF SOCIOLOGY. v.1–6, 1962–1971. Bucharest, Publishing House of the Academy of the Romanian People's Republic.
Issued by the National Committee of Sociology, the Academy. Title varies: 1964–65, *The Rumanian Journal of Sociology*. In Rumanian, English and French.
Indexed: Int. Bibl. Soc.

1630 ROMANIAN SCIENTIFIC ABSTRACTS. SOCIAL SCIENCES. v.1– , Jan. 1964–. Bucharest. Bimonthly.
Issued by the Centrul de Informáre si Documentáre in Ştiintele Sociale şi Politice, Académia. Title varies: *Rumanian Scientific Abstracts. Social Sciences.*

1631 Rome (City). Università. Istituto di Demografia. PUBBLICAZIONI. 1– , 1959– . Roma. Irreg. Ceased publication.
In Italian.
Monograph series.

1632 Rosario, Argentina. Universidad Nacional del Litoral. Istituto de Sociologia de Educación, Paraná. TRABAJOS E INVESTIGACIÓNES. no.1–14, 1963–1965. Parana
In Spanish.
Monograph series.

1633 Royal Asiatic Society. Ceylon Branch. JOURNAL. v,1– , 1958– . Colombo. Annual.

1634 RUCH PRAWNICZY, EKONOMICZNY I SOCJOLOGICZNY. v.1– , 1921– . Poznań. Quarterly.
Issued by the Wydział Prawa, Uniwersytet, and Wydział Prawa, Akademia Ekonomiczna (called, 1929–38, Wyższa Szkoła Handlowa, subsequently Wýsza Szkoła Ekonomiczna). Title varies: 1921–59, *Ruch Prawniczy i Ekonomiczny*. In Polish; table of contents in English and Russian.
Indexed: Int. Bibl. Soc.

RUCH PRAWNICZY I EKONOMICZNY
See RUCH PRAWNICZY, EKONOMICZNY I SOCJOLOGICZNY

THE RUMANIAN JOURNAL OF SOCIOLOGY
See ROMANIAN JOURNAL OF SOCIOLOGY

RUMANIAN SCIENTIFIC ABSTRACTS. SOCIAL SCIENCES
See ROMANIAN SCIENTIFIC ABSTRACTS. SOCIAL SCIENCES

1635 RUMANIAN STUDIES. v.1– , 1970– . Leiden, E. J. Brill. Annual; some volumes combine two or three years.
Issued by the Department of History, University of Illinois. In English and French. Subtitle reads: 'An international annual of the humanities and social sciences'.

1636 RURAL AFRICANA. no.1–31, Mar. 1967–1976; n.s. no.1– , spring 1978– . East Lansing, Mich. Three issues a year; subsequently quarterly.
Issued by the African Studies Center with the Department of Political Science, Michigan State University.

1637 RURAL AMERICA. v.1–19, no.5, Mar/Apr. 1923–May 1941. New York.
Issued by the American Country Life Association. Title varies: 1–2, 1923–24, *Country Life Bulletin.*

1638 RURAL COMMUNITY STUDIES IN EUROPE. v.1– , Apr. 1980– . Oxford, Pergamon Press. Irreg.

1639 RURAL DEMOGRAPHY. 1– , summer 1974– . Dacca, Bangladesh. Semi-annual.
Issued by the Institute of Statistical Research and Training, University of Dacca.

1640 RURAL INSTITUTIONS AND PLANNED CHANGE. 1–8, 1969–1976. Geneva.
Issued by the Research Institute of Social Development, United Nations. Title varies: 1, 1969, *Rural Institutions as Agents of Planned Change.*

RURAL INSTITUTIONS AS AGENTS OF PLANNED CHANGE
See RURAL INSTITUTIONS AND PLANNED CHANGE

RURAL LIFE STUDIES
See United States. Bureau of Agricultural Economics. RURAL LIFE STUDIES

1641 RURAL SOCIOLOGICAL MONOGRAPHS. no.1, 1938. Baton Rouge, La., University of Louisiana. One volume published.
Issued by the Rural Society of America.

1642 Rural Sociological Society. MONOGRAPH. 1– , 1972– . Morgantown, W.Va., University Bookstore. Irreg.
Monograph series.

1643 RURAL SOCIOLOGY. v.1– , Mar. 1936– . Baton Rouge, La.; subsequently Brookings, S.Dak. Quarterly.
Issued by the Section of Rural Sociology, American Sociological Association, and published at Baton Rouge, La.; subsequently by the Rural Sociological Society and the Department of Rural Sociology, South Dakota State University.
Indexed: Bull. sig. soc. eth.; Int. Bibl. Soc.; Int. Pol. Sc. Abstr.; PAIS; PHRA; Pop. Ind.; Psych. Abstr.; SSCI; Sage Fam. Stud. Abstr.; Soc. Abstr.; Soc. Work Res. Abstr.

RURAL SOCIOLOGY MIMEOGRAPHS
See Ohio. State University. Agricultural Economics and Rural Sociology Department. ESS [ECONOMIC AND SOCIOLOGIC SERIES]

RURAL SOCIOLOGY PAMPHLET
See South Dakota. State College of Agriculture and Mechanics. RURAL SOCIOLOGY PAMPHLET

RURAL SOCIOLOGY REPORT
See Iowa. State University of Science and Technology. RURAL SOCIOLOGY REPORT

RURAL SOCIOLOGY SERIES
See Alabama. Agricultural Research Station, Auburn. Department of Agricultural Economics and Sociology. RURAL SOCIOLOGY SERIES

1644 Rutgers University. Center for Alcohol Studies. MONOGRAPHS. 4– , 1964– . New Brunswick, N.J. Irreg.
Continues: Yale University. Center for Alcohol Studies. *Monographs.*

SIP PAPER
See Organisation of Sociologists in Polytechnics and Cognate Institutions. SIP PAPER

SSCI JOURNAL CITATION REPORTS
See SOCIAL SCIENCES CITATION INDEX

SSRC NEWSLETTER
See Social Science Research Council (Gt. Britain). RESEARCH SUPPORTED BY SSRC

1645 SWS NETWORK. v.9, no.2– , 1980– . New Albany, Ind.
Issued by the Sociologists for Women in Society. Continues: Sociologists for Women in Society. *Newsletter.*

1646 Sagamore Sociological Conference. REPORT. 1st–10th, 1907–1917. Boston. Annual.
No meeting in 1915.

1647 SAGE ANNUAL REVIEWS OF COMMUNICATION RESEARCH. v.1– , 1972– . Beverly Hills, Calif., Sage Publications.

1648 SAGE ANNUAL REVIEWS OF STUDIES IN DEVIANCE. .1– , 1977– . Beverly Hills, Calif., Sage Publications.

1649 SAGE FAMILY STUDIES ABSTRACTS. v.1– , Feb. 1979– . Beverly Hills, Calif., Sage Publications. Quarterly.

1650 SAGE PROFESSIONAL PAPERS IN CONTEMPORARY POLITICAL SOCIOLOGY. v.1– , 1976– . Beverly Hills, Calif., London, Sage Publications. Eight issues a year.

1651 SAGE RACE RELATIONS ABSTRACTS. 1– , Nov. 1975– . Beverly Hills, Calif., London, Sage Publications.

1652 SAGE READERS IN CROSS-NATIONAL RESEARCH. v.1–2, 1971–1972? Beverly Hills, Calif., London, Sage Publications. Irreg.

1653 SAGE RESEARCH PROGRESS SERIES IN CRIMINOLOGY. v.1– , 1977– . Beverly Hills, Calif., Sage Publications. Irreg.

1654 SAGE SERIES ON ARMED FORCES AND SOCIETY. [v.1]– , May 1971– . Beverly Hills, Calif., Sage Publications. Irreg.
Sponsored by the Inter-University Seminar on Armed Forces and Society.
Monograph series; unnumbered.

1655 SAGE SERIES ON CROSS-CULTURAL RESEARCH AND METHODOLOGY. Beverly Hills, Calif., Sage Publications. Irreg.

1656 SAGE STUDIES IN AFRICAN MODERNIZATION AND DEVELOPMENT. v.1– , Oct. 1976– . Beverly Hills, Calif., Sage Publications. Irreg.
Monograph series.

1657 SAGE STUDIES IN INTERNATIONAL SOCIOLOGY. v.1– , 1975– . Beverly Hills, Calif., Sage Publications. Irreg.
Sponsored by the International Sociological Association.
Monograph series.

1658 SAGE STUDIES IN SOCIAL AND EDUCATIONAL CHANGE. 1– , 1974– . Beverly Hills, Calif., Sage Publications. Irreg.
Monograph series. Some vols. are translations.

1659 SAGE UNIVERSITY PAPER: QUANTITATIVE APPLICATIONS IN THE SOCIAL SCIENCES. no.1– , 1976– . Beverly Hills, Calif., Sage Publications.

1660 SAGE URBAN STUDIES ABSTRACTS. v.1– , Feb. 1973– . Beverly Hills, Calif., Sage Publications. Quarterly.

1661 SAGE YEARBOOKS IN WOMEN'S POLICY STUDIES. v.1– , 1976– . Beverly Hills, Calif., Sage Publications. Irreg.
Monograph series.

1662 SAHOEHAK YON'GU. JOURNAL OF EWHA SOCIOLOGY. v.1– , 1962– . Seoul, Korea. Annual.
Issued by Sahoehak-hoe, Mullikwa Taehak, Ihwa Yoja Taehakkyo Sinch'on-dong. In Korean; table of contents in English.

SAIKIN NO JINKŌ DŌTAI
See Japan. Kōseishō. Daijin Kambō. Tōkei Jōhōbu. SAIKIN NO JINKŌ DŌTAI

ST. ELIZABETH'S CHRONICLE
See INTERRACIAL REVIEW; A JOURNAL FOR CHRISTIAN DEMOCRACY

1663 Salford. University. Department of Sociology. LEISURE STUDIES AND RESEARCH PROGRAMME PUBLICATIONS. no.1– , 1973– . Salford. Irreg.
Series of papers.

1664 Salisbury, Zimbabwe. University. Department of Sociology. OCCASIONAL PAPER. no.1–8, 1961–1965. Salisbury. Irreg.
Superseded by the University's *Series in Social Studies. Occasional Paper.*
Series of papers.

1665 Salisbury, Zimbabwe. University. Department of Sociology. SERIES IN SOCIAL STUDIES. OCCASIONAL PAPER. no.1, 1974. Salisbury. One issue published.
Supersedes its *Occasional Paper.*

1666 SANGKHOMSAT PORITHAT. v.1– , 1953/1954– . Bangkok. Quarterly, 1953–60; monthly, 1961– .
Issued by the Samakhom Sangkhomsat haeng Prathet Thai. Title in English: *The Social Science Review.* In Thai.

1667 Santiago, Chile. Universidad Catolica. Centro de Investigaciónes Sociologicas. PUBLICACIÓN. no.1, 1962. Santiago, Biblioteca Central, Sección Canje y Donaciónes, Universidad Catolica. Irreg. No more information available.

SBORNIK NAUCHNYKH TRUDOV. SERIIA OBSHCHESTVENNYKH NAUK
See Erivan. Armianskii gosudarstvennyi pedagogicheskii institut. NAUCHNYE TRUDY. SERIIA OBSHCHESTVENNYKH NAUK

SBORNIK PRACI. RADA SOCIALNI VĚDY (G)
See Brünn. Univerzita. Filozofická fakultá. SBORNIK PRACI. RADA SOCIALNI VĚDY (G)

SBORNIK ÚSTAVU VĚDECKO-TECHNICKÝCH INFORMACI MZLVH. SERIE SOCIOLOGIE A HISTORIE ZEMĚDĚLSTVI
See SOCIOLOGIE A HISTORIE ZEMĚDĚLSTVI

SBORNIK ÚVTIZ — SOCIOLOGIE
See SOCIOLOGIE ZEMĚDĚLSTVI

SCANDINAVIAN MIGRATION AND ETHNIC MINORITY REVIEW
See INVANDRARE OCH MINORITETER

SCANDINAVIAN REVIEW OF SOCIOLOGY
See ACTA SOCIOLOGICA. SCANDINAVIAN REVIEW OF SOCIOLOGY

1668 SCANDINAVIAN STUDIES IN CRIMINOLOGY. 1– , 1965– . Oslo, Universitetsforlaget.
Issued by the Scandinavian Research Center for Criminology.
Monograph series.

SCANDINAVIAN STUDIES IN SOCIOLOGY
See NORDISKE STUDIER I SOCIOLOGI

SCANDINAVISCHE ZEITSCHRIFT FÜR SOZIOLOGIE
See SCANDINAVIAN REVIEW OF SOCIOLOGY

SCHRIFTEN
See Cologne. Forschungsinstitut für Sozial- und Verwaltungswissenschaften. Soziologische Abteilung. SCHRIFTEN

1669 SCHRIFTEN ZUR INDUSTRIESOZIOLOGIE UND ARBEITSWISSENSCHAFT. no.1–?, 1964–?. Linz. Ceased publication.

Issued by the Institut für Soziologie, Hochschule für Sozial- und Wirtschaftswissenschaften.
Monograph series.

1670 SCHRIFTEN ZUR MITTELSTANDFORSCHUNG. no.1– , 1962– . Köln, Westdeutscher Verlag. Irreg.
Title varies: no.1–45, 1962–1971, *Abhandlungen zur Mittelstandforschung.*

SCHRIFTENREIHE
See Graz. Universität. Institut für Soziologie. SCHRIFTENREIHE

SCHRIFTENREIHE
See Institut für Empirische Soziologie. SCHRIFTENREIHE

SCHRIFTENREIHE
See Institut für Konfliktforschung. SCHRIFTENREIHE

SCHRIFTENREIHE DER HOCHSCHULE FÜR POLITISCHE WISSENSCHAFT
See POLITISCHE STUDIEN

1671 SCHWEIZERISCHE ZEITSCHRIFT FÜR SOZIOLOGIE. REVUE SUISSE DE SOCIOLOGIE. 1– , Nov. 1975– . Geneva. Three issues a year.
Issued by the Schweizerische Gesellschaft für Soziologie. In English, French and German; summaries in these languages.
Indexed: Soc. Abstr.

1672 SCIENCE AND CULTURE. v.1– , June 1935– . Calcutta. Monthly.
Issued by the Indian Science News Association. Subtitle reads: 'A monthly journal of natural and cultural sciences'.
Indexed: Peace Res. Abstr. J.; Soc. Abstr.

1673 SCIENCE AND SOCIETY. v.1– , 1936– New York, Science and Society. Quarterly.
Issued at the John Jay College, City University of New York. Subtitle reads: 'An independent journal of Marxism'.
Indexed: Bull. sig. soc. eth.; Int. Bibl. Soc.; Int. Pol. Sc. Abstr.; Soc. Sc. Hum. Ind.; Soc. Sc. Ind.; Soc. Abstr.; Wom. Stud. Abstr.

1674 SCIENCE AND SOCIETY. Oxford, Pergamon Press. Irreg.
Monograph series.

1675 SCIENCE AND SOCIETY. 1– , 1978– . West Lafayette, Ind.
Issued by the Purdue University.

1676 Science Council of Canada. STUDY ON POPULATION AND TECHNOLOGY. PERCEPTION. 1– , Nov. 1975– . Ottawa.
Published also in French: *Étude sur la Population et la Technologie. Perceptions.*

LA SCIENCE DANS LA RÉPUBLIQUE POPULAIRE ROUMAINE
See REVUE ROUMAINE DES SCIENCES SOCIALES. SÉRIE DE SOCIOLOGIE

1677 SCIENCE FOR PEOPLE. v.1– , 1973– . London. Quarterly.
Issued by the British Society for Responsibility in Science.

SCIENCE, MEDICINE AND MAN
See ETHICS IN SCIENCE AND MEDICINE

1678 SCIENCE OF SCIENCE. v.1– , 1980– . Dordrecht, D. Reidel Publishing Co. Quarterly.
Issued by the Committee of the Science of Science, Polish Academy of Sciences. Subtitle reads: 'An international journal on scientific reasoning and scientific enterprise'. Supersedes: *Problems of the Science of Science.* Summaries in English, French, German and Russian.
Indexed: Soc. Abstr.

SCIENCE POLICY BULLETIN
See SCIENCE POLICY REVIEWS

1679 SCIENCE POLICY REVIEWS. v.1–5, no.4, Oct. 1967–Dec. 1972. Columbus, Ohio.
Issued by the Battelle Memorial Institute. Title varies: Oct. 1967–70, *Science Policy Bulletin.*

1680 LA SCIENCE SOCIALE, SUIVANT LA MÉTHODE D'OBSERVATION. 1–36, 1886–1903; ser. 2, no.1–144, 1904–1924; ser. 3, no.1–10, 1925–May 1928. Paris.
Title varies slightly. Vols. 23–56, 1897–1903 contain supplements. Continued as individual issues of *Études Sociales,* bearing also its own title and issue numbering.

SCIENCE STUDIES
See SOCIAL STUDIES OF SCIENCE

1681 SCIENCES HUMAINES AFRICANISTES. 1– , 1965– . Paris. Annual.
Issued by the Centre d'Études Africaines, École Pratique des Hautes Études.

1682 SCIENCES SOCIALES. v.1– , 1970– . Moskva, Mezhdunarodnaia kniga. Quarterly.
In French; published also in English, *Social Sciences,* and Spanish editions.
Indexed: Bull. sig. soc. eth.; Int. Bibl. Soc.

1683 SCIENTIFIC AMERICAN. v.1–14, Aug. 28, 1845–June 25, 1859; n.s. v.1– , July 2, 1859– . New York. Weekly, 1845–Oct. 15, 1921; Monthly, 1921– .

Absorbed: *People's Journal,* Nov. 1854, and *Scientific American Monthly,* Nov. 1921. Indexes: v.178, no.5–v.197, May 1948–Dec. 1957.

Indexed: Int. Bibl. Soc.; Int. Pol. Sc. Abstr.; Soc. Abstr.; Soc. Work Res. Abstr.

SCIENTIFIC REPORTS
See World Fertility Survey. SCIENTIFIC REPORTS

1684 SCIENTOMETRICS. v.1– , Jan. 1979– . Amsterdam, Elsevier Scientific Publishing Co. Bimonthly.

Subtitle reads: 'An international journal for all quantitative aspects of the science of science and social policy'.

Indexed: Soc. Abstr.

1685 THE SCOTTISH JOURNAL OF SOCIOLOGY. v.1–4, no.2, Nov. 1976–May 1980. Stirling, Scotland. Two issues a year.

Issued by the University of Stirling. Superseded by: *The International Journal of Sociology and Social Policy.*

1686 SEARCH; HUMAN ECOLOGY. 1– , 1970– . Ithaca, N.Y., New York State Agricultural Experiment Station, Geneva. Two or three issues a year.

Issued by the College of Human Ecology, Cornell University. Supersedes, in part, the Station's *Bulletin Series* issued at Geneva, and its *Memoir Series* issued at Ithaca.

1687 SEGREGATION AND DISCRIMINATION IN SPORT. 1975– . Waterloo, Ont. Three issues a year.

Issued by the SIRLS, Faculty of Human Kinetics and Leisure Studies, University of Waterloo.

SELECCIÓNES DE POBLACIÓN
See Population Reference Bureau. SELECCIÓNES DE POBLACIÓN

1688 SELECTED HIGHLIGHTS OF CRIME AND DELINQUENCY LITERATURE. Oct. 1968–1969. New York.

Issued by the Information Center, National Council on Crime and Delinquency. Merged with: *Information Review on Crime and Delinquency,* to form *Crime and Delinquency Literature.*

SELECTED ITEMS FROM THE URBAN REFERENCE
See Princeton University. Bureau of Urban Research. THE URBAN REFERENCE

SELECTED POLITICAL AND SOCIOLOGICAL TRANSLATIONS ON COMMUNIST CHINA
See United States. Joint Publication Research Service. SELECTED POLITICAL AND SOCIOLOGICAL TRANSLATIONS ON COMMUNIST CHINA

SELECTED POLITICAL AND SOCIOLOGICAL TRANSLATIONS ON EASTERN EUROPE
See United States. Joint Publications Research Service. SELECTED POLITICAL AND SOCIOLOGICAL TRANSLATIONS ON EASTERN EUROPE

SELECTIVE SOVIET ANNOTATED BIBLIOGRAPHIES. SOVIET SOCIETY
See SOVIET PERIODICAL ABSTRACTS. SOVIET SOCIETY

SEMAINE SOCIALE
See Instituts Solvay. Institut de Sociologie. SEMAINE SOCIALE UNIVERSITAIRE

SEMAINE SOCIALE UNIVERSITAIRE
See Instituts Solvay. Institut de Sociologie. SEMAINE SOCIALE UNIVERSITAIRE

SEMINAR SERIES
See Minnesota. University. Center for Youth Development and Research. SEMINAR SERIES

SERIA PRACE STATYSTYCZNO-SOCJOLOGICZNE
See Poland. Główny Urząd Statystyczny. PRACE STATYSTYCZNO-SOCJOLOGICZNE

SERIA SOCJOLOGIA
See Posen. Uniwersytet. Wydział Filozoficzno-Historyczny. PRACE SERIA SOCJOLOGIA

1689 SERIA STUDIÓW SOCJOLOGICZNYCH I SAMORZĄDOWYCH. no.1– , 1971– . Warszawa, Zakład Wydawnictw CRS. Irreg.

Issued by the Spółdzielczy Instytut Badawczy. In Polish.

SERIE A.
See United Nations. Latin American Demographic Center (CELADE), Santiago, Chile. SERIE A.

SERIE C.
See United Nations. Latin American Demographic Center (CELADE), Santiago, Chile. SERIE C.

SERIE D.
See United Nations. Latin American Demographic Center (CELADE), Santiago, Chile. SERIE D.

SERIE G.
See United Nations. Latin American Demographic Center (CELADE), Santiago, Chile. SERIE G.

SERIE ANTROPOLOGIA SOCIAL
See Inter-American Indian Institute. SERIE ANTROPOLOGIA SOCIAL

1690 SERIE DE DOCUMENTOS Y ESTUDIOS SOCIALES. no.1, 1969. Quito.
Issued by the Escuela de Sociologia, Universidad Central del Ecuador. In Spanish.
Monograph series.

1691 SERIE DE ESTUDIOS SOCIOLOGICOS. no.1– , 1972– . Mayaguez. Irreg.
Issued by the Universidad de Puerto Rico. In Spanish.
Monograph series.

1692 SERIE DE SOCIOLOGIA. no.1– , 1973– . Lima, Peru. Irreg.
Issued by the Departamento de Ciencias Sociales, Pontificio Universidad Catolica del Peru. In Spanish.

SERIE ECONOMIA E SOCIOLOGIA
See Instituto do Algodão de Moçambique. SERIE ECONOMIA E SOCIOLOGIA

SERIE ESTUDIOS. SECCIÓN SOCIOLOGIA
See Mendoza, Argentina (City). Universidad Nacional de Cuyo. Faculdad de Ciencias Económicas. SERIE ESTUDIOS. SECCIÓN SOCIOLOGIA

SERIE LATINOAMERICANA
See Colombia. Universidad Nacional. Faculdad de Sociologia. SERIE LATINOAMERICANA

SERIE URBANIZACIÓN, MIGRACIÓNES Y CAMBIOS EN SOCIEDAD PERUANA
See URBANIZACIÓN. MIGRACIÓNES Y CAMBIOS EN SOCIEDAD PERUANA: PUBLICACIÓN

SERIES 1: ANNUAL AND PROGRESS REPORT
See Manitoba. University. Center for Settlement Studies. SERIES 1: ANNUAL AND PROGRESS REPORT

SERIES 2: RESEARCH REPORTS
See Manitoba. University. Center for Settlement Studies. SERIES 2: RESEARCH REPORT

SERIES 3: BIBLIOGRAPHY AND INFORMATION
See Manitoba. University. Center for Settlement Studies. SERIES 3: BIBLIOGRAPHY AND INFORMATION

SERIES 4: PROCEEDINGS
See Manitoba. University. Center for Settlement Studies. SERIES 4: PROCEEDINGS

SERIES 5: OCCASIONAL PAPERS
See Manitoba. University. Center for Settlement Studies. SERIES 5: OCCASIONAL PAPERS

1693 SERIES ON THE DEVELOPMENT OF SOCIETIES. 1– , 1976– . The Hague, Nijhoff. Irreg.
Issued by the Institute of Social Studies.
Monograph series.

SERIIA SOTSIOLOGICHESKAIA
See Gorky. Universitet. UCHENYE ZAPISKI. SERIIA SOTSIOLOGICHESKAIA. SOTSIOLOGIIA VYSHSHEI SHKOLY

SERVICES TO AND CHARACTERISTICS OF UNWED MOTHERS
See Florence Crittenton Association of America. UNWED MOTHERS

1694 Severo-Kavkazskii nauchnyi tsentr vyshshei shkoly. IZVESTIIA. SERIIA OBSHCHESTVENNYKH NAUK. 2– , 1974– . Rostov-on-Don.
In Russian.

1695 SEX ROLES. v.1– , 1975– . New York, Plenum Publishing Corp. Bimonthly. Indexed: Sage Fam. Stud. Abstr.; Soc. Abstr.

SHAKAI KAGAKU KENKYUJO
See Tokyo Daigaku. SHAKAI KAGAKU KENKYUJO

1696 SHAKAI SHISO SHI KENKYU. 1– , 1977– . Kyoto. Annual.
Issued by the Minaruva Shobo. Title in English: *Annals of the Society for the History of Social Thought.* In Japanese.

1697 SHAKAIGAKU HYORON. REVIEW OF SOCIOLOGY. v.1– , July 1948– . Tokyo. Quarterly.
Issued by the Nihon Shakai Gakkai, and the Department of Sociology, Tokyo University. Other title in English: *Sociological Review.* In Japanese; summaries in English.
Indexed: Int. Bibl. Soc.

1698 SHAKAIGAKU KENKYU. 1–8, Oct. 1956–Mar. 1966; no.9– , Mar. 1968– . Tokyo.
Issued by the Hitotsubashi Daigaku. In Japanese.

1699 SHAKAIGAKU KENKYŪ. THE STUDY OF SOCIOLOGY. no.1–27, July 1950–July 1966; no.28– , July 1967– . Tōhoku.
Issued by the Tōhoku Shakaigaku Kenkyū-kai and Tōhoku Daigaku. In Japanese; table of contents in Japanese and English.

1700 SHAKAIGAKU NENSHI. no.1–8, Apr. 1956–Dec. 1965; no.9– , Dec. 1967– . Tokyo. Three issues a year.
Issued by the Waseda Daigaku Shakai Gakkai. Title in English: *Annual Bulletin of Sociology*. In Japanese.

1701 SHAKAIGAKU RONSO. no.1–35, 1953–Dec. 1966; no.36– , Mar. 1967– . Tokyo. Three issues a year (occasionally irregular).
Issued by the Nihon Daigaku Bunrigakubu Shakai Kenkyū-shitsu. In Japanese.

1702 SHE HUI K'O HSÜEH K'AN. SOCIOLOGICAL JOURNAL. no.1–6, July 1929–Jan. 1948. Shanghai. In Chinese.
Issued by the Shih chieh she chu.

1703 SHE HUI K'O HSÜEH LUN TS'UNG. JOURNAL OF SOCIAL SCIENCE. v.1– , Apr. 1950– . Taipei.
Issued by the T'ai-wan ta hsüeh fa hsüeh yüan (College of Law, National Taiwan University). In Chinese and English.

1704 SIERRA LEONE STUDIES. 1922–1970. Freetown, University of Sierra Leone Press. Semi-annual.
Issued by the University of Sierra Leone.

1705 SIGNS; JOURNAL OF WOMEN IN CULTURE AND SOCIETY. v.1– , autumn 1975– . Chicago, Ill., University of Chicago Press. Quarterly.
Issued by the Barnard College.
Indexed: Soc. Abstr.

1706 SIMULATION AND GAMES. v.1– , Mar. 1970– . Beverly Hills, Calif., Sage Publications. Quarterly.
Subtitle reads: 'An international journal of theory, design and research'.
Indexed: Int. Bibl. Soc.; Int. Pol. Sc. Abstr.; PAIS; PHRA; Psych. Abstr.; SSCI; Soc. Sc. Ind.; Soc. Abstr.

1707 Singapore. University. Department of Sociology. WORKING PAPER. no.1– , 1972– . Singapore. About ten issues a year.
Series of papers. Mimeographed.

1708 Singapore. University. Social Science Society. JOURNAL. v.1– , 1961– . Singapore. Annual.

1709 SISYPHUS. v.1– , 1981– . Warszawa, Państwowe Wydawnictwo Naukowe. Irreg.
Issued by the Instytut Filozofii i Socjologii, Polska Akademia Nauk. In English.

1710 SMALL GROUP BEHAVIOR. v.4– , Feb. 1974– . Beverly Hills, Calif., Sage Publications. Quarterly.
Continues: *Comparative Group Studies.*

1711 Smithsonian Institution. Research Institute on Immigration and Ethnic Studies. RIIE BIBLIOGRAPHIC STUDIES. no.1– , 1976– . Washington, D.C. Irreg.

1712 Smithsonian Institution. Research Institute on Immigration and Ethnic Studies. RIIE RESEARCH NOTES. no.1– , 1976– . Washington, D.C. Irreg.

SOC[IOLOGY] AND AN[THROPOLOGY] REPORT
See Mississippi. State University, Department of Sociology and Anthropology. SOC[IOLOGY] AND AN[THROPOLOGY] REPORT

SOCIAAL KOMPAS
See SOCIAL COMPASS

1713 SOCIAL ACTION. v.1– , 1951– . Delhi. Quarterly.
Issued by the Indian Social Institute, earlier called the Indian Institute of Social Order. Subtitle reads: 'A quarterly review of social trends'.
Indexed: Bull. sig. soc. eth.; Int. Bibl. Soc.; PAIS; Peace Res. Abstr. J.; Soc. Abstr.

1714 SOCIAL BEHAVIOR AND PERSONALITY. 1– , 1972– . Wellington, N.Z., Historical Services Ltd. Semi-annual.
Issued by the Society for Personality Research.

1715 SOCIAL BIOLOGY. v.1– , Mar. 1954– . New York. Quarterly.
Issued by the American Eugenics Society; subsequently by the Society for the Study of Social Biology. Title varies: v.1–15, 1954–68, *Eugenics quarterly*.
Indexed: Int. Bibl. Soc.; Soc. Sc. Ind.; Soc. Abstr.; Urb. Aff. Abstr.; Wom. Stud. Abstr.

SOCIAL BIOLOGY AND HUMAN AFFAIRS
See BIOLOGY AND HUMAN AFFAIRS

1716 SOCIAL CASEWORK. v.1– , Mar. 1920– . New York. Monthly, except Aug. and Sep.
Issued by The Family Service Association of America. Title varies: v.1–20, 1920–Feb. 1940,

Family; v.21–27, no.5, Mar. 1940–July 1946, *Family: Journal of Social Casework;* v.27, no.6–v.30, Oct. 1946–Dec. 1949, *Journal of Social Casework.*
Indexed: Bull. sig. soc. eth.; Int. Bibl. Soc.; PHRA; Psych. Abstr.; Sage Fam. Stud. Abstr.; Soc. Sc. Ind.; Soc. Abstr.; Soc. Work. Res. Abstr.; Wom. Stud. Abstr.

1717 SOCIAL CHANGE. 1– , Apr. 1971– . New Delhi. Three issues a year.
Issued by the Council for Social Development.

1718 SOCIAL CHANGE. v.1– , 1973– . New York, Gordon and Breach. Quarterly.
Issued by the Center for the Study of Social Change. Supersedes: *Human Relations Training News.*

SOCIAL CHANGE AND REVOLUTION
See SOCIALE VERANDERING EN REVOLUTIE

1719 SOCIAL CHANGES. 1927–1939. Chicago, The University of Chicago Press.
Title varies: 1927, *Recent Social Changes in the United States since the War and particularly in 1927;* 1928–32, *Social Changes;* 1933, *Social Changes and the New Deal;* 1934, *Social Changes during Depression and Recovery (Social Changes in 1934).* Includes reprints from *American Journal of Sociology.*

SOCIAL CHANGES AND THE NEW DEAL
See SOCIAL CHANGES

SOCIAL CHANGES DURING DEPRESSION AND RECOVERY (SOCIAL CHANGES IN 1934)
See SOCIAL CHANGES

1720 SOCIAL COMPASS. 1– , May/June 1953– . Louvain. Bimonthly.
Title varies: *Sociaal Kompas.* Other titles: *Busola Social; Compas Sociale; Sociaal Compass; Sozialer Kompass.* Subtitle reads: 'Revue internationale des études socio-religieuses. International review of socio-religious studies'. In English and French; summaries in German and Spanish. Indexes: Vols. 1–10, 1953–1963, in v.10.
Indexed: Bull. sig. soc. eth.; Int. Bibl. Soc.; Int. Pol. Sc. Abstr.; SSCI; Soc. Abstr.; Urb. Aff. Abstr.

1721 SOCIAL DEMOCRACY. v.1– , 1969– . New Delhi, R. K. Puram. Quarterly.

1722 SOCIAL DYNAMICS. no.1– , June 1975– . Cape Town. Semi-annual.
Issued by the Faculty of Social Science, University of Cape Town.
Indexed: Soc. Abstr.

1723 SOCIAL ECOLOGY NEWSLETTER. no.1– , May 1972– . Boston, Mass.
Issued by the Research Committee on Social Ecology, International Sociological Association.

SOCIAL ECONOMIC INDICATORS
See Portugal. Instituto Nacional de Estatistica. Servicos Centrais. INDICADORES ECONOMICO-SOCIAIS

1724 SOCIAL FORCES. v.1– , 1922– . Chapel Hill, N.C., University of North Carolina Press. Bimonthly except July, v.1–3; quarterly.
Issued by the University of North Carolina. Title varies: v.1–3, *The Journal of Social Forces.* Cumulative indexes: v.1–50, 1922–72, 1 v.
Indexed: Int. Bibl. Soc.; Int. Pol. Sc. Abstr.; Psych. Abstr.; Sage Fam. Stud. Abstr.; Soc. Sc. Ind.; Soc. Abstr.; Soc. Work Res. Abstr.

SOCIAL HISTORY
See HISTOIRE SOCIAL

SOCIAL HYGIENE
See JOURNAL OF SOCIAL HYGIENE

SOCIAL INDICATORS
See Indonesia. Biro Pusat Statistik. INDIKATOR SOSIAL

1725 SOCIAL INDICATORS RESEARCH. no.1– , May 1974– . Dordrecht, Reidel Publishing Co. Four issues a year.
Indexed: Int. Bibl. Soc.; PHRA; Sage Urb. Abstr.; Soc. Abstr.

1726 SOCIAL ISSUES IN THE SEVENTIES. 1– , 1973– . London, Tavistock Publications. Irreg.
Monograph series.

1727 SOCIAL NETWORKS. 1– , Aug. 1978– . Lausanne, Switzerland, Elsevier Sequoia, S.A. Quarterly.
Published in cooperation with the International Network for Social Network Analysis (INSNA). Summaries in English. Subtitle reads: 'International journal of structural analysis'.
Indexed: Soc. Abstr.

1728 SOCIAL ORDER. v.1–13, no.10, Jan. 1951–Dec. 1963. St. Louis, Mo.
Issued by the Institute of Social Order. Vol.1, 1951 called also 'old ser. IV' in continuation of I.S.O. *Bulletin.*

1729 SOCIAL POLICY. v.1– , May/June 1970– . White Plains, N.Y., International Arts & Sciences Press. Bimonthly.
Indexed: Int. Bibl. Soc.; Soc. Sc. Ind.; PHRA; Soc. Abstr.; Soc. Work Res. Abstr.; Wom. Stud. Abstr.

1730 SOCIAL PRAXIS. v.1– , 1973– . The Hague, Mouton. Quarterly.
Summaries in French.
Indexed: SSCI.

1731 SOCIAL PROBLEMS. v.1– , June 1953– . Buffalo, N.Y., subsequently Ridgefield, Conn. Five issues a year.
Issued by the Society for the Study of Social Problems.
Indexed: Abstr. Soc. Work.; Int. Bibl. Soc.; Int. Pol. Sc. Abstr.; Psych. Abstr.; Soc. Sc. Ind.; Soc. Abstr.; Wom. Stud. Abstr.

A SOCIAL PROFILE OF DETROIT
See Michigan. University. Detroit Area Profile. A SOCIAL PROFILE OF DETROIT

1732 SOCIAL PROGRESS; A YEARBOOK AND ENCYCLOPEDIA OF ECONOMIC, INDUSTRIAL, AND RELIGIOUS STATISTICS. 1904–1906. New York. The Baker and Taylor Co.

1733 SOCIAL PSYCHIATRY. 1– , 1974– . New York, Grune & Stratton. Annual.
Issued by the American Association for Social Psychiatry.

1734 SOCIAL PSYCHOLOGY. v.41, 1978. Washington, D.C.
Issued by the American Sociological Association. Continues: *Sociometry*. Continued by: *Social Psychology Quarterly*.
Indexed: Psych. Abstr.; Soc. Sc. Ind.; SSCI; Soc. Work Res. Abstr.

1735 SOCIAL PSYCHOLOGY QUARTERLY. v.42– , Mar. 1979– . Washington, D.C. Quarterly.
Issued by the American Sociological Association. Continues: *Social Psychology*.
Indexed: Psych. Abstr.; Soc. Sc. Ind.; SSCI.

1736 SOCIAL RESEARCH. v.1– , Feb. 1934– . New York. Quarterly,
Issued by the Graduate Faculty of Political and Social Science, New School for Social Research. Subtitle reads: 'An international quarterly of politics and social science'. Occasionally includes supplements.
Indexed: Bull. sig. soc. eth.; Int. Bibl. Soc.; Int. Pol. Sc. Abstr.; PAIS; Peace Res. Abstr. J.; SSCI; Soc. Sc. Ind.; Soc. Abstr.; Wom. Stud. Abstr.

1737 SOCIAL RESEARCH; AN INTERNATIONAL QUARTERLY OF POLITICS AND SOCIAL SCIENCE. SUPPLEMENT. 1–5, 1938–1943. New York. Irreg.
Issued by the New School for Social Research. Monograph series.

SOCIAL RESEARCH SERIES
See Christian Institute for the Study of Religion and Society. SOCIAL RESEARCH SERIES

1738 SOCIAL REVIEW. no.1– , Sep. 1978– . Cape Town, S.A. Eight issues a year.
Issued by the Social Research Agency.

1739 SOCIAL SCIENCE. v.1– , Nov. 1925– . Winfield, Kans. Quarterly.
Issued by the National Social Science Honour Society Pi Gamma Mu, and the National Academy of Economics and Political Science (1951–).
Indexed: Abstr. Soc. Work; Curr. Cont.; Int. Bibl. Soc.; Int. Pol. Sc. Abstr.; PAIS; Peace Res. Abstr. J.; SSCI; Soc. Abstr.

SOCIAL SCIENCE
See SOCIAL SCIENCE REVIEW (New York)

1740 SOCIAL SCIENCE ABSTRACTS. v.1–5, no.1, Mar. 1929–Jan. 1933. Menasha, Wis.
Index: v.1–4, 1929–32, as v.5, no.1.

SOCIAL SCIENCE ABSTRACTS
See INTERDISCIPLINE

SOCIAL SCIENCE ABSTRACTS
See Tokyo Daigaku. SHAKAI KAGAKU KENKYUJO. ANNALS

1741 SOCIAL SCIENCE & MEDICINE. v.1–12, Apr. 1967–1978. Oxford, Pergamon Press. Quarterly.
Continued by: *Social Science & Medicine. A: Medical Psychology & Sociology; Social Science & Medicine. B: Medical Anthropology; Social Science & Medicine. C: Medical Economics; Social Science & Medicine. D: Medical Geography*. In English, French, German and Spanish; summaries in one of these languages.
Indexed: Bull. sig. soc. eth.; Int. Bibl. Soc.; Int. Pol. Sc. Abstr.; Psych. Abstr.; Soc. Abstr.; Urb. Aff. Abstr.

1742 SOCIAL SCIENCE & MEDICINE. A: MEDICAL PSYCHOLOGY & SOCIOLOGY. v.12–14, Jan. 1978–1980. Oxford, Pergamon Press. Quarterly.
Continues, in part, *Social Science & Medicine*. Continued by: *Social Science & Medicine. Part A: Medical Sociology,* and *Social Science & Medicine. Part E: Medical Psychology*.

1743 SOCIAL SCIENCE & MEDICINE. PART A: MEDICAL SOCIOLOGY. v.15– , Jan. 1981– . Oxford, New York, Pergamon Press. Bimonthly.
Continues, in part, *Social Science & Medicine. A: Medical Psychology & Sociology*.

SOCIAL SCIENCE BIBLIOGRAPHY, INDIA
See ASIAN SOCIAL SCIENCE BIBLIOGRAPHY WITH ANNOTATIONS AND ABSTRACTS

SOCIAL SCIENCE BIBLIOGRAPHY, INDIA, PAKISTAN
See ASIAN SOCIAL SCIENCE BIBLIOGRAPHY, WITH ANNOTATIONS AND ABSTRACTS

SOCIAL SCIENCE BULLETIN
See Brigham Young University. Department of Sociology. SOCIAL SCIENCE RESEARCH BULLETIN

1744 SOCIAL SCIENCE DATA ARCHIVES IN THE UNITED STATES. 1967. New York.
Issued by the Council of Social Science Data Archives.

1745 SOCIAL SCIENCE DATA INVENTORY. REPERTOIRE DES DONNEES EN SCIENCES SOCIALES. 1– , 1977– . Ottawa.
Issued by the Data Clearinghouse for the Social Sciences.

SOCIAL SCIENCE INFORMATION
See International Social Science Council. SOCIAL SCIENCE INFORMATION

1746 SOCIAL SCIENCE INFORMATION STUDIES. SSIS. v.1– , Oct. 1980– . London, Butterworth. Quarterly.

1747 SOCIAL SCIENCE JOURNAL. 1973– . Seoul, Korea. Annual.
Issued by the Korean National Commission for Unesco.
Indexed: Int. Bibl. Soc.

SOCIAL SCIENCE NOTES
See Canada. Department of Indian Affairs and Northern Development. Northern Science Research Group. SOCIAL SCIENCE NOTES

1748 SOCIAL SCIENCE QUARTERLY. v.1– , 1920– . Austin, Tex., University of Texas Press. Quarterly.
Issued by the Southwestern Social Science Association. Title varies: 1920–23, *Southwestern Political Science Quarterly;* 1923–31, *Southwestern Political and Social Science Quarterly;* 1931–68, *Southwestern Social Science Quarterly.*
Indexed: Curr. Cont.; Int. Bibl. Soc.; Int. Pol. Sc. Abstr.; PAIS; SSCI; Sage Fam. Stud. Abstr.; Soc. Sc. Ind.; Soc. Abstr.

1749 SOCIAL SCIENCE RESEARCH. 1971– . Port Moresby, Papua New Guinea. Annual.
Issued by the Department of Social Development and Home Affairs, Papua New Guinea.

SOCIAL SCIENCE RESEARCH BULLETIN
See Brigham Young University. Department of Sociology. SOCIAL SCIENCE RESEARCH BULLETIN

1750 Social Science Research Council. ANNUAL REPORT. 1925– . New York.

1751 Social Science Research Council. BULLETIN. no.1– , Dec. 1930– . New York.
Includes 'Critiques of Research in the Social Sciences', issued by the Council's Committee on Appraisal of Research, Social Science Research Council.
Series of papers.

1752 Social Science Research Council (Gt. Britain). Postgraduate Award Division. RESEARCH SUPPORTED BY THE SSRC. 1968– . London. Annual.
Includes supplement: *SSRC Newsletter*.

1753 Social Science Research Council (Gt. Britain). REVIEWS OF CURRENT RESEARCH. 1– , 1968– . London, Heinemann Educational Books. Irreg.

1754 Social Science Research Council (Gt. Britain). Research Unit on Ethnic Relations. WORKING PAPERS ON ETHNIC RELATIONS. no.1– , 1977– . London. Irreg.
Series of papers. Mimeographed.

1755 Social Science Research Council of Canada. REPORT. 1940/1941–1975/1976. Ottawa. Annual, 1940–54; biennial 1954/56–1975/76. Reports for 1940/41–1954/56 issued by the Council under its earlier name, Canadian Social Science Research Council. Continued by: Social Science Federation of Canada. *Annual Report.*

1756 SOCIAL SCIENCE REVIEW. v.1–3, no.4, 1887–1901. New York.
Title varies: v.1, no.1–19, 1887, *Social Science.*

1757 THE SOCIAL SCIENCE REVIEW. no.1– , fall 1961– . New York. Two issues a year.
Issued by the Social Science Division, Queen's College.
Indexed: Soc. Abstr.

SOCIAL SCIENCE REVIEW
See EPITHEORÉSIS KOINONIKON EREUNON

SOCIAL SCIENCE REVIEW
See RIV'ON LE-MEḤKAR ḤEVRATI

SOCIAL SCIENCE REVIEW
See SANGKHOMSAT PORITHAT

1758 SOCIAL SCIENCE REVIEW AND JOURNAL OF THE SCIENCES. 1–2, 1862–1863; n.s. v.1–6, no. 32, 1864–1866. London.

1759 SOCIAL SCIENCE SERIES. no.1– , 1962– . El Paso, Tex., Texas Western Press. Irreg.
Monograph series.

1760 SOCIAL SCIENCE SERIES. 1– , 1972– . St. Paul, Minn., Windflower. Irreg.
Monograph series.

1761 SOCIAL SCIENCES. 1– , 1970– . Moskva, Mezhdunarodnaia kniga. Bimonthly.
Issued by the Akademiia nauk SSSR. Published also in French, *Sciences Sociales,* and Spanish editions. Includes 'Special Supplement' published irregularly.

SOCIAL SCIENCES
See Institute of Sociology, London. REPORTS OF ANNUAL CONFERENCES

1762 SOCIAL SCIENCES AND HUMANITIES INDEX. [v.1–61], Mar. 1913–Mar. 1974. New York, Wilson Co. Quarterly, with annual cumulations.
Title varies: 1913–19, *Readers' Guide to Periodical Literature. Supplement;* 1920–55, *International Index to Periodicals;* 1956–65, *International Index.* Issues for 1913–1949/50 numbered v.1–37. Superseded by: *Humanities Index,* and *Social Sciences Index.*

1763 SOCIAL SCIENCES CITATION INDEX. 1973– . Philadelphia, Pa. Three issues a year, with annual cumulation.
Issued by the Institute for Scientific Information. Consists of three sections: 'Citation Index'; 'Source Index: Corporate Address Index'; and 'Permuterm Subject Index'. Includes *SSCI Journal Citation Reports;* first report for 1977, published in 1978.

1764 SOCIAL SCIENCES IN CHINA. v.1– , Mar. 1980– . Beijing, China, The Social Science Publishing House of China. Quarterly.
Issued by the Chinese Academy of Social Sciences. In English. Published also in a Chinese edition, *Chung-kuo she hui k'o hsüeh yüan.*

1765 SOCIAL SCIENCES INDEX. 1– , June 1974–. New York, Wilson Co. Quarterly, with annual cumulation.
Supersedes, in part, *Social Sciences & Humanities Index.*

1766 No entry.

SOCIAL SCIENCES. RURAL SOCIOLOGY
See Cornell University. Agricultural Experiment Station. SOCIAL SCIENCES. RURAL SOCIOLOGY

1767 SOCIAL STATISTICS FOR METROPOLITAN NEW YORK. no.1– , Feb. 1965– . New York.
Issued by the Graduate School of Social Work, New York University. Each issue has also a distinctive title.

1768 SOCIAL STRATEGIES: MONOGRAPHS ON SOCIOLOGY AND SOCIAL POLICY. MONOGRAPHIEN ZUR SOZIOLOGIE UND GESELLSCHAFTSPOLITIK. 1– , 1974– . Basel, Switzerland. Irreg.
Issued by the Social Strategies Cooperative Society. In English, French and German.
Monograph series.

1769 SOCIAL STRUCTURE AND SOCIAL CHANGE. 1– , 1977– . Cambridge, Mass., MIT Press. Irreg.

1770 THE SOCIAL STUDIES. v.1– , Sep. 1909– . Philadelphia, Pa.; subsequently Washington, D.C., Heldref Publications. Bimonthly.
Indexed: Soc. Abstr.

1771 SOCIAL STUDIES: IRISH JOURNAL OF SOCIOLOGY. v.1– , Jan. 1972– . Maynooth. Bimonthly.
Issued by the Department of Sociology, St. Patrick's College. Supersedes: *Christus Rex Journal.* Jan. 1972 issue preceded by v.0, no.0 in Oct. 1971.
Indexed: PAIS; Peace Res. Abstr. J.; SSCI.

1772 SOCIAL STUDIES OF SCIENCE. v.1– , 1971– . London, Macmillan; subsequently Beverly Hills, Calif., Sage Publications. Quarterly.
Title varies: v.1–4, 1971–74, *Science Studies.* Subtitle reads: 'An international review of research in the social dimensions of science and technology'.
Indexed: ABC Pol. Sc.; Curr. Cont.

1773 SOCIAL TEXT. THEORY. CULTURE. IDEOLOGY. 1– , winter 1979– . Madison, Wis., Coda Press. Three issues a year.
Indexed: Soc. Abstr.

1774 SOCIAL THEORY AND PRACTICE. v.1– , spring 1970– . Tallahassee, Fla. Quarterly.
Issued by the Center for Social Philosophy, Florida State University. Subtitle reads: 'An international and interdisciplinary journal of social philosophy'.

Indexed: Bull. sig. soc. eth.; Int. Bibl. Soc.; Int. Pol. Sc. Abstr.; LLBA; SSCI; Soc. Sc. Ind.; Soc. Abstr.

SOCIAL TRENDS
See Gt. Britain. Office of Population Censuses and Surveys. SOCIAL TRENDS

1775 SOCIAL WELFARE, SOCIAL PLANNING POLICY, SOCIAL DEVELOPMENT. AN INTERNATIONAL DATA BASE. v.1– , June 1979– . San Diego, Calif., Sociological Abstracts.
An abstracting service of a very broad scope.

1776 SOCIAL WORK RESEARCH & ABSTRACTS. v.13, no.2– , summer 1977– . New York. Quarterly.
Issued by the National Association of Social Workers. Continues: *Abstracts for Social Workers.*

1777 SOCIALA MEDDELANDEN. v.1– , 1903– . Stockholm. Eight issues a year.
Issued by the Kungl. Socialstyrelsen. In Swedish.
Indexed: Int. Bibl. Soc. Cult. Anth.

SOCIALE GEOGRAFIE
See Utrecht. Rijksuniversiteit. Geografisch Instituut. PUBLIKATIES. SERIE A. SOCIALE GEOGRAFIE

1778 SOCIALE VERANDERING EN REVOLUTIE. MUTATION SOCIALE ET RÉVOLUTION. SOCIAL CHANGE AND REVOLUTION. 1– , 1971– . Antwerp.
Issued by the Nationaal Hoger Instituut voor Bouwkunst en Stedebouw. In Flemish and French.

1779 SOCIALIZATION AND LEISURE. 1975– . Waterloo, Ont. Three issues a year.
Issued by the SIRLS, Faculty of Human Kinetics and Leisure Studies, Waterloo University.

1780 SOCIALIZATION AND SPORT. 1975– . Waterloo, Ont. Three issues a year.
Issued by the SIRLS, Faculty of Human Kinetics and Leisure Studies, Waterloo University.

SOCIÁLNI PROBLÉMY
See SOCIOLOGIE A SOCIÁLNI PROBLÉMY: REVUE PRO SOCIÁLNI THEORII E PRAKSI

SOCIATRY
See GROUP PSYCHOTHERAPY AND PSYCHODRAMA

1781 SOCIETÀ. 1–17, no.6, Dec. 1945–1961, Firenze, Parenti. Irreg.

1782 SOCIETÀ RURALE. v.1, no.1–2/3, Mar/June–Sep. 1964. Bologna, Edagricole. Quarterly.
Subtitle reads: 'Rivista di Sociologia agraria, di economia e politica agraria'. Supersedes: *Quaderni di Sociologia.* Merged with *Rivista di Economia Agraria* in Jan. 1965. In Italian.
Indexed: Soc. Abstr.

SOCIÉTÉ
See SOCIETY

1783 Société Canadienne de Sociologie et d'Anthropologie. BULLETIN. 1960–Jan. 1976. Montréal. Semi-annual.
Superseded by: *Society*. In English and French.

1784 Société Canadienne de Sociologie et d'Anthropologie. MONOGRAPH SERIES. SOCIOLOGY. no.1– , 1975– . Montreal. Irreg.
Monograph series.

SOCIÉTÉ ET IDÉOLOGIES
See SOCIÉTÉ: MOUVEMENTS SOCIAUX ET IDÉOLOGIES. 1e SÉRIE: ÉTUDES

1785 Société Francaise de Sociologie. BULLETIN. June 1974– . Paris. Irreg.

1786 Société Internationale de Science Sociale. BULLETIN. no.1–137, 1904–July 1918; 3e periode, no.1–10, 1925–1928. Paris.

1787 Société Jean Bodin pour l'Histoire Comparative des Institutions. RECUEILS. 1– , 1936– . Bruxelles.
No. 1 issued as no.6, 1936, of *Revue,* issued by the Institut de Sociologie, Instituts Solvay.

1788 SOCIÉTÉ, MOUVEMENTS SOCIAUX ET IDÉOLOGIES. 1– , 1973– . Paris, Mouton. Irreg.
Monograph series.

1789 SOCIÉTÉ, MOUVEMENTS SOCIAUX ET IDÉOLOGIES. 1e SÉRIE: ÉTUDES. 1– , 1960– . Paris, Mouton. Irreg.
Issued by the Division des Affaires Culturelles, École Pratique des Hautes Études. Title varies: v.1–6, *Société et Idéologies*.
Monograph series.

1790 SOCIÉTÉ, MOUVEMENTS SOCIAUX ET IDÉOLOGIES. 2e SÉRIE: DOCUMENTS ET TEMOIGNAGES. 1– , 1959– . Paris, Mouton. Irreg.
Monograph series.

1791 SOCIÉTÉ, MOUVEMENTS SOCIAUX ET IDÉOLOGIES. 3e SÉRIE: BIBLIOGRAPHIES. 1– , 1963– . The Hague, Mouton. Irreg.
Monograph series.

1792 SOCIÉTIÉS. 1– , 1976– . Toulouse. Irreg.
Issued by the University of Toulouse. Subseries of: Toulouse. Université-le-Mirail. *Annales. nouv. sér.*

1793 SOCIETY. v.9, no.4– , Feb. 1972– . New Brunswick, N.J., Transaction Periodicals Consortium. Monthly, except July/Aug. and Nov/Dec.
Issued by the Rutgers State University. Continues: *Transactions; Social Science and Modern Society.*
Indexed: Curr. Cont.; PHRA; SSCI; Soc. Sc. Ind.; Soc. Abstr.; Soc. Work. Res. Abstr.

1794 SOCIETY AND LEISURE. no.1– , 1969– . Prague, European Centre for Leisure and Education. Four issues a year; two issues in 1969.
Subtitle reads: 'Bulletin of sociology of leisure, education and culture'.

SOCIETY AND LEISURE
See LOISIR ET SOCIÉTÉ

1795 The Society for the Social History of Medicine. BULLETIN. no.1— , June 1970– . Nottingham, c/o Medical Library. Two issues a year.

1796 Society of Ethnic and Racial Studies. JOURNAL. 1– , Jan. 1977– . Blacksburg, Va. Annual.

1797 SOCIETY. SOCIÉTÉ. 1– , Jan. 1977– . Montréal.
Issued by the Canadian Sociology and Anthropology Association. Supersedes the Association's *Bulletin.* Text in English; preliminary materials and notes in English and French.

1798 SOCIO-ECONOMIC PLANNING SCIENCES. v.1– , Sep. 1967– . New York, Pergamon Press. Quarterly.
Issued by the Graduate Center, City University of New York.
Indexed: Int. Bibl. Soc.; Int. Pol. Sc. Abstr.; Soc. Abstr.

1799 Socio-Economic Research Institute. BULLETIN. v.1–2, Jan/Mar. 1960–1966. Calcutta. Irreg.

1800 SOCIOLINGUISTICS NEWSLETTER. 1– , 1966– . Boulder, Colo., subsequently Missoula, Scholar Press. Irreg.
Issued by the Research Committee on Sociolinguistics, International Sociological Association. Text mainly in English and French.
Indexed: LLBA.

1801 SOCIOLINGUISTICS SERIES. 1– , 1971– . Edmonton, Alberta. Irreg.
Monograph series.

1802 SOCIOLOG. v.1– , 1953– . New Delhi, Ghandewalan. Quarterly.
Text in English and Hindi. Title in Hindi: *Vanyajati.*

1803 SOCIOLOG. 1– , 1971– . Washington, D.C. Ten issues a year.
Issued by the American Sociological Association.

1804 SOCIOLOGIA. Mar. 1939–1966. São Paulo. Quarterly.
Issued by the Fundação Escola de Sociologia e Politica de São Paulo. Subtitle reads: 'Revista dedicada a teoria e a pesquisa das ciências sociais'. In Portuguese, English, French and Spanish.
Indexed: Soc. Abstr.

1805 No entry.

1806 SOCIOLOGIA. v.1– , 1967– . Roma. Three issues year.
Issued by the Istituto di Luigo Sturzo. Continues: *Bolletino di Sociologia dell'Istituto Luigi Sturzo.* Subtitle reads: 'Rivista di scienze sociali'.
Indexed: Bull. sig. soc. eth.; Soc. Abstr.

1807 SOCIOLOGIA. 1– , 1969– . Bratislava, Vydavatelstvo SAV.
Issued by the Sociologický ústav, Slovenská akadémia vied. In Slovak.
Indexed: Bull. sig. soc. eth.

1808 SOCIOLOGIA. 1– , 1970– . Otavalo, Ecuador.'
Issued by the Instituto Otavaleno de Antropologia. Subseries of: *Breviarios de Cultura.* In Spanish.

SOCIOLOGIA
See Asociación Venezolana de Sociologia. SOCIOLOGIA

SOCIOLOGIA
See Bilbao, Spain. Universidad de Deusto. Instituto de Ciencias Sociales. SOCIOLOGIA

SOCIOLOGIA
See Cluj. Universitatea Babes-Bolyai. Biblioteca Centrala Universitara. STUDIA. SOCIOLOGIA

1809 SOCIOLOGIA I. no.1–11, 1946–1969. São Paulo. Irreg.
Issued by the Faculdade de Filosofia, Ciências e Letras, Universidade do São Paulo. Subseries of: Universidade. Faculdade de Filosofia, Ciências e Letras. *Boletim.* In Portuguese.

1810 SOCIOLOGIA II. 1958–1964– . São Paulo. Irreg.
Issued by the Faculdade de Filosofia, Ciências e Letras, Universidade do São Paulo. Subseries of: São Paulo. Universidade. Faculdade de Filosofia, Ciências e Letras. *Boletim*. In Portuguese.

SOCIOLOGIA BRASILEIRA
See COLEÇÃO SOCIOLOGIA BRASILEIRA

1811 SOCIOLOGIA CRIMINAL. [1]–2, 1962–1969. Rio de Janeiro.
Issued by the Sociedade Brasileira de Criminologia, in collaboration with the Faculdade de Dereito, Instituto de Criminologia, Universidade do Estado da Guanabara. In Portuguese.

1812 SOCIOLOGIA DEL DESARROLLO. 1– , Oct. 1971– . Barranguilla. In Spanish.

1813 SOCIOLOGIA DEL DIRITTO. 1– , 1974– . Milano, A. Giuffré. Semi-annual.
Issued by the Commissione Permanente di Sociologia del Diritto, Centro Nazionale di Prevenzione e Difesa Sociale. In Italian; summaries in English.
Published under the auspices of the Commissione Permanente di Sociologia del Diritto, Centro Nazionale de Prevenzione e Diffesa Sociale. In Italian.

1814 SOCIOLOGIA DEL LAVORO. no.1– , 1978– . Bologna, Franco Angeli. Quarterly.
Issued by the University of Bologna. In Italian.

1815 SOCIOLOGIA DELL'ORGANIZAZIONE. 1– , Jan/June 1973– . Padova, Marsiglio. Semi-annual.
In Italian.

1816 SOCIOLOGIA DELLA LETTERATURA. v.1– , 1975– . Roma, Bulzoni. Semi-annual.
In Italian.

1817 SOCIOLOGIA E POLITICA. 1– , 1975– . Lisboa. Irreg.
In Portuguese.
Monograph series.

1818 SOCIOLOGIA EN MEXICO. Apr. 1951–Oct. 1969. Mexico, D.F.
Issued by the Seminario Mexicano de Sociología. In Spanish.

1819 SOCIOLOGIA INDICA. v.1– , no.1/2–, May 1977– . Calcutta.
Issued by the Indian Institute of Sociology.

1820 SOCIOLOGIA INTERNATIONALIS: INTERNATIONALE ZEITSCHRIFT FÜR SOZIOLOGIE UND SOZIALPSYCHOLOGIE. v.1– , 1963– . Berlin, Duncker & Humblot. Two issues a year.
In various languages; summaries in English, French, German and Spanish.
Indexed: Bull. sig. soc. eth.; Int. Pol. Sc. Abstr.; Soc. Abstr.

1821 SOCIOLOGIA MLÁDEŽE. 1969–1970/1971. Bratislava, Smena. Annual.
Subtitle reads: 'Slovenska ročenka pre teoriu a vyskúm mládeže'. Subseries of *Edicia Aktuality*. In Slovak; summaries in English.

1822 SOCIOLOGIA NEERLANDICA. v.1–11, winter 1962/1963–Jan/July 1976. Assen, Van Gorcum. Semi-annual.
Issued by the Netherlands Sociological Society and by the Netherlands' Sociological and Anthropological Society, 1972–75. In English; summaries in French, German and occasionally Spanish. Continued by: *Netherlands Journal of Sociology*.
Indexed: Bull. sig. soc. eth.; Int. Bibl. Soc.; Soc. Abstr.; Urb. Aff. Abstr.

1823 SOCIOLOGIA RELIGIOSA. no.1–?, 1959–197?. Padova; subsequently Milano, Memo Editore. Semi-annual. Ceased publication.
Subtitle reads: Rivista di storia e sociologia delle religioni'. In Italian, English, French and Spanish.
Indexed: Int. Bibl. Soc.; Soc. Abstr.

1824 SOCIOLOGIA RELIGIOSA. no.1– , 1971– . Petropolis, Brazil, Editora Vozes. Irregular.
Issued by the Centro de Investigação e Divulgação. In Portuguese.

1825 SOCIOLOGIA ROMÂNIEI. v.1–7, 1940–1946. Bucureşti. Irreg.
Issued by the Institutuul Social Roman. In Rumanian.
Monograph series.

1826 SOCIOLOGIA RURALIS. spring 1960–1969. Assen, Van Gorcum. Semi-annual.
Issued by the European Society for Rural Sociology. In English, French and German; summaries in English, French and German.
Indexed: Bull. sig. soc. eth.; Int. Bibl. Soc.; Int. Pol. Sc. Abstr.; PAIS; Soc. Abstr.

1827 SOCIOLOGIA. STUDI E RICERCHE. 1– , 1972– . Roma, Bulzoni. Irreg.
In Italian.
Monograph series.

1828 SOCIOLOGIA. TEMI E TESTI DI STORIA DELLA SOCIOLOGIA. 1– , 1973– . Roma, Bulzoni. Irreg.
In Italian.
Monograph series.

1829 SOCIOLOGIA URBANA E RURALE. 1– , 1979– . Milan, Franco Angeli Editore. Semi-annual.
Other title: *Collana di Sociologia Urbana e Rurale.* In Italian.

1830 SOCIOLOGICA. v.1, 1969. Olomouc.
Issued by the Pedagogická fakulta, Universita Palackého. In Czech; summaries in English.
Indexed: Soc. Abstr.

1831 SOCIOLOGICA. 1– , 1973– . Roma.
Issued by the Pontificum Institutum Studiorum Ecclesiasticorum.
In Italian.

SOCIOLOGICA
See STUDIA SOCIOLOGICA

1832 SOCIOLOGICAL ABSTRACTS. v.1– , Nov. 1952– . New York, subsequently San Diego, Calif., Sociological Abstracts, Inc. Six issues a year; the sixth issues consist of annual cumulative indexes: Author; subject, and a list of publications abstracted. Decennial index, 1953–1962. *User's Reference Manual* (1977–) is planned for updating. Includes separately numbered supplements (beginning with 1962): 'Abstracts of papers delivered at the annual meeting of the . . .:
American Society of Criminology
American Sociological Association
Association for the Humanist Sociology
Association for the Sociology of Religion
Canadian Sociology and Anthropology Association
Eastern Sociological Society
Georgia Sociological and Anthropological Association
Illinois Sociological Association
International Institute of Sociology Congress
International Society for Research on Aggression
International Symposium on Victimology
Mid-South Sociological Association
Midwest Sociological Society
North Central Sociological Association
Pennsylvania Sociological Association
Rural Sociological Association
Society for the Study of Social Problems
Southern Association of Agricultural Scientists. Rural Sociology Section.
Southern Sociological Society
Southwestern Sociological Association
World Congress of Rural Sociology
and abstracts of papers from the World Congress of Sociology. Also included as supplements:
International Review of Publications in Sociology (includes 'Book Review Bibliography')
Newsletter of the International Sociological Association
Newsletter of the International Society for the Sociology of Knowledge

1833 SOCIOLOGICAL ANALYSIS. v.1– , Mar. 1940– . Worcester, Mass., subsequently River Forest, Ill. Quarterly (irreg.).
Issued by the American Catholic Sociological Society. Title varies: 1940–63, *The American Catholic Sociological Review.*
Indexed: Cath. Per. Ind.; Curr. Cont.; SSCI; Soc. Abstr.; Wom. Stud. Abstr.

SOCIOLOGICAL ANALYSIS
See SOCIOLOGICAL ANALYSIS & THEORY

1834 SOCIOLOGICAL ANALYSIS & THEORY. v.1– , Oct. 1970– . Beverly Hills, Calif., London, Sage Publications. Three issues a year.
Issued by the Department of Sociological Studies, University of Sheffield. Title varies: v.1–3, 1970–73, *Sociological Analysis.*
Indexed: Int. Bibl. Soc.; Soc. Abstr.

1835 Sociological Association of Ireland. Cumann Sochelaiochta na h Eirieann. PROCEEDINGS OF THE ANNUAL CONFERENCE. 1st– , 1974– . Belfast.
Issued by the Department of Social Studies, Queen's University of Belfast. 2nd and 5th publ. 1976; 1st and 4th publ. 1978.

1836 SOCIOLOGICAL BULLETIN. v.1– , 1952– . Bombay. Two issues a year.
Issued by the Indian Sociological Society.
Indexed: Bull. sig. soc. eth.; Int. Bibl. Soc.; SSCI; Soc. Abstr.

SOCIOLOGICAL CONTRIBUTIONS
See SOZIOLOGISCHE ARBEITEN

1837 SOCIOLOGICAL CONTRIBUTIONS FROM FLANDERS. 1967– . Antwerpen, Standaard Wetenschappelijke Uitgiverij. Irreg.
Issued by the Organisatie voor Vlaamse Sociologen. Includes summaries of doctoral dissertations. In English.

1838 SOCIOLOGICAL FOCUS. v.1–2, fall 1967–1970? Columbus, Ohio. Department of Sociology, University of Cincinnati, Ohio. Quarterly.

Issued by the Ohio Valley Sociological Society, The North Central Sociological Association, and Department of Sociology, University of Akron. Supersedes: *The Ohio Valley Sociologist.* Continued by: *Utah State University Journal of Sociology.*

1839 SOCIOLOGICAL FORUM. v.1–3, fall 1978–1980. New Brunswick, N.J., Transaction Periodicals. Semi-annual.
Issued by the Mid-South Sociological Association. Merged with *Sociological Symposium* to form *Sociological Spectrum.*
Indexed: Soc. Abstr.

1840 SOCIOLOGICAL INQUIRY. v.1– , 1930– . Urbana, Ill. Semi-annual, 1930–1952; quartery, 1953– .
Issued by the Alpha Kappa Delta, National Sociology Honor Society. Title varies: *AKD Quarterly; Alpha Kappa Delta Quarterly; Alpha Kappa Deltian.*
Indexed: Bull. sig. soc. eth.; Int. Bibl. Soc.; SSCI; Soc. Abstr.

1841 SOCIOLOGICAL JOURNAL. 1– , Oct. 1971– . Kampala. Annual.
Issued by the Sociological Society, and the Makerere University.

SOCIOLOGICAL JOURNAL
See SHE HUI HSÜEH K'AN

1842 SOCIOLOGICAL LABORATORY JOURNAL. v.1–2, no.2, Oct. 1960–1961. Lakeland, Fla.
Issued by the Florida Southern College.

1843 SOCIOLOGICAL METHODOLOGY. 1969– . San Francisco, Jossey-Bass. Annual.
Issued by the American Sociological Association.

1844 SOCIOLOGICAL METHODS AND RESEARCH. v.1– , Aug. 1972– . Beverly Hills, Calif., Sage Publications. Quarterly.
Issued by the Department of Sociology, Queen's College, City University of New York.
Indexed: Int. Bibl. Soc.; PAIS; SSCI; Soc. Abstr.; Urb. Aff. Abstr.

1845 SOCIOLOGICAL MICRO-JOURNAL. 1– , 1967– . Copenhagen. Annual.
Issued by the Sociologisk Institut, Københavns Universitet. In English, French and German.
Indexed: Soc. Abstr.

1846 SOCIOLOGICAL OBSERVATIONS. 2– , 1977– . Beverly Hills, Calif., Sage Publications. Irreg.
Monograph series.

SOCIOLOGICAL PAPERS
See Sociological Society, London. SOCIOLOGICAL PAPERS

1847 SOCIOLOGICAL PRACTICE. 1– , spring 1976– . New York, Human Science Press. Semi-annual.
Indexed: Soc. Abstr.

1848 SOCIOLOGICAL PRAXIS. CURRENT ROLES AND SETTINGS. Jan. 1976. Beverly Hills, Calif., Sage Publications.
In *Sage Studies in International Sociology*, 3.
Indexed: Soc. Abstr.

1849 THE SOCIOLOGICAL QUARTERLY. v.1– , Jan. 1960– . Carbondale, Ill., Southern Illinois University Press. Quarterly.
Issued by the Midwest Sociological Society; subsequently by the Department of Sociology, University of Missouri, Columbia. Supersedes: *The Midwest Sociologist.*
Indexed: Int. Bibl. Soc.; Int. Pol. Sc. Abstr.; PAIS; Psych. Abstr.; SSCI; Soc. Sc. Hum. Ind.; Soc. Sc. Ind.; Soc. Abstr.; Soc. Work. Res. Abstr.

1850 SOCIOLOGICAL REVIEW. v.1–44, 1908–1952; n.s. v.1– , July 1953– . Manchester; subsequently London, and Keele, England. Quarterly, 1908–40; irreg. 1940–45; three issues a year, 1953– .
Issued by the Institute of Sociology, 1908–52, University College of North Staffordshire, 1953– . Supersedes the Institute's *Sociological Papers*. Indexes: 1953–75, 1 v.
Indexed: Brit. Hum. Ind.; Bull. sig. soc. eth.; Int. Bibl. Soc.; Int. Pol. Sc. Abstr.; Psych. Abstr.; SSCI; Sage Fam. Stud. Abstr.; Sage Urb. Abstr.; Soc. Abstr.; Urb. Aff. Abstr.

SOCIOLOGICAL REVIEW
See PRZEGLĄD SOCJOLOGICZNY

SOCIOLOGICAL REVIEW
See REVIJA ZA SOCIOLOGIJU

SOCIOLOGICAL REVIEW
See SHAKAIGAKU HYORON

SOCIOLOGICAL REVIEW
See SOCIOLOGICKÁ REVUE

SOCIOLOGICAL REVIEW
See SOCIOLOGICKÝ ČASOPIS

SOCIOLOGICAL REVIEW
See SOCIOLOŠKI PREGLED

SOCIOLOGICAL REVIEW
See SOSYOLOJI DERGISİ

1851 SOCIOLOGICAL REVIEW. MONOGRAPHS. no.1–, 1958– . Keele, England. Irreg.
Issued by the University College of North Staffordshire.
Monograph series.
Indexed: Soc. Abstr.

SOCIOLOGICAL SERIES
See Duke University, Durham, N.C. SOCIOLOGICAL SERIES

1852 Sociological Society, London. SOCIOLOGICAL PAPERS. v.1–3, 1904–1906. London. Irreg.
Superseded by: *Sociological Review*.

Sociological Society, London.
See also Institute of Sociology, London.

1853 SOCIOLOGICAL STUDIES. 1–4, 1962–1972. London, Cambridge University Press. Irreg.
Monograph series.

1854 SOCIOLOGICAL STUDIES. no.1– , 1974– . Birmingham, Ala. Irreg.
Issued by the Bureau of Public Administration, University of Alabama.

1855 SOCIOLOGICAL STUDIES IN ROMAN HISTORY. v.1– , 1978 [published 1980]– . London, Cambridge University Press. Irreg.
Monograph series.

SOCIOLOGICAL STUDY SERIES
See Mississippi. University. Bureau of Governmental Research. SOCIOLOGICAL STUDY SERIES

1856 SOCIOLOGICAL SYMPOSIUM. v.1-8, fall 1968–1972. Bowling Green, Oreg., subsequently Blacksburg, Va. 1973– . Semi-annual, 1968–fall 1975; quarterly, 1976– .
Issued by the Department of Sociology and Anthropology, Western Kentucky University, no.1–8; subsequently by the Virginia Polytechnic Institute and State University, no.9– . Issues are numbered consecutively in one sequence. Cumulative index, 1969–78, publ. 1979. Merged with *Sociological Forum* to form *Sociological Spectrum*.
Indexed: Curr. Cont.; Psych. Abstr.; SSCI; Soc. Anthr.; Soc. Work. Res. Abstr.

1857 SOCIOLOGICAL THEORIES IN PROGRESS. v.1–2, 1966–1972. Boston, Mass., Houghton Mifflin. Annual.

SOCIOLOGICAL TRANSLATIONS ON EASTERN EUROPE
See United States. Joint Publications Research Service. SOCIOLOGICAL TRANSLATIONS ON EASTERN EUROPE

1858 SOCIOLOGICAL YEARBOOK ON RELIGION IN BRITAIN. v.1–8, 1968–1975. London, SCM Press. Annual.
Issued by the London School of Economics and Political Science, University of London. Includes a section titled: 'Bibliography of Work in the Sociology of British Religion'.
Indexed: Bull. sig. soc. eth.; Int. Bibl. Soc.

SOCIOLOGICAS
See Centro Colombiano de Investigaciónes Psico-Sociologicas. SOCIOLOGICAS. PUBLICACIÓN

1859 SOCIOLOGICKÁ KNIHOVNA: MENŠI ŘADA. no.1–10, 1925–1927. Praha.
Issued by the Masarykova sociologická společnost v Praze. In Czech.

1860 SOCIOLOGICKÁ REVUE. REVUE DE SOCIOLOGIE. SOCIOLOGICAL REVIEW. SOZIOLOGISCHE REVUE. 1–15, 1930–1948. Brno.
Issued by the Sociologický seminar, Masarykova univerzita, and Masarykova sociologická společnost. In Czech.

1861 SOCIOLOGICKÝ ČASOPIS. v.1– , 1965– . Praha. Six issues a year.
Issued by the Vědecke kolegium filozofie, subsequently by the Filozofický ústav, Československa akademie věd. Title in English: *Sociological Review*. In Czech and Slovak; summaries in English and Russian. Table of contents in English, French, German and Russian.
Indexed: Bull. sig. soc. eth.; Int. bibl. Soc.; Int. Pol. Sc. Abstr.; SSCI; Soc. Abstr.

SOCIOLOGIE
See Bucharest. Universitatea. ANALELE. SOCIOLOGIE

1862 SOCIOLOGIE A HISTORIE ZEMĚDĚLSTVI. 1–10, June 1965–1974. Praha. Two issues a year.
Issued by the Ústav vědecko-technických informací, Ministerstvo zemědělství, lesniho a vodniho hospodarstvi. Subseries of *Sbornik UVTI* [Ústav vědeckotechnických informaci]. In Czech; summaries in English, German and Russian. Continued by: *Sociologie zemědělstvi*.
Indexed: Soc. Abstr.

1863 SOCIOLOGIE A SOCIÁLNI PROBLÉMY; REVUE PRO SOCIÁLNI TEORII E PRAKSI. 1–6, 1931–1938? Praha.
Title varies: 1–5, *Sociálni problémy*. In Czech.

1864 SOCIOLOGIE CATHOLIQUE. 1–14, Mar. 1892–Nov. 1908. Montpellier.

LA SOCIOLOGIE CONTEMPORAINE
See CURRENT SOCIOLOGY

SOCIOLOGIE DE L'ÉDUCATION
See Paris. École Pratique des Hautes Études. Centre de Sociologie Européenne. CAHIERS. SOCIOLOGIE DE L'ÉDUCATION

1865 SOCIOLOGIE DU DÉVELOPPEMENT. v.1– , 1968– . Paris, Éditions Gauthier-Villars.
Sub-series of: *Collection de l'Institut d'Économie Régionale du Sud-Ouest*, and of *Techniques Économiques Modernes*. Vol.1 of this publication is no.27 of *Techniques Économiques Modernes*.

1866 SOCIOLOGIE DU TRAVAIL. 1– , Oct/Dec. 1959– . Paris, Éditions du Seuil.
Issued by the Association pour le Développement de la Sociologie du Travail.
Indexed: Int. Bibl. Soc.; Int. Pol. Sc. Abstr.; Urb. Aff. Abstr.

1867 SOCIOLOGIE EN SAMENLEVING. 1– , 1963– . Utrecht, Bijleveld. Irreg.
In Dutch.
Monograph series.

1868 SOCIOLOGIE ET CONNAISSANCE. 1970– . Paris, Éditions Anthropos. Irreg.
Monograph series.

1869 SOCIOLOGIE ET DROIT SLAVES. [v.1]–[4], no.1–9, Dec. 1945–1948. Paris.
Issued under the auspices of Institut International de Sociologie, and Société Legislation Comparée, in cooperation with several institutes of the University of Paris.

1870 SOCIOLOGIE ET SOCIÉTÉS. REVUE THÉMATIQUE. v.1– , May 1969– . Montréal, Les Presses de l'Université de Montréal. Two issues a year.
Issued by the Département de Sociologie, Université de Montréal. In French; summaries in English, French and Spanish.
Indexed: Bull. sig. soc. eth.; Int. Bibl. Soc.; Int. Pol. Sc. Abstr.; SSCI; Soc. Abstr.

1871 SOCIOLOGIE ET TIERS-MONDE. 1– , 1969– . Paris, Éditions Anthropos. Irreg.
Monograph series; unnumbered.

SOCIOLOGIE HAITIENNE
See ECONOMISTE HAITIEN; REVUE HAITIENNE D'ÉCONOMIE PURE ET APPLIQUÉE

1872 SOCIOLOGIE NOUVELLE. SITUATIONS. 1– , 1972. Gemloux, Duculet. Irreg.
Monograph series.

1873 SOCIOLOGIE PERMANENTE. 1978– . Paris, Éditions du Seuil. Irreg.
Monograph series.

1874 SOCIOLOGIE ROMÂNESCĂ. 1936–1939; 1947–? Bucureşti. Ceased publication.
Subtitle reads: 'Revista Institutului de Stiinte Sociale al Romaniei'. In Rumanian.

1875 SOCIOLOGIE ZEMĚDĚLSTVÍ. 11– , 1975– . Praha. Semi-annual.
Issued by the Ústav vědecko-technických informacii, and Československá akademie zemědělská. Continues: *Sociologie a historie zemědělstvi*. Subseries of *Sbornik ÚVTIZ — Sociologie*. In Czech; summaries in English and Russian.

1876 SOCIOLOGIJA. Zagreb. Irreg.
Monograph series, unnumbered.

1877 SOCIOLOGIJA; CASOPIS ZA DRUSTVENE NAUKE. v.1– , 1959– . Beograd. Quarterly.
Issued by the Jugoslovensko udruženje za sociologiju. Continues the sociological part of *Jugoslovenski casopis za filozofiju i sociologiju.* Subtitle varies slightly. In Serbo-Croatian. Table of contents and summaries in English.
Indexed: Bull. sig. soc. eth.; Int. Bibl. Soc.; Int. Pol. Sc. Abstr.; Soc. Abstr.

1878 SOCIOLOGIJA SELA. v.1– , July/Sep. 1963– . Zagreb. Quarterly.
Issued by the Agrarni institut. In Serbo-Croatian. Summaries in English and Russian; table of contents in English and Russian.

1879 SOCIOLOGISCH BULLETIN. 1947–1972. s-Gravenhage, Boekcentrum N.V. Quarterly.
Issued by the Sociologisch Instituut (called Sociologisch Instituut van de Stichting 'Kerk en Wereld', 1947–57). In Dutch.
Indexed: Soc. Abstr.

1880 SOCIOLOGISCH JAARBOEK. 1–13, 1947–1959. Leiden, E. J. Brill.
Issued by the Nederlandse Sociologische Vereniging. In Dutch. Continued as monographs without a series title.

1881 SOCIOLOGISCHE EN SOCIOGRAFISCHE STUDIEN. 1–3, 1949–1952. Leiden. Irreg.
In Dutch.
Monograph series.

1882 SOCIOLOGISCHE GIDS; TIJDSCHRIFT VOOR SOCIOLOGIE EN SOCIAAL ONDERZOEK. 1953– . Meppel, Netherlands, J. A. Boom en Zoon. Bimonthly.
In Dutch, English and German; summaries in English.
Indexed: Int. Bibl. Soc.; Soc. Abstr.

1883 SOCIOLOGISCHE MONOGRAFIEËN. no.1– , 1970– . Leuven, Uitgave van het Sociologisch Onderzoeksinstituut Katholieke Universiteit Leuven. Irreg.

Other title: *Reeks Sociologische Monografieën.* In Flemish.

Monograph series; includes some works in translation.

1884 SOCIOLOGISCHE VERKENNINGEN. no.1–4, 1971–1973. Leuven, Leuven University Press. Irreg.

In Flemish.

Monograph series.

1885 SOCIOLOGISK FORSKNING. 1– , 1964– . Uppsala. Quarterly.

Issued by the Sveriges Sociologförbund. In Swedish.

Indexed: SSCI; Soc. Abstr.; Urb. Aff. Abstr.

1886 SOCIOLOGISKE MEDDELELSER; A DANISH SOCIOLOGICAL JOURNAL. ser.1– , 1952– . København. One or two issues a year.

Issued by the Statistisk-Økonomisk Laboratorium, Sociologisk Institut, Københavns Universitet. In English and the Scandinavian languages; summaries in one other of these languages.

Indexed: Int. Bibl. Soc.; Soc. Abstr.

1887 SOCIOLOGIST. 1–3, Jan. 1883–1885? Knoxville, Tenn.

1888 SOCIOLOGIST. v.1– , 1969– . Chambersburg, Pa., subsequently Washington, D.C. Monthly.

Issued by the District of Columbia Sociological Society. A processed bulletin.

1889 SOCIOLOGIST. 1– , 1968– Ibadan. Annual.

Issued by the University of Ibadan and the Sociological Society.

1890 Sociologists for Women in Society. NEWSLETTER. v.1–9, no.1, Mar. 1971–1980. San Francisco, Calif., subsequently Brooklyn, N.Y., Washington, D.C., and New Albany, Ind.

Continued by: *SWS Network.*

1891 SOCIOLOGNYTT. 1962– . Uppsala.

Issued by the Sveriges Sociologförbund.

1892 LE SOCIOLOGUE. 1– , 1966– . Paris, Presses Universitaires de France. Irreg.

Subseries of *Collection SUP.*

Monograph series.

1893 SOCIOLOGUS: ZEITSCHRIFT FÜR EMPIRISCHE SOZIOLOGIE UND ETHNOLOGISCHE FORSCHUNG. A JOURNAL FOR EMPIRICAL SOCIOLOGY, SOCIAL PSYCHOLOGY AND ETHNIC RESEARCH. n.F. v.1– , 1951– . Berlin, Duncker & Humblot. Two issues a year.

Continues: *Sociologus* and *Archiv für Anthropologische Völkerforschung und Kolonialen Kulturwandel.*

Indexed: Afr. Abstr.; Bull. sig. soc. eth.; Int. Bibl. Soc.; Int. Pol. Sc. Abstr.; Soc. Abstr.

1894 SOCIOLOGUS; ZEITSCHRIFT FÜR VÖLKERPSYCHOLOGIE UND SOZIOLOGIE. 1–9, Mar. 1925–Dec. 1933. Leipzig, Hirschfeld. Quarterly.

Title varies: 1925–Dec. 1931, *Zeitschrift für Volkerpsychologie und Soziologie.* Continued by: *Sociologus; Zeitschrift für Empirische Soziologie, Sozialpsychologie und Ethnologische Forschung.*

1895 SOCIOLOGY. v.1– , Jan. 1967– . London, Oxford University Press. Three issues a year.

Issued by the British Sociological Association.

Indexed: Brit. Hum. Ind.; Bull. sig. soc. eth.; Int. Bibl. Soc.; Int. Pol. Sc. Abstr.; SSCI; Soc. Ed. Abstr.; Soc. Sc. Ind.; Soc. Abstr.; Urb. Aff. Abstr.

SOC[IOLOGY] AND AN[THROPOLOGY] REPORT

See Mississippi. State University. Department of Sociology and Anthropology. SOC[IOLOGY] AND AN[THROPOLOGY] REPORT

1896 SOCIOLOGY AND EASTERN EUROPE. 1968–1969? Boston, Mass.

Issued by the Department of Sociology, Boston University, in cooperation with the Subcommittee on Liaison with East European Sociologists. Committee on International Cooperation, American Sociological Association.

SOCIOLOGY AND RURAL LIFE

See Mississippi. Agricultural Experiment Station. SOCIOLOGY AND RURAL LIFE

1897 SOCIOLOGY AND SOCIAL RESEARCH. v.1– , 1916– . Los Angeles, Calif. Bimonthly, subsequently quarterly.

Issued by the University of Southern California, Los Angeles. Title varies: v.1–5, (no.1–19), *Studies in Sociology; Sociological Monographs*; v.6–11, *Journal of Applied Sociology.* Absorbed: *News Notes* of Southern California Sociological Society, in October 1921, and *Bulletin of Social Research* of the Department of Sociology, University of Southern California, in Sep. 1927.

Indexed: Bull. sig. soc. eth.; Int. Bibl. Soc.; Int. Pol. Sc. Abstr.; PAIS; Psych. Abstr.; SSCI; Soc. Sc. Hum. Ind.; Soc. Sc. Ind.; Soc. Abstr.; Soc. Work Res. Abstr.

SOCIOLOGY FELLOWSHIP NEEDS
See Yenching University, Peking. Department of Sociology and Social Work. SOCIOLOGY FELLOWSHIP NEEDS

1898 SOCIOLOGY, LAW AND LEGAL THEORY. 1, 1974. Rotterdam, Rotterdam University Press.

1899 SOCIOLOGY OF EDUCATION. v.1– , Sep. 1927– . Washington, D.C. Monthly, 1927–63; subsequently quarterly.
Issued by the Department of Sociology, University of California at Berkeley. Title varies: v.1–36, 1927–Mar. 1963, *The Journal of Educational Sociology*.
Indexed: Int. Bibl. Soc.; SSCI; PAIS; Psych. Abstr.; Soc. Abstr.

1900 SOCIOLOGY OF EDUCATION. no.1– , 1970– . New Dehli.
Issued by the National Council of Educational Research and Training.

1901 SOCIOLOGY OF EDUCATION ABSTRACTS. v.1– , 1965– . Liverpool. Quarterly.
Issued by the School of Education, University of Liverpool; Department of Social Science and Education, and Department of Sociology, Edgehill College of Education.

SOCIOLOGY OF FERTILITY SERIES
See Calcutta. Institute of Social Studies. Research Division. SOCIOLOGY OF FERTILITY SERIES

1902 SOCIOLOGY OF HEALTH & ILLNESS; A JOURNAL OF MEDICAL SOCIOLOGY. v.1— , June 1979– . London, Routledge & Kegan Paul. Quarterly.
Indexed: Soc. Abstr.

SOCIOLOGY OF LAW
See HOSHAKAIGAKU

1903 SOCIOLOGY OF PLAY AND GAMES. 1975– . Waterloo, Ont. Three issues a year.
Issued by the SIRLS, Faculty of Human Kinetics and Leisure Studies, University of Waterloo.

SOCIOLOGY OF RURAL LIFE
See Minnesota. Agricultural Experiment Station, St. Anthony Park. SOCIOLOGY OF RURAL LIFE

1904 SOCIOLOGY OF SPORT AND LEISURE ABSTRACTS; A REVIEW OF SOCIAL SCIENCE LITERATURE. 1– , 1980– . Amsterdam, Elsevier Scientific Publishing Co. Three issues a year.

1905 SOCIOLOGY OF THE SCIENCES. 1– , 1977– . Dordrecht, D. Reidel. Annual.
Indexed: Soc. Abstr.

1906 SOCIOLOGY OF WORK AND OCCUPATIONS. 1– , Feb. 1974– . Beverly Hills, Calif., Sage Publications. Quarterly.
Indexed: Int. Bibl. Soc.; Psych. Abstr.; SSCI; Sage Fam. Stud. Abstr.; Soc. Abstr.

1907 SOCIOLOGY RESEARCH MONOGRAPHS no.1– , 1978– . Armidale, Australia. Irreg.
Issued by the University of New England, Australia.
Monograph series.

1908 SOCIOLOGY; REVIEWS OF NEW BOOKS. v.1– , Oct. 1973– . Washington, D.C., Heldref Publications. Bimonthly.
Issued by the Educational Association.
Indexed: Soc. Abstr.

SOCIOLOGY SERIES
See Auckland, N.Z. University. SOCIOLOGY SERIES

SOCIOLOGY SERIES
See Georgia. University. Institute of Community and Area Development. SOCIOLOGY SERIES

SOCIOLOGY SERIES
See Kansas. Fort Hays. State College. STUDIES. SOCIOLOGY SERIES

1909 SOCIOLOGY THESES REGISTER. Ed.1– , 1976– . London.
Issued by the Social Science Research Council and the British Sociological Association.

1910 SOCIOLOŠKA IN POLITOLOŠKA KNJIŽNICA. 1–2, 1973. Maribor, Obzoria. Irreg.
Issued by the Fakultet za socjologiju, Univerzitet. In Slovenian.
Monograph series.

1911 SOCIOLOŠKE TEME. 1–6, 1962–1968. Beograd. Two issues a year.
Issued by the Savez Studenata sociologije beogradskog univerziteta. In Serbo-Croatian.

1912 Sociološki institut. ZBORNIK RADOVA. v.1– , 1967– . Beograd.
In Serbo-Croatian.

1913 SOCIOLOSKI PREGLED. v.1–?, 1938–1939? Beograd. Ceased publication.
In Serbo-Croatian. No more information available.

1914 SOCIOLOSKI PREGLED. v.1– , 1965– . Beograd.
Issued by the Srpsko sociološki drustvo. Title in English: *Sociological Review*. Not published 1966–67. In Serbo-Croatian; some summaries in English.
Indexed: Soc. Abstr.

1915 SOCIOMETRY. v.1–40, July/Oct. 1937–Dec. 1977. Washington, D.C., American Sociological Association. Quarterly.
Issued by the Department of Sociology, University of California at Los Angeles. Continued by: *Social Psychology*.
Indexed: Int. Bibl. Soc.; Int. Pol. Sc. Abstr.; SSCI; Soc. Sc. Ind.; Soc. Abstr.; Urb. Aff. Abstr.; Wom. Stud. Abstr.

1916 SOCIOMETRY MONOGRAPH. no.1–41, 1941–1960. New York, Beacon House, Irreg.
Monograph series.

1917 SOCIOTECHNOLOGY; AN INTERNATIONAL JOURNAL. v.1– , 1978– . Elmsford, N.Y. Pergamon Press. Quarterly.
Indexed: Psych. Abstr.

1918 SOCJOLINGWISTYKA. 1– , 1977– . Katowice. Irreg.
Issued by the Uniwersytet Śląski w Katowicach. Subseries of: *Prace Naukowe Uniwersytetu Śląskiego w Katowicach*.

1919 SOCJOLOGIA. 1– , 1974– . Toruń. Irreg.
Issued by the Uniwersytet in Toruń. Subseries of: the Uniwersytet's *Zeszyty Naukowe. Nauki Humanistyczno-Społeczne*. In Polish; summaries in English and French.

1920 SOCJOLOGIA W POLSCE: PUBLIKACJE ZWARTE I CIĄGŁE. 1976– . Warszawa.
Issued by the Ośrodek Dokumentacji i Informacji Naukowej, Instytut Filozofii i Socjologii, Polska Akademia Nauk. In Polish. Continues : *Prace Badawcze i Publikacje z Zakresu Socjologii w Polsce*.

1921 SOCJOLOGIA WYCHOWANIA. 1– , 1976– . Toruń. Irreg.
Issued by the Uniwersytet Mikołaja Kopernika. Subseries of: *Acta Universitatis Nicolai Copernici. Nauki Humanistyczno-Społeczne*. In Polish; summaries in English.

1922 SOCJOLOGICZNE PROBLEMY PRZEMYSŁU I KLASY ROBOTNICZEJ. 1– , 1966– . Warszawa, Państwowe Wydawnictwo Naukowe. Irreg.
Issued by the Zakład Badań Społeczynch Przemysłu i Klasy Robotniczej, Wyższa Szkoła Nauk Społecznych przy KC PZPR.

1923 SOGO TOSHI KENKYU. 1– , Nov. 1977– . Tokyo.
Issued by the Tokyo Toritsu Daigaku Toshi Kenkyū Senta. Title in English: *Comprehensive Urban Studies*. In Japanese; summaries in English.

1924 SOME CURRENT RESEARCH IN EAST AFRICA. Nov. 1964– . Nairobi. Irreg.
Issued by the East African Staff College.

1925 SONDAGES. v.1– , June 1939– . n.s. Oct. 1944–Aug. 1945. Paris, Éditions de Chanselier. Quarterly.
Issued by the Institut Francaise d'Opinion. Title varies: 1939–Aug. 1945, *Bulletin d'Information*. Suspended 1941–Oct. 1, 1944. Subtitle reads: 'Revue francaise de l'opinion publique'.
Indexed: Bull. sig. soc. eth.; Int. Bibl. Soc.; Soc. Abstr.

SOOCHOW JOURNAL OF SOCIAL & POLITICAL SCIENCES
See TUNG WU CHENG CHIH SHE HUI HSÜEH HUI HSÜEH PAO

1926 SOROKIN LECTURES. no.1– , 1968– . Saskatoon, Sas. Annual.
Issued by the University of Saskatchewan.
Series of papers.

1927 SORT OF SOCIOLOGY. no.1– , winter 1975/1976– . Rochdale, England. Panparameter Ltd.
Subtitle reads: 'The new behavioural science quarterly'.

1928 SOSHIOROJI. v.1– , Jan. 1952– . Kyoto. Semi-annual.
Issued by the Shakaigaku Kenkyū-kai. In Japanese.

SOSIOGRAFI INDONESIA
See SOSIOGRAFI INDONESIA DAN HUKUM ADAT

1929 SOSIOGRAFI INDONESIA DAN HAKUM ADAT. v.1– , 1959– . Jogjakarta, Jajasan Pembina Hukum Adat. Semi-annual.
Title varies: v.1, 1959, *Sosiografi Indonesia*; v.2, 1960, *Madjalah Hukum Adat*. In Indonesian; some special issues in English.

1930 SOSIOLOGIA. v.1– , 1964– . Helsinki. Quarterly.
Issued by the Westermarck-Samfundet. Includes some Ph.D. dissertations in sociology. In Finnish.
Indexed: Int. Bibl. Soc.; Soc. Abstr.

1931 SOSYOLOJI DERGISİ. SOCIOLOGICAL REVIEW. REVUE DE SOCIOLOGIE. ZEITSCHRIFT FÜR SOZIOLOGIE. 1– , 1942– . İstanbul. Irreg.
Issued by the Edebiyat Fakültesi Yayinlari, İstanbul Üniversitesi. In English, French and German.
Indexed: Soc. Abstr.

1932 ŞOSYOLOJI DUNYASI. v.1– , 1962– . İstanbul, Işil Matbaasi. Annual.
Issued by the Türk Sosyoloji Cemiyetinin Resmi Dergisi. In Turkish.

1933 SOTSIAL'NAIA PSIKHOLOGIIA I FILOSOFIIA. 1– , 1971– . Leningrad.
In Russian.

1934 SOTSIAL'NYE ISSLEDOVANIIA. [1]– , 1965– . Moskva, Izdatel'stvo 'Nauka'.
Issued by the Institut filosofii, Akademiia nauk SSSR, and Sovetskaia sotsialisticheskaia assotsiatsiia. In Russian.

1935 SOTSIOLOGICHESKI IZSLEDOVANIIA. 1, 1968. Sofia.
Issued by the Institut po sotsiologii, Bulgarska akademiia na naukite, in cooperation with Sotsiologichesko druzhestvo v NRB. Superseded by: *Sotsiologicheski problemi*. In Bulgarian.
Indexed: Soc. Abstr.

1936 SOTSIOLOGICHESKI PROBLEMI. 1– , 1969– . Sofia, Publishing House of the Bulgarian Academy of Sciences. Bimonthly.
Issued by the Institut po sotsiologiia, Bulgarska akademiia na naukite. Supersedes: *Sotsiologicheski izsledovaniia*. In Bulgarian. Summaries in English and Russian.
Indexed: Bull. sig. soc. eth.; Soc. Abstr.

1937 SOTSIOLOGICHESKIE ISSLEDOVANIIA. June/Sep. 1974– . Moskva, Izd-vo 'Nauka'. Quarterly.
Issued by the Institut sotsiologicheskikh issledovanii, Akademiia nauk SSSR. In Russian.
Indexed: Soc. Abstr.

SOTSIOLOGICHESKIE ISSLEDOVANIIA
See Sverdlovsk. Ural'skii gosudarstvennyi universitet. SOTSIOLOGICHESKIE ISSLEDOVANIIA

SOTSIOLOGICHESKIE PROBLEMY NARODNOGO OBRAZOVANIIA
See Sverdlovsk. Gosudarstvennyi pedagogicheskii institut. SOTSIOLOGICHESKIE PROBLEMY NARODNOGO OBRAZOVANIIA

1938 SOTSIOLOGICHESKII SBORNIK. 1– , 1970– . Makhal-Kala.
Issued by the Institut istorii, iazyka i literatury, Dagestanskii filial, Akademiia nauk SSSR. In Russian.

1939 SOTSIOLOGIIA KUL'TURY. no.1– , 1974– . Moskva, Izd. Sovetskaiia Rossiia.
Issued by the Otdel sosiologicheskikh issledovanii, Nauchno-issledovatel'skii institut kultury. Subseries of: Nauchno-issledovatel'skii institut kultury. Otdel sotsiologicheskikh issledovanii. *Trudy*. In Russian.

SOTSIOLOGIIA VYSHSHEI SHKOLY
See Gorky. Universitet. UCHENYE ZAPISKI. SERIIA SOTSIOLOGICHESKAIA. SOTSIOLOGIIA VYSHSHEI SHKOLY

1940 South Africa. Department of Statistics. VERSLAG VOR HUWELIKE EN EGSKEIDINGS: SUID-AFRIKA. REPORT ON MARRIAGES AND DIVORCES: SOUTH AFRICA. 1972– . Pretoria.
Continues: South Africa. Department of Statistics. *Verslag vir Huwelike: Suid-Afrika*. Subseries of: *Verslag* — Department van Statistiek. In Afrikaans and English.

1941 South African Institute of Race Relations. ANNUAL REPORT. 1– , 1930– . Johannesburg.

1942 South African Institute of Race Relations. A FACT PAPER. no.1, 1958. Johannesburg. One volume published.

1943 South African Institute of Race Relations. MONOGRAPH SERIES. 1938–1965. Johannesburg. Irreg.
Monograph series.

THE SOUTH AFRICAN JOURNAL OF SOCIOLOGY
See SUID-AFRIKAANSE TYDSKRIF VIR SOCIOLOGIE

SOUTH AND SOUTHEAST ASIA URBAN AFFAIRS ANNUALS
See SOUTH AND SOUTHEAST ASIA URBAN AFFAIRS BI-ANNUALS

1944 SOUTH AND SOUTHEAST ASIA URBAN AFFAIRS BI-ANNUALS. 1– , 1971– . Beverly Hills, Calif., Sage Publications. Biennial.
Title varies: v.1–2, 1971–74, *South and Southeast Asia Urban Affairs Annuals*.

1945 SOUTH ASIA SOCIAL SCIENCE ABSTRACTS. 1–7, 1952–1958. Calcutta.
Issued by the South Asia Science Cooperation Office of the United Nations Educational, Scientific and Cultural Organization, 1952–53; by the Research Centre on Social and Economic Development in Southern Asia, Unesco, 1954–58. Absorbed by: *Asian Social Science Bibliography with Annotations and Abstracts*.

SOUTH ASIA SOCIAL SCIENCE BIBLIOGRAPHY
See ASIAN SOCIAL SCIENCE BIBLIOGRAPHY WITH ANNOTATIONS AND ABSTRACTS

1946 SOUTH ATLANTIC URBAN STUDIES. 1– , 1977– . Charleston, S.C., University of South Carolina Press. Annual.
Issued by the Urban Studies Center, College of Charleston.

1947 SOUTH CAROLINA URBAN & REGIONAL REVIEW. 1– , Mar. 1971– . Columbia, S.C. Irreg.
Issued by the Bureau of Urban and Regional Affairs, South Carolina University.

1948 South Dakota. State College of Agriculture and Mechanics, Brookings. RURAL SOCIOLOGY PAMPHLET. 1–109, 1940–1943. Brookings, S.D.

1949 SOUTHEAST ASIAN JOURNAL OF SOCIAL SCIENCE. 1– , 1973– . Singapore, University of Education Press. Semi-annual.
Formed by the merger of: *South-east Asian Journal of Sociology*, and *Southeast Asian Journal of Economic Development and Social Change*.

1950 SOUTH-EAST ASIAN JOURNAL OF SOCIOLOGY. May 1968–1972. Singapore. Annual.
Issued by the Singapore Sociology Society, and the Department of Sociology, University of Singapore. Merged with: *Southeast Asian Journal of Economic Development and Social Change*, to form *Southeast Asian Journal of Social Science*.

SOUTHEASTERN ASIA SOCIAL SCIENCE BIBLIOGRAPHY
See ASIAN SOCIAL SCIENCE BIBLIOGRAPHY WITH ANNOTATIONS AND ABSTRACTS

1951 SOUTHEASTERN REVIEW. 1– , Dec. 1973– . Charlottesville, Va., University of Virginia Printing Office. Semi-annual.
Subtitle reads: 'Journal of sociology and anthropology'.
Indexed: Soc. Abstr.

1952 SOUTHERN QUARTERLY. v.1– , 1962– . Hattiesburg, Miss. Quarterly.
Issued by the University of Southern Mississippi. Subtitle reads: 'A scholarly journal in the humanities and social sciences'.
Indexed: Int. Bibl. Soc.; Int. Pol. Sc. Abstr.; Soc. Abstr.

1953 THE SOUTHERN SOCIOLOGIST. v.1– , 1968– . Blacksburg, Va. Quarterly.
Issued by the Southern Sociological Society, and the Department of Sociology, Virginia Polytechnic Institute and State University.
Indexed: Soc. Abstr.

SOUTHWESTERN POLITICAL AND SOCIAL SCIENCE QUARTERLY
See SOCIAL SCIENCE QUARTERLY

SOUTHWESTERN POLITICAL SCIENCE QUARTERLY
See SOCIAL SCIENCE QUARTERLY

SOUTHWESTERN SOCIAL SCIENCE QUARTERLY
See SOCIAL SCIENCE QUARTERLY

1954 Southwestern Sociological Association. PROCEEDINGS. v.1–21, 1952–1970. Dallas. Annual.

SOVIET CULTURE
See SURVEY; A QUARTERLY REVIEW OF CULTURAL TRENDS

1955 SOVIET PERIODICAL ABSTRACTS; SOVIET SOCIETY. v.1–6, no.3/4, May 1861–June 1967. White Plains, N.Y. Quarterly.
Issued by the Slavic Language Research Institute, Inc. Title varies: v.1, 1961–Mar. 1962, *Selective Soviet Annotated Bibliographies; Soviet Society*.

1956 THE SOVIET REVIEW. v.1– , Aug. 1960– . White Plains, N.Y., International Arts and Sciences Press. Quarterly.
Subtitle reads: 'A journal of translation'. Supersedes: *Soviet Highlights*.
Indexed: Soc. Sc. Ind.; Soc. Abstr.

1957 SOVIET SOCIOLOGY. v.1– , 1962– . White Plains, N.Y., International Arts and Sciences Press. Quarterly.
Articles translated from Soviet journals.
Indexed: Bull. sig. soc. eth.; Curr. Cont.; Int. Bibl. Soc.; SSCI; PAIS: Soc. Abstr.

1958 SOVIET STUDIES. v.1– , June 1949– . Oxford, Blackwell. Quarterly.
Subtitle reads: 'A quarterly journal of the social and economic institutions of the USSR'.
Indexed: Brit. Hum. Ind.; Bull. sig. soc. eth.; Int. Pol. Sc. Abstr.; PAIS; Soc. Abstr.

SOVIET SURVEY
See SURVEY; A QUARTERLY REVIEW OF CULTURAL TRENDS

1959 SOZIALE WELT; ZEITSCHRIFT FÜR SOZIALWISSENSCHAFTLICHE FORSCHUNG UND PRAXIS. 1– , 1949– . Göttingen, Verlag Otto Schwartz. Quarterly.
Issued by the Sozialforschungsstelle, Universität Münster, in cooperation with various institutes of sociology in universities in West Germany. Indexes: v.11–30, 1960–79, 1 v.
Indexed: Bull. sig. soc. eth.; Int. Bibl. Soc.; Peace Res. Abstr. J.; Soc. Abstr.

SOZIALER KOMPAS
See SOCIAL COMPASS

1960 SOZIALISATION UND KOMMUNIKATION. no.1– , 1974– . Stuttgart, Ferdinand Enke Verlag. Irreg.
Issued by the Sonderforschungsbereich Sozialisations- und Kommunikationsforschung des Sozialwissenschaftlichen Forschungszentrum, Universität Erlangen-Nürnberg.
Monograph series.

1961 SOZIALSTATISTIK; JAHRBUCH. STATISTIQUES SOCIALES: ANNUAIRE. 1960– . Luxembourg.
Issued by the Statistical Office of the European Community (Statistisches Amt der Europäischen Gemeinschaften). Title varies: 1960–61, no.2, *Informations Statistiques. Statistiques Sociales*; 1961, no.3–1962, no.2, *Statistiques Sociales*. Other titles, *Jahrbuch der Sozialstatistik*, and *Annuaire des Statistiques Sociales*.

SOZIALWISSENSCHAFTLICHES LITERATURBLATT
See BIBLIOGRAPHIE DER SOZIALWISSENSCHAFTEN

1962 SOZIOLOGIE DER GEGENWART. MATERIALLEN ZUR MODERNEN GESELLSCHAFTSKUNDE. 1– , 1977– . Heidelberg. Irreg.
Monograph series.

1963 SOZIOLOGIE DER SCHULE. 1– , 1974– . Weinheim. Irreg.
Monograph series.

1964 SOZIOLOGIE IN DER SCHWEITZ. 1– , 1974– . Stuttgart, Hans Huber. Irreg.
Issued by the Schweizerische Gesellschaft für Soziologie. Other title: *Reihe Soziologie in der Schweitz*.
Monograph series.

1965 SOZIOLOGIE (JAHRESKATALOG). Berlin Werbegemeinschaft Elwert & Meuer GmbH. Annual.

1966 SOZIOLOGIE UND SOZIALPHILOSOPHIE. 1–7, 1926–1928. Wien, Leipzig. Irreg.
Issued by the Soziologische Gesellschaft in Wien.
Monograph series.

SOZIOLOGISCHE ABHANDLUNGEN
See Berlin (West). Freie Universität. Wirtschafts- und Sozialwissenschaftliche Fakultät. SOZIOLOGISCHE ABHANDLUNGEN

1967 SOZIOLOGISCHE ARBEITEN. TRAVAUX SOCIOLOGIQUES. SOCIOLOGICAL CONTRIBUTIONS. 1– , 1966– . Bern und Stuttgart, Verlag Hans Huber. Annual.
Issued by the Schweizerische Gesellschaft für Praktische Sozialforschung. In German, French and English.

1968 SOZIOLOGISCHE ARBEITBERICHTE: CAUSA. 1– , 1975– . Kiel. Irreg.
Issued by the Christian-Albrechts-Universität.

SOZIOLOGISCHE ARBEITSHEFTE
See Berlin (West). Technische Universität. Institut für Soziologie. SOZIOLOGISCHE ARBEITSHEFTE

SOZIOLOGISCHE FORSCHUNG IN DER DDR. INFORMATIONEN
See INFORMATIONEN ZUR SOZIOLOGISCHEN FORSCHUNG IN DER D[EUTSCHEN] D[EMOCRATISCHEN] R[EPUBLIK]

1969 SOZIOLOGISCHE GEGENWARTSFRAGEN. 1–2, 1932; n.F. 1– , 1957– . Stuttgart, Ferdinand Enke Verlag. Irreg.
Monograph series.

SOZIOLOGISCHE LEHREBEISPIELE
See BEITRÄGE ZUR SOZIALKUNDE. SERIE B: STRUKTUR UND WANDEL DER GESELLSCHAFT

SOZIOLOGISCHE REVUE
See SOCIOLOGICKÁ REVUE

1970 SOZIOLOGISCHE REVUE. BESPRECHUNGEN NEUER LITERATUR. v.1– , Jan. 1978– . München, Oldenbourg Verlag. Quarterly.

1971 SOZIOLOGISCHE SCHRIFTEN. v.1–5, 1964–1967. Berlin, Duncker & Humblot. Irreg.
Monograph series.

1972 SOZIOLOGISCHE STUDIEN. 1– , 1971– . Aachen. Irreg.
Issued by the Institut für Soziologie der Rheinisch-Westfällischen Hochschule.

1973 SOZIOLOGISCHE TEXTE. 1– , 1959– . Neuwied, H. Luchterhand. Irreg.
Monograph series; some works are translations, some in second editions.

1974 Spain. Consejo Superior de Investigaciónes Cientificas. Instituto Balmes de Sociologia. ESTUDIOS DEMOGRAFICOS. 1– , 1945– . Madrid. Irreg.
In Spanish.

1975 Spain. Consejo Superior de Investigaciónes Cientificas. Instituto Balmes de Sociologia. ESTUDIOS SOCIOLOGICOS INTERNACIONALES. 1– , 1956– . Madrid. Irreg.
In Spanish.

1976 Spain. Instituto Nacional de Investigaciónes Agrarias. ANALES. ECONOMIA Y SOCIOLOGIA AGRARIAS. no.1– , 1971– . Madrid. Annual.
Supersedes, in part, Spain. Instituto Nacional de Investigaciónes Agronomicas. *Anales*. In Spanish; summaries in English and Spanish.

SPECIAL PAPERS
See Philippine Sociological Society. SPECIAL PAPERS

SPECIAL REPORT
See JOURNAL OF INTERGROUP RELATIONS

SPOMENIK
See Akademija nauka i umjetnosti. Odeljenie drustvenih nauka. SPOMENIK

1977 SPORT AND SOCIAL INSTITUTIONS (EXCLUDING POLITICS AND EDUCATION). 1975– . Waterloo, Ont. Three issues a year.
Issued by the SIRLS, Faculty of Human Kinetics and Leisure Studies, University of Waterloo.

1978 SPORT AND SOCIAL STRATIFICATION. 1975– . Waterloo, Ont. Three issues a year.
Issued by the SIRLS, Faculty of Human Kinetics and Leisure Studies, University of Waterloo.

1979 SPORT AND THE SMALL GROUP. 1975– . Waterloo, Ont. Three issues a year.
Issued by the SIRLS, Faculty of Human Kinetics and Leisure Studies, University of Waterloo.

1980 SPORT AS A MACRO-SOCIAL SYSTEM. 1975– . Waterloo, Ont. Three issues a year.
Issued by the SIRLS, Faculty of Human Kinetics and Leisure Studies, University of Waterloo.

1981 SPORT, LEISURE AND DEVIANT BEHAVIOUR. 1975– . Waterloo, Ont. Three issues a year.
Issued by the SIRLS, Faculty of Human Kinetics and Leisure Studies, University of Waterloo. Processed.

1982 SPORT, LEISURE AND LIFE STYLE IN CANADA. 1975— . Waterloo, Ont. Three issues a year.
Issued by the SIRLS, Faculty of Human Kinetics and Leisure Studies, University of Waterloo. Processed.

1983 SPORT OCCUPATIONS AND CARRIER PATTERNS. 1975– . Waterloo, Ont. Three issues a year.
Issued by the SIRLS, Faculty of Human Kinetics and Leisure Studies, University of Waterloo. Processed.

1984 SPORTS SOCIOLOGY. BULLETIN. v.1–6, no.1, 1972–spring 1977. Park Forest South, Ill. Semi-annual.
Issued by the College of Human Learning and Development, Governor's State University. Processed.

1985 SRI LANKA JOURNAL OF SOCIAL SCIENCES. 1– , June 1978– . Colombo. Semi-annual.
Issued by the Social Science Research Centre, National Science Council of Sri Lanka.

STAND UND ENTWICKLUNG DER BEVÖLKERUNG
See Germany (Federal Republic). Statistisches Bundesamt. BEVÖLKERUNG UND ERWERBSSTÄTIGKEIT. REIHE 1.1: STAND UND ENTWICKLUNG DER BEVÖLKERUNG

1986 STANFORD SOCIOLOGICAL SERIES. no.1, 1955. Stanford, Calif. One volume published.

1987 STANFORD STUDIES IN SOCIOLOGY. 1–2, 1960–1962. Stanford, Calif.

1988 Stanford University. Institute for Communication Research. STUDIES IN THE UTILIZATION OF BEHAVIORAL SCIENCE. v.1–2, 1951–1963. Stanford, Calif.

STATISTICAL BULLETIN. INTERNATIONAL MIGRATION
See Papua New Guinea. Bureau of Statistics. STATISTICAL BULLETIN. INTERNATIONAL MIGRATION

STATISTICAL REPORT
See Intergovernmental Committee for European Migration. STATISTICAL REPORT

STATISTIQUE DU MOUVEMENT DE LA POPULATION. NOUVELLE SÉRIE
See France. Institut National de la Statistique et des Études Économiques. STATISTIQUE DU MOUVEMENT DE LA POPULATION. NOUVELLE SÉRIE

STATISTIQUE DU MOUVEMENT DE LA POPULATION, PENDANT L'ANNÉE . . .
See Greece. Genike statistike hyperesia. STATISTIQUE DU MOUVEMENT DE LA POPULATION PENDANT L'ANNÉE . . .

1989 STATISTIQUE INTERNATIONALE DES GRANDES VILLES. INTERNATIONAL STATISTICS OF LARGE TOWNS. SERIES A-B-C-D-E. 1954–1970. La Haye.
Issued by the Institut International de Statistique. In five parts, each with separate title page and separate pagination: A. Population; B. Lodgement; C. Données économiques; D. Services Publiques; E. Statistique culturelle et des sports. In English and French.

STATISTIQUES DÉMOGRAPHIQUES
See Belgium. Institut National de Statistique. STATISTIQUES SOCIALES

STATISTIQUES DÉMOGRAPHIQUES
See Portugal. Instituto Nacional de Estatistica. STATISTIQUES DÉMOGRAPHIQUES

STATISTIQUES SOCIALES: ANNUAIRE
See SOZIALSTATISTIK; JAHRBUCH

1990 STOCKHOLM STUDIES IN SOCIOLOGY. 1–3, 1956–1965. Stockholm, Almqvist & Wiksell. Irreg.
Issued by the University of Stockholm. Subseries of: *Acta Universitatis Stockholmiensis*.
Monograph series.

STRATIFICAZIONE E CLASSI SOCIALI IN ITALIA
See Fondazione Giovanni Agnelli. Progetto Stratificazione e Classi Sociali in Italia. QUADERNI DI RICERCHE DEL PROGETTO STRATIFICAZIONE E CLASSI SOCIALI IN ITALIA DELLA FONDAZIONE GIOVANNI AGNELLI

1991 STRUCTURES SOCIALES ET INSTITUTIONELLES DE L'AFRIQUE. 1– , 1972– . Paris, Éditions Klinsieck. Irreg.
Issued by the Federal University of Cameroun.
Monograph series.

1992 STUDI DI ECONOMIA E SOCIOLOGIA URBANA. 1966– . Torino, Editore Boringhieri. Irreg.
In Italian.
Monograph series.

1993 STUDI DI SOCIOLOGIA. v.1– , Jan/Mar. 1963– . Milano, Vita e Pensiero. Quarterly.
Issued by the Università Cattolica del Sacro Cuore. In Italian, French and English; summaries in English, French and Italian. Indexes: v.1–5, 1963–67, in v.6.
Indexed: Afr. Abstr.; Bull. sig. soc. eth.; Int. Bibl. Soc.

1994 STUDI DI SOCIOLOGIA DEL DIRITTO. 1– , 1974?– . Milano, A. Giuffre. Irreg.
Issued by the Istituto de Filosofia e Sociologia del Diritto, Facolta di Jurisprudenza, Università di Milano. In Italian.
Monograph series.

1995 STUDI DI SOCIOLOGIA DELLA RELIGIONE. 1– , 1967– . Roma.
Issued by the Centro Internazionale di Studi Umanisti. In Italian.

1996 STUDI E RICERCHE DI SOCIOLOGIA DELL'ARTE E DELLA LETTERATURA. 1– , 1974– . Pisa. Irreg.
In Italian.

1997 STUDI E RICERCHE SOCIOLOGICHE. 1976– . Milano, Franco Angeli Editore. Irreg.
In Italian.
Monograph series.

1998 STUDI EMIGRAZIONE. ÉTUDES MIGRATIONS. v.1– , Oct. 1963– . Roma, Morcelliana Editrice. Three issues a year.
Issued by the Centro Studi Emigrazione. In English, French, German, Italian and Spanish. Summaries in English and French.
Indexed: Int. Bibl. Soc.

STUDI SI CERCETĂRI ŞTIINŢIFICE: SERIA 3: ŞTIINŢE SOCIALE
See Academia Republicii Populare Romîne. Filiala Cluj. STUDI ŞI CERCETĂRI ŞTIINŢIFICE: SERIA 3: ŞTINŢE SOCIALE

1999 STUDIA DEMOGRAFICZNE. 1– , 1963– . Warszawa, Państwowe Wydawnictwo Naukowe. Quarterly.

Issued by the Komitet Nauk Demograficznych, Polska Akademia Nauk (Polish Academy of Sciences. Committe on Demography). In Polish. Summaries and table of contents in English and Russian.
Indexed: Int. Bibl. Soc.

2000 STUDIA KRYMINOLOGICZNE, KRYMINALISTYCZNE I PENITENCJARNE. 1974– . Warszawa, Państwowe Wydawnictwo Naukowe. Two issues a year.
Issued by the Instytut Problematyki Przestępczości. In Polish.

2001 STUDIA SOCIOLOGICA. 1, 1969. Bratislava.
Issued by the Sociologický ústav, Slovenska akadémia vied. In Slovak.

2002 STUDIA SOCIOLOGICA. 1– , 1968?–. Praha.
Issued by the Univerzita Karlova. Subseries of *Acta Universitatis Carolinae. Philosophica et Historica*. Other title: *Sociologica*. In Czech; summaries in English, German and Russian.

2003 STUDIA SOCIOLOGICA UPPSALIENSIA. 1– , 1962– . Uppsala. Irreg.
Issued by the University of Uppsala. Subseries of: *Acta Universitatis Uppsaliensis*. In Swedish.
Monograph series.

2004 STUDIA SOCJOLOGICZNE. no.1– , 1961– . Warszawa, Państwowe Wydawnictwo Naukowe. Quarterly.
Issued by the Instytut Filozofii i Socjologii, Polska Akademia Nauk. In Polish; table of contents and summaries also in English and Russian.
Indexed: Bull. sig. soc. eth.; Int. Bibl. Soc.; Psych. Abstr.; Soc. Abstr.

2005 STUDIA SOCJOLOGICZNO-POLITYCZNE. 1–24, 1956–1967? Warszawa, Państwowe Wydawnictwo Naukowe. Irreg.
In Polish; table of contents and summaries also in English and Russian.
Indexed: Int. Pol. Sc. Abstr.; Soc. Abstr.

STUDIA UNIVERSITATIS BABES-BOLYAI. SOCIOLOGIA
See Cluj. Universitatea. Biblioteca Centrala Universitara. STUDIA UNIVERSITATIS BABES-BOLYAI. SOCIOLOGIA

2006 STUDIA Z SOCJOLOGII MLODZIEŻY I WYCHOWANIA. 1– , 1973– . Kraków, Państwowe Wydawnictwo Naukowe. Irreg.
Issued by the Uniwersytet Jagielloński. In Polish; summaries in English and Russian. Subseries of the University's *Zeszyty Naukowe. Prace Socjologiczne*.

STUDIEN UND BERICHTE
See Tübingen. Universität. Soziologisches Seminar. STUDIEN UND BERICHTE

2007 STUDIEN ZUM WANDEL VON GESELLSCHAFT UND BILDUNG IM 19. JAHRHUNDERT. v.1– , 1971– . Göttingen, Vandenhoeck & Ruprecht. Irreg.
Monograph series.

2008 STUDIEN ZUR MASSENKOMMUNIKATION. 1– , 1966– . Hamburg, Verlag Hans Bredow-Institut. Irreg.
Monograph series.

2009 STUDIEN ZUR SOZIOLOGIE. 1–3, 1948–1949. Mainz, Internationale Universum Verlag. Irreg.
Monograph series.

2010 STUDIEN ZUR SOZIOLOGIE. v.1– , 1963– . München, R. Piper & Co. Verlag. Irreg.
Monograph series.

2011 STUDIEN ZUR SOZIOLOGIE DER REVOLUTION. 1– , 1961– . Berlin, Dietrich Reimer Verlag. Irreg.
Monograph series.

2012 STUDIEN ZUR SOZIOLOGIE DES BILDUNGSWESENS. v.1– , 197 – . Weinheim und Basel, Beltz Verlag. Irreg.
Issued by the Deutsches Institut für Internationale Pädagogische Forschung. Some volumes in translation.

STUDIES
See Canada. Royal Commission on Bilingualism and Biculturalism. STUDIES

2013 STUDIES AND DOCUMENTS ON IMMIGRATION AND INTEGRATION IN CANADA. no.1–12, May 1962–1970. Montreal. Quarterly.
Issued by the Jewish Immigrant Aid Services in Canada.

STUDIES EN DOKUMENTATION
See Belgium. Ministère de la Santé Publique et de la Famille. Centre d'Études de la Population et de la Famille. STUDIES EN DOKUMENTATION

2014 STUDIES IN COMPARATIVE INTERNATIONAL DEVELOPMENT. v.1– , 1965– . New Brunswick, N.J., Transaction Periodicals Consortium. Three issues a year.
Issued by the Rutgers University.
Indexed: Bull. sig. soc. eth.; Int. Bibl. Soc.; Int. Pol. Sc. Abstr.; PAIS; Soc. Abstr.

2015 STUDIES IN DEMOGRAPHY. no.1– , 1973– . Bombay, Tata McGraw-Hill Publishing Co. Irreg.
Monograph series; some works in revised editions.

STUDIES IN DEMOGRAPHY
See Demographic Research Centre, Kerala. STUDIES IN DEMOGRAPHY

STUDIES IN DEVELOPMENT
See Indiana. University. International Development Research Center. STUDIES IN DEVELOPMENT

2016 STUDIES IN EUROPEAN SOCIETY, 1– , July 1973– . The Hague, Mouton. Irreg.
Monograph series.

STUDIES IN FAMILY PLANNING
See Population Council, New York. STUDIES IN FAMILY PLANNING

2017 STUDIES IN HUMAN ECOLOGY. 1– , 1973– . Warsaw. Irreg.
Issued by the Instytut Ekologii, Polska Akademia Nauk. In English; summaries in Polish.

2018 STUDIES IN PEACEFUL CHANGE, no.1–2, 1968. London, London University Press. Irreg.
Monograph series. Continued as unnumbered series.

2019 STUDIES IN POLITICAL AND SOCIAL PROCESSES. no.1– , 1977– . Washington, D.C.
Issued by the American Enterprise Institute for Public Policy Research.

2020 STUDIES IN POPULATION AND URBAN GEOGRAPHY. 1– , 1975– . Westport, Conn., Greenwood Press. Irreg.
Issued by the International Population and Urban Research, University of California at Berkeley.

2021 STUDIES IN PUBLIC COMMUNICATION. no.1–4, summer 1957–autumn 1962. Chicago, The University of Chicago Press.
Issued by the Committee on Communication, the University of Chicago.

2022 STUDIES IN PUBLIC POLICY. no.1– , 1977– . Glasgow. Irreg.
Issued by the Centre for the Study of Public Policy, University of Strathclyde.
Series of papers. Processed.

2023 STUDIES IN RACE AND NATIONS. v.1–6, no.3, 1969/1970–1975. Denver, Colo. Quarterly.
Issued by the Center of International Race Relations, University of Denver. Each issue is thematic.

2024 STUDIES IN SEX AND SOCIETY. 1– , 1966– . New York, Basic Books. Irreg.
Issued by the Institute for Sex Research, Indiana University.

2025 STUDIES IN SOCIAL ANTHROPOLOGY. v.1– , 1966– . The Hague, Mouton. Irreg.
Monograph series.

2026 STUDIES IN SOCIAL LIFE. 1– , 1953– . The Hague, Nijhoff. Irreg.
Monograph series.
Indexed: SSCI

2027 STUDIES IN SOCIAL POLICY. no.1– , 1977– . Glasgow. Irreg.
Issued by the Centre for the Study of Public Policy, University of Strathclyde.
Series of papers.

2028 STUDIES IN SOCIETY. 1– , 1978– . Melbourne, Sydney, Allen & Unwin. Irreg.
Supersedes: New South Wales. University, Kensington. School of Sociology. *Studies in Sociology*.

STUDIES IN SOCIETY
See Oslo. Universitet. Institutt för Sosiologi. STUDIES IN SOCIETY

2029 STUDIES IN SOCIOLOGY. v.1–4, June 1936–1939/1940. Dallas, Tex.
Issued by the Department of Sociology, Southern Methodist University.

2030 STUDIES IN SOCIOLOGY. 1– , 1977– . London, George Allen & Unwin. Irreg.
Monograph series; some works in second editions.

2031 STUDIES IN SOCIOLOGY. no.1– , 1967– . New York, Praeger; subsequently International Publications Service. Irreg.
Monograph series.

2032 STUDIES IN SOCIOLOGY. [1]– , 1969– . Jaipur, India. Irreg.
Issued by the University of Rajasthan.
Monograph series.

2033 STUDIES IN SOCIOLOGY. 1– , 1971– . Delhi, Hindustan Publishing Co. Irreg.
Issued by the Asian Research Centre, Institute of Economic Growth. Title varies: v.1–2, 1971–1974, *Studies in Asian Social Development*.

2034 STUDIES IN SOCIOLOGY. 1– , 1972– . Manchester, Manchester University Press. Irreg.
Monograph series.

STUDIES IN SOCIOLOGY
See Catholic University of America. STUDIES IN SOCIOLOGY

STUDIES IN SOCIOLOGY
See Colorado. University. STUDIES. SERIES D. STUDIES IN SOCIOLOGY

STUDIES IN SOCIOLOGY
See ESTUDIOS DE SOCIOLOGIA

STUDIES IN SOCIOLOGY
See New South Wales. University, Kensington. School of Sociology. STUDIES IN SOCIOLOGY

STUDIES IN SOCIOLOGY
See Oregon. University. UNIVERSITY OF OREGON MONOGRAPHS. STUDIES IN SOCIOLOGY

STUDIES IN SOCIOLOGY
See RANDOM HOUSE STUDIES IN SOCIOLOGY

STUDIES IN SOCIOLOGY, ECONOMICS, POLITICS AND HISTORY
See Iowa. University. STUDIES IN THE SOCIAL SCIENCES

STUDIES IN SOCIOLOGY; SOCIOLOGICAL MONOGRAPHS
See SOCIOLOGY AND SOCIAL RESEARCH

2035 STUDIES IN SOVIET SOCIETY. v.1–2, 1966–1969. London, Tavistock Publications. Irreg.
Monograph series.

2036 STUDIES IN SYMBOLIC INTERACTION. v.1– , 1978– . Greenwich, Conn., JAI Press. Annual.

STUDIES IN THE SOCIAL SCIENCES
See Iowa. University. STUDIES IN THE SOCIAL SCIENCES

2037 STUDIES IN THE STRUCTURE OF POWER; DECISION-MAKING IN CANADA. 1–5, 1964–1972. Toronto, University of Toronto Press. Irreg.
Monograph series.

2038 STUDIES IN THE THIRD WORLD SOCIETIES. no.1– , 1976– . Williamsburg, Va., Bosell Print and Publ. Co. Quarterly.
Issued by the Department of Anthropology, College of William and Mary.

STUDIES IN THE UTILIZATION OF BEHAVIORAL SCIENCE
See Stanford University. Institute for Communication Research. STUDIES IN THE UTILIZATION OF BEHAVIORAL SCIENCE

STUDIES IN URBAN CHANGE. REPORT
See Emory University, Atlanta. Center for Research in Social Change. STUDIES IN URBAN CHANGE

STUDIES OF ANTI-SOCIAL BEHAVIOR
See ACTA CRIMINOLOGICA

STUDIES OF THE CITY
See YALE STUDIES OF THE CITY

2039 STUDIES ON SOCIETY IN CHANGE. no.1– , 1975– . New York, distributed by the Columbia University Press.
Issued by the Department of History, Brooklyn College.
Monograph series.

STUDIES ON SOCIOLOGY
See TILBURG STUDIES IN SOCIOLOGY

STUDIES ON THE FAMILY
See International Seminar on Family Research. RECHERCHES SUR LA FAMILLE

2040 STUDIES ON THE LEFT. v.1–7, no.2, fall 1959–Mar/Apr. 1967. Madison, Wis. Three issues a year, 1959–62; quarterly.
Subtitle reads: 'A journal of research, social theory and review'.
Indexed: Soc. Abstr.

STUDIES. SERIES D. STUDIES IN SOCIOLOGY
See Colorado. University. STUDIES. SERIES D. STUDIES IN SOCIOLOGY

STUDIES. SOCIOLOGY SERIES
See Kansas. Fort Hays State College, Hays. STUDIES. SOCIOLOGY SERIES

THE STUDY OF SOCIOLOGY
See SHAKAIGAKU KENKYU

STUDY ON POPULATION AND TECHNOLOGY. PERCEPTION
See Science Council of Canada. STUDY ON POPULATION AND TECHNOLOGY. PERCEPTION

2041 THE SUBTERRANEAN SOCIOLOGY NEWSLETTER. v.1– , July 1967– . Ann Arbor, Mich. Three issues a year (irreg.).
Issued by the University of Michigan. Processed.

2042 Sucre, Bolivia (City). Universidad Mayor Real y Pontificiade San Francisco Xavier. Instituto de Sociologia Boliviana. REVISTA. July/Dec. 1941–1957? Sucre, Imprenta Universitaria de Sucre. Annual.
In Spanish.

2043 SUDAN JOURNAL OF ECONOMIC AND SOCIAL STUDIES. 1– , summer 1971– . Khartoum, Khartoum University Press. Semi-annual.
Issued by the Faculty of Economic and Social Studies, University of Khartoum.

2044 SUDAN SOCIETY. v.1– , 1962– . Khartoum. Annual.
Issued by the Social Studies Society, and the Faculty of Economic and Social Studies, University of Khartoum. In English and Arabic.
Indexed: Anth. Ind.; Int. Bibl. Soc. Cult. Anth.

SUICIDE
See SUICIDE AND LIFE-THREATENING BEHAVIOR

2045 SUICIDE AND LIFE-THREATENING BEHAVIOR. 1– , spring 1971– . New York, Behavioral Publications. Quarterly.
Issued by the American Association of Suicidiology. Title varies: v.1–4, 1971–74, *Life-Threatening Behavior*. Other title: *Suicide*.
Indexed: Sage Fam. Stud. Abstr.; Soc. Abstr.

2046 DIE SUID-AFRIKAANSE TYDSKRIF VIR SOSIOLOGIE. THE SOUTH AFRICAN JOURNAL OF SOCIOLOGY. no.1– , Nov. 1970– . Pretoria. Semi-annual.
Issued by the South African Sociological Association and the Department of Sociology, University of Pretoria. In English, Afrikaans and Dutch.
Indexed: LLBA; Soc. Abstr.

2047 SUMMATION. v.1– , June 1968– . East Lansing, Mich. Semi-annual.
Issued by the Social Science Research Bureau, Michigan State University.
Indexed: Soc. Abstr.

Sun Yat-Sen University. JOURNAL; SOCIAL SCIENCES
See Guangshou. Zhongshan Daxue Xuebao. CHUNG-SHAN TA HSÜEH HSÜEH PAO; SHE HUI K'O HSÜEH

SUPPLEMENT
See COMPARATIVE STUDIES IN SOCIETY AND HISTORY. SUPPLEMENT

SUPPLEMENT
See CURRENT SOCIOLOGY. SUPPLEMENT

SUPPLEMENT
See JOURNAL OF EXPERIMENTAL & SOCIAL PSYCHOLOGY. SUPPLEMENT

2048 SURVEY; A JOURNAL OF EAST AND WEST STUDIES. no.1– , Jan. 1956– . London, Oxford University Press. Quarterly.
Issued by the Congress for Cultural Freedom, no.1–77, 1956–70; International Association for Cultural Freedom, no.78– . Title varies: no.1–8. Jan–Sep. 1956, *Soviet Culture*; no.9–19, Oct. 1956–Sep. 1957, *Soviet Survey*; no.20/22, Oct–Nov/Dec. 1957, *Survey; An Analysis of Culture Trends in the Soviet Orbit*. No. 78 called also v.16, no.1.
Indexed: Int. Bibl. Soc.; Int. Pol. Sc. Abstr.; Soc. Sc. Ind.; Soc. Abstr.; Urb. Aff. Abstr.

SURVEY; AN ANALYSIS OF CULTURAL TRENDS IN THE SOVIET ORBIT
See SURVEY; A JOURNAL OF EAST & WEST STUDIES

2049 SURVEY OF METROPOLITAN PLANNING. 1966–1968. Albany, N.Y. Annual.
Issued by the Graduate School of Public Affairs, State University of New York.

2050 A SURVEY OF RACE RELATIONS IN SOUTH AFRICA. 1951/1952– . Johannesburg. Annual.
Issued by the South African Institute of Race Relations. Information for the period 1946–50 included in the Institute's *Annual Report*.

2051 Sverdlovsk. Gosudarstvennyi pedagogicheskii institut. SOTSIOLOGICHESKIE PROBLEMY NARODNOGO OBRAZOVANIIA. Sverdlovsk. Irreg.
Subseries of its *Uchenye zapiski*.

2052 Sverdlovsk. Ural'skii gosudarstvennyi universitet. SOTSIOLOGICHESKIE ISSLEDOVANIIA. no.1– , 1966– . Sverdlovsk. Irreg.
Indexed: Soc. Abstr.

2053 Sweden. Statistiska Sentralbyrån. BEFOLKNINGS FÖRÄNDRINGAR. 1967– . Stockholm. Annual.
Subseries of its *Sveriges officiella Statistik*.

2054 Switzerland. Statistisches Amt. BEVÖLKERUNGSBEWEGUNG IN DER SCHWEITZ. MOUVEMENT DE LA POPULATION EN SUISSE. Bern.
Subseries of its *Statistische Quellenwerke der Schweitz*.

2055 SYMBOLIC INTERACTION. 1– , fall 1977– . Minneapolis, ISSS Press. Quarterly, semi-annual, 1981– .
Issued by the Society for the Study of Symbolic Interaction (ISSS).

2056 SYNTHESE. v.1–2, 1956–1957. Köln, Westdeutscher Verlag.
Subtitle reads: 'Gesellschaft und Wirtschaft, Geist und Kultur'.
Indexed: Int. Bibl. Soc.; Soc. Abstr.

2057 Syracuse University. Youth Development Center. DELINQUENCY PROFILE OF SYRACUSE AND ONANDAGA COUNTY, N.Y. 1957/1958– . Syracuse, N.Y.

2058 SZOCIOLÓGIA. 1972– . Budapest.
Issued by the Szociológiai Bizottságának Folyóirata, Magyar Tudományos Akadémia. Table of contents in Hungarian, English and Russian; summaries in English and Russian.
Indexed: Bull. sig. soc. eth.; Int. Bibl. Soc.

2059 SZOCIOLÓGIAI INFORMÁCIÓ. 1972– . Budapest, Fövárosi Szabó Ervin Könyvtár. Four issues a year.
In Hungarian.

2060 SZOCIOLÓGIAI TANULMÁNYOK. no.1– , 1966– . Budapest, Akadémiai Kiadó. Irreg.
Issued by the Magyar Tudományos Akadémia. In Hungarian.
Monograph series.

2061 SZOCIOLÓGICA. 1– , 1974– . Szeged, Az MTA Szociológiai Bizotságának Folyórata. Four issues a year.
Issued by the Central Library, Attila Jozsef University at Szeged. In Hungarian.
Indexed: Soc. Abstr.

2062 T.D.I. TEORIA, DEBATE E INFORMAÇÃO. Apr. 1976– . Belém.
Issued by the Asociação Regional dos Sociologos (A.R.S.). In Portuguese.

TESG
See TIJDSCHRIFT VOOR ECONOMISCH EN SOCIALE GEOGRAFIE

TABULATION OF RESULTS
See Institute of Student Opinion. INSTITUTE OF STUDENT OPINION POLL.

2063 TAIWAN DEMOGRAPHIC FACT BOOK. 1963– . Taichung, Taiwan
Issued by the Department of Civil Affairs. In Chinese and English.

TAIWAN DEMOGRAPHIC QUARTERLY
See China (Republic of China — Nei sheng pu). CHUNG-HUA MIN K'UO T'AI-WAN JEN K'OU T'UNG CHI CHI K'AN

2064 T'ai-wan ta Hsüeh, T'ai-pei. T'AI-WAN TA HSÜEH SHE HUI HSÜEH K'AN. 1– , Dec. 1963– . Taipei. Annual.
Title in English: *National Taiwan University Journal of Sociology*. Supplements accompany some issues. In Chinese and English.

TANY MALAGASY
See TERRE MALGACHE

2065 TÁRSADALOMTUDOMÁNY. v.1–24, 1929–1944. Budapest. Társadalomtudományi Társulat. Quarterly.
In Hungarian.

2066 TÁRSADALOMTUDOMÁNYI KÖZLEMÉNYEK. 1st– , Oct. 1971– . Budapest, Társadalomtudományi Intézet.
Issued by the Institute of Sociology. In Hungarian.

2067 Tartu. Ülikool. Sotsioloogia Laboratorium. TRUDY PO SOTSIOLOGII. 2– , 1972– . Tartu.
In Estonian and Russian.

2068 TEACHING SOCIOLOGY. v.1– , 1973– . Beverly Hills, Calif., Sage Publications. Quarterly.
Indexed: Curr. Cont.; SSCI; Sage Fam. Stud. Abstr.; Soc. Abstr.

TECHNICAL BULLETIN
See Michigan. State University, East Lansing. Institute for Community Development and Services. TECHNICAL BULLETIN

TECHNICAL REPORT
See Michigan. State University, East Lansing. Department of Communication. DIFFUSION OF INNOVATIONS IN RURAL SOCIETIES. TECHNICAL REPORT

TECHNOLOGICAL FORECASTING
See TECHNOLOGICAL FORECASTING AND SOCIAL CHANGE

2069 TECHNOLOGICAL FORECASTING AND SOCIAL CHANGE. v.1– , June 1969– . New York, American Elsevier Publishing Co. Quarterly.
Title varies: 1969–70, *Technological Forecasting*.
Indexed: Int. Bibl. Soc.; Int. Pol. Sc. Abstr.

2070 TECHNOLOGY AND CULTURE. v.1– , winter 1959– . Detroit; subsequently Chicago, The University of Chicago Press. Quarterly.
Issued by the Society for the History of Technology and the Case Institute of Technology. Includes 'Current Bibliography in the History of Technology', an annual section arranged by historical periods and in subject groups.
Indexed: Abstr. Anth.; Soc. Abstr.; Wom. Stud. Abstr.

2071 TECHNOLOGY AND DEMOCRATIC SOCIETY. 1– , 1967– . Assen, Van Gorcum, and London, Tavistock Publications. Irreg.
Monograph series.

2072 TECHNOLOGY AND SOCIETY. New York, Institute of Electrical and Electronic Engineers.
Issued by the Committee on Social Implications of Technology, Institute of Electrical and Electronic Engineers. Other title: *IEEE Technology and Society*. Continues: *IEEE Newsletter*.

2073 TELOS; A QUARTERLY JOURNAL OF RADICAL SOCIAL THEORY. no.1– , spring 1968– . St. Louis, Mo.
Issued by the Department of Sociology, Washington University.
Indexed: Soc. Abstr.

2074 TEMAS SOCIALES. no.1–5, Sep/Oct. 1968–Mar. 1970. La Paz. Monthly.
Issued by the Sección Sociologia, Faculdad de Derecho, Ciencias Politicas y Sociales, Universidad Mayor de San Andres. In Spanish.
Indexed: Int. Bibl. Soc.

2075 TERRE MALGACHE. TANY MALAGASY. v.1–16, 1966–1974. Tananarive, Hachette. Semi-annual.
Issued by the École Nationale Supérieure Agronomique, Université de Madagascar. In French.
Indexed: Bull. sig. soc. eth.; Int. Bibl. Soc.

2076 TERROR AND SOCIETY. 1, 1969. New York, Oxford University Press. One volume published.
Monograph series.

2077 TERRORISM. 1– , Sep. 1977– . New York, Crane, Russak & Co. Quarterly.
Issued by the State University of New York at Oneonta.
Indexed: Soc. Abstr.

2078 Texas. Agricultural and Technical University. Department of Agricultural Economics and Sociology. DEPARTMENTAL TECHNICAL REPORT. no.1– , 1957– . College Station, Tex. Irreg.
Series of papers. Processed.

2079 Texas. University. Bureau of International Business Research. POPULATION SERIES. no.1– , 1964– . Austin, Tex. Irreg.
Monograph series.

2080 Texas. University. Bureau of International Business Research. Population Research Center. INTERNATIONAL CENSUS BIBLIOGRAPHY. no.1–6, 1965–1967. Austin, Tex.
Continued by its *Supplement*, listed separately.

2082 TEXTES DE SOCIOLOGIE, D'ANTHROPOLOGIE ET DE PSYCHOLOGIE SOCIALE. 1– . , 1970– . Paris, Librarie Droz. Irreg.
Monograph series.

LES TEXTES SOCIOLOGIQUES
See Paris. École Pratique des Hautes Études. 6e Section des Sciences Économiques et Sociales. LES TEXTES SOCIOLOGIQUES

2081 Texas. University. Bureau of International Business Research. Population Research Center. INTERNATIONAL CENSUS BIBLIOGRAPHY. SUPPLEMENT. 1968– . Austin, Tex.
Continues the Bureau's *International Census Bibliography* and lists current general population censuses.

2083 TEXTOS BRASILEIROS DO SOCIOLOGIA. 1– , 1957– . Rio de Janeiro. Irreg. Ceased publication.
Issued by the Instituto Superior de Estudos Brasileiros. In Portuguese.

TEXTOS DO SOCIOLOGIA
See Rio de Janeiro. Universidad do Brasil. Instituto de Ciências Sociais. TEXTOS DO SOCIOLOGIA

2084 THEORIES OF CONTEMPORARY CULTURE. 1– , 1977– . Milwaukee, Wis. Irreg.
Issued by the Center for Twentieth Century Studies, University of Wisconsin at Milwaukee.

2085 THEORY AND DECISION. v.1– , Oct. 1970– . Dordrecht, Reidel Publishing Co. Four issues a year.
Subtitle reads: 'An international journal for philosophy and methodology of the social sciences'.
Indexed: Bull. sig. soc. eth.; Int. Pol. Sc. Abstr.; Soc. Abstr.

2086 THEORY AND SOCIETY. v.1– , 1974– . Amsterdam, Elsevier Scientific Publishing Co. Quarterly.
Indexed: Int. Bibl. Soc.; Soc. Abstr.

2087 THIRD WORLD REVIEW. 1–4, no.2, 1974–fall 1978. Courtland, N.Y. Semi-annual.
Issued by the Department of Sociology — Anthropology, State University of New York at Courtland.

2088 TIERS-MONDE; CROISSANCE — DÉVELOPPEMENT — PROGRÈS. v.1– , Jan/June 1960– . Paris, Presses Universitaires de France. Quarterly.

Issued by the Institut d'Étude du Développement Économique et Sociale, Université de Paris. Title on cover: *Revue Tiers-Monde*. Table of contents in English, French, German, Russian and Spanish.
Indexed: Int. Bibl. Soc.; Int. Pol. Sc. Abstr.

2089 TIJDSCHRIFT VOOR ECONOMIE EN SOCIOLOGIE. May 1935–1939? Ghent.
Issued by the Vereeniging voor Economische Wetenschappen. In Flemish.

2090 TIJDSCHRIFT VOOR ECONOMISCHE EN SOCIALE GEOGRAFIE. JOURNAL OF ECONOMIC AND SOCIAL GEOGRAPHY. 1– , Jan. 15, 1910– . Rotterdam, Van Waesberge, Heregewerff & Richards. Monthly.
Issued by the Nederlandse Vereeniging voor Economische en Sociale Geografie (called earlier Nederlandse Vereeniging voor Economische Geografie); subsequently by the Koninklijk Nederlands Aardrijskundig Genootschap. Title varies: 1910–Feb/Mar. 1948, *Tijdschrift voor Economische Geografie*. Title in other languages: *Netherlands Journal of Economic and Social Geography; Revue Nederlandaise de Géographie Économique et Sociale; Zeitschrift für Wirtschafts- und Sozialgeographie; Revista Hollandesa de Geografia Económica y Social*. In Dutch and English.
Indexes: v.1–25, 1910–34, in v.25.
Indexed: Soc. Abstr.

TIJDSCHRIFT VOOR ECONOMISCHE GEOGRAFIE
See TIJDSCHRIFT VOOR ECONOMISCHE EN SOCIALE GEOGRAFIE

2091 TIJDSCHRIFT VOOR OPVOEDKUNDE. v.1– , 1909– . Nijmegen, Standaard Boekhandel. Bimonthly.
Title varies: 1909–19, *Vlasms Opvoekundig Tijdschrift;* 1919–55, *Tijdschrift voor Zielkunde en Opvoedingsleer*. In Dutch.
Indexed: Soc. Abstr.

2092 TIJDSCHRIFT VOOR SOCIALE WETENSCHAPPEN. v.1– , June 1956– . Ghent. Quarterly.
Issued by the Studie-en-Onderzoekcentrum voor Sociale Wetenschappen, Rijksuniversiteit, Ghent. In Flemish.
Indexed: Bull. sig. soc. eth.; Int. Bibl. Soc.; Soc. Abstr.

TIJDSCHRIFT VOOR ZIELKUNDE EN OPVOEDINGSLEER
See TIJDSCHRIFT VOOR OPVOEDKUNDE

2093 TILBURG STUDIES IN SOCIOLOGY. v.1– , 1973– . Tilburg, Universitaire Pers Tilburg. Irreg.
Issued by the Institute of Labor Studies, Tilburg School of Economics, Social Sciences and Law. Other title: *Studies on Sociology*. In English and Dutch.
Monograph series. Some works are translations into Dutch.

2094 TINERETUL ŞI LUMEA DE MÎINE. SERIA A: SOCIOLOGIA TINERETULUI. 1– , 1970– . Bucureşti, Editura Academiei Republicii Socialiste România. Irreg.
Issued by the Centrul de Cercetări pentru Problemele Tineretului, Academia Republicii Socialiste România. In Rumanian; summaries in English, French, German and Russian.
Monograph series.

2095 Tōkyō Daigaku. SHAKAI KAGAKU KENKYŪJO. ANNALS. no.1– , 1953– . Tokyo.
Issued by the Institute of Social Science, University of Tokyo. Title varies: no.1–6, *Social Science Abstracts*. In English.

2096 TOKYO GAKUGEI DAIGAKU KENKYU HOKOKU. Ser.1–17, Nov. 1949–Mar. 1966. Tokyo. Annual.
Issued by the Tokyo University. Subseries of the University's *Bulletin*. Continued by: *Tōkyō Gakukei Daigaku Kiyō dai 3-bumon Shakai Kagaku*. In Japanese.

2097 TOKYO GAKUKEI DAIGAKU KIYO DAI 3-BUMON SHAKAI KAGAKU. ser.18– , Nov. 1966– . Tokyo. Annual.
Issued by the University of Tokyo. Continues: *Tōkyō Gakukei Daigaku Kenkyū Hōkoku*. In Japanese.

2098 TOKYO JOSHI DAIGAKU SHAKAI GAKKAI KIYO-KEIZAI TO SHAKAI. no.1– , Oct. 1965– . Tokyo. Annual.
Issued by the Tokyo Women's University Sociological Society. In Japanese.

2099 TOOLS AND METHODS OF COMPARATIVE RESEARCH. no.1–3, 1964–1966. New Haven, Conn., Yale University Press. Irreg.
Issued by the International Social Science Committee and International Committee for Social Science Documentation. Includes proceedings of conferences.

2100 Toronto. Bureau of Municipal Research. CENTENNIAL STUDY AND TRAINING PROGRAMME ON METROPOLITAN PROBLEMS. PAPER. no.1–11, 1967. Toronto. Irreg.
Series of papers.

2101 Toronto. University. Centre for Urban and Community Studies. BIBLIOGRAPHIC SERIES. no.1– , Jan. 1969– . Toronto. Irreg.
Monograph series. Processed.

2102 Toronto. University. Centre for Urban and Community Studies. RESEARCH PAPER. no.1– , Sep. 1968– . Toronto. Irreg.
Includes subseries: *Component Study*.
Series of papers. Processed.

2103 Toronto. University. Institute for the Quantitative Analysis of Social and Economic Policy. POLICY PAPER SERIES. no.1– , 1968– . Toronto. Irreg.
Series of papers.

2104 Toronto. University. Institute for the Quantitative Analysis of Social and Economic Policy. WORKING PAPER. 1–12, Dec. 1951–1964; [n.s.]1– , 1965– . Toronto. Irreg.
Series of papers.

2105 TÖRTÉNETI DEMOGRÁFIAI TANULMÁNYOK. 1–2, 1966–1968. Budapest.
Subseries of: *Nepeszegtudományi Kutató Intézet Közleményi.* In English, French and German.
Monograph series.

TRABAJOS E INVESTIGACIÓNES
See Rosario, Argentina. Universidad Nacional del Litoral. Instituto de Sociologia de Educación, Paraná. TRABAJOS E INVESTIGACIÓNES

TRABAJOS E INVESTIGACIÓNES. PUBLICACIÓN INTERNA
See Buenos Aires. Universidad Nacional Autonoma. Instituto de Sociologia. TRABAJOS E INVESTIGACIÓNES. PUBLICACIÓN INTERNA

2106 TRANS-ACTION. v.1–9, no.3, Nov. 1963–Jan. 1972. St. Louis; subsequently Fulton, Mo.
Issued by the Community Leadership Project, Washington University. Subtitle reads: 'Social science and modern society'. Continued by: *Society*.
Indexed: Soc. Abstr.; Urb. Aff. Abstr.

2107 TRANSACTION STUDIES IN SOCIAL POLICY. SP. 1– , 1971– . New Brunswick, N.J., Transaction Books. Irreg.
Monograph series; some volumes are collections of papers delivered at conferences.

TRANSACTIONS
See AMERICAN ANTHROPOLOGIST

TRANSACTIONS
See Westermarck Society. TRANSACTIONS

TRANSACTIONS
See World Congress of Sociology. TRANSACTIONS

2108 TRANSFORMATION; THEORY AND PRACTICE OF SOCIAL CHANGE. v.1– , 1972– . Toronto, Transformation Publishers. Six issues a year.

2109 TRANSITION. 1– , 1978– . Turkeyen, Georgetown. Two issues a year.
Issued by the Faculty of Social Sciences, University of Guyana.
Indexed: Soc. Abstr.

TRAVAUX
See Brussels. Université Libre. Institut de Sociologie. Centre de Sociologie du Travail. TRAVAUX

TRAVAUX
See Instituts Solvay. Institut de Sociologie. TRAVAUX

TRAVAUX
See Liège. Université. Institut de Sociologie. TRAVAUX

TRAVAUX DES GROUPES D'ÉTUDES DE LA RECONSTRUCTION NATIONALE
See Instituts Solvay. Institut de Sociologie. TRAVAUX DES GROUPES D'ÉTUDES DE LA RECONSTRUCTION NATIONALE

TRAVAUX DU GROUPE D'ETHNOLOGIE SOCIALE
See FAMILLE ET HABITATION

TRAVAUX ET DOCUMENTS
See Centre d'Études Sociologiques. TRAVAUX ET DOCUMENTS

TRAVAUX ET DOCUMENTS
See France. Centre Nationale de la Recherche Scientifique. Centre d'Études Sociologiques. TRAVAUX ET DOCUMENTS

TRAVAUX ET DOCUMENTS. CAHIERS
See France. Institut Nationale d'Études Démographiques. TRAVAUX ET DOCUMENTS. CAHIERS

TRAVAUX SOCIOLOGIQUES
See SOZIOLOGISCHE ARBEITEN

2110 Trinidad and Tobago. Central Statistical Office. ESTIMATED INTERNAL MIGRATION BULLETIN. 1– , 1973– . Port of Spain.
Subseries of its *Continuous Sample of Survey of Population*. In Spanish.

TROPICAL HOUSING AND PLANNING MONTHLY BULLETIN
See EKISTICS

TRUDY KAFEDR OBSHCHESTVENNYKH NAUK
See Barnaul. Barnaul'skii gosudarstvennyi pedagogicheskii institut. TRUDY KAFEDR OBSHCHESTVENNYKH NAUK

TRUDY PO SOTSIOLOGII
See Tartu. Ülikool. Sotsioloogia Laboratorium. TRUDY PO SOTSIOLOGII

TRUDY. SERIIA A. OBSHCHESTVENNYE NAUKI
See Lietuvos Mokslu Akademija, Vilnius. TRUDY. SERIIA A: OBSHCHESTVENNYE NAUKI

2111 Tucumán, Argentina. Universidad. Instituto de Sociografia y Planeación. CUADERNOS DE SOCIOGRAFIA Y PLANEACIÓN. 1– , 1951– . Tucumán.
Subseries of its *Publicaciónes*. In Spanish; summaries in English.

TUDOMÁNUOK OSZTÁLYÁNAK KÖZLEMÉNYI
See Magyar Tudományos Akadémia. Társadalmitörténeti. TUDOMÁNYOK OSZTÁLYÁNAK KÖZLEMÉNYI

2112 Tudományos Ismeretterjesztö Társulat. VÁLÓSAG. v.1– , 1958– . Budapest, Gondalat Könyv-Lapkiadó es Terjesztö Vállalat. Monthly.
In Hungarian.
Indexed: LLBA; Soc. Abstr.

2113 TUNG WU CHENG CHIH SHE HUI HSÜEH HUI HSÜEH PAO. no.1– , 1977– . Taipei. Annual.
Issued by the Tung Wu ta hsüeh. In Chinese and English. Other title: *Soochow Journal of Social & Political Sciences.*

2114 Tunis. Centre d'Études et de Recherches Économiques et Sociales. Al-Jāmi'ah al-Tūnisīyah. CAHIERS DU C.E.R.E.S. SÉRIE DÉMOGRAPHIQUE. no.1– , June 1967– . Tunis.

TUTKIMUKSIA. RESEARCH REPORTS
See Helsinki. Yliopisto. Sociologian Laitos. TUTKIMUKSIA. RESEARCH REPORTS

2115 Tübingen. Universität. Max Weber Institut. VERÖFFENTLICHUNGEN. 1– , 1967– . Tübingen, J.C.B. Mohr (Paul Siebeck). Irreg.
Monograph series.

2116 Tübingen. Universität. Soziologisches Seminar. STUDIEN UND BERICHTE AUS DEM SOZIOLOGISCHEN SEMINAR DER UNIVERSITÄT TÜBINGEN. STUDIEN. v.1– , 1963– . Tübingen. Irreg.

2117 TYDSKRIF VIR MAATSKAPLIKE NAVORSING. JOURNAL FOR SOCIAL RESEARCH. v.1– , July 1950– . Pretoria. Semiannual.
Issued by the Departement van Onderwys, Kuns en Wetensap, Nasionale Raad vir Sociale Navorsing. In English and Afrikaans. In v.1–3, no.1, title in English preceded by title in Afrikaans; subsequently title positions reversed, volume by volume.

2118 TYDSKRIF VIR RASSE-AANGELEENTHEDE. JOURNAL OF RACIAL AFFAIRS. v.1– , 1949– . Pretoria. Quarterly.
Issued by the Suid-Afrikaanse Buro vir Rasse-Aangeleenthede. In English and Afrikaans.

UCHENYE ZAPISKI
See Irkutsk, Siberia. Irkutskii gosudarstvennyi pedagogicheskii institut inostrannykh iazykov. Kafedra istorii KPSS i politicheskoi ekonomii. UCHENYE ZAPISKI

UCHENYE ZAPISKI
See Leningrad. Universitet. Nauchno-issledovatel'skii institut kompleksnykh sotsiologicheskih issledovanii. UCHENYE ZAPISKI

UCHENYE ZAPISKI
See PROBLEMY SOTSIAL'NYKH ISSLEDOVANII

UCHENYE ZAPISKI
See Sverdlovsk. Gosudarstvennyi pedagogicheskii institut. SOTSIOLOGICHESKIE PROBLEMY NORODNOGO OBRAZOVANIIA

UCHENYE ZAPISKI. SERIIA OBSHCHESTVENNYE NAUKI
See Vladimir, Russia. Vladimirskii pedagogicheskii institut. UCHENYE ZAPISKI. SERIIA OBSHCHESTVENNYE NAUKI

UCHENYE ZAPISKI. SERIIA SOTSIOLOGICHESKAIA. SOTSOLOGIIA VYSHSHEI SHKOLY
See Gorky. Universitet. UCHENYE ZAPISKI. SERIIA STOSTIOLGICHESKAIA. SOTSIOLOGIIA VYSHSHEI SHKOLY

2119 Union of Capitals of the European Community. EUROPA DES CAPITALES. EUROPE OF THE CAPITALS. 1– , 1973– . Bruxelles.
In English, French, Italian, Dutch and German.

UNION'S LIAISON AND INFORMATION BULLETIN
See FAMILLES DANS LE MONDE

UNITAR NEWS
See United Nations. Institute for Training and Research. UNITAR NEWS

UNITAR PS
See United Nations. Institute for Training and Research. UNITAR PS

2120 United Nations. Centro Latinoamericano de Demografia. BOLETIN INFORMATIVO. 1961–1972. Santiago, Chile. Four issues a year.
Superseded by: *Notas de Población*. In Spanish.

2121 United Nations. Department of Economic and Social Affairs. POPULATION BULLETIN. no.1– , Dec. 1951– . New York.
Nos. 1–4 issued by the Department of Social Affairs, Population Division.

2122 United Nations. Department of Economic and Social Affairs. Population Division. POPULATION NEWSLETTER. no.1– , Apr. 1968– . New York. Quarterly.

2123 United Nations. Department of Social Affairs. Population Division. POPULATION STUDIES. no.1– , 1958– . New York.
No.1–20 issued by the Department of Social Affairs, Population Division. No.1 lacks symbol of the United Nations Document. Title varies: no.1–2, *Reports on the Population of Trust Territories*. (United Nations (Document) ST/SOA/SER.A).

2124 United Nations. Economic Commission for Western Asia. POPULATION BULLETIN. no.1– , June 1971– . Beirut. Irreg.
Issues no.1–5, 1971–73 were issued by the U.N.'s Economic and Social Office in Beirut.

2125 United Nations. Economic Commission for Africa. Population Programme Centre. AFRICAN POPULATION NEWSLETTER. v.1– , May 1970 . Addis Ababa.

2126 United Nations. Institute for Training and Research. UNITAR NEWS. v.1– , 1969– . New York.

2127 United Nations. Institute for Training and Research. UNITAR PS. no.1– , 1971– . New York. Irreg.
No.10, 1977, the latest issue published.
Monograph series; some works prepublished in mimeographed form.

2128 United Nations. Regional Centre for Demographic Training and Research in Latin America. BOLETIN DEMOGRAFICO. v.1– , Jan. 1968– . Santiago, Chile. Semi-annual.
In Spanish; table of contents in English and Spanish.

2129 United Nations. Latin American Demographic Center (CELADE). SERIE A. no.1– , 1962– . Santiago, Chile. Irreg.
Early issues issued by the Regional Centre for Demographic Training and Research in Latin America.
In Spanish.

2130 United Nations. Latin American Demographic Center (CELADE). SERIE C. no.1– , 1963– . Santiago, Chile. Irreg.
Early issues issued by the Regional Centre for Demographic Training and Research in Latin America.
No.161, March 1976, the latest issue published. In Spanish.

2131 United Nations. Latin American Demographic Center (CELADE). SERIE D. no.1– , 1962– . Santiago, Chile. Irreg.
Early issues issued by the Regional Centre for Demographic Training and Research in Latin America.
In Spanish. Issued with added designation E/CN CELADE/D.

2132 United Nations. Regional Centre for Demographic Training and Research in Latin America. SERIE G. no.1– , 196 – . Santiago, Chile.
In Spanish.

2133 United Nations Educational, Scientific and Cultural Organization. POPULATION AND CULTURE SERIES. no.1– , 1954– . Paris. Irreg.
Monograph series.

2134 United States. Agency for International Development. RESEARCH AND DEVELOPMENT ABSTRACTS. Jan.1967–Dec.1968. Washington, D.C. Monthly.
Some volumes issued by the Agency's Reference Center, and the Bureau for Technical Assistance under its variant name, Technical Assistance Bureau. Continues: United States. Agency for International Development. Reference Center. *A.I.D. Research Abstracts*.

2135 United States. Bureau of Agricultural Economics. RURAL LIFE STUDIES. 1–6, 1941–1943. Washington, D.C.

2136 United States. Bureau of the Census. CURRENT POPULATION REPORTS; POPULATION ESTIMATES AND PROJECTIONS. SERIES P–26. Washington, D.C.

Subseries of *The Current Population Survey*. Continues the Bureau's *Current Population Reports; Population Estimates; Series P–25*.

2137 United States. Interagency Committee on Population Research. INVENTORY AND ANALYSIS OF FEDERAL POPULATION RESEARCH. 1976/1977– . Washington, D.C. Annual.

Subseries of: *DHEW Publication NIH*. At head of title 1976–77, *Population Sciences*. Supersedes: *Inventory of Federal Population Research* and *Analysis of Population Research Report* issued by the Interagency Committee on Population Research. Prepared by the Interagency Committee on Population Research. Prepared by the Office of Planning and Evaluation, in cooperation with the Center of Population Research, National Institute of Child Health and Human Development.

2138 United States. Joint Publications Research Service. POLITICAL AND SOCIOLOGICAL REPORT ON ALBANIA. 1– , Oct. 4, 1958– . New York. Irreg.

Subseries of its *JPRS/NY*.

2139 United States. Joint Publications Research Service. SELECTED POLITICAL AND SOCIOLOGICAL TRANSLATIONS ON COMMUNIST CHINA. New York. Irreg.

Subseries of its *JPRS–N*.

2140 United States. Joint Publications Research Service. SELECTED POLITICAL AND SOCIOLOGICAL TRANSLATIONS ON EASTERN EUROPE. Dec. 9, 1958– . Washington, D.C. Semi-monthly.

Subseries of its *JPRS/DC*.

2141 United States. Joint Publications Research Service. SOCIOLOGICAL TRANSLATIONS ON EASTERN EUROPE. 1959– . Washington, D.C., Office of Technical Services. Irreg.

Subseries of its *JPRS/DC*.

2142 United States. National Center for Health Statistics. VITAL AND HEALTH STATISTICS. SERIES 14: DATA FROM THE NATIONAL VITAL STATISTICS SYSTEM, DATA ON NATALITY, MARRIAGE AND DIVORCE. Washington, D.C. Irreg.

Monograph series.

2143 United States. National Science Foundation. REVIEW OF DATA ON RESEARCH AND DEVELOPMENT. no.1–44, Dec. 1956–Feb. 1964. Washington, D.C.

Superseded by: *Reviews of Data on Science Resources*, issued by the Foundation's Office of Economic and Manpower Studies.

2144 United States. National Science Foundation. Office of Economic and Power Studies. REVIEWS OF DATA ON SCIENCE RESOURCES. v.1– , Dec. 1964– . Washington, D.C.

Supersedes: *Review of Data on Research & Development* and *Scientific Manpower Bulletin* issued by the National Science Foundation.

2145 United States. National Science Foundation. Office of Special Studies. CURRENT PROJECTS ON ECONOMIC AND SOCIAL IMPLICATIONS OF SCIENCE AND TECHNOLOGY. 1959– . Washington, D.C.

Title varies slightly.

2146 UNIVERSITÀ E SOCIETÀ. 1– , 1974– . Milano. Irreg.

Issued by the Università Cattolica del Sacro Cuore. Subseries of the University's *Pubblicazioni*. In Italian.

UNIVERSITY OF CALIFORNIA PUBLICATIONS IN CULTURE AND SOCIETY
See California. University. UNIVERSITY OF CALIFORNIA PUBLICATIONS IN CULTURE AND SOCIETY

UNIVERSITY OF CALIFORNIA PUBLICATIONS IN SOCIOLOGY
See California. University. UNIVERSITY OF CALIFORNIA PUBLICATIONS IN SOCIOLOGY

UNIVERSITY OF CALIFORNIA PUBLICATIONS IN SOCIOLOGY AND SOCIAL INSTITUTIONS
See California. University. UNIVERSITY OF CALIFORNIA PUBLICATIONS IN SOCIOLOGY AND SOCIAL INSTITUTIONS

2147 University of Cape Town. Centre for African Studies. COMMUNICATIONS. no.1– , 1977– . Cape Town. Irreg.

Supersedes: University of Cape Town. School of African Studies. *Communications*.

2148 University of Cape Town. School of African Studies. COMMUNICATIONS. no.1–37, 1942–1976. Cape Town. Irreg.

Superseded by: University of Cape Town. Centre for African Studies. *Communications*.

THE UNIVERSITY OF MICHIGAN INDEX TO LABOR UNION PERIODICALS
See THE MICHIGAN INDEX TO LABOR UNION PERIODICALS

University of North Wales, Bangor
See Bangor. University of North Wales

UNIVERSITY OF OREGON MONOGRAPHS. STUDIES IN SOCIOLOGY
See Oregon. University. UNIVERSITY OF OREGON MONOGRAPHS. STUDIES IN SOCIOLOGY

University of Rhodesia
See Salisbury, Zimbabwe. University.

UNIVERSITY OF WASHINGTON JOURNAL OF SOCIOLOGY
See Washington (State). University. Department of Sociology. UNIVERSITY OF WASHINGTON JOURNAL OF SOCIOLOGY

University of Zambia
See Zambia. University.

2149 UNTERSUCHUNGEN ÜBER GRUPPEN UND VERBÄNDE. 1– , 1964– . Berlin, Duncker & Humblot. Irreg.
Monograph series.

UNWED MOTHERS
See Florence Crittenton Association of America. UNWED MOTHERS

2150 UOMO E LA SOCIETÀ. 1– , 1969– . Roma, M. Bulzoni. Irreg.
In Italian.
Monograph series.

2151 Uppsala. Universitet. Sociologiska Institutionen. RESEARCH REPORTS OF THE DEPARTMENT OF SOCIOLOGY. 1– , 196 – . Uppsala. Irreg.
Includes subseries: *Special Series — Family Research*. In English and Swedish.
Monograph series. Processed.

2152 URBAN ABSTRACTS. Apr. 1974– . London. Monthly.
Issued by the Greater London Council. Supersedes: *Planning and Transportation Abstracts*.

2153 URBAN AFFAIRS ABSTRACTS. 1– , Aug/Dec. 1971– . Washington, D.C. Weekly, with quarterly and annual cumulations.
Issued by the National League of Cities, and the United States Conference of Mayors. Issues for 1971 are unnumbered but constitute v.1.

2154 URBAN AFFAIRS ANNUAL REVIEW. v.1– , 1967– . Beverly Hills, Calif., London, Sage Publications. Irreg.
Issued by the Department of Urban Affairs, University of Wisconsin.
Indexed: Int. Bibl. Soc.

2155 URBAN AFFAIRS QUARTERLY. v.1– , Sep. 1965– . Ann Arbor, Mich., subsequently Beverly Hills, Calif., Sage Publications. Quarterly.
Sponsored by the City University of New York; subsequently by the Institute of Public Policy Studies, University of Michigan, Ann Arbor.
Indexed: Bull. sig. soc. eth.; Int. Bibl. Soc.; Int. Pol. Sc. Abstr.; PAIS; Soc. Sc. Ind.; SSCI; Soc. Abstr.

URBAN AND REGIONAL REFERENCES
See Canadian Council on Urban and Regional Research. URBAN AND REGIONAL REFERENCES

URBAN AND REGIONAL STUDIES
See Birmingham. University. Centre for Urban and Regional Studies. URBAN AND REGIONAL STUDIES

2156 URBAN AND RURAL PLANNING THOUGHT. v.1– , Jan. 1958– . New Delhi. Quarterly.
Issued by the School of Planning and Architecture (formerly School of Town and Country Planning). Title varies: *A Journal of Urban and Rural Planning Thought*.
Indexed: Int. Bibl. Soc.; Soc. Abstr.

2157 THE URBAN & SOCIAL CHANGE REVIEW. v.1– , 1967– . Chestnut Hill, Mass. Semi-annual.
Issued by The Institute of Human Sciences, Boston College; subsequently by the Graduate School of Social Work, Boston College. Title varies: v.1–2, 1967–68, Institute of Human Sciences. *Review*.
Indexed: Int. Bibl. Soc.; Int. Pol. Sc. Abstr.; LLBA; Sage Fam. Stud. Abstr.; Soc. Work. Res. Abstr.; Soc. Abstr.

2158 URBAN ANTHROPOLOGY. v.1– , spring 1972– . Brockport, N.Y.; subsequently New York, Plenum Publishing Co. Two issues a year, later quarterly.
Issued by the Department of Anthropology, State University of New York at Brockport; subsequently by the Institute for the Study of Man, Inc. Includes section 'Urban Anthropology Newsletter', 1974– .
Indexed: Curr. Cont.; PHRA; Sage Urb. Abstr.; SSCI; Soc. Abstr.

2159 URBAN ANTHROPOLOGY BIBLIOGRAPHY. no.1–, 1973. Brockport, N.Y. One issue published.
Issued by the Department of Anthropology, State University of New York at Brockport.

2160 URBAN ANTHROPOLOGY NEWSLETTER. v.1–3, no.3, 1972–fall 1974. Dallas, Tex.
Issued by the Department of Anthropology, Southern Methodist University. Continued as a supplement to *Urban Anthropology*, 1974– .

URBAN COMMUNITY SCIENCES
See AMERICAN MEN AND WOMEN OF SCIENCE. URBAN COMMUNITY SCIENCES

2161 URBAN ENVIRONMENT. no.1, 1971. New York, Macmillan. Irreg.
Monograph series.

2162 URBAN FORUM. v.1– , spring 1975– . Ottawa. Quarterly.
Issued by the Urban Research Council of Canada. Title in French: *Colloque Urbain*. Supersedes: *Urban Research Bulletin*. In English and French.

2163 URBAN INFORMATION SERIES. no.1– , 1972– . College Park, Md., Urban Information Interpreters, Inc. Irreg.
Called also *Urban Information Specialist Series*.
Monographic series of bibliographic guides and directories.

URBAN INFORMATION SPECIALIST SERIES
See URBAN INFORMATION SERIES

2164 URBAN LIFE. v.1– , Apr. 1972– . Beverly Hills, Calif., Sage Publications. Quarterly.
Title varies: v.1–3, 1972–74, *Urban Life and Culture*. Subtitle reads: 'A journal of bibliographic research'.
Indexed: Curr. Cont.; PAIS; PHRA; Sage Urb. Abstr.; SSCI; Soc. Sc. Ind.; Soc. Abstr.; Urb. Aff. Abstr.

URBAN LIFE AND CULTURE
See URBAN LIFE

2165 Urban Policy Conference. PROCEEDINGS. 1st– , 1965– . Iowa City.
Issued by the Institute of Public Affairs, University of Iowa, and the League of Iowa Municipalities. Each issue has also a distinctive title.

URBAN POPULATION GROWTH SERIES
See URBAN POPULATION SERIES

2166 URBAN POPULATION SERIES. no.1– , 1972– . Washington, D.C.
Issued by the Technical Department, Inter-American Development Bank, no.1–3; by its General Studies Division, no.4. Title varies: no.1–2, *Urban Population Growth Series*.
Series of papers.

URBAN REFERENCE
See Princeton University. Bureau of Urban Research. THE URBAN REFERENCE

URBAN RENEWAL IN CONNECTICUT
See Connecticut. Community Development Division. Urban Renewal Section. URBAN RENEWAL IN CONNECTICUT. REPORT

URBAN RENEWAL IN CONNECTICUT. STATISTICAL REPORT
See Connecticut. Community Development Division. Urban Renewal Section. URBAN RENEWAL IN CONNECTICUT. STATISTICAL REPORT

2167 URBAN RESEARCH BULLETIN. Apr. 1969–1974. Ottawa.
Issued by the Canadian Council on Urban and Regional Research. Title in French: *Bulletin de Recherches Urbaines*. Superseded by: *Urban Forum*.

2168 URBAN RESEARCH NEWS. v.1–11, no.1–16, Nov. 16, 1966–1977. Beverly Hills, Calif., Sage Publications. Biweekly.

2169 URBAN STUDIES. no.1– , May 1964– . Beverly Hills, Calif., Sage Publications. Three issues a year.
Issued by the Department of Social and Economic Research, University of Glasgow. Indexes: 1964–1975.
Indexed: Brit. Hum. Ind.; Int. Bibl. Soc.; Int. Pol. Sc. Abstr.; PHRA; Soc. Sc. Ind.; Soc. Abstr.

2170 URBAN STUDIES BULLETIN. 1–3, Jan. 1973–1976. Ithaca, N.Y. Semi-annual.
Issued by the Center for Urban Development Research, Cornell University. Processed.

2171 URBAN STUDIES STUDENT REVIEW. spring 1974– . New Brunswick, N.J. Annual.
Issued by the Department of Community Development, Livingston College.

2172 URBAN SYSTEMS. v.2–4, 1977–1979. New York., Pergamon Press. Quarterly.
Continues: *Computers & Society*. Continued by: *Computers, Environment and Urban Systems*. Some issues have distinctive titles.

2173 URBANISM; PAST AND PRESENT. winter 1975/1976– . Milwaukee, Wis. Semi-annual.
Issued by the University of Wisconsin at Milwaukee. Supersedes: *Urban History Group Newsletter*.

2174 URBANIZACIÓN, MIGRACIÓNES Y CAMBIOS EN SOCIEDAD PERUANA: PUBLICACIÓN. no.1– , 1966– . Lima, Peru. Irreg.
Issued by the Instituto de Estudios Peruanos. Other title: *Serie Urbanización, Migraciónes y Cambios en Sociedad Peruana*. In Spanish.

2175 URBANIZATION, PLANNING HUMAN ENVIRONMENT IN EUROPE. v.1– , 1972– . The Hague, Nijhoff. Irreg.
In English.
Monograph series.

2176 URBANIZATION POLICY PLANNING ESSAYS. [1]– , 1973– . Seattle, Wash. Irreg.
Issued by the Department of Urban Planning, University of Washington. Subseries of the Department's *Urban Planning & Development Notes*.

2177 Utah. State University of Agriculture and Applied Science, Logan. UTAH STATE UNIVERSITY JOURNAL OF SOCIOLOGY. v.3–4, 1972–1973. Logan. Annual.
Continues: *Sociological Focus*. Continued by: *Western Sociological Review*.

UTAH STATE UNIVERSITY JOURNAL OF SOCIOLOGY
See Utah. State University of Agriculture and Applied Science, Logan. UTAH STATE UNIVERSITY JOURNAL OF SOCIOLOGY

UTAH STATE UNIVERSITY JOURNAL OF SOCIOLOGY
See WESTERN SOCIOLOGICAL REVIEW

2178 UTOPIE. v.1– , 1967– . Paris, Éditions Anthropos. Semi-monthly.

2179 Utrecht. Rijksuniversiteit. Geografisch Instituut. PUBLIKATIES. SERIE A. SOCIALE GEOGRAFIE. HUMAN GEOGRAPHY. v.1– , 1955– . Utrecht. Irreg.
Includes some reprinted works. In Dutch; some works with summaries in English and French.
Monograph series.

2180 VÄESTÖNTUTKIMUKSEN VUOKSIKIRJA YEARBOOK OF POPULATION RESEARCH IN FINLAND. v.1– , 1946– . Helsinki, Väestöpoliitinen Tutkimuslaitos. Annual.
Title varies: v.1–5, 1946–59, *Yearbook of the Finnish Population and the Family Welfare Federation*. In Finnish; some articles in English.
Indexed: Soc. Abstr.

VÁLOSAG
See Tudományos Ismeretterjesztö Társulat. VÁLÓSAG

2181 Vanderbilt Sociology Conference. PROCEEDINGS. 1st– , 1969– . Nashville, Tenn. Irreg.

VANYAJATI
See SOCIOLOG

VERHANDLUNGEN DES DEUTSCHEN SOZIOLOGENTAGES
See Deutsche Gesellschaft für Soziologie. SCHRIFTEN REIHE 1. SER

VERHANDLUNGEN. VORTRÄGE UND DISKUSSIONEN IN DER HAUPT VERSAMMLUNG UND IN DEN SITZUNGEN DER UNTERGRUPPEN
See Deutscher Soziologentag. VERHANDLUNGEN, VORTRÄGE UND DISKUSSIONEN IN DER HAUPT VERSAMMLUNG UND IN DEN SITZUNGEN DER UNTERGRUPPEN

VERÖFFENTLICHUNGEN
See München. Universität. Max Weber Institut. VERÖFFENTLICHUNGEN

VERÖFFENTLICHUNGEN
See Tübingen. Max Weber Institut. VERÖFFENTLICHUNGEN

VERSLAG VIR HUWELIKE EN EGSKEIDINGS: SUID-AFRIKA
See South Africa. Department of Statistics. VERSLAG VIR HUWELIKE EN EGSKEIDINGS: SUID-AFRIKA

VESTNIK. OBSHCHESTVENNYE NAUKI
See Erivan. Universitet. VESTNIK. OBSHCHESTVENNYE NAUKI

VESTNIK OBSHCHESTVENNYKH NAUK
See Akademiia nauk Armianskoii S.S.R. VESTNIK OBSHCHESTVENNYKH NAUK

VESTSI. SERYIA HRAMADSKIKH NAVUK
See Akademiia navuk B.S.S.R., Minsk. VESTSI. SERYIA HRAMADSKIKH NAVUK

2182 VIE CONTEMPORAINE; REVUE DE PSYCHOLOGIE SOCIALE. v.1–2, no.4, 1907–Apr. 1908. Paris.
Title varies: v.1–2, no.1, *Revue de Psychologie Sociale*; v.2, no.2, *Revue de Psychologie*.

2183 LA VIE URBAINE. 1–16, Mar. 1919–Sep/Dec. 1939; n.s. no.55– , Jan/Mar. 1950– . Paris. Four issues a year.
Issued by the Institut d'Urbanisme de Paris, Université de Paris-Val-de-Marne. Not published 1924–25, 1931, 1940–Dec. 1949. v.1–7, 1919–28 also as no.1–35; v.8–16, Jan. 1930–39 also as no.1–54.

2184 VIERTELJAHRESSCHRIFT FÜR WISSENSCHAFTLICHE PHILOSOPHIE UND SOZIOLOGIE. v.26–49, 1902–1916. Leipzig.
Supersedes: *Vierteljahresschrift für Wissenschaftliche Philosophie* (1877–1901).

2185 VIITORUL SOCIAL; REVISTĂ DE SOCIOLOGIE ȘI ȘTIINȚE POLITICE. 1– , 1972– . Bucuresti, Editura Academiei Republicii Socialiste România. Quarterly.
Issued by the Academia de Științe Sociale și Politice, Academia 'Stefan Gheorghiu', and Asociatia Româna de Științe Politice. In Rumanian.
Indexed: Int. Bibl. Soc.; Soc. Abstr.

VISNIK; SERIIA SUSPIL'NYKH NAUK
See Lvov. Universitet. VISNIK; SERIIA SUSPIL'NYKH NAUK

VITA HUMANA
See HUMAN DEVELOPMENT

VITAL AND HEALTH STATISTICS. SERIES 14: DATA FROM THE NATIONAL VITAL STATISTICS SYSTEM, DATA ON NATALITY, MARRIAGE AND DIVORCE
See United States. National Center for Health Statistics. SERIES 14: DATA FROM THE NATIONAL VITAL STATISTICS SYSTEM, DATA ON NATALITY, MARRIAGE AND DIVORCE

VLAAMS OPVOEDKUNDIG TIJDSCHRIFT
See TIJDSCHRIFT VOOR OPVOEDKUNDE

2186 Vladimir, Russia. Vladimirskii pedagogicheskii institut. UCHENYE ZAPISKI. SERIIA OBSHCHESTVENNYE NAUKI. no.1– , 196?– . Vladimir. In Russian.
Subseries of its: *Uchenye zapiski*.

2187 VOPROSY FILOSOFII I SOTSIOLOGII. no.1– , 1969– . Leningrad, Izdatel'stovo Leningradskogo universiteta. Annual.
Issued by the Leningradskii universitet. In Russian.

2188 VOPROSY OBSHCHESTVENNYKH NAUK. no.1– , 1970– . Kiev, Isd-vo Kievskogo universiteta.
Issued by the Kievskii universitet. In Russian.
Indexed: Int. Bibl. Soc.

2189 VOPROSY SOTSIOLOGII I OBSHCHESTVENNOI PSIKHOLOGII. 1– , 1970– . Moskva.
Issued by the Moskovskii universitet. In Russian.

VORTRÄGE UND DISKUSSIONEN IN DER VERSAMMLUNG UND IN DEN SITZUNGEN DER UNTERGRUPPEN
See Deutscher Soziologentag. VERHANDLUNGEN. VORTRÄGE UND DISKUSSIONEN IN DER VERSAMMLUNG UND IN DEN SITZUNGEN DER UNTERGRUPPEN

2190 VOX POPULORUM. v.1–4, no.1–26, May 1, 1922–Feb. 1926. Torino, Roma.
Issued by the Institut International de Sociologie et des Réformes Politiques et Sociales. In Italian.

VREEMDE ARBEIDERS
See Louvain. Université Catholique. Sociologisch Onderzoeksinstituut. VREEMDE ARBEIDERS

WSR WESTERN SOCIOLOGICAL REVIEW
See WESTERN SOCIOLOGICAL REVIEW

WANDERUNGEN IN BERLIN (WEST)
See Berlin (West). Statistisches Landesamt. DIE WANDERUNG IN BERLIN

DIE WANDERUNGSBEWEGUNG IN BERLIN (WEST)
See Berlin (West). Statistisches Landesamt. DIE WANDERUNG IN BERLIN

2191 WARSAN SANGHKHOMWITTHAYAMANUTWITTHAYA. v.1– , 2510/2511– . [i.e. 1967/1968–]. Chiang Mai Khana Sankhomsat, Mahawitthayalai Chiang Mai.
Title in English: *The Journal of Sociology and Anthropology*. In Thai.

2192 Washington (State). University. Center for Urban and Regional Research. MONOGRAPH. no.1– , 1969– . Seattle. Irreg.
Monograph series.

2193 Washington (State). University. Department of Sociology. UNIVERSITY OF WASHINGTON JOURNAL OF SOCIOLOGY. v.1– , 1969– . Seattle. Annual.
Issued in cooperation with The Washington Chapter of Alpha Kappa Delta.

2194 Washington (State). University. Urban Data Center. PROCEEDINGS. 5th– , 1964– . [Place of publications varies] Irreg.

Proceedings of the fifth conference issued in Houston, Texas University. Public Affairs Research Center. *Occasional Paper*, no.2.

2195 Washington (State). University. Urban Data Center. RESEARCH REPORT. no.1– , 1964– . Seattle. Irreg.
Monograph series.

2196 Washington University, St. Louis. Institute for Urban and Regional Studies. WORKING PAPER. ESS. 1, 1968. St. Louis, Mo. One issue published.
Processed.

2197 Washington University, St. Louis. Institute for Urban and Regional Studies. WORKING PAPER. HMS SERIES. 1–7, 1953–1975. St. Louis, Mo. Irreg.
Series of papers. Processed.

2198 Washington University, St. Louis. Institute for Urban and Regional Studies. WORKING PAPER. INS. 1– , 1967– . St. Louis, Mo. Irreg.
Series of papers. Processed.

2199 Washington University, St. Louis. Institute for Urban and Regional Studies. WORKING PAPER. SSF. 1, 1969. St. Louis, Mo. One issue published.
Processed.

2200 WASHINGTON UNIVERSITY STUDIES. NEW SERIES. SOCIAL AND PHILOSOPHICAL SCIENCES. no.1–9, 1927–1952. St. Louis, Mo.
Supersedes, in part, *Washington University Studies. Humanities Series*. Superseded by the University's unnumbered series titled *Washington University Studies*, 1955– .

2201 WELSH SOCIAL TRENDS. no.1– , 1977– . Cardiff. Annual.
Issued by the Welsh Office.

2202 THE WEST AFRICAN JOURNAL OF SOCIOLOGY AND POLITICAL SCIENCE. v.1– , Oct. 1975– . Exeter, England. Quarterly (irreg.).
Issued by the Department of Politics, University of Exeter.

2203 Westermarck Society. TRANSACTIONS. v.1– , 1947– . København, Munksgaard, subsequently Helsinki.
Indexed: Soc. Abstr.

2204 Western Association of Sociology and Anthropology. Meeting. PROCEEDINGS. 11th– , 1969– . Edmonton, Alberta. Annual.
Each issue has also a distinctive title.

2205 WESTERN SOCIOLOGICAL REVIEW. v.5– , 1974– . Logan, Utah. Annual.
Issued by the Department of Sociology, Social Work and Anthropology, Utah State University; co-sponsored by the Utah Sociological Society. Continues: *Utah State University Journal of Sociology*. Title on cover: *WSR Western Sociological Review*.
Indexed: Soc. Abstr.

2206 Wien. Hochschule für Welthandel. Institut für allgemeine Soziologie und Wirtschaftssoziologie. BERICHTE. no.1–6, 1972–1973. Wien. Irreg.
The Institut was earlier called Institut für allgemeine Soziologie.

2207 WIENER STUDIEN ZUR AGRARPOLITIK UND AGRARSOZIOLOGIE. v.1– , 1957– . Göttingen. Irreg.
Monograph series.

2208 WIRTSCHAFT UND GESELLSCHAFT. 1– , 1975– . Tübingen, J. C. B. Mohr (Paul Siebeck). Irreg.
Monograph series.

2209 Wisconsin. Department of Administration. Management and Information Section. WISCONSIN POPULATION PROJECTIONS. 1st– , 1969– . Madison. Annual.

2210 Wisconsin. University. Department of Rural Sociology. POPULATION SERIES. no.1–24, Feb. 1961–June 1970. Madison.
Title varies: *Wisconsin's Population Series*.

2211 Wisconsin. University. Department of Rural Sociology. Applied Population Laboratory. FAMILY ADJUSTMENT IN SELECTED LOW INCOME AREAS. PRELIMINARY REPORT. no.1–2, Apr. 1968–Oct. 1968. Madison. Irreg.
Monograph series. Processed.

2212 Wisconsin. University. Department of Rural Sociology. Applied Population Laboratory. POPULATION NOTES 1960. no.1–12, Sep. 1961–Aug. 1970. Madison. Irreg.

2213 Wisconsin. University. Department of Rural Sociology. Applied Population Laboratory. POPULATION NOTES 1970. no.1–9, Mar. 1973–June 1979. Madison. Irreg.

WISCONSIN POPULATION PROJECTIONS *See* Wisconsin. Department of Administration. Management and Information Section. WISCONSIN POPULATION PROJECTIONS

2214 WISCONSIN SOCIOLOGIST. v.1– , spring 1962– . Madison. Quarterly.

Issued by the Wisconsin Sociological Association; 1962–65 in cooperation with the University of Wisconsin at Milwaukee. Supersedes a publication of the same title, 1960–62. The issue for spring 1962 called also 'new series'. Processed.

Indexed: Psych. Abstr.; Soc. Abstr.

WISCONSIN'S POPULATION SERIES
See Wisconsin. University. Department of Rural Sociology. Applied Population Laboratory. POPULATION SERIES 1960, and POPULATION SERIES 1970

2215 WISSENSCHAFT UND GESELLSCHAFT. v.1– , 1973– . Berlin (East), Akademie Verlag. Irreg.

Issued by the Institut für Wissenschaftstheorie und Organisation, Akademie für Wissenschaften der DDR.

Monograph series.

2216 DAS WISSENSCHAFTLICHE TASCHENBUCH; ABT. SOZIOLOGIE. München, Goldman. Irreg.

Monograph series of popular works.

WOMAN AND SOCIETY
See FRAU UND GESELLSCHAFT

2217 WOMEN IN CANADIAN SOCIOLOGY/ANTHROPOLOGY. FEMMES ET SOCIOLOGIE/ANTHROPOLOGIE CANADIENNE. bulletin. 4– , 1977– . Downsview, Ont.

Issued by the Department of Sociology, York University. Continues: *Women in Canadian Sociology. Bulletin. Femmes et Sociologie Canadienne. Bulletin.*

2218 WOMEN IN CANADIAN SOCIOLOGY. BULLETIN. FEMMES ET SOCIOLOGIE CANADIENNE. BULLETIN. 1–3, 1974–76. Downsview, Ont.

Issued by the Department of Sociology, York University. Continued by: *Women in Canadian Sociology†Anthropology. Femmes et Sociologie† Anthropologie Canadienne. Bulletin.*

2219 WOMEN, SPORT, AND LEISURE. 1975– , Waterloo, Ont. Three issues a year.

Issued by the SIRLS, Faculty of Human Kinetics and Leisure Studies, University of Waterloo.

2220 WOMEN TODAY. v.1–6, Dec. 1954–Dec. 1963. London. Semi-annual.

Issued by the Department of Education in Tropical Areas, Institute of Education, University of London. Title varies: 1954–Dec. 1962, *African Women*. Subtitle reads: 'A journal for women in changing societies'.

2221 WOMEN'S STUDIES. v.1– , 1972– . London, Gordon and Breach. Semi-annual.

Indexed: Soc. Abstr.; Wom. Stud. Abstr.

2222 WOMEN'S STUDIES ABSTRACTS. v.1– , winter 1972– . Rush, N.Y. Quarterly, with annual subject index.

2223 WOMEN'S STUDIES INTERNATIONAL QUARTERLY. v.1– , 1978– . Oxford, New York, Pergamon Press. Quarterly.

Some issues are thematic.

Indexed: Soc. Abstr.

WORK PAPER
See Florida. University, Gainesville. Urban and Regional Development Center. WORK PAPER

WORKING PAPER
See California. University. University at Los Angeles. Institute of Urban and Regional Development. WORKING PAPER

WORKING PAPER
See Columbia University. Center for Advanced Research in Urban and Environmental Affairs. WORKING PAPER

WORKING PAPER
See Haifa. Technion — Israel Institute of Technology. Center for Urban and Regional Studies. WORKING PAPER

WORKING PAPER
See International Union for the Scientific Study of Population. WORKING PAPER

WORKING PAPER
See Liverpool. University. Department of Geography. African Population Mobility Project. WORKING PAPER

WORKING PAPER
See London. University. University College. School of Environmental Studies. Planning Methodology Unit. WORKING PAPER

WORKING PAPER
See London. University. University College. Planning Methodology Research Unit. WORKING PAPER

WORKING PAPER
See Princeton University. Research Center for Urban and Environmental Planning. WORKING PAPER

WORKING PAPER
See Singapore. University. Department of Sociology. WORKING PAPER

WORKING PAPER
See Toronto. University. Institute for the Quantitative Analysis of Social and Economic Policy. WORKING PAPER

WORKING PAPER. ESS
See Washington University, St. Louis. Institute for Urban and Regional Studies. WORKING PAPER. ESS

WORKING PAPER. HMS
See Washington University, St. Louis. Institute for Urban and Regional Studies. WORKING PAPER. HMS

WORKING PAPER. INS
See Washington University, St. Louis. Institute for Urban and Regional Studies. WORKING PAPER. INS

WORKING PAPER, SSF
See Washington University, St. Louis. Institute for Urban and Regional Studies. WORKING PAPER. SSF

WORKING PAPERS
See Massachusetts Institute of Technology. Migration and Development Study Group. WORKING PAPERS

2224 WORKING PAPERS FOR A NEW SOCIETY. 1– , spring 1973– . Cambridge, Mass. Quarterly.
Issued by the Cambridge Policy Studies Institute.
Indexed: Soc. Abstr.

2225 WORKING PAPERS IN COMPARATIVE SOCIOLOGY. no.5– , 1975– . Auckland, N.Z. Irreg.
Issued by the Department of Sociology, University of Auckland. Continues the University's *Papers in Comparative Sociology*.

2226 WORKING PAPERS IN CULTURAL STUDIES. [no.1]– , 1971– . Birmingham, England. Irreg.
Issued by the Centre for Contemporary Cultural Studies, University of Birmingham.

2227 WORKING PAPERS IN SOCIOLOGY AND ANTHROPOLOGY. v.1– , Oct. 1967– . Athens, Ga. Irreg.
Issued by the Department of Sociology, University of Georgia.
Series of papers.

WORKING PAPERS ON ETHNIC RELATIONS
See Social Science Research Council (Gt. Britain). Research Unit on Ethnic Relations. WORKING PAPERS ON ETHNIC RELATIONS

WORLD AGRICULTURAL ECONOMICS ABSTRACTS
See WORLD AGRICULTURAL ECONOMICS AND RURAL SOCIOLOGY ABSTRACTS

2228 WORLD AGRICULTURAL ECONOMICS AND RURAL SOCIOLOGY ABSTRACTS. v.1– , Apr. 1959– . Farnham Royal, Slough, Bucks. Quarterly, 1959–72; monthly, 1973– ; with annual cumulations and geographical index.
Issued by the Commonwealth Bureau of Agricultural Economics, Commonwealth Agricultural Bureau. Title varies: 1958–59, *World Agricultural Economics Abstracts*. Supersedes: *Digest of Agricultural Economics and Marketing*. Includes a section 'Rural sociology'.

2229 World Congress of Sociology. TRANSACTIONS. 2nd– , 1951– . [Place of publication varies] Quadrennial.
Issued by the International Sociological Association. Transactions of the first congress not published.
Indexed: Soc. Abstr.

2230 World Fertility Survey. BASIC DOCUMENTATION. no.1– , Mar. 1975– . Voorburg, Netherlands.
Issued in cooperation with the Information Office, International Statistical Office.

2231 World Fertility Survey. OCCASIONAL PAPERS. 1– , Oct. 1973– . Voorburg, Netherlands. Irreg.
Issued by the International Union for the Study of Population.
Monograph series.

2232 World Fertility Survey. [REPORT] 1972–1975– . Voorburg, Netherlands.
First report covers the period Jan. 1972–Jan. 1975.

2233 World Fertility Survey. SCIENTIFIC REPORTS. 1977– . The Hague, Irreg.
Issued by the International Union for the Study of Population, in cooperation with the International Statistical Office.

2234 World Fertility Survey. WORLD FERTILITY SURVEY NEWSLETTER. no.1– , Oct. 1973– . Voorburg, Netherlands.

WORLD FERTILITY SURVEY NEWSLETTER
See World Fertility Survey. WORLD FERTILITY SURVEY NEWSLETTER

WORLD INDEX TO SOCIAL SCIENCE INSTITUTIONS

See INTERNATIONAL SOCIAL SCIENCE JOURNAL

2235 WRITING SOCIOLOGY. no.1– , Oct. 1976– . London. Irreg.
Issued by the Department of Sociology, University of London. Goldsmith's College.
Indexed: Soc. Abstr.

Wrocław
See Breslau

2236 Wyoming. University. Division of Business and Research. DEMOGRAPHIC SERIES. no.1–2, 1965. Laramie.

2237 YAGL-AMBU. 1– , 1974–. Port Moresby, Papua New Guinea. Two issues a year.
Issued by the Department of Econmics, University. Subtitle reads: 'Papua and New Guinea journal of the social sciences and the humanities'.

2238 YALE SERIES OF WORKING PAPERS IN SOCIOLOGY. 1– , 1979– . New Haven, Conn. Irreg.
Issued by the Department of Sociology, Yale University.

2239 YALE SOCIOLOGY JOURNAL. 1– , spring 1971– . New Haven, Conn. Semi-annual.
Issued by Graduate Students of the Department of Sociology, Yale University.

2240 YALE STUDIES IN ATTITUDE AND COMMUNICATION. v.1–4, 1957–1961. New Haven, Conn. Irreg.
Issued by the Institute of Human Relations.
Monograph series.

2241 YALE STUDIES OF THE CITY. 1, 1969. New Haven, Conn., Yale University Press. Irreg.
Other title: *Studies of the City*.
Monograph series.

2242 Yale University. Center of Alcohol Studies. MEMOIRS. no.1–6, 1944–1948. New Haven, Conn. Quarterly.

2243 Yale University. Center of Alcohol Studies. MONOGRAPHS. no.1–3, 1958. New Haven, Conn. Irreg.
Continued by: Rutgers University. Center of Alcohol Studies. *Monographs*.

2244 THE YEAR BOOK OF SOCIAL POLICY IN BRITAIN. 1971– . London, Routledge & Kegan Paul. Annual.
Indexed: Int. Bibl. Soc.; Int. Pol. Sc. Abstr.

YEARBOOK OF POPULATION STUDIES IN FINLAND
See VÄESTÖNTUTKIMUKSEN VUOKSIRJA

YEARBOOK OF THE FINNISH POPULATION AND FAMILY WELFARE FEDERATION
See VÄESTÖNTUTKIMUKSEN VUOKSIRJA

YEARBOOK OF THE NORTHERN ASSOCIATION OF CRIMINALISTS
See NORDISK KRIMINALISTISK ÅRSBOK

2245 THE YENCHING JOURNAL OF SOCIAL STUDIES. v.1– , June 1938– . Peking.
Publication suspended Aug. 1941–Aug. 1948. Ceased publication.

2246 Yenching University, Peking. Department of Sociology. SOCIOLOGY FELLOWSHIP NEEDS. no.1–11, 1930–1932. Peking.

2247 YOUTH AND SOCIETY. v.1– , Sept. 1969– . Beverly Hills, Calif., Sage Publications. Quarterly.
Issued by the Youth Study Center, University of Southern California, Los Angeles.
Indexed: Int. Bibl. Soc.; PHRA; SSCI; Sage Fam. Stud. Abstr.; Soc. Abstr.; Urb. Aff. Abstr.

YOUTH IN TRANSITION
See Michigan. University. Survey Research Center. YOUTH IN TRANSITION

2248 Yugoslavia. Savezni zavod za statistiku. DEMOGRAFSKA STATISTIKA. 1956– . Beograd.
Supersedes the Institute's *Vitalna statistika*, 1950–55. In Serbo-Croatian.

2249 Z BADAŃ KLASY ROBOTNICZEJ I INTELIGENCJI. 1958–1969. Wrocław, Zakład Narodowy im. Ossolińskich. Irreg.
In Polish.
Monograph series.

Z HISTORICKO-DEMOGRAFICKÝCH STUDII
See HISTORICKÁ DEMOGRAFIE

ZAGADNIENIA NAUKOZNAWSTWA
See PROBLEMS OF THE SCIENCE OF SCIENCE

2250 ZAMBEZIA. 1– , Jan. 1969– . Salisbury, Zimbabwe. Publications Department, University of Rhodesia. Annual.

Issued by the University of Zimbabwe. Subtitle varies: 1969–74, 'A journal of social studies in Southern and Central Africa'; 1975– , 'The journal of the University of Rhodesia'.
Indexed: Abstr. Anth.

2251 Zambia. University. Institute for African Studies. COMMUNICATION. no.7– , 1971– . Lusaka. Irreg.
Continues its Institute for Social Research. *Communication*. Each issue has also a distinctive title.

2252 Zambia. University. Institute for Social Research. BULLETIN. no.1– , Jan. 18, 1966– . Lusaka. Annual.
Supersedes: Rhodes-Livingstone Institute. *Proceedings,* 1958–63.
Indexed: Anth. Ind.

2253 Zambia. University. Institute for Social Research. COMMUNICATION. no.1–6, 1966–1970. Lusaka. Irreg.
Supersedes: Rhodes-Livingstone Institute. *Communications,* 1943–65. Superseded by: Zambia. University. Institute for African Studies. *Communication.*

2254 ZAMBIAN URBAN STUDIES. no.1–3, 1969–1970. Lusaka.

2255 ZASSHI KIJI SAKUIN. JIMBUN SHAKAIHEN. v.1– , 1948– . Tokyo. Monthly, 1948–74; semi-annual, 1975; quarterly, with annual cumulative index, 1976– .
Issued by the National Diet Library. Title in English: *Japanese Periodical Index. Humanities and Social Sciences Section.* In Japanese.

ZBORNIK
See Institut za kriminološka i sociološka istraživanja. ZBORNIK

ZBORNIK RADOVA
See Sociološki institut. ZBORNIK RADOVA

2256 ZEITSCHRIFT FÜR AGRARGESCHICHTE UND AGRARSOZIOLOGIE. 1– , Apr. 1953– . Frankfurt-am-Main, DLG Verlag GmbH. Semi-annual.
Includes supplements titled *Sonderband*
Indexed: Int. Bibl. Soc.; Soc. Abstr.

2257 ZEITSCHRIFT FÜR AGRARESCHICHTE UND AGRARSOZIOLOGIE. SONDERBAND. 1– , 1958– . Frankfurt-am-Main, DLG Verlag GmbH. Irreg.
Supplement to *Zeitschrift für Agrargeschichte und Agrarsoziologie.*
Monograph series.

2258 ZEITSCHRIFT FÜR BEVÖLKERUNGSWISSENSCHAFT. DEMOGRAPHIE. 1975– . Wiesbaden, Deutsche Verlags-Anstalt GmbH. Quarterly.
Issued by the Bundesinstitut für Bevölkerungsforschung.

2259 ZEITSCHRIFT FÜR DEMOGRAPHIE UND STATISTIK DER JUDEN. 1–17, 1905–1923; n.s. v.1–3, 1924–1926. Berlin. Monthly.

2260 ZEITSCHRIFT FÜR SOZIALPSYCHOLOGIE. v.1– , 1970– . Frankfurt-am-Main, Akademische Verlagsgesellschaft. Quarterly.
Indexed: Int. Bibl. Soc.

2261 ZEITSCHRIFT FÜR SOZIOLOGIE. 1– , Jan. 1972– . Bielefeld, Ferdinand Enke Verlag. Quarterly.
Issued by the Fakultät der Soziologie, Universität. In English and German.
Indexed: Bull. sig. soc. eth.; Curr. Cont.; SSCI; Soc. Abstr.

ZEITSCHRIFT FÜR SOZIOLOGIE
See SOSYOLOJI DERGISI

2262 ZEITSCHRIFT FÜR STAATSSOZIOLOGIE, WIRTSCHAFT, KULTUR, ERZIEHUNG. v.1–18, no.4, 1953–1971. Freiburg, Themis Verlag. Quarterly.

2263 ZEITSCHRIFT FÜR STADTGESCHICHTE, STADTSOZIOLOGIE ND DENKMALPFLEGE. 1–4, 1974–1977. Stuttgart.
Continued by: *Alte Stadt.*

ZEITSCHRIFT FÜR VÖLKERPSYCHOLOGIE UND SOZIOLOGIE
See SOCIOLOGUS: ZEITSCHRIFT FÜR VÖLKERPSYCHOLOGIE UND SOZIOLOGIE

ZEITSCHRIFT FÜR WIRTSCHAFTS- UND SOZIALGEOGRAPHIE
See TIJDSCHRIFT VOOR ECONOMISCHE EN SOCIALE GEOGRAFIE

ZENTRALARCHIV FÜR EMPIRISCHE FORSCHUNG
See Cologne. Universität. ZENTRALARCHIV FUR EMPIRISCHE SOZIALFORSCHUNG

2264 Zürich. Universität. Soziologisches Institut. BULLETIN. no.1– , Nov. 1966– . Zürich. Semi-annual.
The June 1967 issue prepared in cooperation with the Departamento de Sociologia, Fundación Bariloche. In English and German; summaries in English. Also an edition in Spanish, titled *Boletin.*
Indexed: Int. Bibl. Soc.

Supplement I

2265 AMSTERDAM SOCIOLOGISCH TIJDSCHRIFT. v.1– , May 1974– . Groningen, Wollers-Noordhaff. Annual.
In Dutch.

ANNUAL REPORT
See International Sociological Association. ANNUAL REPORT

2266 ARTS IN SOCIETY. v.1– , Jan. 1958– . Madison, Wis. Frequency varies.
Issued by the Extension Division, University of Wisconsin. Index to v.1–3, 1958–summer 1966, in v.3, no.4.

2267 BEITRÄGE ZUR SOZIOLOGIE DER GEMEINDEN. 1957–1960. Köln, Westdeutscher Verlag. Four volumes published.

2268 BI-SOCIOLOGIE. v.8– , 1978– . Bucureşti. Bimonthly.
Issued by the Centrul de Informáre si Documentare in Ştiinţe Sociale şi Politice, Academia Reipublicii Ştiinţe România. Continues, in part, its *Bulletin de Informáre Ştiinţifica-Filozofie, Sociologie, Psihologie*. In Rumanian.

2269 BURAKU MONDAI KENKYU. no.1– , 1956– . Kyoto.
Issued by the Institute of Buraku Problems. In Japanese; table of contents in English.

2270 CHU HAI SHU ŸAN HUI HSÜEH CHI SHE HUI KUNG TSO HSÜEH HSI. 1– , June 1971– . Kowloon.
Issued by the Department of Sociology and Social Work, Hsi Institute. In Chinese. Title in English: *Sociological Review*.

2271 COLLECTION SOCIOLOGIE ET PASTORALE. 1– , 1956– . Montréal. Irreg.
Monograph series.

2272 Congreso Nacional de Sociologia (Colombia). MEMORIA. 1st, 1963. Bogotá.
In Spanish.

2273 CROSSROADS; TRENDS & ISSUES OF CONTEMPORARY SOCIETY. [no.1]– , autumn 1978– . Jerusalem. Quarterly.
Issued by the Israel Research Institute of Contemporary Society. First issue unnumbered.

2274 CURRENT PERSPECTIVES IN SOCIAL THEORY; A RESEARCH ANNUAL. v.1– , 1980– . Greenwich, Conn., JAI Press.

2275 ESTUDIOS SOCIOLÓGICOS. 1, 1902. Lima, Impr. la Industria. One monograph published.
In Spanish.

2276 HABITAT. v.1–2, no.3/4, June 1976–1977. Oxford, New York, Pergamon Press. Bimonthly.
Published in cooperation with the World Environment Resources Council (WERC). Continued by: *Habitat International*.

2277 International Sociological Association. ANNUAL REPORT. RAPPORT ANNUEL. 1964– . Geneva. Annual.

2278 JOURNAL OF AFRICAN AFRO-AMERICAN AFFAIRS. v.1– , 1977– . Flint, Mich. Annual.
Supersedes: *The Journal of Afro-American Issues* (listed no.1021).

2279 KULTURELLER WANDEL. 1974– . Meisenheim, Verlag Anton Jain. Irreg.
Monograph series.

2280 Olomouc, Moravia. Univerzita Palackého. SBORNIK. SOCIOLOGIE-HISTORIE. 1967. Olomouc, Statni pedagogické nakladetelstvi.
Issued by the Pedagogická fakulta, Univerzita Palackého. In Czech.

2281 Oslo. Universitet. Institutt for Sosiologi. SKRIFTSERIE. 1– , 1973– . Oslo. Irreg.
In Norwegian.
Monograph series.

2282 POLITIK UND SOZIOLOGIE. 1– ?, 1966– ?. Villingen, Neckar-Verlag. Irreg. Ceased publication.
Monograph series.

2283 RESEARCH IN SOCIAL STRATIFICATION AND MOBILITY. v.1– , 1981– . Greenwich, Conn., JAI Press. Annual.
Subtitle reads: 'a research annual'.

2284 RESEARCH IN THE SOCIOLOGY OF WORK. v.1– , 1981– . Greenwich, Conn. Annual.
Subtitle reads: 'a research annual'.

SBORNIK. SOCIOLOGIE-HISTORIE
See Olomouc, Moravia. Universita Palackého. SBORNIK. SOCIOLOGIE-HISTOIRE

SKRIFTSERIE
See Oslo. Universitet. Institutt for Sosiologi. SKRIFTSERIE

2285 SOCIOLOGI ED ECONOMISTI. 1– , 1948– . Torino, Unione Tip., Editrice Torinese. Irreg.
In Italian.
Monograph series.

2286 SOCIOLOGIA BOLIVIANA CONTEMPORANEA. 1– , 1977– . La Paz, Empresa Editora 'Universo'. Irreg.
In Spanish.
Monograph series.

2287 SOCIOLOGIA DEL DIRITTO. 1– , 1980– . Milano, F. Angeli. Irreg.
In Italian.
Monograph series.

2288 SOCIOLOGIA DEL LAVORO E DEL'ORGANIZAZIONE. 1– , 1979– . Milano, F. Angeli. Irreg.
In Italian.
Monograph series.

2289 SOCIOLOGIA DELLA LETTERATURA; LETTERE CRITICHE. SERIE DI SOCIOLOGIA. 1– , 1977– . Milano, Mursia Editore. Irreg.
In Italian.
Monograph series.

2290 SOCIOLOGICAL OBSERVATIONS. 1– , 1977– . Beverly Hills, Calif., Sage Publications. Irreg.
Monograph series.

SOCIOLOGICAL REVIEW
See CHU HAI SHU ŸAN HUI HSÜEH CHI SHE HUI KUNG TSO HSÜEH HSI

2291 SOCIOLOGICAL SPECTRUM. v.1– , Jan. 1981– . Washington, D.C., Hemisphere Publishing Corporation. Quarterly.
Issued by the Mid-South Sociological Association. Formed by the merger of *Sociological Forum* and *Sociological Symposium*.
Indexed: Soc. Abstr.

2292 SOCIOLOGICAL STUDIES. no.1– , 1971– . Birmingham, Ala. Irreg.
Issued by the Bureau of Public Administration, University of Alabama. Irreg.

2293 SOCIOLOGICKÝ SBORNIK. 1–2, 1946–1947. Turciansky Sv. Martin.
In Czech.

2294 SOCIOLOGY OF COOPERATION MONOGRAPH. no.1–4, 1955–1959. Glen Gardner, N.J. Irreg.
Monograph series.

2295 SOSIOLOGIAN TUTKIMUKSIA. 1– , 1977– . Turku. Irreg.
Issued by the Turun Yliopisto (University of Turku). In Finnish.
Monograph series.

2296 SOZIOLOGIE. 2– , 1974– . Wiesbaden, Otto Harrassowitz. Semi-annual.

2297 SOZIOLOGIE. no.1– , 1977– . Stuttgart, F. Enke Verlag. Two issues a year.

2298 SOZIOLOGENKORRESPONDENZ. v.1– , 1970– . Aachen, H. J. Halle.

2299 STUDIES IN SOCIAL ORGANIZATION. 1, 1964. New York. One volume published.
Issued by the Russell Sage Foundation.

2300 WELSH SOCIOLOGIST. v.1– , 1972–? Caerwys, Flintshire; now in Austria. One or two issues a year.
Issued by the Gwasg Gwenffrwd in association with the ASTIC Forschung (ASTIC Research Associates) for private distribution. In various languages.

2301 WIENER SOZIOLOGISCHE STUDIEN. 1–3, 1933–1936. Wien. Irreg.

Supplement II

2302 ACRACIA; REVISTA SOCIOLOGICA. v.1, no.1–30, Jan. 1886–1888. Barcelona. Weekly (irreg.).
In Spanish.

2303 COLLANA DI SOCIOLOGIA. 1– , 197 – . Milano, F. Angeli. Irreg.
In Italian.
Monograph series.

2304 COLLANA DI STUDI E RICERCHE SOCIOLOGICHE. 1– , 1976– . Milano, F. Angeli. Irreg.
In Italian.
Monograph series.

2305 FOLIA SOCIOLOGICA. 1– , 1980– . Łódź. Irreg.
Issued by the Uniwersytet Łódzki. Irreg. Subseries of *Acta Universitatis Lodziensis*. In English. Summaries in Polish, Russian and Spanish.

2306 SERJA SOCJOLOGIA. no.1– , 197 – . Poznań. Irreg.
Issued by the Uniwersytet in Poznan. In Polish.
Monograph series.

2307 SOCIOLOGIA E METODOLOGIA DELLA RICERCHA. 1– , 1974– . Roma, ELTA. Irreg.
In Italian.
Monograph series.

2308 SOCIOLOGIE NOUVELLE. THEORIES. 1– , 197 – . Gembloux, Duculet. Irreg.
Monograph series.

2309 Oslo. Universitet. Institutt for Rettssosiologi. STENSILSKRIFTER. no.1– , 1968– . Oslo. Irreg.

In Norwegian.

2310 SOTSIOLOGICHESKIE PROBLEMY OBRAZOVANIIA I DUKHOVNOI KULTURY. no.1– , 1975– . Sverdlovsk. Irreg.

Issued by the Sverdlovskii pedagogicheskii institut.

In Russian.

STENSILSKRIFTER
See Oslo. Universitet. Institutt for Sosiologi. STENSILSKRIFTER

2311 STUDIES IN ISRAELI SOCIETY. v.1– , 1980– . New Brunswick, N.J., Transaction.

Sponsored by the Israel Sociological Society.

Subject Index